Essentials

AutoCAD®
Map 3D 2021

November 2020

AUTODESK.
Authorized Publisher

Trademarks

The following are registered trademarks or trademarks of Autodesk, Inc., and/or its subsidiaries and/or affiliates in the USA and other countries: 123D, 3ds Max, Alias, ATC, AutoCAD LT, AutoCAD, Autodesk, the Autodesk logo, Autodesk 123D, Autodesk Homestyler, Autodesk Inventor, Autodesk MapGuide, Autodesk Streamline, AutoLISP, AutoSketch, AutoSnap, AutoTrack, Backburner, Backdraft, Beast, BIM 360, Burn, Buzzsaw, CADmep, CAiCE, CAMduct, Civil 3D, Combustion, Communication Specification, Configurator 360, Constructware, Content Explorer, Creative Bridge, Dancing Baby (image), DesignCenter, DesignKids, DesignStudio, Discreet, DWF, DWG, DWG (design/logo), DWG Extreme, DWG TrueConvert, DWG TrueView, DWGX, DXF, Ecotect, Ember, ESTmep, FABmep, Face Robot, FBX, Fempro, Fire, Flame, Flare, Flint, ForceEffect, FormIt 360, Freewheel, Fusion 360, Glue, Green Building Studio, Heidi, Homestyler, HumanIK, i-drop, ImageModeler, Incinerator, Inferno, InfraWorks, Instructables, Instructables (stylized robot design/logo), Inventor, Inventor HSM, Inventor LT, Lustre, Maya, Maya LT, MIMI, Mockup 360, Moldflow Plastics Advisers, Moldflow Plastics Insight, Moldflow, Moondust, MotionBuilder, Movimento, MPA (design/logo), MPA, MPI (design/logo), MPX (design/logo), MPX, Mudbox, Navisworks, ObjectARX, ObjectDBX, Opticore, P9, Pier 9, Pixlr, Pixlr-o-matic, Productstream, Publisher 360, RasterDWG, RealDWG, ReCap, ReCap 360, Remote, Revit LT, Revit, RiverCAD, Robot, Scaleform, Showcase, Showcase 360, SketchBook, Smoke, Socialcam, Softimage, Spark & Design, Spark Logo, Sparks, SteeringWheels, Stitcher, Stone, StormNET, TinkerBox, Tinkercad, Tinkerplay, ToolClip, Topobase, Toxik, TrustedDWG, T-Splines, ViewCube, Visual LISP, Visual, VRED, Wire, Wiretap, WiretapCentral, XSI.

NASTRAN is a registered trademark of the National Aeronautics Space Administration.

All other brand names, product names, or trademarks belong to their respective holders.

Disclaimer

Published by:

ASCENT Center for Technical Knowledge
630 Peter Jefferson Parkway, Suite 175
Charlottesville, VA 22911
866-527-2368
www.ascented.com

Contents

Introduction v

Exercise Files vii

Chapter 1: Getting Started 1
    Lesson: AutoCAD Map 3D User Interface 2
    Exercise: Exploring the AutoCAD Map 3D User Interface 7

Chapter 2: Creating and Editing Geometry 11
    Lesson: Using Coordinate Geometry 12
    Exercise: Use Coordinate Geometry to Draw a Parcel 17
    Lesson: Performing Drawing Cleanup 20
    Exercise: Clean Up the Water Mains Drawing 26

Chapter 3: Drawing-Based Attribute Data 31
    Lesson: Creating and Attaching Object Data 32
    Exercise: Create an Object Data Table 37
    Exercise: Attach Object Data to Objects 39
    Lesson: Editing and Managing Object Data 41
    Exercise: Edit Object Data 45
    Lesson: Creating Dynamic Annotation 46
    Exercise: Creating Annotation in AutoCAD Map 3D 49
    Lesson: Connecting to a Database 53
    Exercise: Attach an External Database Table and Use Data View 57
    Lesson: Defining a Link Template and Linking Records to Objects ... 60
    Exercise: Define a Link Template and Generate Links 63
    Lesson: Using Database Information in a Drawing 66
    Exercise: Using Database Information in a Drawing 69

Chapter 4: Object Classification 73
    Lesson: Setting Up Object Classifications 74
    Exercise: Set Up an Object Class 79
    Lesson: Classify, Select, and Create Classified Objects 83
    Exercise: Classify, Select, and Create Classified Objects 87

Chapter 5: Importing and Exporting Data **91**

    Lesson: Importing and Exporting Data **92**

        Exercise: Import an ArcView ShapeFile 98

        Exercise: Export an Autodesk SDF File 100

Chapter 6: Establishing a Geospatial Environment **105**

    Lesson: Connecting to a Feature Source **106**

    Lesson: Using Coordinate Systems **116**

        Exercise: Re-project Geospatial Data 124

    Lesson: Working with Point Data **126**

        Exercise: Attach an ODBC Point Source 130

    Lesson: Query Features on Connect **133**

        Exercise: Use an Attribute Filter with an SDF 137

Chapter 7: Editing Features **141**

    Lesson: Editing Feature Attributes and Geometry **142**

        Exercise: Edit Geometry and Attributes 151

    Lesson: Moving Data Between DWG Objects and FDO Features **154**

        Exercise: Convert DWG Objects into FDO Features 158

    Lesson: Merging and Splitting Features **161**

        Exercise: Split a Zoning Feature 165

        Exercise: Merge Waterline Features 168

    Lesson: Enhanced Data Exchange **170**

        Exercise: Save Current Map to AutoCAD 172

Chapter 8: Raster Images **175**

    Lesson: Inserting Raster Images **176**

        Exercise: Inserting Raster Images 179

    Lesson: Modifying Inserted Raster Image Properties and Behavior **180**

        Exercise: Change Inserted Image Properties 182

    Lesson: Connecting to Raster Images **183**

        Exercise: Connect to a Raster Feature Source 184

    Lesson: Working with DEM Files **186**

        Exercise: Attach and Stylize a DEM 195

        Exercise: Create Contour Lines from a DEM 198

Chapter 9: Source Drawings **201**

    Lesson: Attaching Source Drawings **202**

    Lesson: Working with Coordinate Systems **211**

        Exercise: Create a Drive Alias 215

        Exercise: Attach Source Drawings 216

Chapter 10: Source Drawing Queries **219**

  Lesson: Define Property and Location Queries **220**
  Exercise: Define a Property and Location Query. 230
  Lesson: Altering Properties During Queries **233**
  Exercise: Alter Properties During a Query 238
  Lesson: Using the Query Library **241**
  Exercise: Save and Run a Saved Query 245
  Lesson: Save Back to Queried Drawings **248**
  Exercise: Save Queried and New Objects to Source Drawing 255

Chapter 11: Stylizing **261**

  Lesson: About the Display Manager **262**
  Exercise: Create a Display Map from Existing Drawings and Add Elements 270
  Exercise: Add Styles to Display Map Elements. 273
  Lesson: Stylizing FDO Features **276**
  Exercise: Stylize FDO Features. 283
  Exercise: Move Text Between a Drawing and an FDO Data Store. 288

Chapter 12: Plotting Maps **291**

  Lesson: Prepare a Layout Sheet for Review **292**
  Exercise: Create a Layout for a Display Map 295
  Lesson: Map Books **298**
  Exercise: Create a Template for Map Books 301
  Exercise: Generate a Map Book 305

Chapter 13: Survey Data **311**

  Lesson: Creating Survey Data Stores **312**
  Exercise: Creating Parcel Survey Data Store. 316
  Lesson: Working with Survey Data Stores **318**
  Exercise: Working with Survey Data Stores. 323

Chapter 14: Industry Models **327**

  Lesson: Open, Edit, and Create an Industry Model **328**
  Exercise: Open and Edit an Industry Model 331
  Exercise: Start a New Drawing from an Industry Model Template 334
  Exercise: Import Data into the Industry Model from an FDO Data Store 336

Appendix A: Additional Exercises **339**

  Exercise: Connect to a Feature Source 340
  Exercise: Use a Spatial Filter with a SHP 343
  Exercise: Convert Drawings into the Current Project Coordinates. 345
  Exercise: Querying Objects Based on Object and SQL Data 347
  Exercise: Performing a Compound Query. 350
  Exercise: Create a Thematic Map 352
  Exercise: Create a Legend 355
  Lesson: Point Clouds **356**

Introduction

The *AutoCAD® Map 3D 2021: Essentials* learning guide is designed for use in Authorized Training Centers (ATC) locations, corporate training settings, and other classroom settings. Although this courseware is designed for instructor-led courses, you can also use it for self-paced learning.

This introduction covers the following topics:

- Course Objectives
- Prerequisites
- Using This Learning Guide
- Downloading and Installing the Exercise Files
- Feedback
- Free Autodesk Software for Students and Educators

This learning guide is complementary to the software documentation. For detailed explanations of features and functionality, refer to the Help in the software.

Course Objectives

After completing this course, you will be able to:

- Understand the AutoCAD Map 3D user interface.
- Create and edit mapping geometry.
- Link and manage drawing-based attribute data.
- Use object classification.
- Connect to geospatial features.
- Edit geospatial features.
- Import and export drawing-based data.
- Work with raster images.
- Work with source drawings.
- Use source drawing queries.
- Stylize drawings and geospatial features.
- Create Map Books and plot maps.
- Use Survey Data with AutoCAD Map 3D's Survey Data Stores.
- Work with AutoCAD Map 3D's Industry Models.

Prerequisites

- Note: This guide is designed for the Windows version of AutoCAD® 2021. It may not be compatible with the Mac version of AutoCAD 2021.
- Access to the AutoCAD Map 3D 2021 Windows version of the software. The exercises and files included with this guide might not be compatible with prior versions.
- Experience with AutoCAD or AutoCAD-based products and a sound understanding and knowledge of Mapping and GIS terminology.
- Working knowledge of Microsoft® Windows® software.

Using this Learning Guide

The lessons are independent of each other. However, it is recommended that you complete these lessons in the order that they are presented unless you are familiar with the concepts and functionality described in those lessons.

Each chapter contains:

- **Lessons -** Usually two or more lessons in each chapter.
- **Exercises -** Practical, real-world examples for you to practice using the functionality you have just learned. Each exercise contains step-by-step procedures and graphics to help you complete the exercise successfully.

Downloading and Installing the Exercise Files

The Exercise Files page in this learning guide contains a link and instructions to download and install all of the data required to complete the exercises.

Feedback

We always welcome feedback on the learning guides. After completing this course, if you have suggestions for improvements or want to report an error in the learning guide or with the exercise files, please send your comments to *feedback@ASCENTed.com*.

Students and Educators Can Access Free Autodesk Software and Resources

Autodesk challenges you to get started with free educational licenses for professional software and creativity apps used by millions of architects, engineers, designers, and hobbyists today. Bring Autodesk software into your classroom, studio, or workshop to learn, teach, and explore real-world design challenges the way professionals do.

Note: Free products are subject to the terms and conditions of the end-user license and services agreement that accompanies the software. The software is for personal use for education purposes and is not intended for classroom or lab use.

Get started today. Register at the Autodesk Education Community and download one of the many Autodesk software applications available.

Visit www.autodesk.com/joinedu/

Exercise Files

To download the exercise files for this learning guide, use the following steps:

1. Type the URL *exactly as shown below* into the address bar of your Internet browser, to access the Course File Download page.

   Note: If you are using the ebook, you do not have to type the URL. Instead, you can access the page simply by clicking the URL below.

   ## http://www.ascented.com/getfile?id=bagroides

2. On the Course File Download page, click the **DOWNLOAD NOW** button, as shown below, to download the .ZIP file that contains the practice files.

3. Once the download is complete, unzip the file and extract its contents.

The recommended exercise files folder location is:
C:\Autodesk Learning\Map 3D Essentials

Note: It is recommended that you do not change the location of the practice files folder. Doing so may cause errors when completing the practices.

This emulates proper CAD procedures by having project files stored in a common folder structure. For training purposes, the folders reside on the local C drive. However, in practice these folders should be on a shared network drive so that the whole project team has access to them.

Getting Started

The AutoCAD® Map 3D software is based on the AutoCAD® software and contains all of that software's functionality. It also contains its own powerful tools designed for mapping and geographic information systems (GIS) professionals.

Objectives

After completing this chapter, you will be able to:

- Describe the elements of the AutoCAD Map 3D user interface.
- Explore the AutoCAD Map 3D user interface.

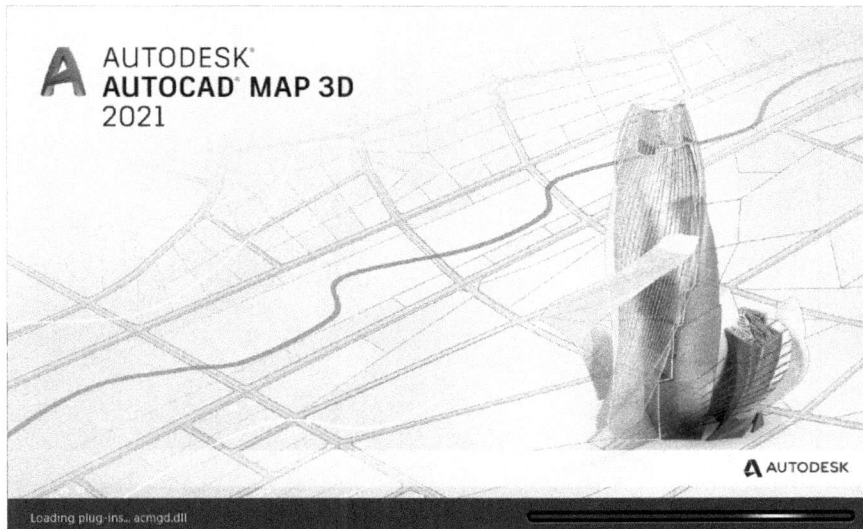

Lesson: AutoCAD Map 3D User Interface

Overview

The AutoCAD Map 3D software provides a robust environment with several ways of viewing its many ribbons and workspaces. You view the various ways of customizing the interface according to the type of work you are planning to perform.

Map Explorer is a key element of the user interface, as shown in the following illustration.

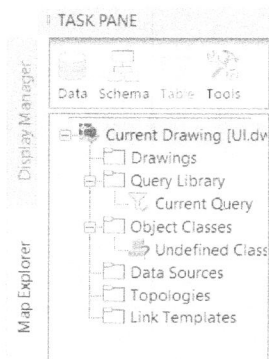

Objectives

After completing this lesson, you will be able to:

- Describe the elements of the AutoCAD Map 3D user interface.
- Explore the AutoCAD Map 3D user interface.

About the AutoCAD Map 3D User Interface

This first time you open the AutoCAD Map 3D software, you are prompted to select your default workspace. The software provides three workspace options, as shown in the following illustration.

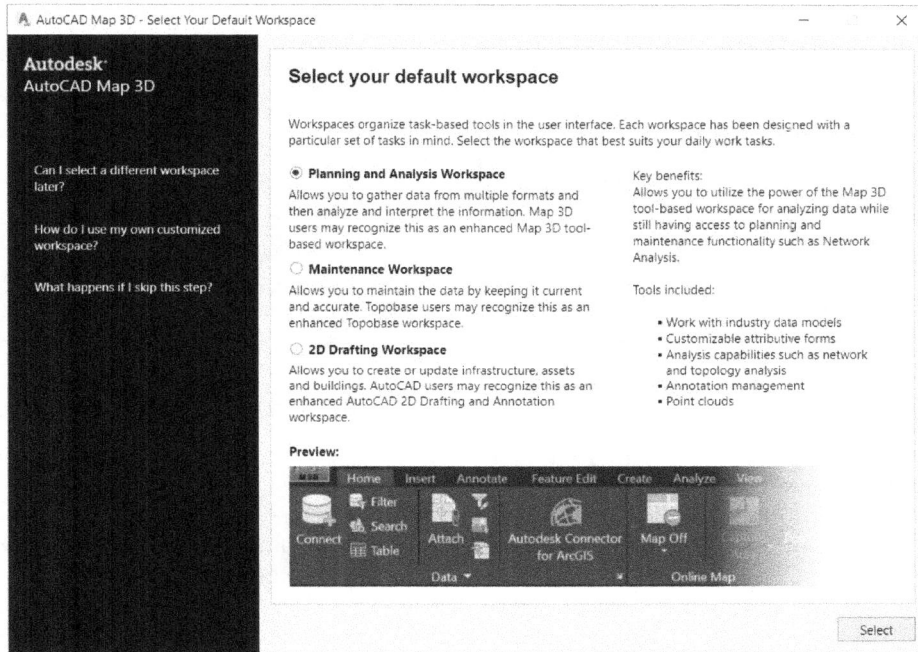

The Planning and Analysis Workspace has replaced the tool based workspace containing tools from the AutoCAD Map 3D software. It enables the gathering of data from multiple formats and the analyzing of that data. It also has maintenance and planning functionality. This workspace is used throughout this learning guide, with the exception of the last chapter covering Industry Models.

The Maintenance Workspace is an enhanced Topobase workspace that enables you to work with and maintain different data models from a range of formats all in one workspace. This will be used in the last chapter covering Industry Models.

The 2D Drafting Workspace provides the familiar 2D Drafting and Annotation workspace from the AutoCAD software, while adding the Map 3D functionality. It includes the creation and editing tools, annotation management, and clean up tools from the AutoCAD software while still providing Data Connect functionality for planning and maintenance.

A fourth workspace is available, which will be familiar to legacy AutoCAD Map 3D users, called Map Classic. This workspace provides menus and floating toolbars to access tools rather than the ribbon interface that will be used throughout this learning guide.

The AutoCAD Map 3D software contains a wide array of tools to help you interact with the application. Your familiarity with these tools helps you decide how to access the various available functions.

When a drawing is not open, or if you click ⊡ (New Tab) in the File Tabs area, the Start tab displays in the model window. It contains two content frames: Learn and Create, as shown below.

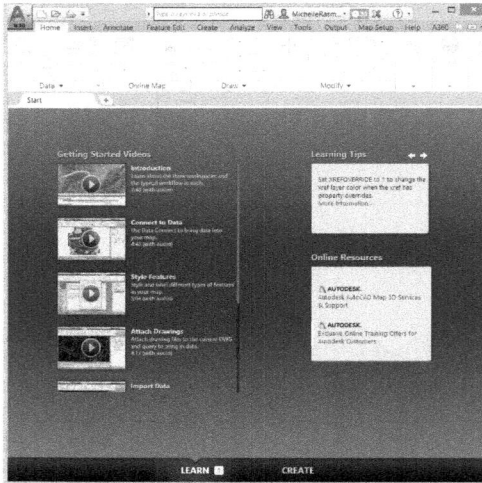

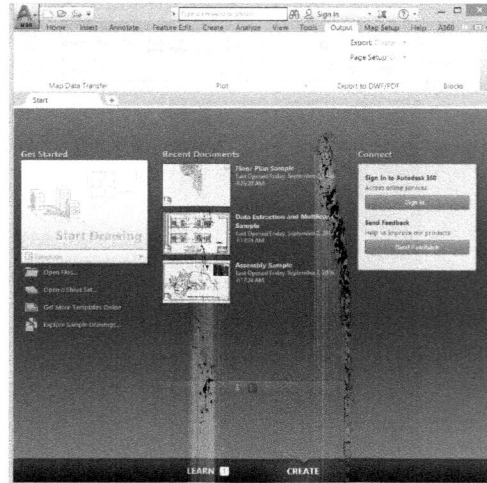

- **Learn**: Contains Getting Started Videos and Online Resources to help you quickly get up to speed with the AutoCAD Map 3D software.
- **Create**: Provides options on starting a new drawing from a template, or opening an existing drawing or sheet set. It also enables you to connect with other users online via the Autodesk 360 service and send feedback to Autodesk to help improve the product.

The following illustration shows the user interface in the AutoCAD Map 3D software. The key parts are called out below.

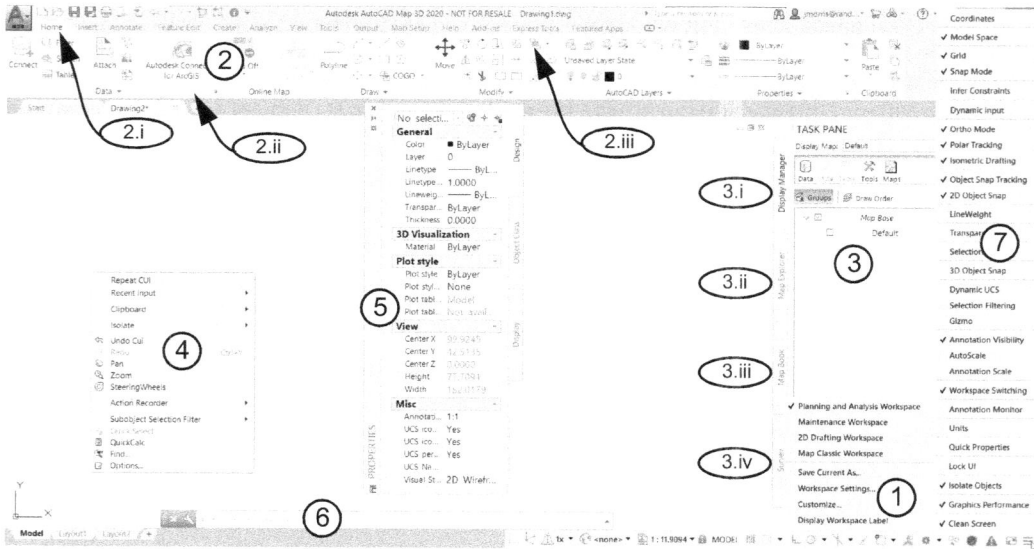

Key Parts of the User Interface

The following is a summary of the various user interface tools in the AutoCAD Map 3D software:

1. Four primary workspaces are available: Planning and Analysis, Maintenance, 2D Drafting, and Map Classic.

2. The Planning and Analysis Workspace continues to use the collection of ribbons, some combining tools that work with Geospatial Features or AutoCAD Objects in the AutoCAD Map 3D software. It is divided logically into specific areas of functionality:

    i. Ribbon (or Tab)
    ii. Panel
    iii. Tool

3. The Task pane includes tabs to access:

    i. **Map Explorer** - Provides the main access to critical functions in the AutoCAD Map 3D software. The tree structure includes branches for Drawings, Query Library, Feature Sources, Feature Classes, Data Sources, Topologies, and Link Templates. Shortcut buttons at the top of Map Explorer (Data, Schema, Table, Tools, and Remove) offer quick access to common tasks.
    ii. **Display Manager** - Used to create stylized versions of maps.
    iii. **Map Book Tasks** - Used to create plot sets.
    iv. **Survey** - Used to create and store point data.

4. Right-clicking on most items in the user interface provides you with instant access to a wide array of commands and functions.

5. The Properties dialog box in the AutoCAD software plays a critical role in the AutoCAD Map 3D user interface. Double-clicking on an object opens the Properties palette, which displays the object's properties from the AutoCAD software and AutoCAD Map 3D software.

6. Press <Ctrl>+<9> and click **Yes** in the *Command Line - Close Window* dialog box to confirm to toggle the command line at the bottom of the window in the AutoCAD Map 3D software.

7. Customize which commands display in the Status Bar by clicking ≡ (Customization) on the Status Bar and selecting items from the list.

8. A legacy Map menu is available by loading the Map Classic Workspace, as shown in the following illustration.

Online Map Services

Coordinate zones play an important role in Map 3D and help to unify a variety of different drawings and GIS information. Coordinate zones are discussed in detail in a later chapter. Once a coordinate zone is assigned to a drawing, the Online Map service becomes available (but an Autodesk account is required for access).

The online maps are geolocated. They have the following characteristics:

- The map is temporary (below we will examine options to "capture" a map).
- The map displays behind all other objects in the drawing, thus no need for changing display orders.
- The map covers a large area: the extents of the coordinate zone assigned to the drawing.
- As the map is temporary, you cannot plot the map unless you have previously captured it.

The first time you access the Online Map service, you are greeted with a splash screen outlining the "fine print" along with a link to the **Terms of Service**. You need to accept these by clicking **Yes** in order to use this service, as shown in the following illustration.

You can select the **Remember my choice** checkbox to avoid seeing this splash screen in the future. If you have checked the box previously but want to restore the splash screen, you can go through the Systems tab in the Options dialog box to change the Hidden Messages setting.

Exercise: Exploring the AutoCAD Map 3D User Interface

Map object data displayed in the AutoCAD Properties palette.

1. Open ...\1-Getting Started\UI.dwg, as shown in the following illustration.

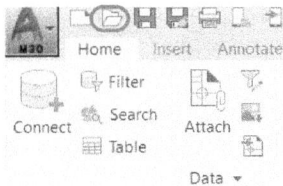

2. If a splash screen appears asking if you want to use the Online Map Data, click **No**. Do not click the **Remember my choice** checkbox.

Geolocation - Online Map Data

Do you want to use Online Map Data?

Online Map Data enables you to use an online service to display maps in AutoCAD. Please sign into your Autodesk account to access online maps.

By accessing or using this service, you understand and agree that you will be subject to, have read and agree to be bound by the terms of use and privacy policies referenced therein: Online Map Data - Terms of Service.

☐ Remember my choice   Yes   No

3. Click the View ribbon. Under Palettes, click Map Task Pane, as shown in the following illustration. The Task Pane is toggled on or off by default on the right side of the screen.

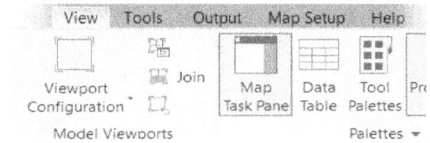

4. Look through the items in Map Explorer tab. Click Data, Schema, and Tools at the top, as shown in the following illustration. Note the tree structures for critical Map items and functions.

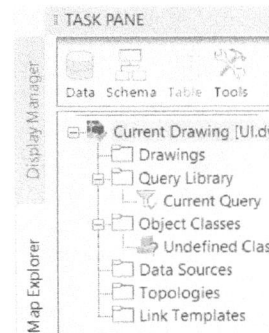

5. Select the Display Manager tab.
   - Look through the Display Manager. This is where you compose special display configurations.
   - Click Data, Tools, and Maps at the top, as shown in the following illustration, to see the items that you can access through them.

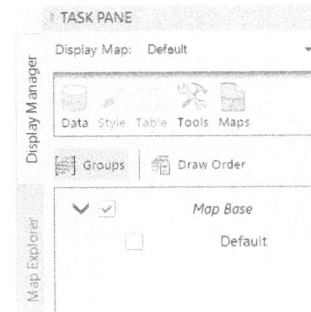

6. Select the Map Book tab, as shown in the following illustration, in which you will compose special Map plot configurations called Map Books.

7. Select the Survey tab, as shown in the following illustration, in which you can create Survey Data Stores with imported point information.

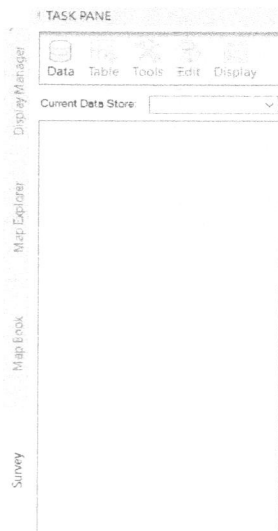

8. Click through the following tabs across the top:

- Home
- Annotate (Map Annotation panel)
- Feature Edit
- Create
- Analyze
- Tools (Map Edit panel)
- Map Setup

Look through each to see what functions can be accessed through them.

9. At the bottom of the Task Pane, as shown in the following illustration, click the workspace switching tool.

10. Select the Maintenance Workspace. Note that the ribbons change so that the tools are more familiar to Topobase users, as shown in the following illustration.

11. Select the Map Classic Workspace. Note the menus and floating toolbars that are available, as shown in the following illustration.

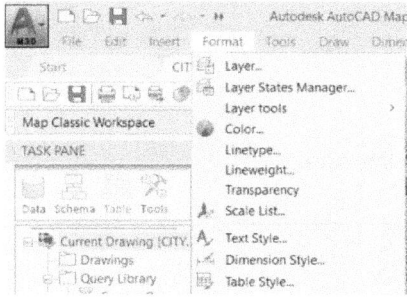

12. Select the Planning and Analysis Workspace.

13. Click the Tools ribbon.

- Under Customization, click User Interface, as shown in the following illustration.

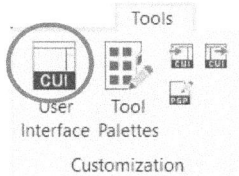

14. In the Customize User Interface dialog box:

- Under Workspaces, right-click on Planning and Analysis Workspace (current).
- Click Set Default, as shown in the following illustration.
- Click OK.

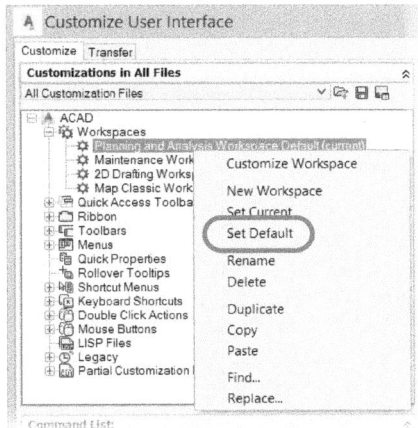

15. On the keyboard, press <Ctrl>+<9>. This will toggle the Command Line on and off. At the bottom of the screen, note the command line disappear and reappear. The Command line is shown in the following illustration.

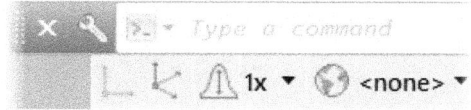

16. In the drawing editor:

- Click on a red line in the model that represents a road centerline.
- Right-click and click Properties. Note the Map data displayed in the AutoCAD Properties palette, as shown in the following illustration.

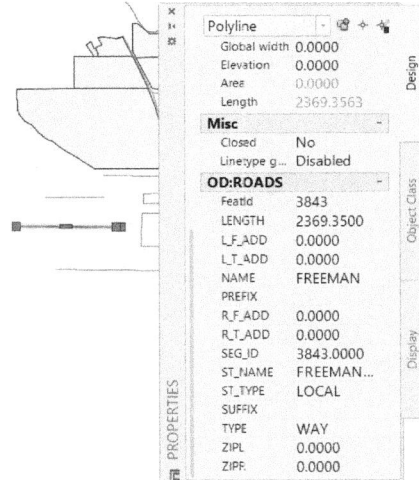

17. Save and close the drawing.

Chapter Summary

Having completed this chapter, you can:

- Describe the elements of the AutoCAD Map 3D user interface.
- Explore the AutoCAD Map 3D user interface.

Creating and Editing Geometry

The lessons in this chapter cover coordinate geometry and drawing cleanup.

The Coordinate Geometry feature is a series of input and inquiry commands that help you to calculate point locations on a drawing. Use input commands to create objects using accurate geometry. Use inquiry commands to obtain accurate geometric information about objects in your drawing, such as angles, bearings, lines, arcs, slopes, elevations, and azimuth values.

The AutoCAD® Map 3D software provides drawing cleanup tools to help you clean up and edit your maps so that they are accurate and suitable for topology, mapping, or plotting.

Objectives

After completing this chapter, you will be able to:

- Use coordinate geometry to draw a parcel and to list line and arc information.
- Use drawing cleanup to fix errors in a drawing.

Lesson: Using Coordinate Geometry

Overview

This lesson covers the coordinate geometry commands in the AutoCAD Map 3D software, a series of input and inquiry commands that you use to draw coordinate geometry and to list coordinate geometry information about existing objects.

The following illustration shows the coordinate geometry Input draw commands toolbar in the Home tab.

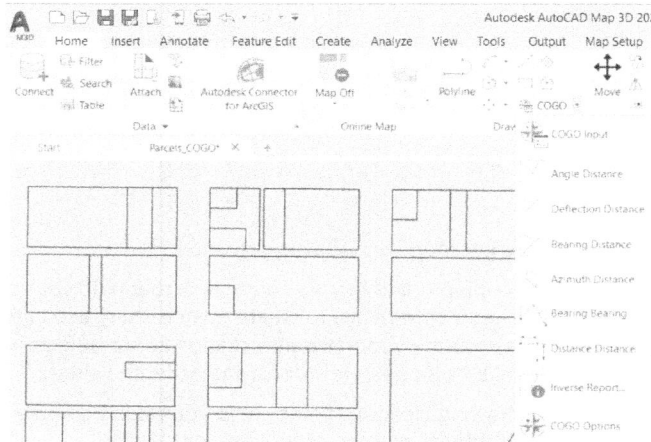

Objectives

After completing this lesson, you will be able to:

- Describe the coordinate geometry commands.
- List the coordinate geometry commands.
- Decide when to use coordinate geometry.
- Draw a parcel using coordinate geometry.

About Coordinate Geometry

You can use the standard commands in the AutoCAD software to create objects in a map, or you can use coordinate geometry input and inquiry commands. Depending on the source of your information, such as survey information or legal descriptions, coordinate geometry commands might be the only method that you can use to accurately reflect the source of your information.

Coordinate Geometry Defined

Coordinate geometry commands are a series of input and inquiry commands. Input commands run transparently in a geometry creation command and you can execute inquiry commands to gather information about existing objects. Unlike standard commands in the AutoCAD software, coordinate geometry commands can use bearings, azimuth, and deflection combined with distances to create geometry in your map.

The following illustration shows a parcel being drawn with the Bearing and Distance coordinate geometry command.

Note: When using Cogo input commands, toggle off Dynamic Input.

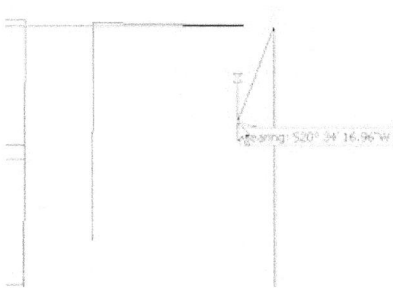

Example of Using Coordinate Geometry

You can use coordinate geometry to create objects that are documented with bearings and distances. For example, you can use coordinate geometry commands to draw the lines, as shown in the following illustration.

Coordinate Geometry Commands

The transparent coordinate geometry commands are called transparent COGO commands to differentiate them from the AutoCAD transparent commands. You can use transparent COGO commands in nearly all of the AutoCAD commands that prompt for a point.

The following illustration shows an example of the command line during a transparent COGO command.

```
Specify next point or [Undo] _PD
Quadrants - NE = 1  SE = 2  SE = 3  NW = 4
>>Specify quadrant (1-4)  1
```

Input Commands

The following lists some of the commonly used transparent COGO commands.

Command	Definition
Angle Distance	Specifies a point based on an angle from a reference line, and a distance from a point on the reference line.
Bearing Distance	Specifies a point based on a bearing and a distance from a reference point.
Azimuth Distance	Specifies a point based on an azimuth and a distance from a reference point.
Bearing-Bearing	Specifies a point using the projections from two existing lines or points and two bearings.
Distance-Distance	Specifies a point using two points and two distances to the new point.

Note: When using the Bearing commands, you need to understand the quadrant values that the software is looking for. The following illustration shows the numbers required for each quadrant.

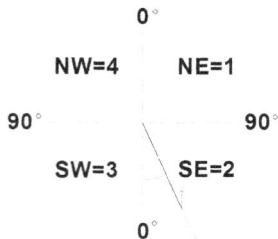

Inquiry Commands

The following lists commonly used inquiry commands.

Command	Definition
Line and Arc Information	Displays coordinate geometry information for lines and arcs, including curve details.
Angle Information	Displays acute and obtuse angle information between intersecting lines.
Add Distance	Displays a running total of distances between disjunctive points or selected text with numeric values.

COGO Input

All COGO input that is launched transparently can also be entered though the COGO Input dialog box, as shown in the following illustration. It enables you to pick the existing point or enter the new points.

When to Use Coordinate Geometry Commands

Your decision to use coordinate geometry input is usually based on the source of the data you receive, or on how you are asked to report information about objects in the drawing.

Follow these guidelines when deciding to use coordinate geometry commands.

- If you are required to create geometry based on the legal description of a property or survey data, use coordinate geometry commands.
- If you need to report the course or bearing of a line, use coordinate geometry inquiry commands.
- If you need to report the added distances of more than one line or add distances based on textual numeric data, use coordinate geometry commands.

Example of Coordinate Geometry Inquiry

The following illustration shows how the same arc is reported using the AutoCAD Map 3D properties and the coordinate geometry Line & Arc Information inquiry command. The AutoCAD software's standard properties display in the Properties palette, and the COGO inquiry information displays on the command line, as shown in the following illustration.

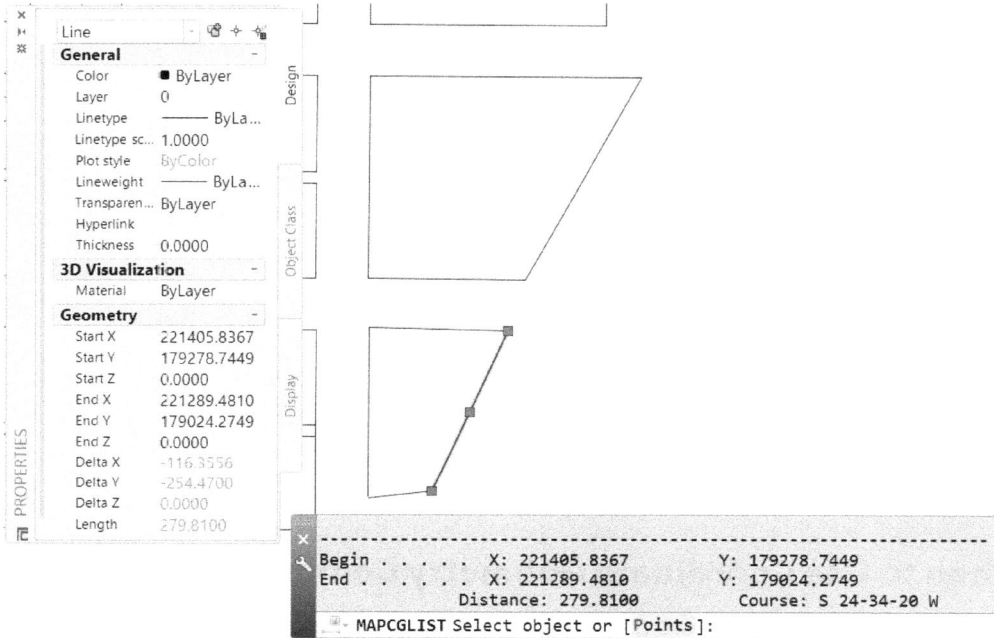

Exercise: Use Coordinate Geometry to Draw a Parcel

In this exercise, you will draw a parcel in an existing map using bearings and distances, as shown in the following illustration. You will also list information about lines and distances.

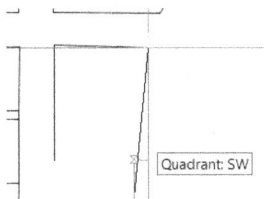

Quadrant: SW

1. Open ...\2-Creating and Editing Geometry\ Parcels_COGO.dwg.

2. Ensure that you are in the Planning and Analysis Workspace, as shown in the following illustration.

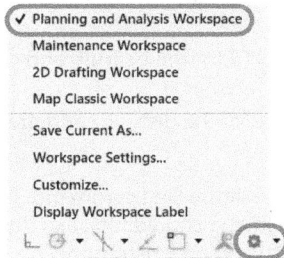

✓ Planning and Analysis Workspace
Maintenance Workspace
2D Drafting Workspace
Map Classic Workspace

Save Current As...
Workspace Settings...
Customize...
Display Workspace Label

3. To start the Line command, in the Home tab, under Draw, select Line, as shown in the following illustration.

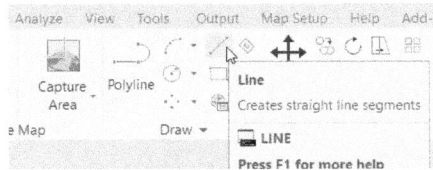

4. For the first point of the line, at the command line:

    - Enter **221192.44**, **179015.61**.
    - Press <Enter>.
    - Ensure that dynamic input is toggled off by clicking ⌷ in the Status Bar or by pressing F12.

5. While still in Draw Line mode, in the Home tab, under Draw, click the arrow next to COGO>Bearing Distance, as shown in the following illustration. This becomes the default tool for COGO.

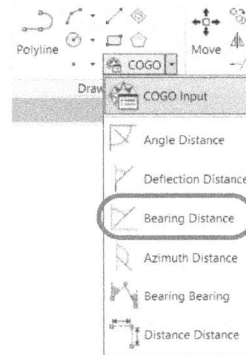

COGO Input
Angle Distance
Deflection Distance
Bearing Distance
Azimuth Distance
Bearing Bearing
Distance Distance

Note: If the command sticks on the quadrant, you can use an apostrophe and the capital letters from the command's drop-down. For instance, 'bd would be used for the COGO Bearing Distance option. It is typical for it to stick if dynamic input is toggled on.

6. At the command line:

    - If prompted for a Starting point, enter **221192.44**, **179015.61** again, or you can use the Up Arrow key (^) on your keyboard to repeat these values.
    - Enter **1** for the quadrant, as shown in the following illustration. Press <Enter>.
    - Enter **0.09** for the bearing. Press <Enter>.
    - Enter **268.81** for the distance. Press <Enter>.

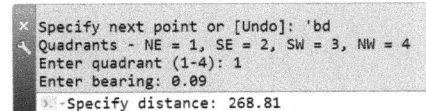

```
Specify next point or [Undo]: 'bd
Quadrants - NE = 1, SE = 2, SW = 3, NW = 4
Enter quadrant (1-4): 1
Enter bearing: 0.09
-Specify distance: 268.81
```

7. Under Draw, click the arrow next to COGO> Bearing Distance, as shown in the following illustration.

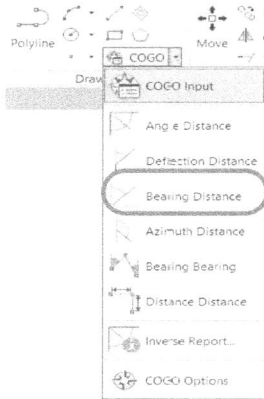

For the second line segment, do the following:

- If prompted for a Starting point, select the top endpoint of the last line you created.
- Enter **2** for the quadrant and press <Enter>.
- Enter **88.4737** for the bearing and press <Enter>.
- Enter **213.05** for the distance and press <Enter>.

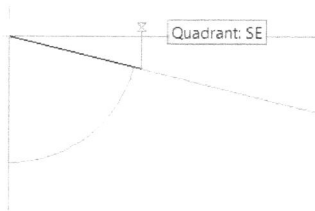

8. For the third line segment, do the following:

- Under Draw, click the arrow next to COGO>Bearing Distance.
- If prompted for a Starting point, select the right endpoint of the last line you created.
- Enter **3** for the quadrant and press <Enter>.
- Enter **24.5721** for the bearing and press <Enter>.
- Enter **279.81** for the distance and press <Enter>.

9. For the fourth line segment, do the following:

- Under Draw, click the arrow next to COGO>Bearing Distance.
- If prompted for a Starting point, select the bottom endpoint of the last line you created.
- Enter **3** for the quadrant and press <Enter>.
- Enter **83.3912** for the bearing and press <Enter>.
- Enter **96.24** for the distance and press <Enter>.

10. Press <Esc> to exit the Line command. When finished, your image should look like that shown in the following illustration.

11. On the Analyze tab, under Inquiry, select Add Distances, as shown in the following illustration.

12. Use the endpoint OSnap and select the second last segment's beginning and end points to add its distance, as shown in the following illustration.

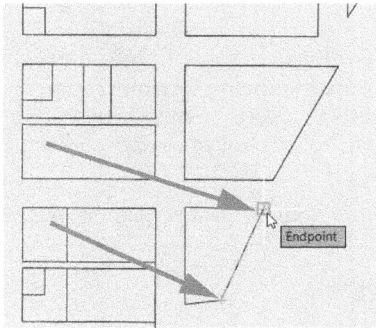

The command line displays the distance for the first segment and the current overall distance, as shown in the following illustration.

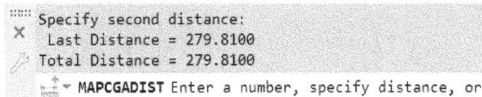

```
 :::::  Specify second distance:
  ×     Last Distance = 279.8100
  ⌐     Total Distance = 279.8100
        ⊢ ⌐ ▾ MAPCGADIST Enter a number, specify distance, or
```

13. Using the running endpoint OSnap, select the beginning and end points for each perimeter segment to add their distance to the overall distance value, as shown in the following illustration.

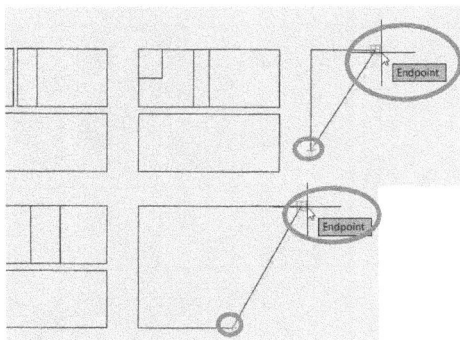

The total distance displays as 952.7752, as shown in the following illustration.

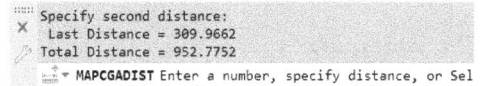

```
 :::::  Specify second distance:
  ×     Last Distance = 309.9662
  ⌐     Total Distance = 952.7752
        ⊢ ⌐ ▾ MAPCGADIST Enter a number, specify distance, or Sel
```

14. Press <Esc>.

15. On the Analyze tab, under Inquiry, select Line & Arc Information, as shown in the following illustration.

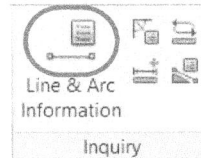

Click the second last segment, as shown in the following illustration, to display the line data.

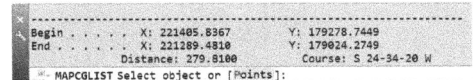

```
 × ------------------------------------------------------
   ¬ Begin . . . . .  X: 221405.8367      Y: 179278.7449
     End . . . . .    X: 221289.4810      Y: 179024.2749
                      Distance: 279.8100  Course: S 24-34-20 W
     ₩¬ MAPCGLIST Select object or [Points]:
```

Note: If your command line is not visible, press F2 to see the results in a text window. Press F2 again to close the text window.

16. Save and close the drawing.

Lesson: Performing Drawing Cleanup

Overview

This lesson covers several cleanup tools and how to use them. Errors can be introduced into maps in several ways. For example, while digitizing or through inaccurate scanning. You must address errors using the drawing cleanup tools before you can create topology or perform map analysis. The AutoCAD Map 3D software has several tools to help you clean up and edit your maps so that they are accurate and suitable for topology, mapping, and plotting.

The following illustration shows the Drawing Cleanup Errors dialog box. In this example, Duplicate lines are identified.

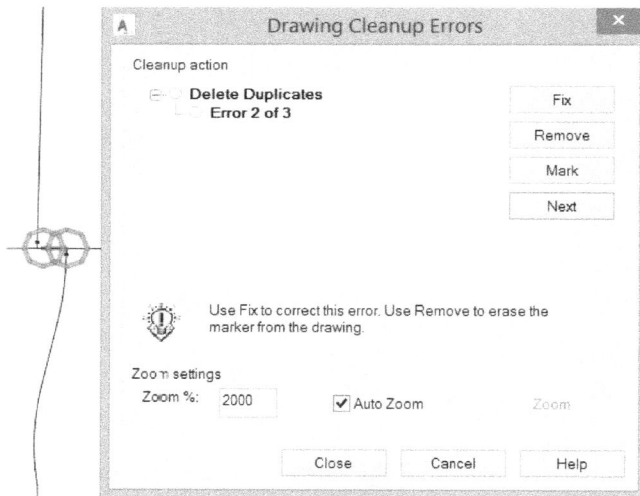

Objectives

After completing this lesson, you will be able to:

- Describe drawing cleanup.
- List common options and settings used in drawing cleanup.
- Decide how to use drawing cleanup.
- Explain the process of drawing cleanup.
- Use drawing cleanup.

About Drawing Cleanup

You can manually clean geometry in a map using the AutoCAD standard editing tools. However, most maps are so extensive and complicated that using manual editing techniques is not only tedious, but is also unlikely to identify every error that needs to be addressed.

The drawing cleanup tools in the AutoCAD Map 3D software automate many of the map-editing tasks, as shown in the following illustration.

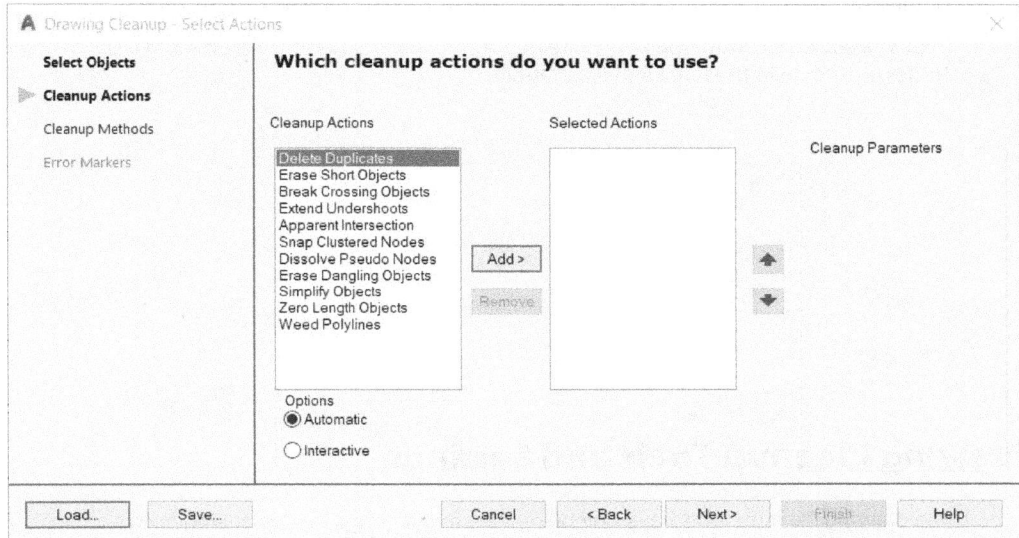

Drawing Cleanup Defined

With the Drawing Cleanup tool, you can specify what type of error you need to fix, the tolerance for the error, and what objects to include in the cleanup operation. The value of using the cleanup tool instead of the AutoCAD standard editing tools is that the cleanup tool examines all or part of the drawing for problems with the geometry and fixes them according to the criteria that you set.

The following illustration shows the typical errors that are encountered in a map.

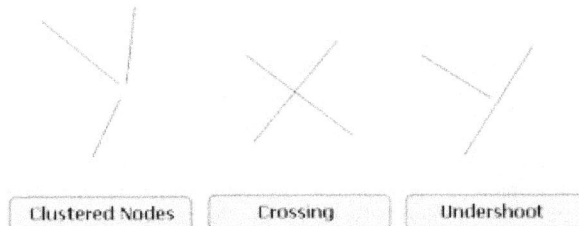

You can think of drawing cleanup as a set of criteria for geometry correctness to which all objects in the drawing must adhere.

Drawing Cleanup Example

To build a polygon topology, the topology must be complete. No links in the topology can cross each other, and multiple line segments that represent a single boundary should be reduced to single polylines. Before building the polygon topology, use drawing cleanup to fix these common errors.

In this example of a simple set of parcels, the small circles represent line endpoints. In the illustration shown on the left, the two lines that cross in the center need to be broken where they cross, the corners of the parcels should be joined, and the corner nodes (pseudo nodes) removed to create a single outside boundary for each parcel, as shown in the illustration on the right.

In this case, two cleanup operations are performed: Break Crossing Objects and Dissolve Pseudo Nodes, as shown in the following illustration.

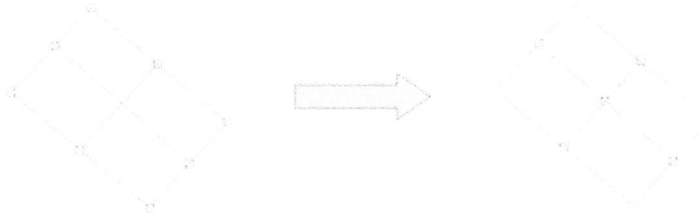

Drawing Cleanup Tools and Settings

The drawing cleanup tools have several options and settings for controlling each cleanup operation. For more information, refer to the AutoCAD Map 3D Help.

Selecting Objects

You can select an entire drawing or subsets of objects in the drawing for cleanup. Two selection methods are available:

- **Layer Filters** - Selects objects on specified layers.
- **Manual** - Selects objects using the AutoCAD standard selection tools.

Cleanup Actions

The following are some of the most common cleanup actions:

Action	Definition
Delete Duplicates	Duplicate lines and geometry can result from queries that produce coincident lines or from the unintentional duplication of layers. These might not be exact duplicates, but if the endpoints fall within a specified tolerance, they are considered duplicates.
Break Crossing Objects	Crossing objects are any lines, arcs, or polylines that cross each other.

Action	Definition
Snap Clustered Nodes	Clustered nodes are the endpoints of lines, arcs, or polylines that approach each other but do not meet within a specified tolerance.
Erase Short Objects	Short objects are usually unintentional objects that represent part of a line segment or result from previous cleanup operations. If they fall within the tolerance, they are removed.

Cleanup Methods

Once you have selected objects and cleanup actions, the following methods of cleanup are available:

Method	Definition
Modify original objects	Modifies the original object and retains as much information as possible.
Retain original objects and create new objects	Does not affect the original objects, but creates new objects on a specified layer.
Delete original objects and create new objects	Deletes any objects that are determined to be errors, and creates new objects on a specified layer.

Anchors

Some objects in a drawing should not be modified. For example, geometry in a drawing might represent a legal boundary or a benchmark. You anchor these objects before performing drawing cleanup.

Tolerance

You use tolerance settings to set a distance that an error must be within to be considered an error. In the following example, four lines are considered clustered nodes. The dashed circle represents a tolerance value. Lines 1, 2, and 3 fall within the tolerance and are considered errors. Line 4 falls outside the tolerance and is not considered an error, as shown in the following illustration.

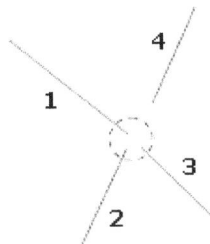

Drawing Cleanup Strategies

Drawing cleanup is not usually a single operation in which you remove all of the errors in the drawing. Depending on the number and type of errors, drawing cleanup is an iterative process in which you clean certain errors and then repeat the process to clean additional errors.

The reason for cleaning a drawing can influence how you approach the cleanup. For example, if you intend to use the drawing for a street network topology, crossing objects can be tolerated and might even be required. However, if you intend to use the drawing to produce a polygon topology, crossing objects cannot be tolerated. You also need to consider any object data or SQL links that are attached to objects in the drawing. Using incorrect methods of cleanup might destroy these links.

Drawing Cleanup Guidelines

When performing drawing cleanup, consider the following issues:

- If objects have object data, hyperlinks, or SQL links associated with them, drawing cleanup might break these associations. You can control this behavior by selecting a cleanup method that either retains or modifies the original object.

- For greater control of the cleanup operation, consider performing one cleanup action at a time and completing one action before moving to another.

- To display the extent and nature of the problems in the drawing, use markers for your first cleanup pass.

- If you are cleaning drawings from a regular source and the same types of problems exist in each drawing, create a profile for the cleanup settings.

- Determine whether any objects in the drawing cannot be changed and anchor them before performing drawing cleanup.

- Start the cleanup operation using small tolerances and review to find out whether the tolerance setting has captured the errors. If the tolerance setting is too low, repeat the cleanup operation with a larger tolerance until the operation recognizes the errors. Be careful when increasing tolerances. If tolerances are set too high, valid geometry can be recognized as errors.

Example Cleanup Strategy

If you are working on data that is going to become a polygon topology, break the crossing objects first, and then dissolve any pseudo nodes that might have been produced. This ensures that all links are broken at intersections. If any broken intersections produce short objects, they are joined by dissolving the pseudo node.

1. Review the existing data. In this case, the simple parcel map displays normal, but there are several problems that prevent the creation of a polygon topology, as shown in the following illustration.

2. Decide to break the crossing objects and view the results with markers, then complete the operation after reviewing the problem locations. In this case, the outside lines are not broken where the inside lines meet them and the two inside lines cross each other in the center, as shown in the following illustration.

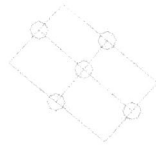

3. Dissolve the pseudo nodes. The outside corners of the parcels need to be joined to produce a single boundary for each parcel. There are also two line segments in the center of the parcels that must be joined, as shown in the following illustration.

Drawing Cleanup Process

Defining an approach to drawing cleanup is critical for success. Part of the process is understanding the effect that any cleanup operation is going to have on your data. Drawing cleanup is a powerful tool that can save significant time in preparing maps, but if used improperly, it can produce unwanted results that might be difficult to undo.

Process: Drawing Cleanup

The Drawing Cleanup wizard guides you through the process of cleaning your data.

1. Start the Drawing Cleanup wizard.
In the Drawing Cleanup wizard, you select the objects to clean, specify the cleanup actions to perform, and specify the methods to use during the cleanup.

2. Use the interactive cleanup method first.
Run drawing cleanup with the required cleanup actions, and use markers to verify what is going to be cleaned.

3. Fix errors.
If the markers represent the required results, run drawing cleanup again and fix the errors.

> The UNDO command undoes a cleanup operation, but it is recommended that you save your drawing before performing any large cleanup operation.

Exercise: Clean Up the Water Mains Drawing

The Water Mains drawing has several errors, including duplicate objects. In this exercise, you will open the Water Main drawing and use the cleanup tools to fix all of the errors, as shown in the following illustration.

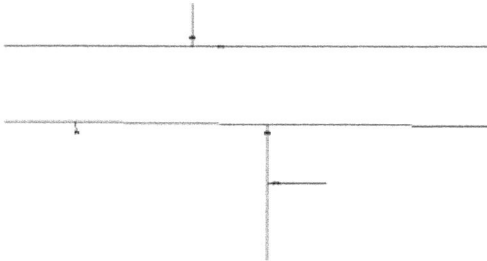

1. Open ...\ *2-Creating and Editing Geometry\ Water_cleanup.dwg*.

2. On the Tools tab, under Map Edit, select Drawing Clean Up, as shown in the following illustration.

3. In the Drawing Cleanup - Select Objects dialog box:

    ■   Under Object To Include In Drawing Cleanup, click Select All.

    ■   For Layers, click the Browse button, as shown in the following illustration. Be sure not to enter anything in the Objects to anchor portion, as show in the following illustration.

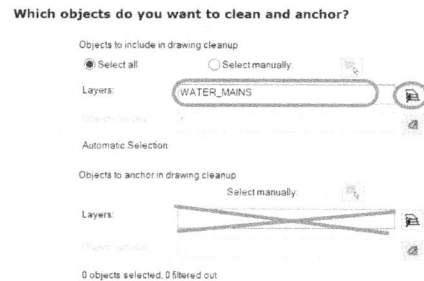

4. In the Select Layers dialog box:

    ■   Select the WATER_MAINS layer, as shown in the following illustration.

    ■   Click Select to return to the Drawing Cleanup - Select Objects window.

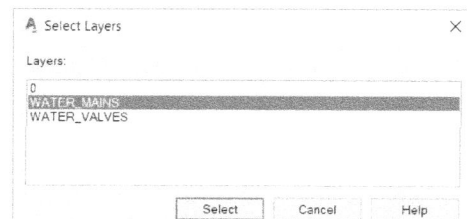

5. In the Drawing Cleanup - Select Objects dialog box, click Next, as shown in the following illustration.

6. In the Drawing Cleanup - Select Actions dialog box:
   - Under Cleanup Actions, select Delete Duplicates, as shown in the following illustration.
   - Click Add.

Which cleanup actions do you want to use?

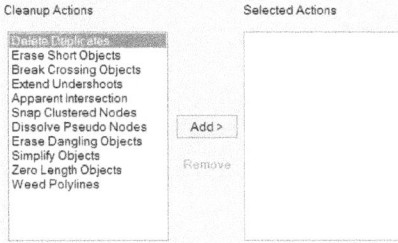

Cleanup Actions		Selected Actions
Delete Duplicates		
Erase Short Objects		
Break Crossing Objects		
Extend Undershoots		
Apparent Intersection		
Snap Clustered Nodes		
Dissolve Pseudo Nodes	Add >	
Erase Dangling Objects		
Simplify Objects	Remove	
Zero Length Objects		
Weed Polylines		

7. Under Options, select Interactive, as shown in the following illustration.
   - Click Next.

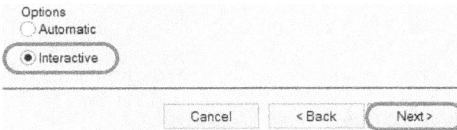

Options
- Automatic
- Interactive

| Cancel | < Back | Next > |

8. In the Drawing Cleanup - Cleanup Methods dialog box, click Next, as shown in the following illustration.

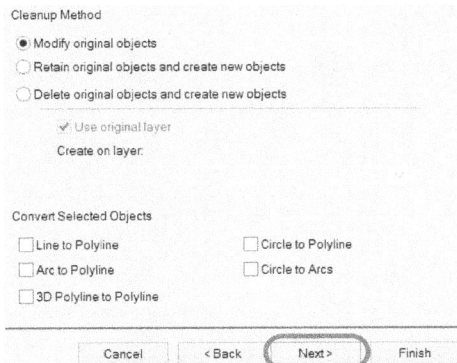

Cleanup Method
- Modify original objects
- Retain original objects and create new objects
- Delete original objects and create new objects
  - Use original layer
  - Create on layer:

Convert Selected Objects
- Line to Polyline
- Arc to Polyline
- 3D Polyline to Polyline
- Circle to Polyline
- Circle to Arcs

| Cancel | < Back | Next > | Finish |

9. In the Drawing Cleanup - Error Markers dialog box:
   - Under Blocks and Colors, change the color for Delete Duplicates from Cyan to Green, as shown in the following illustration.
   - Click Finish.

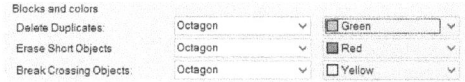

Blocks and colors

Delete Duplicates:	Octagon	Green
Erase Short Objects	Octagon	Red
Break Crossing Objects	Octagon	Yellow

10. To view individual errors with the Drawing Cleanup Errors window:
   - Under Cleanup Action, expand Delete Duplicates, as shown in the following illustration.
   - Select Error 1 of 6.
   - Under Zoom Settings, for Zoom % enter **2000** and press <Enter>.
   - Click Next on the right side of the window to view the next error.
   - Continue clicking Next to review all three errors.

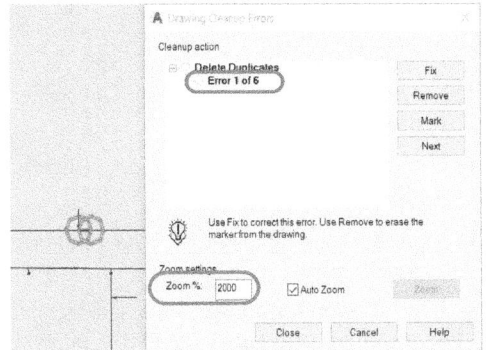

A Drawing Cleanup Errors

Cleanup action
- Delete Duplicates
  - Error 1 of 6

| Fix |
| Remove |
| Mark |
| Next |

Use Fix to correct this error. Use Remove to erase the marker from the drawing.

Zoom settings
Zoom %: 2000   Auto Zoom   Zoom

| Close | Cancel | Help |

11. Under Cleanup Action:

- To correct all found errors, select the Delete Duplicate heading as shown in the following illustration. The options change to focus on a l errors.
- Click Fix All.

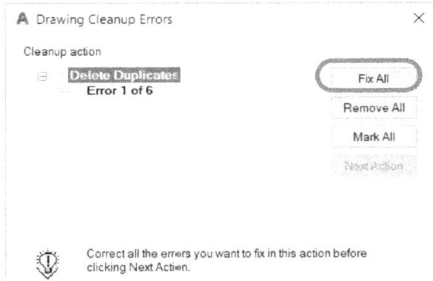

12. In the Drawing Cleanup dialog box, click Close.

The command line indicates that 6 objects were deleted, as shown in the following illustration.

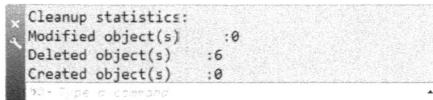

13. On the Tools tab, under Map Edit, select Drawing Clean Up.

14. In the Drawing Cleanup - Select Objects dialog box, click Next.

15. In the Drawing Cleanup - Select Actions dialog box:

- Under Selected Actions, select Delete Duplicates, as shown in the following illustration.
- Click Remove.

Which cleanup actions do you want to use?

16. Under Cleanup Actions:

- Select Snap Clustered Nodes.
- Click Add.
- Under Cleanup Parameters, for Tolerance, enter **0.02**, as shown in the following illustration.
- Under Options, select Automatic.
- Click Next.

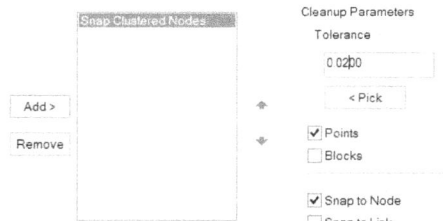

17. In the Drawing Cleanup - Cleanup Methods dialog box, click Finish.

30 objects were modified automatically, as shown in the following illustration.

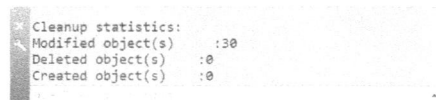

18. Save and close the drawing.

Chapter Summary

Having completed this chapter, you can:

- Use coordinate geometry to draw a parcel and list line and arc information.
- Use drawing cleanup to fix errors in a drawing.

Drawing-Based Attribute Data

The lessons in this chapter describe working with object data, annotations, and external databases.

After acquiring or creating map geometry and objects, the next step is to associate data with those objects. Other than land features, such as contour lines, nearly every object in a map has underlying data that describes or controls the object's attributes, in addition to its location and object type.

Examples include fire hydrants with physical attributes and maintenance records, and streets with speed limits and maintenance records. The underlying data and how it is used or displayed, provides a rich and sophisticated environment for the analysis, display, and reporting of a digital representation of your mapping project.

Objectives

After completing this chapter, you will be able to:

- Create and attach object data.
- Edit and manage object data.
- Add dynamic annotation to a drawing.
- Connect to a database.
- Define a link template and link records to objects.
- Use database information in a drawing.

Lesson: Creating and Attaching Object Data

Overview

Object data is an easy and flexible method of attaching tabular or nongraphic data to objects in the AutoCAD® Map 3D software. This lesson covers creating object data tables and attaching object data to objects in a drawing.

The following illustration shows the object data attached to a water valve that displays in the Properties palette.

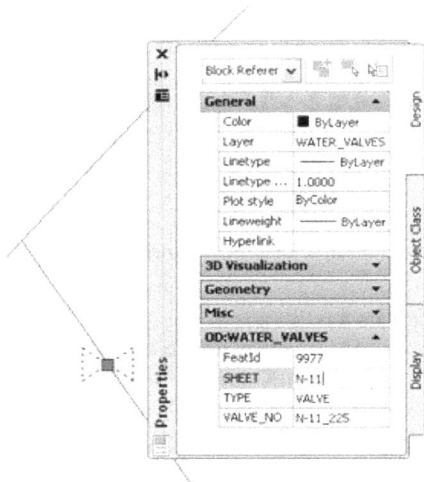

Objectives

After completing this lesson, you will be able to:

- Describe object data.
- Explain the process of creating and attaching object data.
- List object data field types.
- Decide when to use object data.
- Create an object data table.
- Attach object data to objects.

About Object Data

In the AutoCAD Map 3D software, you have multiple options for associating tabular or nongraphic data to the AutoCAD objects, including block attributes, database links, and object data.

Object data is attribute data that is attached to any object in the AutoCAD software and stored in a drawing file. Using object data, you can create a simple table containing text and numeric data, which can be attached to any object in a drawing.

The following illustration shows a single drawing with multiple object data tables defined. In this case, the Water Valve and Water Main tables are user defined and the topology table has been generated by the AutoCAD Map 3D software as a result of creating topology.

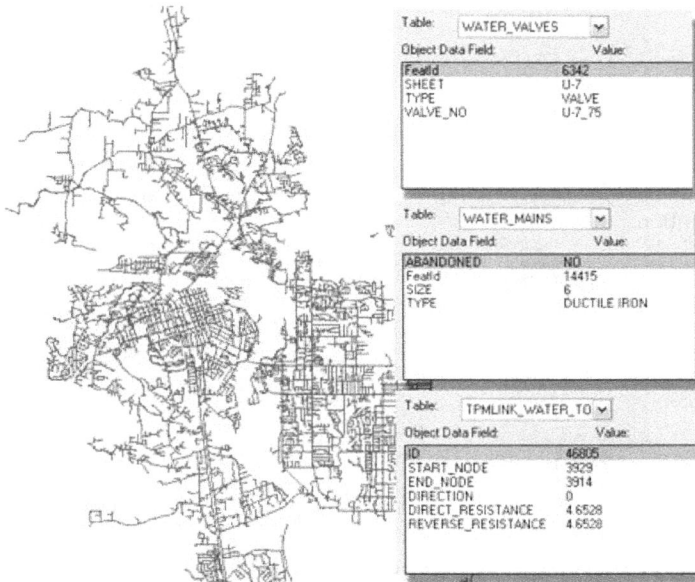

You can think of object data as block attributes, except that you are not limited to attaching the data to a block reference.

You can create object data tables and attach them to the AutoCAD objects for many purposes. These are considered user-defined tables. In addition to user-defined object data tables, the AutoCAD Map 3D software generates object data automatically to:

- Store topology information.
- Store information when you move data into and out of the AutoCAD Map 3D software. For example, when importing data from other file formats, tabular data is imported and associated to the AutoCAD objects with object data.

Examples of Uses for Object Data

The following illustrations show examples of some of the ways in which you might use object data:

- Store information about water valves, as shown in the following illustration.

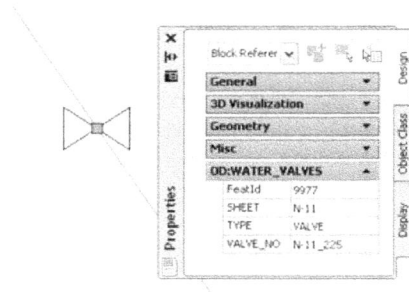

- Store information about soil type polygons imported from other mapping applications, as shown in the following illustration.

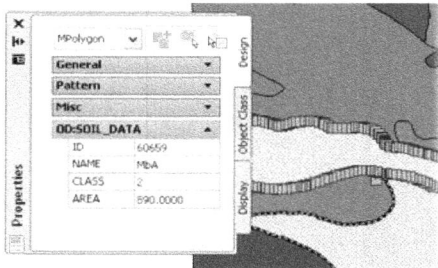

- Access topology information about specific objects, as shown in the following illustration.

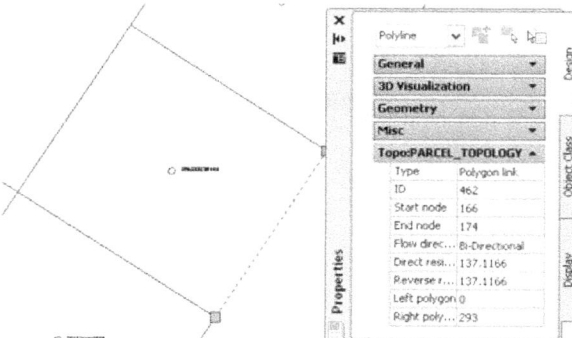

Process of Creating and Attaching Object Data

Getting Started with Object Data

Creating object data is a two-step process:

- Define the object data by creating object data tables and fields.
- Attach the object data to objects in your drawing and populate the table fields with data.

Each time you attach the table to an object, you are prompted to enter the values for each field in the table.

The following illustration shows a defined single object data table and how the table is attached to individual objects in the drawing. When the table is attached to each object, the fields are populated with data that is specific to each object.

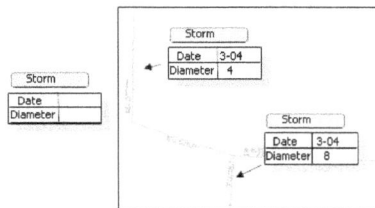

Define Object Data Dialog Box

When you are creating a new object data table, use this information to help you design the table. The following illustration shows the Define Object Data dialog box, which you use to design an object data table.

Naming the Object Data Table and Fields

Valid object data table names are a maximum of 25 alphanumeric characters without any spaces. Each field in the object data table requires a name and a data type. Description and default values are optional. Valid field names are a maximum of 31 alphanumeric characters

Object Data Table Fields

Object data tables contain fields to store each record. The following lists the four types of object data fields and describes the data for each:

Option	Description
Integer	Includes whole numbers between -2, 147, 483, 648 and 2, 147, 483, 647.
Character	Includes all characters and numbers.
Point	A set of three real numbers (separated by commas) that represents a point with X, Y and Z values.
Real	A real number between 1.7E-308 (1.7 times 10t o the powers of -308) and 1.7E=308.

Deciding When to Use Object Data

The AutoCAD Map 3D software provides data linking and association through three primary methods: SQL links, block attributes, and object data. Deciding when to use object data can be based on several factors.

Data Access Outside the AutoCAD Map 3D Software

Object data is only available to users of the AutoCAD Map software. Mapping systems can be designed to separate database functions from the graphic map, usually when the data is accessed and updated regularly. The users responsible for the maintenance of the data use a database program to update the data, which is linked to objects in the AutoCAD Map 3D drawing.

Portability and Ease of Use

Object data provides a simple and flexible method of attaching data to objects. When you save a drawing file with object data, another user of the AutoCAD Map 3D software can open the file and have full access to the object data without using additional databases or files.

Static and Dynamic Data

Object data is best used to document static data that is associated with an object, such as sewer pipe diameter, type, length, etc. This data does not require regular access by non-users of the AutoCAD Map 3D software. Dynamic data, such as maintenance records, often requires multiple records to be associated to a single object. Object data becomes cumbersome when more than one record in the same table is linked to a single object. Many functions, such as query, thematic maps, and the Properties palette, only recognize one record per object, regardless of how many are associated with the object.

External database links are most appropriately used when the data is dynamic in nature. For example, a sewer pipe might have several instances of maintenance. This is an ideal situation in which to use an external database link. The object has a single key, which is related to a record in a database. The database application can then be used to relate this record to other tables that contain additional information.

Exercise: Create an Object Data Table

In this exercise, you will create an object data table and define fields in it, as shown in the following illustration.

1. Open ...\3-Drawing-Based Attribute Data\Creating and Attaching Object Data\Water_OD.dwg, as shown in the following illustration.

2. On the Map Setup ribbon, under Attribute Data, click Define Object Data, as shown in the following illustration.

3. In the Define Object Data dialog box, click New Table, as shown in the following illustration.

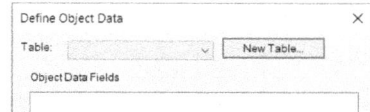

4. For Table Name, enter **WATER_MAINS**, as shown in the following illustration.

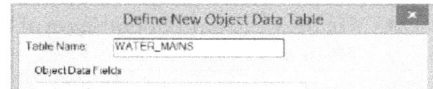

5. To define the first field for the WATER_MAINS table, under Field Definition, do the following:

- For the Field Name, enter **ABANDONED** and press <Enter>.
- For the Type, select Character.
- For the Description, enter **Abandoned Water Main** and press <Enter>.
- For the Default, enter **NO** and press <Enter>.

6. The completed Field Definition should look as shown in the following illustration.

- Click Add.

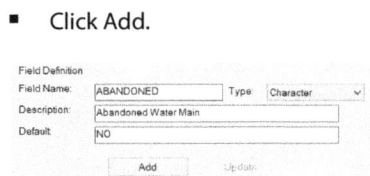

7. To define the second field, do the following:

- For the Field Name, enter **FeatId** and press <Enter>.
- For the Type, select Integer.
- For the Description, enter **Feature Id for Water Mains** and press <Enter>.

8. Click Add.

9. To define the third field, do the following:

- For the Field Name, enter **SIZE** and press <Enter>.
- For the Type, select Character.
- For the Description, enter **Water Main Size** and press <Enter>.

10. Click Add.

11. To define the fourth field, do the following:

- For the Field Name, enter **TYPE** and press <Enter>.
- For the Type, select Character.
- For the Description, enter **Type of Water Main** and press <Enter>.
- For the Default, enter **STEEL** and press <Enter>.

12. Click Add. The four fields should be listed as shown in the following illustration.

13. Click OK.

14. In the Define Object Data dialog box, click Close, as shown in the following illustration.

15. Save and close the drawing.

Exercise: Attach Object Data to Objects

In this exercise, you will use an object data table that has been defined and attach it to multiple objects in a drawing, as shown in the following illustration.

1. Open ...\3-Drawing-Based Attribute Data\Creating and Attaching Object Data\Water_OD2.dwg.

2. On the Create ribbon, under Drawing Object, click Attach/Detach Object Data, as shown in the following illustration.

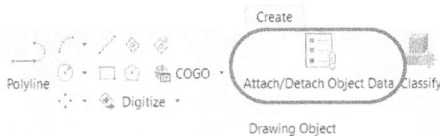

3. In the Attach/Detach Object Data dialog box:
   - For Object Data Field, select Abandoned Water Main, as shown in the following illustration.
   - For Value, the default is NO.
   - Press <Enter> to accept the default.

4. - Select Feature Id for Water Mains.
   - For Value, enter **1** and press <Enter>.

5. - Select Water Main Size.
   - For Value, enter **15** and press <Enter>.

6. - Select Type of Water Main.
   - For Value, ensure the default is STEEL and press <Enter> to accept the default.

7. In the Attach/Detach Object Data dialog box:
   - Click Attach to Objects.
   - Select the Water Main, as shown in the following illustration.
   - Press <Enter>.

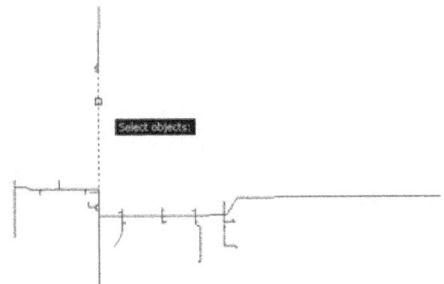

The command line indicates that the data was attached to one object, as shown in the following illustration.

```
Attached data to 1 object(s).

Command:
```

8. Click Create ribbon.
   - Under Drawing Object, click Attach/Detach Object Data.

9. In the Attach/Detach Object Data dialog box:
   - For Object Data Field, select Abandoned Water Main.
   - For Value, enter **YES**.
   - Press <Enter>.

10. Enter the following values for the remaining fields:
    - Feature Id for Water Mains: **2**
    - Water Main Size: **10**
    - Type of Water Main: **STEEL**

    Note: Press <Enter> after each entry.

11. Click Attach to Objects.
    - Select the Water Main, as shown in the following illustration.
    - Press <Enter>.

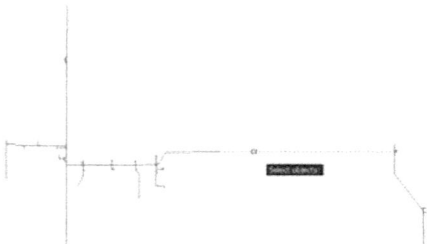

12. On the Create ribbon, under Drawing Objects, click Attach/Detach Object Data.

13. In the Attach/Detach Object Data dialog box:
    - For Object Data Field, select Abandoned Water Main.
    - Press <Enter> to accept the default.

14. Enter the following values for the remaining fields:
    - Feature Id for Water Mains: **3**
    - Water Main Size: **15**
    - Type of Water Main: **PVC**

    Note: Press <Enter> after each entry.

15. Click Attach to Objects.
    - Select the Water Main, as shown in the following illustration.
    - Press <Enter>.

Object data is now attached to three water mains.

16. Save and close the drawing.

Lesson: Editing and Managing Object Data

Overview

In this lesson, you edit pre-existing object data that is attached to objects in the drawing. You learn about the object data tools that are available in addition to using the Properties palette to modify and edit object data.

The following illustration shows the Edit Object Data dialog box.

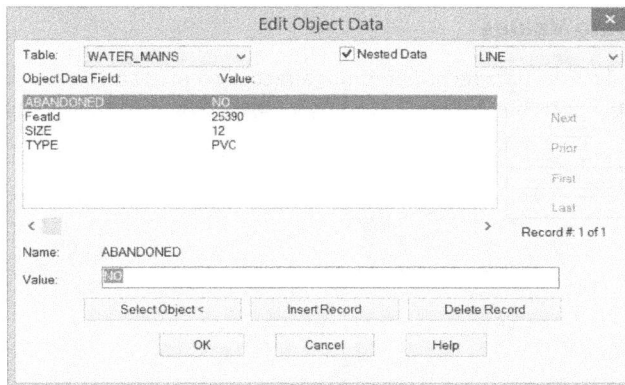

Objectives

After completing this lesson, you will be able to:

- Explain the difference between modifying object data tables and editing object data records.
- List the tools for editing object data.
- Decide the best method for editing object data.
- Edit object data.

About Editing Object Data

After attaching object data tables to objects, you can edit the tables and individual records.

The object data table definition is saved in the drawing file. This definition includes the table name, fields, field types, etc. When you create an object data table and attach it to objects, any changes you make to the table definition affect each instance where the table has been attached to objects.

When you attach a table to an object, all fields in the table are attached as well. An object data record only exists as an attachment. Object data does not provide a method of viewing all records in a table. Therefore, you edit object data by editing the values in the fields of a table that is attached to an object.

Example: Editing Object Data Values

Editing the values in an individual object data record does not affect all records and does not affect the table definition. The following illustration shows that a single object data record has been changed to reflect a new value.

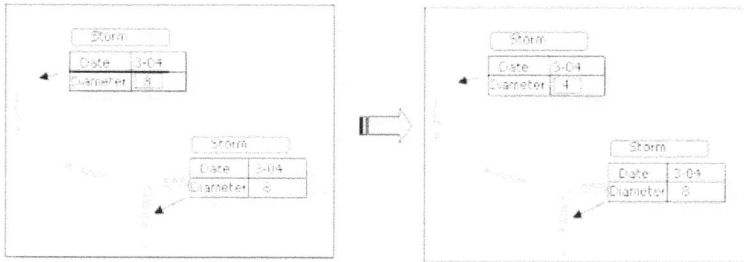

Example: Modifying the Object Data Table

The following illustration shows how object data records are affected when you modify the table. When you change an object data table definition in a drawing, all instances of the table are changed. When you are adding a field, as in this example, this might not have any negative consequences. However, if you change an existing field definition, the new definition might not support the data values that are attached to every object.

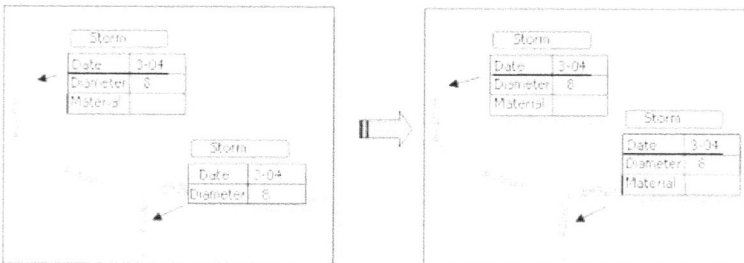

Tools Available to Edit Object Data

You can edit object data in the AutoCAD Map 3D software using the object data tools or the Properties palette. Each has a slightly different approach to object data access.

Edit Object Data Dialog Box

You use the Edit Object Data dialog box to access multiple records from the same table that are attached to a single object, as shown in the following illustration. This dialog box also contains the AutoCAD Map 3D object data tools, which you use to select additional objects and to switch between different tables that are attached to a single object.

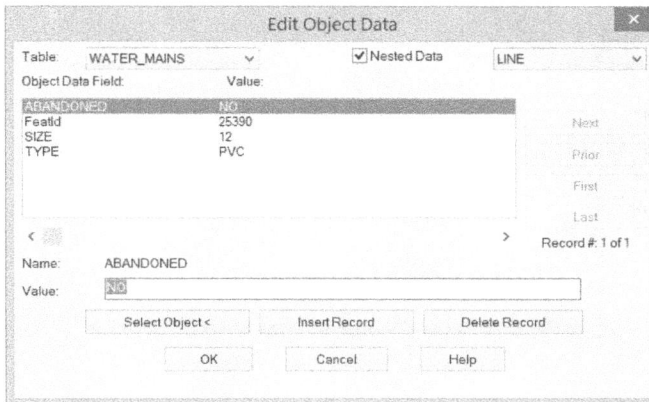

Properties Palette

The Properties palette offers a quick and comprehensive view of all of the properties of an object or set of objects, including object data. A limitation of editing object data with the Properties palette is that if multiple records from the same object data table are attached to the object, only the first record displays. If multiple tables are attached, the first record in each table displays, as shown in the following illustration.

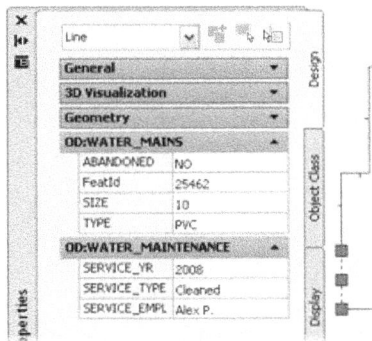

Guidelines for Editing Object Data

When you edit object data, you must decide how to select the objects that you want to edit and how to make the edit.

Multiple Edits Using Queries and Selection Tools

If you want to change an object data value for a set of objects to a common value, you can use selection tools or queries to select the objects. You can then use the Properties palette to change the value for all of the objects, as shown in the following illustration.

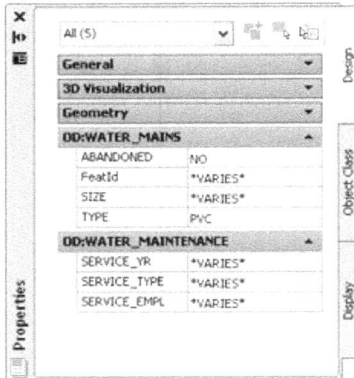

Single-Object Edits

If you are editing object data on a single object, the Properties palette and the Edit Object Data dialog box are equally efficient methods.

Exercise: Edit Object Data

In this exercise, you will work with two object data tables that are attached to a waterline. You will add a record to a maintenance table and edit the record of an additional table that documents the physical characteristics of the waterline.

1. Open ...\3-Drawing-Based Attribute Data\Edit and Manage Object Data\Water_OD.dwg.

2. On the Tools ribbon, under Map Edit, click Edit Object Data, as shown in the following illustration.

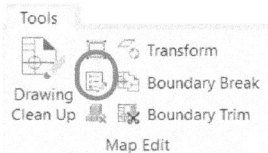

3. Select the water main, as shown in the following illustration. You will need to zoom out and pan to find the area.

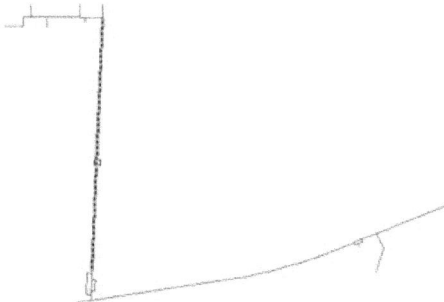

4. In the Edit Object Data dialog box, for Table, select WATER_MAINTENANCE, as shown in the following illustration.

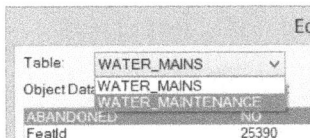

5. Enter the following values for the new record:
   - Year of Service: **2008**
   - Type of Service: **Replacement**
   - Employee Name: **City of Redding**

   Note: Press <Enter> after each entry.

6. Select WATER_MAINS from the Table list.

7. Replace the existing values in this record with the following, as shown in the following illustration:
   - ABANDONED: **NO**
   - FeatId: **25390**
   - SIZE: **15**
   - TYPE: **PVC**

   Note: Press <Enter> after each entry.

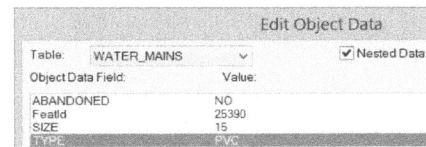

8. Click OK.

9. Select, then right-click on the water main that you just modified and select **Properties** from the right-click menu.

10. You can view and edit the object data in the Properties palette, as shown in the following illustration.

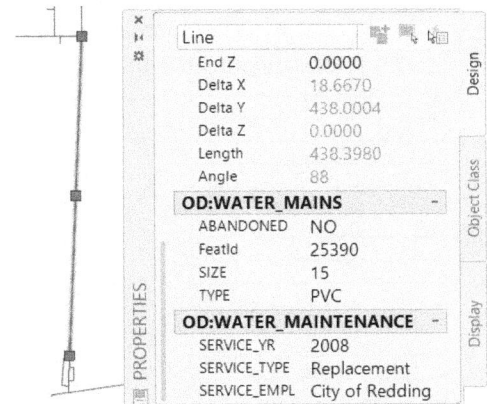

11. Save and close the drawing.

Lesson: Creating Dynamic Annotation

Overview

In this lesson, you add dynamic annotation to a drawing. In the AutoCAD Map 3D software, the term annotation refers to a special function in which data attached to objects is extracted and used to create text. This automation of text creation can be a great time saver.

The following illustration shows a set of parcels with annotation text.

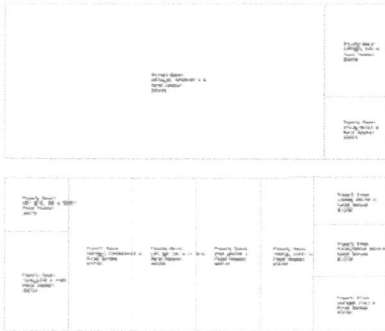

Objectives

After completing this lesson, you will be able to:

- Describe the concept of annotation.
- Decide between annotation and static text.
- Create annotation in the AutoCAD Map 3D software.

About Annotation in the AutoCAD Map 3D Software

Implementing the Annotation feature in the AutoCAD Map 3D software requires a bit of setup and is well worth the effort. The user interface is quite straightforward. To begin, you must have objects in the drawing with some sort of attribute associated with them, either the AutoCAD block attributes, object data, or SQL data stored in external databases.

You must also have an annotation template that provides information about how to create the annotation text: what data should be used, what text properties apply, and the location relative to the object being annotated. When you have created a template, selecting the objects that are to be used generates the annotation.

The template is created in a separate drawing environment. The process is similar to that of the AutoCAD block creation, but one difference is the specification of which data to extract to generate the annotation.

The following illustration shows the settings that control the creation and display of annotation text.

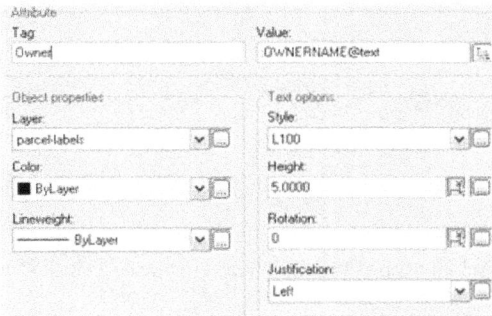

Key Facts about Annotation Templates

- Creation of an annotation template invokes the Block Editor that provides standard drawing commands for designing the template.
- The text that displays as annotation is based on selected attributes.

Example of Annotation

The AutoCAD point objects have been used as centroids for a set of parcels in a polygon topology. An object data table containing the owner's name and address has been attached to each centroid and the specific data entered for each parcel. An annotation template is created that extracts data from the points and labels for each parcel automatically.

About Annotation Versus Static Text

The decision about whether to use Map Annotation or to just place text in a drawing manually is largely based on what you have to work with. If you have a lot of objects that require labels and they already have some form of data attached to them, the use of Map Annotation is probably preferable.

The following illustration shows the object data attached to a polyline from the AutoCAD software.

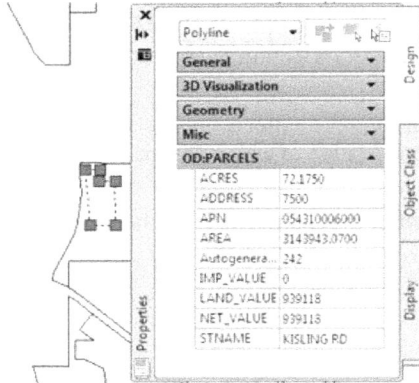

Annotation Guidelines

When using annotation, the following guidelines should be followed:

- An annotation template is designed so that all of the annotation created with a single template will be created the same.
- You might need to use more than one annotation template.
- Additional templates can be made by copying existing ones.
- When you use Insert Annotation, if you select objects that do not carry the data specified in the annotation template, the raw tag value displays.
- Existing annotation can be refreshed or updated if the data or templates change.
- All of the annotations in a drawing that are based on the same template can be erased simultaneously.

Example of Using Multiple Annotation Templates

You can satisfy varying requirements in a single drawing using multiple annotation templates that have different scales, attributes, layers, or colors.

The following illustration demonstrates the use of annotation templates with different scale factors to label parcels of varying sizes.

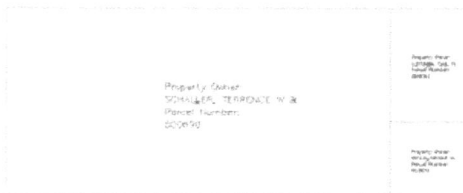

Exercise: Creating Annotation in AutoCAD Map 3D

In this exercise, you will identify the data associated with closed polyline objects in a drawing and design an annotation template for the labels. You will then create the annotation for a set of parcels. Two annotation templates are created using the same object data but at two different scales, as shown in the following illustration.

The completed exercise

1. Open ...\3-Drawing-Based Attribute Data\Annotation\annotation.dwg.

2. Select any polyline, then right-click and select Properties.

    ▪ Note the object data that displays in the lower portion of the Properties palette, as shown in the following illustration.

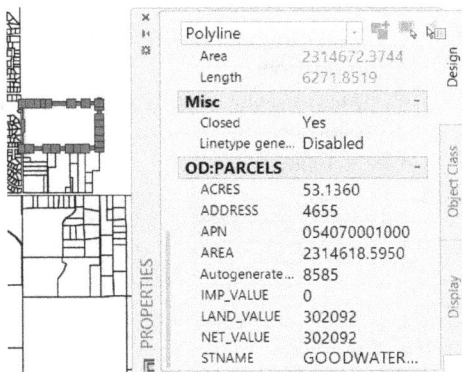

3. On the Annotate ribbon, under Map Annotation, click Define Template, as shown in the following illustration.

4. In the Define Annotation Template dialog box, click New, as shown in the following illustration.

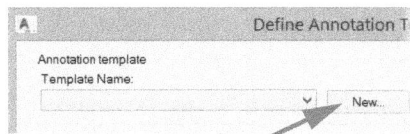

5. In the New Annotation Template Name dialog box:

    ▪ For New Template Name, enter **Parcel_Label**.

    ▪ Click OK.

    The Drawing Editor is replaced with the Block Editor, as shown in the following illustration.

6. If the Block Authoring palette appears, close it.

7. Type **MapAnnText** in the command line.

8. Press <Enter> to open the Annotation Text dialog box.

9. In the Annotation Text dialog box:

    ▪ For Tag, enter **ADDRESS**.

    ▪ For Value, click the Expression Chooser button, as shown in the following illustration.

10. In the Expression Chooser dialog box:

- Expand Object Data.
- Expand PARCELS.
- Click ADDRESS, as shown in the following illustration.
- Click OK.

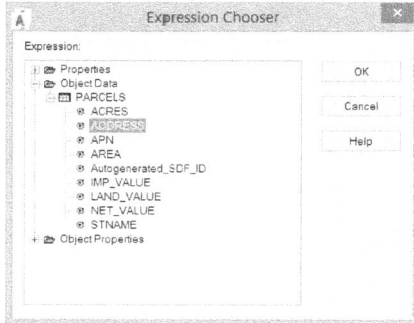

11. In the Annotation Text dialog box:

- Under Object Properties, for Layer, select the PARCEL_ANNO.
- Under Text Options, for Style, select Annotative.
- For Height, enter **2**, as shown in the following illustration.
- Click OK.

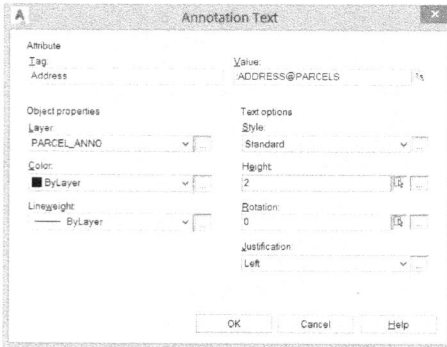

12. When prompted to Specify Left Point Of Text, at the command line:

- Enter **-25, 0**.
- Press <Enter>.

13. Type **MapAnnText** in the command line and press <Enter>.

14. In the Annotation Text dialog box:

- For Tag, enter **ST_NAME**.
- For Value, click the Expression Chooser button.

15. In the Expression Chooser dialog box:

- Expand Object Data.
- Expand PARCELS.
- Click STNAME, as shown in the following illustration.
- Click OK.

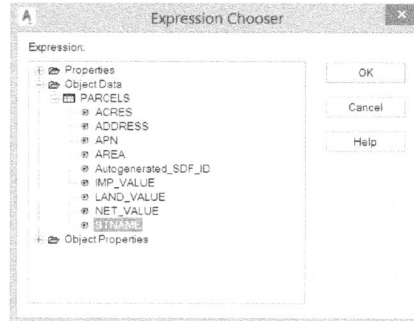

16. In the Annotation Text dialog box:

- Under Object Properties, for Layer, select PARCEL_ANNO.
- Under Text Options, for Style, select Annotative.
- Under Height, enter **2**, as shown in the following illustration.
- Click OK.

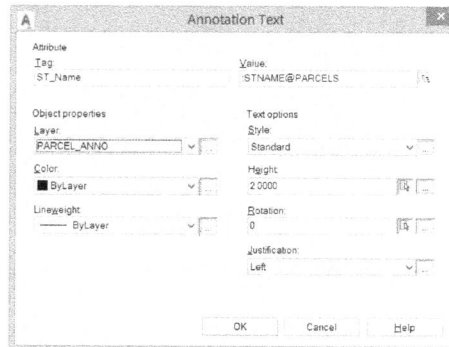

17. When prompted to Specify Left Point of Text:
    - At the command line, enter **-25, -10**.
    - Press <Enter>. The result should be similar to that shown in the following illustration.

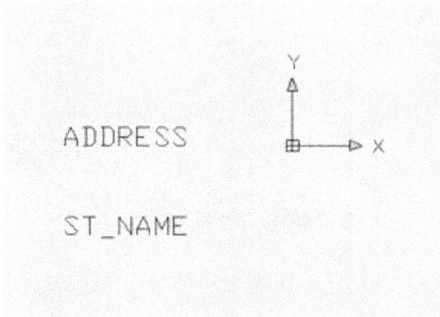

18. On the Block Editor ribbon, click Close Block Editor.

19. In the Block - Changes Not Saved dialog box, select Save the Changes to ACMAP_ANN_TEMPLATE_Parcel_Label.

20. In the Define Annotation Template dialog box:
    - Under Default Properties, for Layer, select PARCEL_ANNO.
    - Under Insertion Point, ensure that .LABELPT is selected, as shown in the following illustration.
    - Click OK.

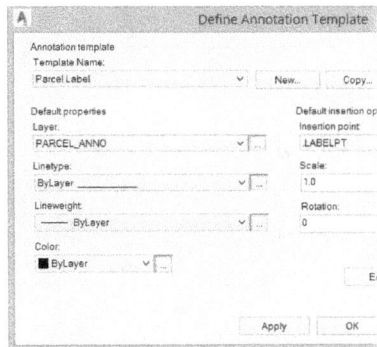

21. On the Annotate ribbon, under Map Annotation, click Insert, as shown in the following illustration.

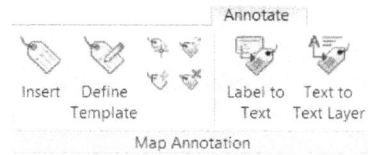

22. In the Insert Annotation dialog box:
    - Click Parcel_Label, as shown in the following illustration.
    - Click Insert.

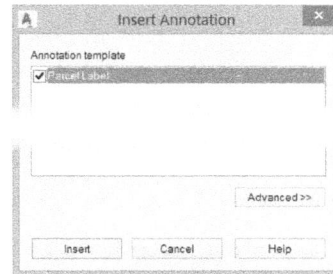

23. In the Drawing Editor:
    - Click several parcel polylines.
    - Press <Enter>.
    - Zoom in to see the results, as shown in the following illustration.

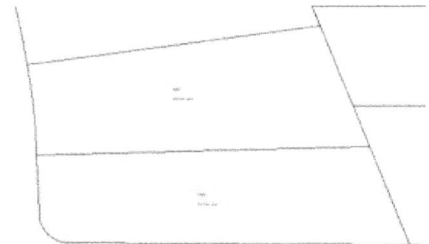

24. On the Annotate ribbon, under Map Annotation, click Define Template.

25. On the Define Annotation Template dialog box, select Parcel_Label in the Template Name drop-down list, and click Copy.

26. In the New Annotation Template Name dialog box:

- For New Template Name, enter **Parcel_Label_2X**.
- Click OK.

27. In the Define Annotation Template dialog box:

- For Scale, enter **2**, as shown in the following illustration.
- Click OK.

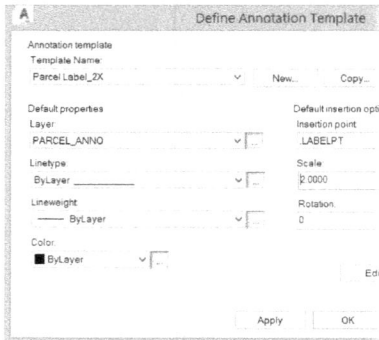

28. On the Annotate ribbon, under Map Annotation, select Insert.

29. In the insert Annotation dialog box:

- Select Parcel_Label_2X, as shown in the following illustration.
- Click Insert.

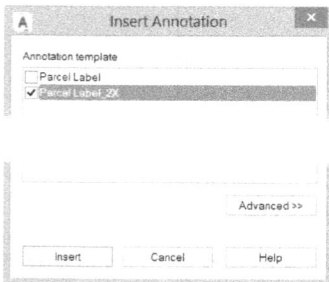

30. In the Drawing Editor:

- Select a few parcel polylines, as shown in the following illustration.
- Press <Enter>.

31. Save and close the drawing.

Lesson: Connecting to a Database

Overview

In this lesson, you learn how to connect external database files to a drawing using a simple drag and drop method. Once the database is attached, you can view the data in the database using Data View. In Data View, the display of the data can be adjusted to make it more useful.

The following illustration shows Data View open in a drawing.

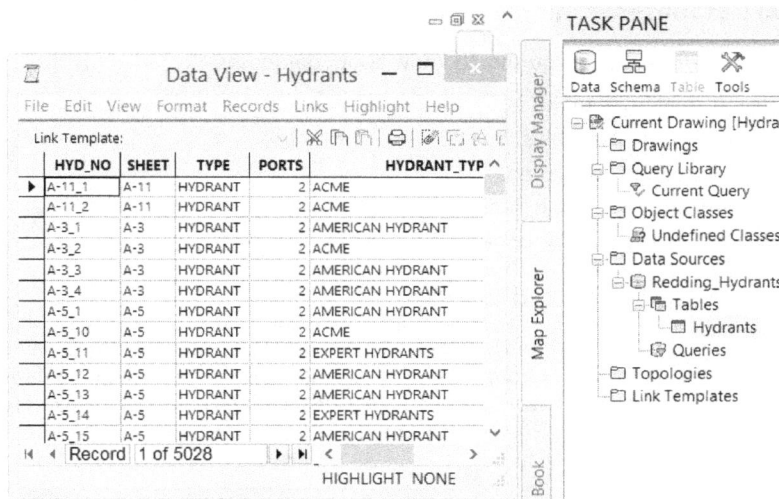

Objectives

After completing this lesson, you will be able to:

- Describe database tables.
- Explain the function of a Universal Data Link file.
- Describe the function of Data View.
- Attach an external database and use Data View.

About External Data

External data is information that is stored in files that are separate from a drawing file. In the AutoCAD Map 3D software, data can also be stored as internal information, such as object data or block attributes. Both internal and external information have advantages and disadvantages.

Some of the common benefits of using external tables are shown in the following list:

- External data can be accessed by individuals without having access to the drawing files.
- External data is better for data that changes frequently, such as maintenance information.
- Drawing file size is not increased if the data is stored externally.

About External Databases

Following are some important things you should know about databases:

- Databases store information in tables.
- Databases can contain multiple tables.
- Tables are made up of rows and columns.
- Rows are also referred to as records or individual items of data.
- Columns are also referred to as fields or general types of data.

Example of a Database Connected to a Map

A map of the sanitary sewer system in a town is linked to an external database that stores maintenance information. A field technician returning from a day of maintenance only works with the database application to update the maintenance work done that day. Because the database is linked to the map, the next time the map is accessed, the new information that was entered into the database displays.

Microsoft Office 365 and the 64 bit ODBC Driver

If you have a 64 bit operating system and have MS Office 365 installed, you will not be able to install the required 64 bit ODBC driver successfully as the installed MS Office 365 will cause it to fail. You MUST install the ODBC driver first. Consult with your IT department to assist you with this if need be.

For more information, consult the Autodesk Knowledge Network on this issue.

About the Universal Data Link

When you drag and drop a database file into the AutoCAD Map 3D Map Explorer task pane to attach it to a drawing, a Universal Data Link (UDL) is automatically created. By default, it is stored in the folder called Data Links in the Application Data folder in the user's Documents and Settings folder.

A UDL for a specific database connection is persistent. If you attach and save a database to a drawing, when the drawing is reopened, the AutoCAD Map 3D software reestablishes the connection using the existing UDL. If you want to attach another drawing to the same database, the new connection should be established through the existing UDL. This is preferred to dragging and dropping the database into the Map Explorer again, as this unnecessarily generates a new UDL file.

The following illustration shows a UDL file providing the information the AutoCAD Map 3D software needs to link an external database to two drawing files.

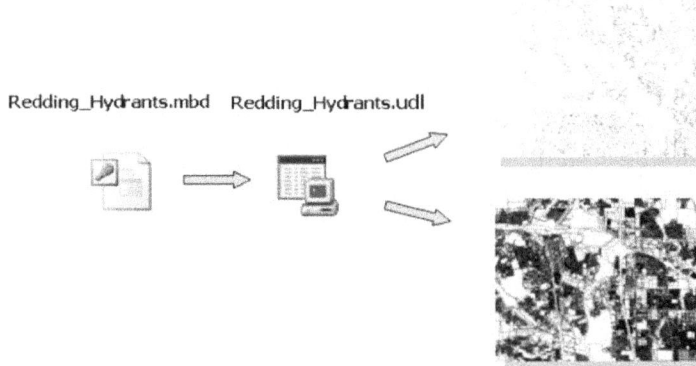

Redding_Hydrants.mbd   Redding_Hydrants.udl

UDL File

A UDL is a file that provides the required information to the AutoCAD Map 3D software to link an external database to a drawing file. A UDL file accomplishes this by storing and supplying to the AutoCAD Map 3D software, information about the type and location of the database that is to be attached, and what driver to use.

Example of a UDL File

If a database called *Utilities.mdb* is attached to a drawing, a file called *Utilities.udl* is created by the AutoCAD Map 3D software. This file stores the information the AutoCAD Map 3D software needs to connect to that database.

About Data View

When you store information about objects in a drawing in an external database, you use Data View to access that data. Without Data View, you would need the application that a database was created in to view the data.

The following illustration shows Data View displaying the contents of an external database table.

Data View Defined

Data View in the AutoCAD Map 3D software provides a way to view information stored in external database tables without the actual database application. In Data View, you can reorder or hide columns and filter the data to show information that meets your specific requirements.

The following illustration shows how to hide a column of data in Data View.

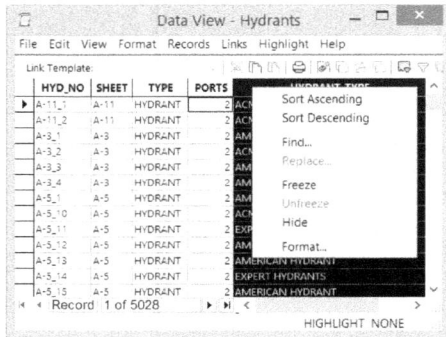

Features of Data View

These are some of the important aspects of Data View:

- Data View enables the viewing of data in external database tables directly in the AutoCAD Map 3D software.
- The database application that the database was originally created in is not required to view data.
- In the Data View, the columns of data can be reordered or hidden.
- In the Data View, filters can be created to only display specific data.

> Depending on your access rights to the database, you might be able to edit records in Data View.

Example of Using Data View to Display Specific Information

If you were to view a database table in Data View that contained three columns for Parcel IDs, Values, and Areas, you could arrange these columns in any order, and/or filter the data to only show the parcels with a value of less than, greater than, or equal to a specified amount, or only parcels with less than a specified area.

Exercise: Attach an External Database Table and Use Data View

In this exercise, you will attach an external database to a drawing, see it in Map Explorer, and select a table to examine in Data View. You will also make some adjustments to the display of the table in Data View, as shown in the following illustration.

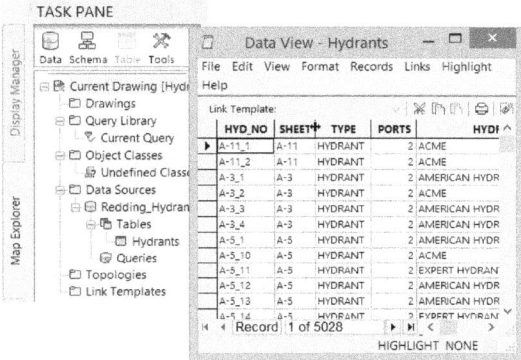

1. Open ...\3-Drawing-Based Attribute Data\ Connecting to a Database\Hydrants.dwg.

2. Open Windows Explorer and locate ...\3-Drawing-Based Attribute Data\ Connecting to a Database\ Redding_Hydrants.mdb.

3. Ensure that the Map Task Pane is open and the Map Explorer tab is the active tab.

   Drag and drop Redding_Hydrants.mdb into Map Explorer, as shown in the following illustration.

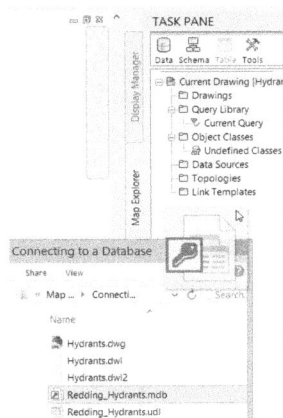

Note: If you receive an error, go to the Microsoft.com site and search for the appropriate Microsoft Access Database Engine for your specific computer setup and follow the steps to set it up, or consult with your IT department.

4. In Map Explorer, note that the Redding_Hydrants database is shown under Data Sources, and that the Hydrants table is shown under Tables, as shown in the following illustration.

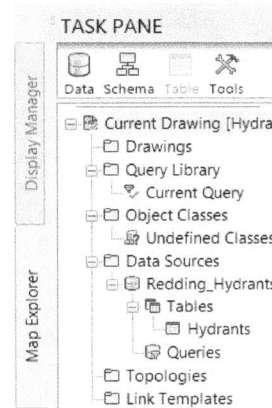

5. Double-click on the Hydrants table to open Data View, as shown in the following illustration.

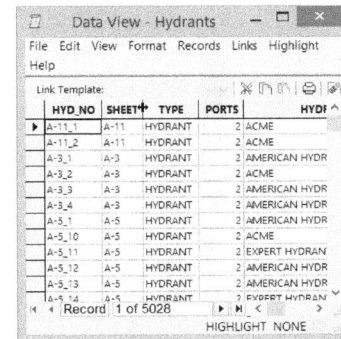

6. Use the scroll bars to examine the information displayed in Data View.

7. To move the PORTS column, click on the header to highlight the column, as shown in the following illustration.

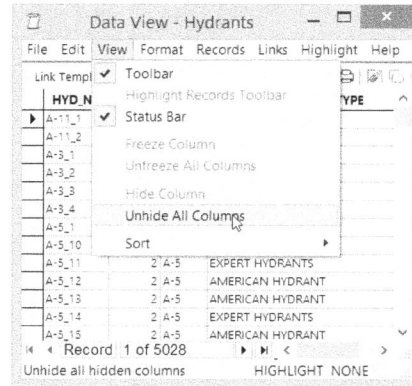

8. In the Data View window:

- Click and hold the left mouse button on the column header. A Move icon displays.
- Drag the PORTS column to the left until a red line displays between the HYD_NO and SHEET columns.
- Release the left mouse button to drop the PORTS column between these two columns.

9. To hide the TYPE column, right-click on the column header. Click Hide, as shown in the following illustration.

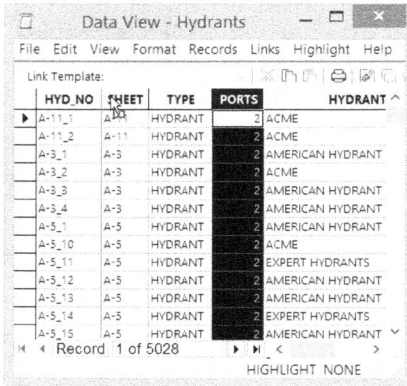

10. To show the TYPE column, click View menu> Unhide All Columns, as shown in the following illustration.

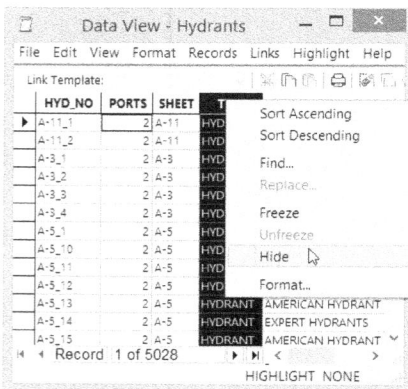

11. Click SQL Filter, as shown in the following illustration.

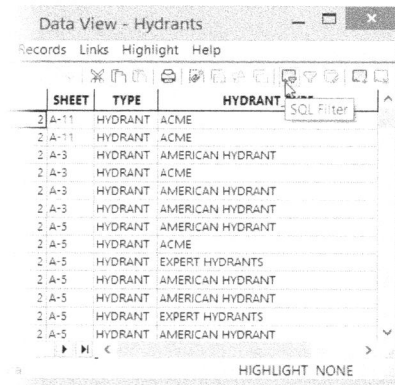

12. In the Table Filter dialog box:

- Under Where Condition, for Column, select PORTS.
- For Operator, select >=.
- For Value, enter **3**, as shown in the following illustration.
- Click Add.
- Click OK.

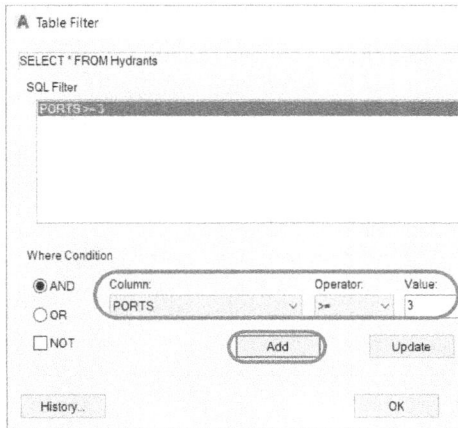

13. Note that only the hydrants with 3 or more ports are now displayed, as shown in the following illustration.

14. Close the drawing without saving.

Lesson: Defining a Link Template and Linking Records to Objects

Overview

In this lesson, you create a link template based on a database and automatically generate links between records in that database and objects in a drawing. A database can store information about real-world artifacts that are represented by objects in a drawing. Linking database records to the corresponding objects in a drawing offers a number of benefits, including a variety of analyses.

The following illustration shows a record in a database and the corresponding hydrant block in a drawing.

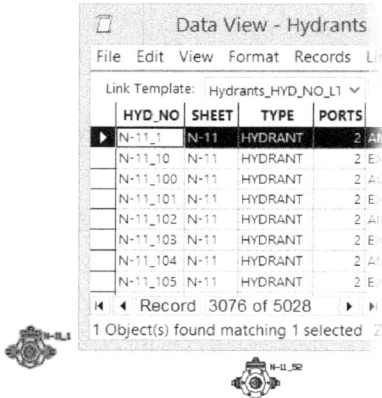

Objectives

After completing this lesson, you will be able to:

- Describe the function of a link template.
- Describe the guidelines for selecting a key field.
- Define a link template and generate links.

About Link Templates

A link template is a component in the AutoCAD Map 3D software that specifies which external database you are linking to, which table in that database, and which column in that table you are using as a key field.

The following illustration shows a link template named APN. This template specifies *Redding.mdb* as the database, Parcels as the table, and APN as the key field. The linked parcel contains a single value for APN that specifies the record in the Redding database to which it is linked.

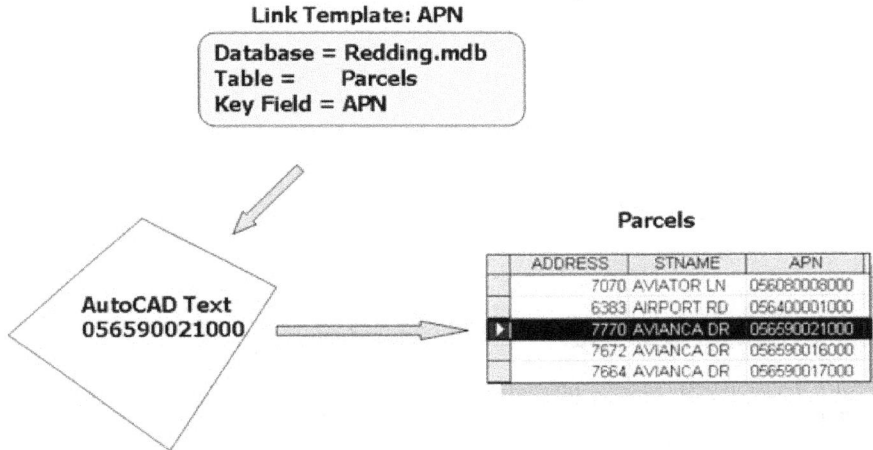

Link Templates

Note the following when linking records in a database to objects in a drawing:

- Link templates are required to link objects in drawings to records in external databases. A specific link template is required for each database table to which you want to link objects.
- A key field is a column or field, in a database table that is used to link specific records in the table to objects in a drawing. For this reason, the values in the key field must be unique for each record.

Example of Selecting a Key Field for a Link Template

The database *Redding.mdb* contains a table called Parcels, with a column APN. Every record (row) in the table has a different or unique APN value. Because of this, APN is a good candidate for a key field. The link template stores the name of the database, the table, and the key field to link drawing objects to records.

Guidelines for Selecting a Key Field

Existing Data

The following illustration shows parcel ID numbers represented as text in the parcels in a drawing. These text values match values in the key field in the database table.

What Makes a Good Key Field?

An important decision you make when preparing to attach database records to drawing objects is which field to use as the key field. One criterion is the relationship of the key field values to existing values on objects in the drawing.

Guidelines for Key Field Selection

The Generate Links process requires that drawing objects have values already associated with them that match the values in the key field of the database. These values can be block attributes or text values. While linking objects manually is a much more tedious process, it does have the advantage that the objects do not require any values associated with them beforehand.

Records can be manually linked to objects in a drawing if no matching values exist to enable the automatic generation of links.

An Example

In the Parcels table in the Redding database, the APN field contains parcel numbers that match values in the Parcels drawing. The values are represented as AutoCAD text in each parcel polygon, represented by a closed polyline. The matching values provide the information required to generate the automatic link.

Exercise: Define a Link Template and Generate Links

In this exercise, you will define a link template and automatically generate links between records in the attached database and objects in the drawing with corresponding values, as shown in the following illustration.

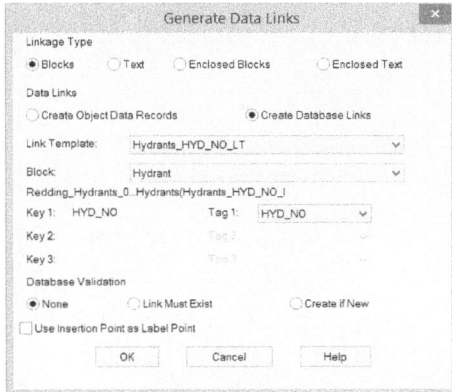

The Generate Data Links dialog box

1. Open ...\3-Drawing-Based Attribute Data\Defining a Link Template, and Linking Records to Objects\Hydrants.dwg.

2. In the drawing editor, double-click on a hydrant. In the Enhanced Attribute Editor, note that each hydrant has block attribute data with a tag called HYD_NO, as shown in the following illustration.

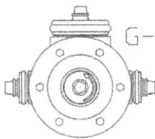

3. Click OK to dismiss the Enhanced Attribute Editor.

4. Double-click on the Hydrants table in Map Explorer to open the table in Data View. Note the values in the HYD_NO column, as shown in the following illustration.

When you use the HYD_NO values to link to matching block attributes in the drawing, the database records will be linked to blocks that have the same attribute value.

5. In Map Explorer, right-click on Link Templates>Define Link Template, as shown in the following illustration.

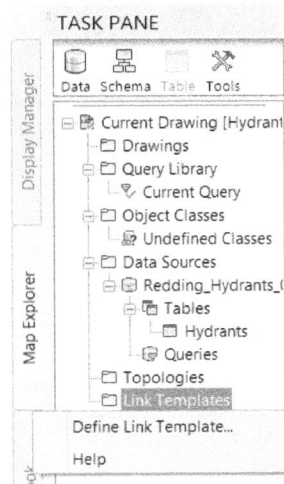

6. In the Define Link Template dialog box:

- Note that the Data Source is Redding_Hydrants and the Table Name is Hydrants.
- For Link Template, enter **Hydrants_HYD_NO_LT**.
- Under Key Selection, check the box for HYD_NO to use this column for the key field, as shown in the following illustration.
- Click OK.

7. In Map Explorer, expand the Link Templates icon to see the newly created link template, as shown in the following illustration.

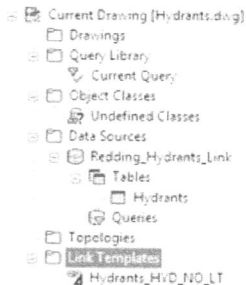

8. In MAP Explorer, right-click on Hydrants_HYD_NO_LT>Generate Links, as shown in the following illustration.

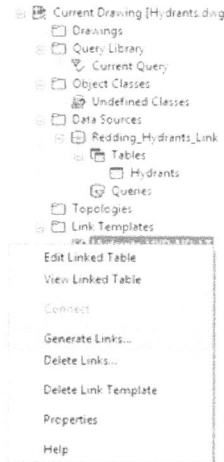

9. In the Generate Data Links dialog box:

- For Linkage Type, click Blocks.
- Under Data Links, click Create Database Links.
- Note that the Hydrants_HYD_NO_LT link template is selected.
- Note that the Hydrant block is selected.
- Note that the HYD_NO is selected for the Block Tag 1.
- Under Database Validation, click None, as shown in the following illustration.
- Click OK.

10. Press <Enter> or click All in the Command line, as shown in the following illustration.

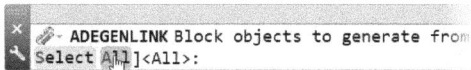

```
× ⌖- ADEGENLINK Block objects to generate from
⌕ Select All]<All>:
```

11. Once the links have been created, double-click on the Hydrants table in Map Explorer.

12. In Data View:

- Click Highlight>AutoZoom.
- Click Highlight>AutoHighlight, as shown in the following illustration.

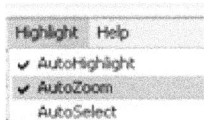

```
Highlight  Help
✓ AutoHighlight
✓ AutoZoom
   AutoSelect
```

13. Click Highlight>Zoom Scale.

14. In the Zoom Scale dialog box:

- Set the scale to 5, as shown in the following illustration.
- Click OK.

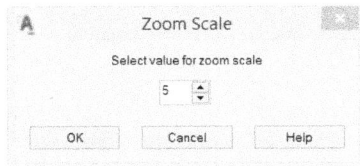

```
A              Zoom Scale
       Select value for zoom scale
              5  ▲
                 ▼
    OK        Cancel      Help
```

15. In Data View:

- Click a record to highlight and zoom to the hydrant block in the drawing to which the record is linked.
- Click another record to view another selected hydrant, as shown in the following illustration.

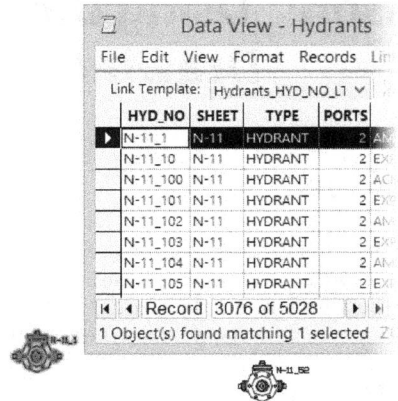

Data View - Hydrants

File Edit View Format Records Lin

Link Template: Hydrants_HYD_NO_L1 ∨

HYD_NO	SHEET	TYPE	PORTS
N-11_1	N-11	HYDRANT	2 AM
N-11_10	N-11	HYDRANT	2 EX
N-11_100	N-11	HYDRANT	2 AC
N-11_101	N-11	HYDRANT	2 EX
N-11_102	N-11	HYDRANT	2 AM
N-11_103	N-11	HYDRANT	2 EX
N-11_104	N-11	HYDRANT	2 AM
N-11_105	N-11	HYDRANT	2 EX

◄ ◄ Record 3076 of 5028 ► ►

1 Object(s) found matching 1 selected Z

16. Save and close the drawing.

Lesson: Using Database Information in a Drawing

Overview

This lesson covers how to use criteria in the database to select objects in a drawing, and how to select records in the database, based on objects in a drawing. When you connect a database to a drawing, define a link template, and create links to objects in the drawing, you can use these relationships to analyze both the database and the drawing.

Objectives

After completing this lesson, you will be able to:

- Describe drawing object selection from Data View.
- Describe database record selection through a drawing.
- Analyze database information in a drawing.

About Object Selection Through a Database

Database information is easily filtered and analyzed based on multiple criteria. When you link each database record to an individual object in a drawing, you extend the same possibility for analysis to the objects in the drawing.

How Object Selection Works

You can use Data View in the AutoCAD Map 3D software to select objects using database filtering to find specific records and identify the objects in the drawings that are linked to those records.

The following illustration shows the result of searching the database. The record is highlighted and the corresponding parcel in the drawing is selected.

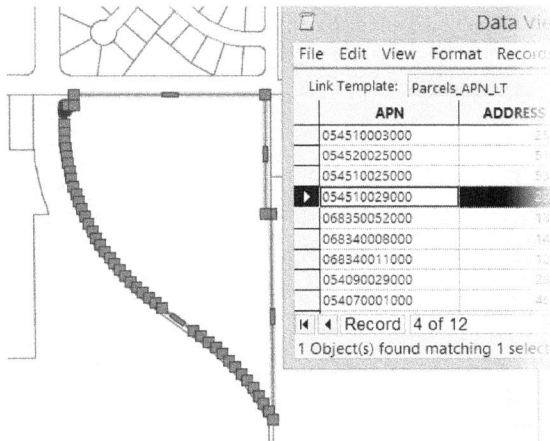

Methods

Drawing objects that are linked to selected database records can be identified in three ways:

- The AutoCAD Map 3D software can zoom to each object at a user-specified scale.
- Linked objects can be highlighted.
- Linked objects can be made into an AutoCAD selection set.

Example of Database Filtering for Object Selection

A database contains information about parcels of property in a town. All of the parcels are drawn on a map of the town and are linked to the corresponding records in the database. All of the parcels that are valued at more than $400,000 are selected with a filter in the Map Data View. The corresponding parcels in the drawing are highlighted so that they can be easily identified.

About Database Record Selection from a Drawing

Just as you can select drawing objects by working in Data View, you can also highlight database records by selecting their corresponding drawing objects. This important feature provides a spatial parameter to database filtering.

How Record Selection Works

Specific records in a database can be identified in Data View by selecting the corresponding objects in a drawing. Standard AutoCAD selection methods provide powerful spatial parameters for searching database records. For example, if you want to identify all of the parcels in a database that are within a street block, you can specify crossing or inclusion selection windows, polylines, or fences. More sophisticated AutoCAD selection methods, such as the Object Filter command or the Quick Filter tool, can also be used.

The following illustration shows an area of parcels selected in a city map.

Methods

Some important facts about selecting objects in the AutoCAD software are:

- Geographic location is the most commonly used selection factor. Simple AutoCAD selection methods are effective in these situations.
- The Quick Filters command can be used to select specific block references and layers.

A Typical Example

You need information about all of the parcels in a town that lie within a 500-foot radius of a school. Looking at a map, you can easily draw the circle that selects the parcels and identifies the linked records.

Exercise: Using Database Information in a Drawing

In this exercise, you will use an SQL Filter to select specific records in a database. The corresponding drawing objects are located. Next, you will select drawing objects in a specific area of the map. The corresponding database records are highlighted in Data View.

1. Open ...\3-Drawing-Based Attribute Data\ Using Database Information In a Drawing\ Parcels.dwg.

2. In the Map Task Pane>Map Explorer tab, double-click on the Parcels table to open Data View.

3. In the Data View dialog box, click the SQL Filter icon, as shown in the following illustration.

4. In the Table Filter dialog box:
   - Under Where Condition, for Column, select LAND_VALUE.
   - Set the Operator to > (Greater than).
   - For Value, enter **200000**, as shown in the following illustration.
   - Click Add.
   - Click OK.

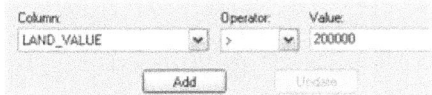

   Twelve records are returned in Data View, as shown in the following illustration.

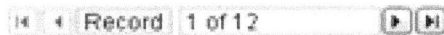

5. In Data View:
   - Click Highlight>AutoHighlight, AutoZoom, AutoSelect.
   - Click Zoom Scale, as shown in the following illustration.

6. In the Zoom Scale dialog box:
   - For Select Value For Zoom Scale, enter **40**, as shown in the following illustration.
   - Click OK.

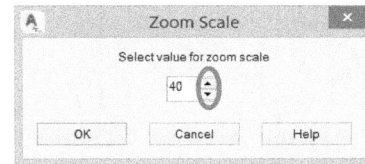

7. Resize the Data View dialog box for a clear view of the Drawing Editor.
   - Click on the cell at the left end of one row. A parcel is now selected for editing in both the database and the drawing, as shown in the following illustration.

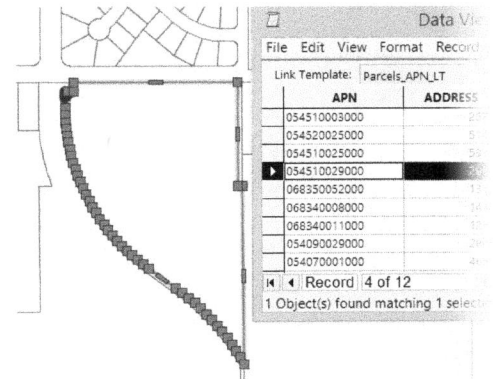

   - Continue to click through the records in Data View to select parcels with a Land Value over 200000.

8. In Data View, click Records>Clear Filter, as shown in the fol owing illustration.

9. Zoom to the drawing extents.

10. In Data View, click Highlight>Show Highlighted Records Only, as shown in the following illustration.

11. In Data View, click Highlight>Highlight Records>Select Objects, as shown in the following illustration.

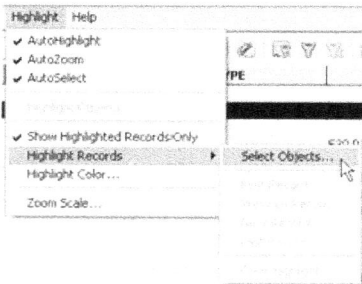

12. Select a group of parcels. Press <Enter>, as shown in the following illustration.

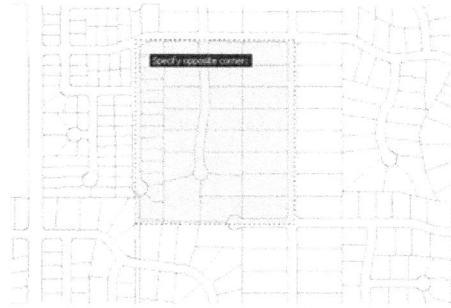

Data View now displays and highlights only the selected parcels, as shown in the following illustration.

APN	ADDRESS	STNAME
068640002000	4684	DANDELION DR
068460008000	1783	EL VERANO ST
068460006000	1730	EL VERANO ST
068490004000	4661	COLUMBINE DR
068490003000	4647	COLUMBINE DR
068540006000	1850	EL VERANO ST
068640001000	4690	DANDELION DR
068460007000	1770	EL VERANO ST

Record 1 of 57

56 record(s) are linked to 56 selected obje SELECT   40%

13. Save and close the drawing.

Chapter Summary

Having completed this chapter, you can:

- Create and attach object data.
- Edit and manage object data.
- Add dynamic annotation to a drawing.
- Connect to a database.
- Define a link template and link records to objects.
- Using database information in a drawing.

Chapter

4

Object Classification

The lessons in this chapter cover how to set up and use object classification.

Objectives

After completing this chapter, you will be able to:

- Set up an object class.
- Create, select, and classify objects.

Chapter

4

Object Classification

The lessons in this chapter cover how to set up and use object classification.

Objectives

After completing this chapter, you will be able to:

- Set up an object class.
- Create, select, and classify objects.

73

Lesson: Setting Up Object Classifications

Overview

An object class is a set of real-world artifacts, such as a road or sewer system, represented in a map by geometry with specific properties. You use object classification to standardize and organize objects in your drawing. When you create an object using object classification, it automatically takes its properties and values from its object classification, creating consistency and establishing standards in your drawings.

In this lesson, you learn what object classification is and how to create an object classification definition file and an object class.

The following illustration shows the properties associated with an object class object.

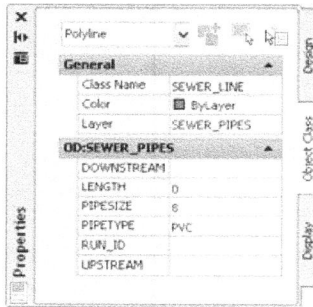

Objectives

After completing this lesson, you will be able to:

- Explain what object classification is.
- State the process of setting up an object classification.
- Decide how to set up object classifications for a specific goal.
- Set up an object class.

About Object Classification

Three main components make up object classification. These components are typically managed by a mapping technician or a CAD manager.

The following illustration shows how object classes are presented in Map Explorer.

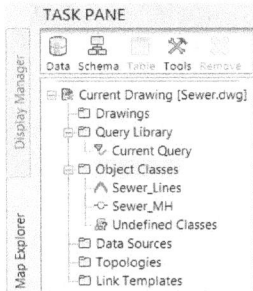

Object Classification Components

Following are the three main components of object classification.

Component	Definition
Object definition file	An XML file that contains one or more object class definitions. This file can be attached to one or more drawings. Typically, in a multiuser environment, object definition files are created by a CAD manager or someone responsible for establishing and managing standards. You must have superuser privileges in the AutoCAD® Map 3D software to create an object definition file.
Object class	A set of definitions used to establish a standard model of a real-world artifact, this is defined and stored in the object definition file. Each object definition file can contain one or more object class definitions. For example, a sewer line object class can include a standard object data table that documents diameter, installer, material, etc. The objects created using the sewer line object class can also force a standard layer and object type.
Object class objects	You can classify existing objects into an object class or create new objects based on an object class. If you create an object based on a class, it adopts all of the definitions of that object class, possibly including an automatic object data table attachment, standard layer, and standard object type.

Object Classification Process Overview

You can use object classification in a single-user environment or in an enterprise-wide mapping system with multiple users and differing roles. In both cases, the process of setting up object classification requires the same steps.

> To create an object definition file, you must have superuser privileges in the AutoCAD Map 3D software.

Process: Setting Up Object Definition Files and Object Classes

This process outlines how to set up object definition files, object classes, and object class objects. Although this process focuses on creating the object class definition file and object classes, creating object class objects is included here to provide a comprehensive overview.

1. Before setting up an object definition file, analyze your mapping system to identify what classes are required and how you want to deploy the definition file, as shown in the following illustration. Create the definition file.

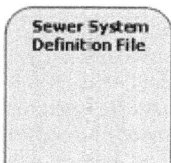

2. Once the definition file has been created, users with the correct privileges can create object classes. When you create a feature class, you use an example object to define the object class. The object class is then created using any properties associated with the example object, including layer, block references, object data, etc. Once the example definitions have been established, as shown in the following illustration, you can modify default values for block insertion, force layers, establish default object data values, etc.

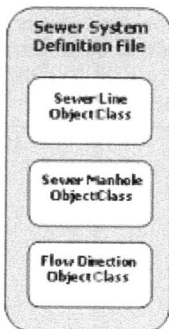

3. When the definition file and feature class are created, users can begin to classify objects, as shown in the following illustration, create objects, and use the object selection tools.

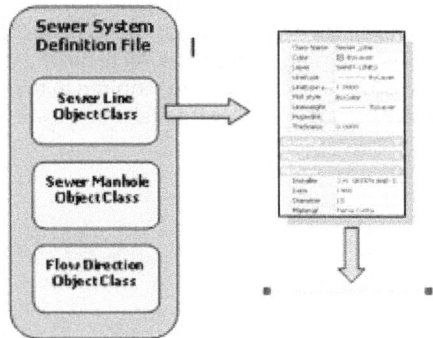

Guidelines for Setting Up Object Classification

In complex mapping systems, object classification is a powerful tool to group objects that are common.

Setting Up the Object Class

You can choose to use object classification for any of several reasons. The purpose of the object classes can range from simply enforcing layering standards to creating sophisticated digital representations of real-world objects. Consider the following guidelines when approaching object class design:

- When you first create the object class, ensure that all definitions are associated with the example object. For example, if the object class is to include an object data table, verify that the object data table is included as part of the example object.
- If you are applying object classification to an existing mapping system, the object class definitions can disqualify some of the existing objects from being included in the object class. For example, if a range of object data values is enforced in the object class, some of the existing objects in the map might not have the required object data values.

Roles and Responsibilities

- If you work in a multiuser or enterprise mapping system, object classes should be designed with the key individuals in the system. For example, if the road network is maintained by a group outside the mapping department, that group should be included in the design of the object class representing roads.
- Object definition files can be shared between users. These files should be maintained by the person who manages the mapping system.

Applying Object Classification to a Mapping System

The example in the following illustration shows how you can use object classification in a multiuser environment. A CAD manager, or someone who is responsible for establishing and maintaining standards, creates the object definition file and object classes. When the object classes are defined, the definition file is attached to drawings used by the mapping technicians. All technicians access the same definition file and use the same object classes. If any changes are required in the object classes, the CAD manager makes the change to a single file, thus updating it for all technicians.

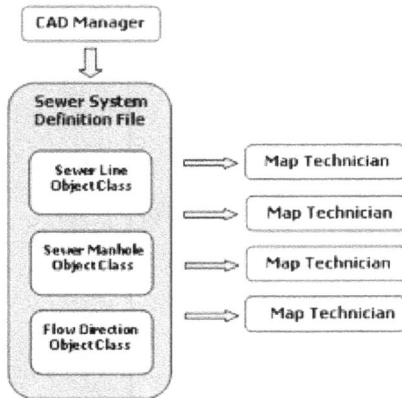

Exercise: Set Up an Object Class

In this exercise, you will create an object definition file and two object classes, as shown in the following illustration.

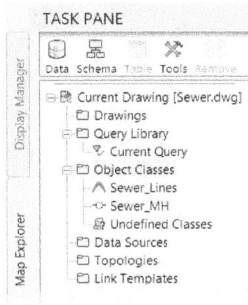

1. Open ...\4-Object Classification\Setting Up Object Classifications\ Sewer-Setup.dwg, as shown in the following illustration.

2. On the Map Setup ribbon, Map panel, beside Map, click the down arrow>User Login, as shown in the following illustration.

3. In the User Login dialog box:
   - For Login Name, enter **Superuser**, as shown in the following illustration.
   - For Password, enter **SUPERUSER**.
   - Click OK.

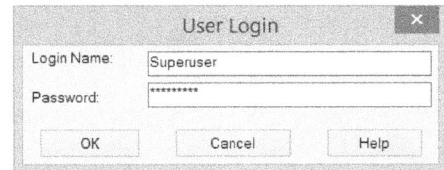

4. In Map Explorer, right-click on Object Classes and select New Definition File, as shown in the following illustration.

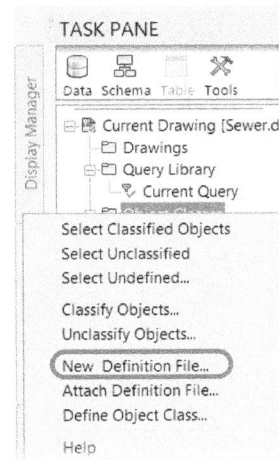

5. In the New Object Class Definition File dialog box:

- Browse to ...\4-ObjectClassification\Setting Up Object Classifications.
- For File Name, enter **Sewer**, as shown in the following illustration.
- Click Save.

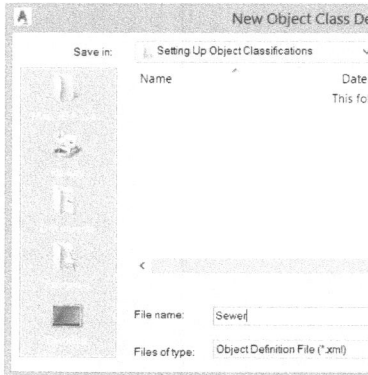

6. In Map Explorer, right-click on Object Classes and select Define Object Class, as shown in the following illustration.

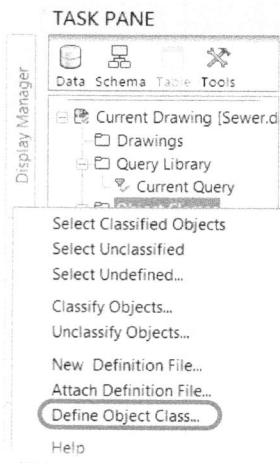

7. When prompted to select an example object:

- Select one of the sewer lines in the drawing, as shown in the following illustration.
- Press <Enter>.

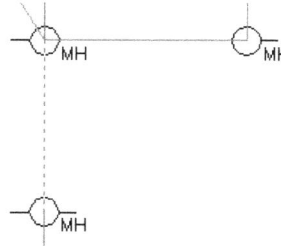

8. In the Define Object Classification dialog box:

- For Class Name, enter **Sewer_Lines**.
- On the Applies To tab, under Object Types, toggle on AcDbPolyline, as shown in the following illustration.

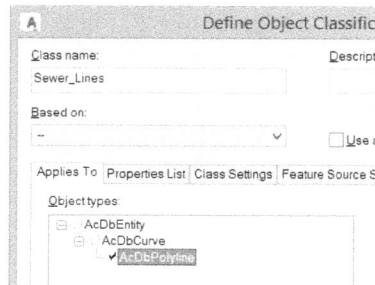

9. On the Properties List tab, for Available Properties:

- Under General, click Layer
- Under OD:SEWER_PIPES, toggle on RUN_ID and UPSTREAM, as shown in the following illustration.

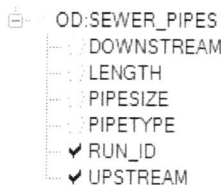

10. Select the Layer property.

   ▪ Under Property Attributes, click Range.
   ▪ Click Browse, as shown in the following illustration.

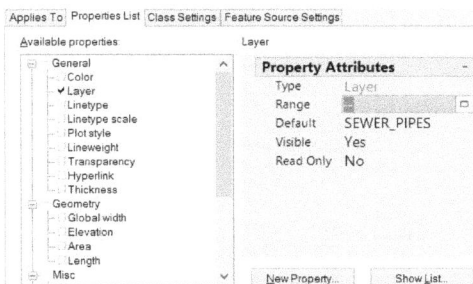

11. In the Layer Range Editor dialog box:

   ▪ Select Choose Specific Layers.
   ▪ Select SEWER_PIPES.
   ▪ Clear all other layer check boxes, as shown in the following illustration.
   ▪ Click OK.

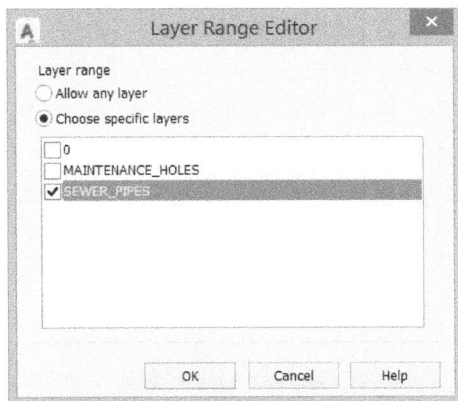

12. Under Available Properties:

   ▪ Under OD:SEWER_PIPES, toggle on DOWNSTREAM.
   ▪ Under Property Attributes, click Default.
   ▪ Clear the default value, as shown in the following illustration.

DOWNSTREAM

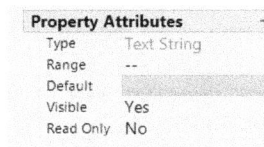

13. Under Available Properties:

   ▪ Under OD:SEWER_PIPES, toggle on LENGTH.
   ▪ For Default, enter **0**.

14. Under Available Properties:

   ▪ Under OD:SEWER_PIPES, toggle on PIPESIZE.
   ▪ For Default, enter **8**.

15. Under Available Properties:

   ▪ Under OD:SEWER_PIPES, toggle on PIPETYPE.
   ▪ For Default, enter **PVC**.
   ▪ For Range, enter **PVC, VCP, RCP, DI, ABS, STL, AC**, as shown in the following illustration.
   ▪ When done, press <Enter>.

PIPETYPE

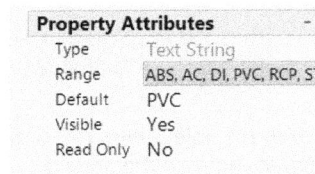

16. Under Available Properties:

   ▪ Under OD:SEWER_PIPES, toggle on RUN_ID.
   ▪ For Default, clear the default value.

17. Under Available Properties:

   ▪ Under OD:SEWER_PIPES, toggle on UPSTREAM.
   ▪ For Default, clear the default value.

18. On the Class Settings tab:
    - Under Class icon, select Browse.
    - Navigate to the ...\4-Object Classification\Setting Up Object Classifications folder.
    - Select the SF.bmp file.
    - Click Open.

19. Click Save Definition, as shown in the following illustration.

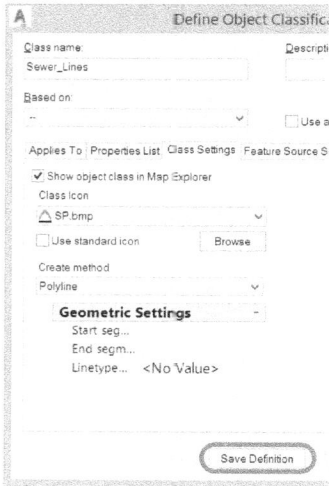

20. Repeat Steps 6 through 19 to define the Sewer_MH object class. Use the following values:
    - For an example object, click one of the maintenance holes in the drawing.
    - For Class Name, toggle on **Sewer_MH**.
    - On the Applies To tab, toggle on AcDbBlockReference>MH.
    - On the Properties List tab, click Layer.
    - Set the range to only the MAINTENANCE_HOLES layer.
    - On the Class Settings tab, under the class icon, browse to and select MH.bmp for the icon.
    - Click Save Definition.

21. Verify that the two new object classes display in Map Explorer, as shown in the following illustration.

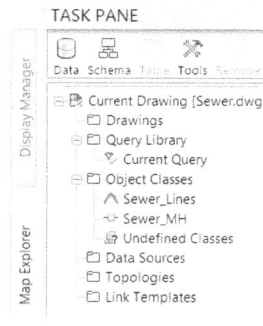

Note: Although you have selected two example objects to create the Sewer_Lines and Sewer_MH Object Classes, no objects in the map are classified yet.

22. Save and close the file.

Lesson: Classify, Select, and Create Classified Objects

Overview

Object classification is a tool you can employ in a large mapping system or single-user environment. In either case, the process of using object classification consists of three primary tasks: create an object definition file, create an object class, and create classified objects. Once a definition file and object class have been created, you can create the classified objects. You can create classified objects by classifying existing objects, or create new classified objects.

The following illustration shows the shortcut menu that is available for object classes. In this lesson, you learn how to create, select, and classify objects from this menu.

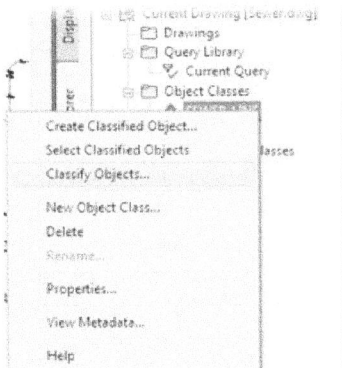

Objectives

After completing this lesson, you will be able to:

- Describe classified objects.
- Decide how to prepare a drawing for object classification.
- Classify, select, and create object class objects.

About Classified Objects

All objects in a drawing have several properties associated to them. For example, individual geometry objects must be on a single layer, or an object data table associated can be associated with an object.

When an object is part of an object class, it means certain definitions are associated to the object as defined by that class. For example, all objects in a specific object class have the same object data table, layer, object type, etc. Therefore, multiple definitions are recognized as a single definition, the object class.

Creating Classified Objects

All maps and the objects in them are designed to create a model of the real world. Digital maps have the added benefit of the information associated with the geometry. This information, along with spatial analysis, is the basis of geographic information systems.

When you create a line, point, or text in a map, it represents something in the real world. You can attach object data, SQL links, or attribute data to this object to better represent the object. Object classification is a method of creating a standard model of the object you are representing. Rather than drawing a line to represent a pipe, you create a pipe object. From a definition perspective, the line is a pipe, not just a line.

Example of Using Object Classes

You design and create an object class to perform a specific function. For example, if you produce road maps, you might want to have a set of standard road objects, such as primary and secondary roads.

Each of these standard objects has a specific set of properties. You might want all of the primary roads to be created using a polyline with a thick lineweight, to be on the Primary Roads layer, and to have object data associated with them that lists values for speed limits and the number of lanes. Similarly, you might want secondary roads to go on the Secondary Roads layer, to use a thin lineweight, and to include information about the surface type.

Guidelines for Classifying Objects

Before you can classify objects, you must create an object class definition file and an object class. The guidelines in this section assume that a definition and object class have already been created and are available to you.

Guidelines

Before you classify objects into an existing object class, you should know how classification works and what behavior to expect. The following guidelines assume that you are classifying existing objects:

Property Alteration

▪ Ensure that the objects you classify reside on the appropriate layer. If the object class you use to classify objects expects them to be on a specific layer, and you classify existing objects that are on a different layer, they are not placed on the layer specified by the object class.

Out of Range

▪ During the classification procedure, you can set options to include or not include objects that are out of range of the object class. For example, if the layer specified in the object class is forced, you cannot classify objects that are not on that layer. The same is true if object data fields expect a range of values and the object you attempt to classify has a value that falls outside that range.

Multiple Layers and Definitions

You can classify objects that are on different layers into the same object class. For example, if you want the entire road network to be recognized as a single object class, you can include all of the objects that make up the road network, regardless of layers or object types.

Objects Rejected During Classification

One important aspect of object classification is the ability to force specific definitions on the objects in the object class. For example, all objects must be on a specific layer, or the object data values must fall within a specific range. In the following example, objects are rejected during the classification process because they do not have one or more of the standard definitions required by the object class.

This object class is defined to only accept specific object data values. In this case, sewer pipe materials can only have values of ABS, AC, DI, PVC, RCP, STL, and VCP, as shown in the following illustration. If any of the sewer lines in the drawing do not have these values, they are rejected during classification and considered out of range.

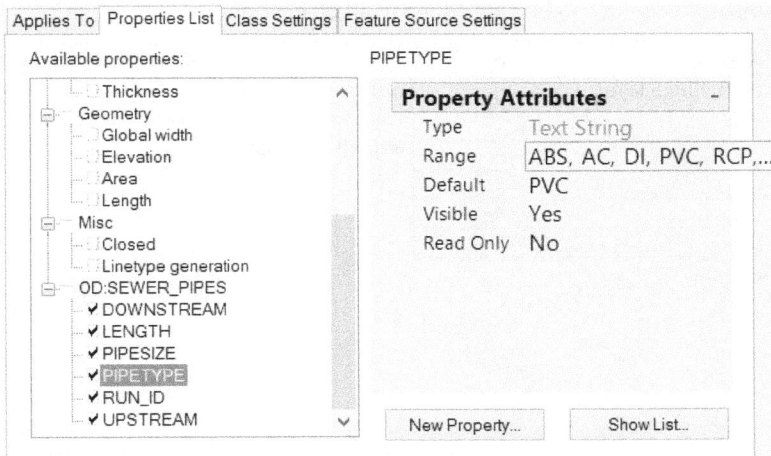

The sewer line shown in the following illustration was rejected during classification because the object data value for materials is outside the range of the object class. In this case, SDR-35 was not a valid PIPETYPE.

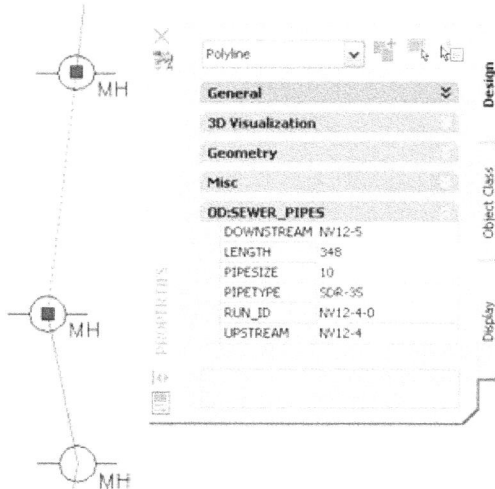

Enforcing Standards

You can use object classification to enforce standards in a mapping system. When you first classify existing objects, you can use the classification process to identify objects that deviate from established standards as defined by the object class.

Classification Example

The following example shows how objects are added to an object class:

This object class is defined to only accept objects that are on the SEWER_PIPES layer.

The following illustration shows a selected object class and all of the objects in it. In this case, all of the objects are on the correct layer and all are classified.

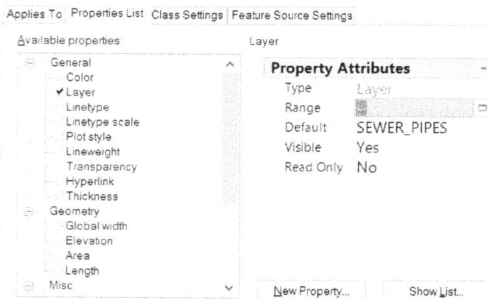

Exercise: Classify, Select, and Create Classified Objects

In this exercise, you will open a drawing with two object classes already defined but no objects classified, as shown in the following illustration. You will classify the objects in the drawing, select them to verify the correct classification, and create new objects.

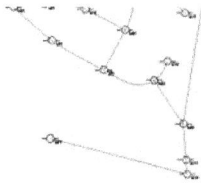

The completed exercise

1. Open ...\4-Object Classification\Classify, Select, and Create Object Class Objects\sewer-Classify.dwg.

2. In the Map Explorer, right-click on SEWER_LINE class and select Classify Objects, as shown in the following illustration.

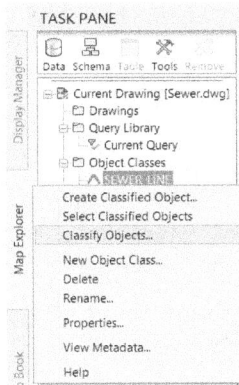

3. In the Classify Objects dialog box:
   - Clear the Include Objects With Missing or Out of Range Property Values check box, as shown in the following illustration.
   - Click OK.

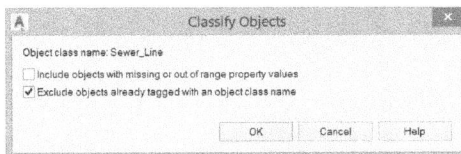

4. When prompted to select objects, at the command line:
   - Enter **ALL**, as shown in the following illustration.
   - Press <Enter> twice.

The drawing contains a total of 15,301 objects, of which 8736 are the wrong object type and 6565 are classified.

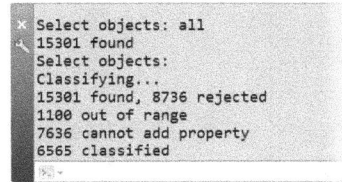

The SEWER_LINE object class was defined to only accept polyline objects that reside on the SEWER_PIPES layer.

5. In the Map Explorer:
   - Right-click on SEWER_LINE class>Select Classified Objects.
   - Note that some of the sewer lines are not selected, as shown in the following illustration. These are the sewer lines that did not conform to the object classification standard, such as the range of pipe types.
   - Press <Esc> to clear the objects.

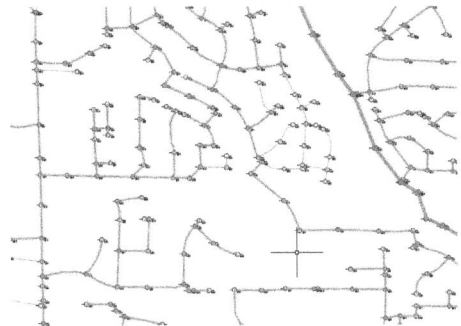

6. Repeat Steps 2 through 5 for the SEWER_MH object class.

Note that 7,636 sewer maintenance holes were classified, as shown in the following illustration. Also, note that several were out of range, meaning that the object data did not conform to the ranges set in the object class definition.

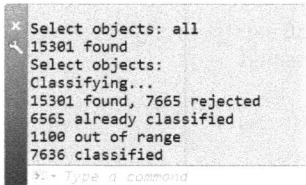

```
Select objects: all
15301 found
Select objects:
Classifying...
15301 found, 7665 rejected
6565 already classified
1100 out of range
7636 classified
>: - Type a command
```

The SEWER_MH object class was designed to only accept objects that reside on the MAINTENANCE_HOLES layer and are the MH block reference.

7. Zoom to the indicated area of the map, as shown in the following illustration.

8. In the Map Explorer:

- Right-click on SEWER_LINE class>Create Classified Object.
- Use an endpoint Osnap to start the feature at the end of the existing sewer line. Draw the line as shown in the following illustration.

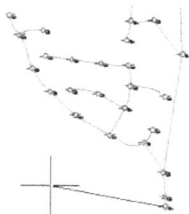

9. To finish the command:

- Press <Enter>.
- Press <Esc>.

The new classified object is created on the correct layer and has the object data table attached with all of the default values, as shown in the following illustration.

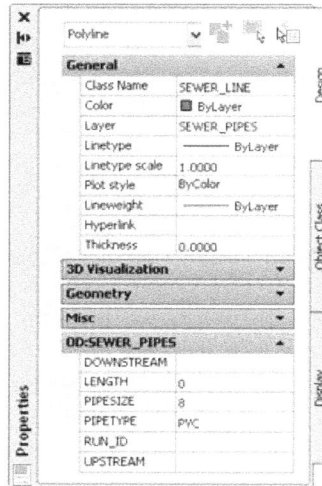

10. Repeat Step 8 for the SEWER_MH object class and add the maintenance hole to the endpoint of the new sewer line.

- When prompted for X ,Y scale factors and rotation, press <Enter> each time to accept the default values.
- Press <Esc> to end the command.

The completed classified object should look, as shown in the following illustration.

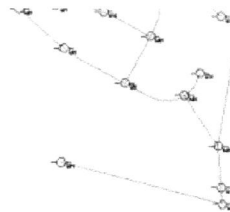

11. Save and close the drawing.

Chapter Summary

Having completed this chapter, you can:

- Set up an object class.
- Create, select, and classify objects.

Importing and Exporting Data

The lesson in this chapter covers importing data into the AutoCAD® Map 3D software. When you work with other departments, companies, or contractors on a mapping project, you must often read data supplied in a different file format from another application. Using the AutoCAD Map 3D software, you can import data from several external file formats. You also learn to export your drawings into the powerful SDF geospatial format.

Objectives

After completing this chapter, you will be able to:

- Import an ArcView Shape file.
- Export an Autodesk® SDF file.

Lesson: Importing and Exporting Data

Overview

In this lesson, you learn how to import and export data from other mapping applications. The AutoCAD Map 3D software maintains the integrity and nature of the data by putting it into a structure that is as similar as possible to the original file structure.

Objectives

After completing this lesson, you will be able to:

- Explain data import and export.
- Describe the import process.
- Describe the export process.
- Import an ArcView Shape file.
- Export an Autodesk SDF File.

About Importing and Exporting Data

One of the most expensive phases of developing a mapping system is acquiring data. In many cases, base map information, such as political boundaries, soils, watersheds, and terrain, is readily available from various agencies. Files containing this data can be in a wide range of formats. The import tools in the AutoCAD Map 3D software give you access to much of this existing data.

Exporting data to SDF is one of the most effective techniques for sharing data with the Autodesk Infrastructure Map Server. SDF is a native Autodesk file-based geospatial format that is optimized for storing large, classified data sets.

The following illustration shows data imported from ArcView. Note that not only is the geometry present, but that the underlying data has also been imported and linked to the object as object data.

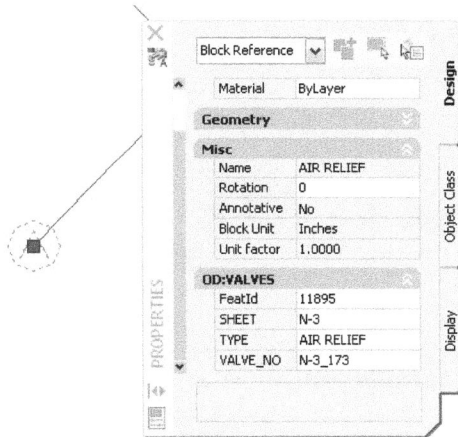

Data Import

Importing mapping or GIS data is more than importing geometry. Mapping and GIS data, by their very nature, include underlying data that is usually as important as what you see on the screen as geometry. When you import data, the following information can be imported:

Information Type	Definition
Geometry	The geometry from other formats can be imported into the AutoCAD Map 3D software. This includes layering and coordinate system information.
Data	Most mapping applications provide a form of underlying data to the geometry. The AutoCAD Map 3D software can read most forms of this data and attach it as either object data or SQL links.

Data Export

Exporting data from the AutoCAD Map 3D software to another file format follows the same principles as importing data. When data is written to another file format, geometry and data integrity are kept as close as possible to the target file format.

Example of Importing Data

Depending on your location and the type of map you are creating, you might find existing land-based data available to you through government agencies. Another typical use is to share imported data between departments or companies that use a different data format.

This example shows how data from an ArcView shape file is imported into the AutoCAD Map 3D software. ArcView uses four file formats: SHP, DBF, PRJ, and SHX. The SHP file contains the geometry, the DBF file contains the data that underlies the geometry, the projection file contains information about which coordinate system the file is in, and the SHX file is an index file. In this example, the shape file is imported and placed on a layer in the AutoCAD Map 3D software that matches the filename. The DBF file information is mapped to object data in the AutoCAD Map 3D file, as shown in the following illustration.

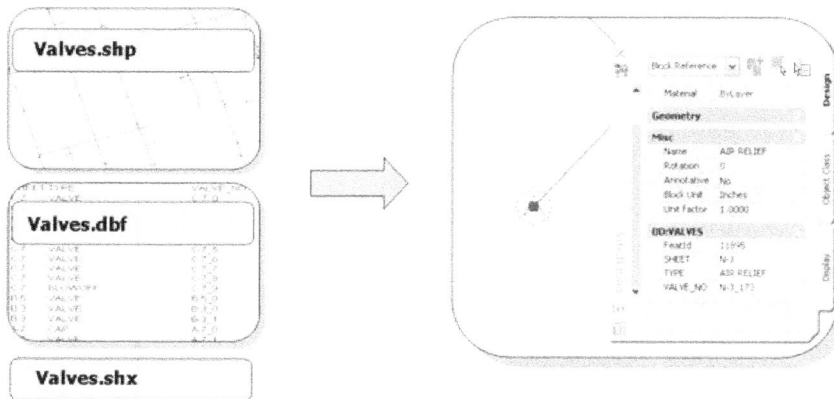

The Import Process

You can import data as an occasional method of acquiring data, or share data with other users on a regular basis. The process for import and export varies with your specific purpose.

The following illustration shows how the AutoCAD Map 3D software is the central point of data acquisition and creation. For example, an ArcView ShapeFile can be imported into the AutoCAD Map 3D software and either be maintained as native drawing data, exported out to another file format, or returned to its original format. Each import and export operation maintains the integrity of the original data as closely as possible. This process of importing and exporting is completely different to the direct connections and editing capability found with the FDO Providers.

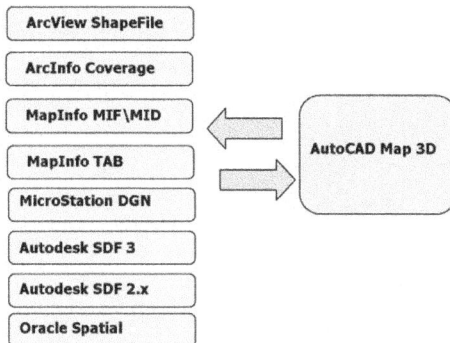

ArcView ShapeFile
ArcInfo Coverage
MapInfo MIF\MID
MapInfo TAB
MicroStation DGN
Autodesk SDF 3
Autodesk SDF 2.x
Oracle Spatial

AutoCAD Map 3D

Setting Up an Import

You can import data into a new drawing or into an existing drawing. The following list shows the common steps you take to import data.

1. **Review the incoming file -** Before starting an import, gather as much information about the incoming data as possible. This might include the coordinate system, what data is on each layer, and what type of database information is available. ESRI users can often provide metadata (data about data) to you with the files to help you know where the data came from and what you can use it for.

2. **Prepare the target drawing -** If you import to an existing drawing and want to map the data to specific layers, ensure that the layers have been created. If you need to convert coordinate systems during the import, assign the correct coordinate system to the target drawing. If you plan to map database information to an existing object data table, verify that the object data table definition is going to accommodate the incoming data.

3. **Perform the import -** Set all of the appropriate options in the Import dialog box to capture all of the data you want to use. Once the import is complete, verify the integrity of the data.

The Export Process

You can export data as a method of sharing data or as a process for converting data into geospatial formats. The export process varies based on the type of data and how the information is going to be used.

The following illustration shows how graphical and attribute information is exported to various formats. For example, the DWG objects that are connected to a database with a Link Template can be exported to an SDF file with the associated database information. Regardless of the attribute information attached, Link Template, Object Data, Classification, or Block Attribute, this information can be exported along with the graphical information.

Various types of exports can be used to move your DWG object into another geospatial format, such as an FDO database, Oracle, SDF files, and Shape files.

This process of exporting is different from the direct connections and editing capability found with the FDO providers that is discussed in other chapters of this learning guide. Once the objects are exported, there is no link back to the original DWG, as shown in the following illustration.

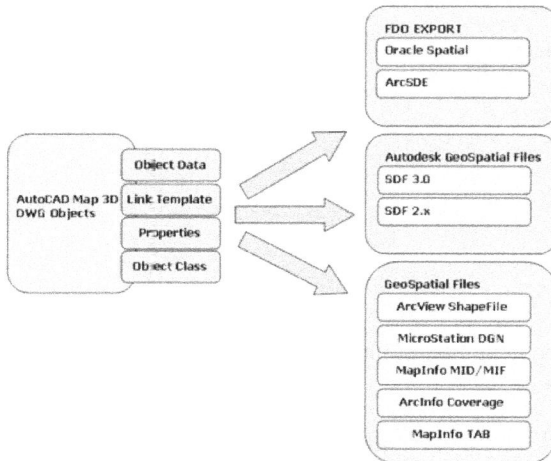

Process: Setting Up an Export

You can export data into FDO, SDF, or most geospatial file formats. The following describes the common steps you take to export data.

1. Choose the type of export.

There are two types of geospatial export: FDO and file-based. Once you choose the type, you choose the file format, such as SDF or SHP, as shown in the following illustration.

2. Filter objects to export.

Decide how you want to filter the exported data. You can limit what you export based on the object's layer or based on an Object Classification, as shown in the following illustration.

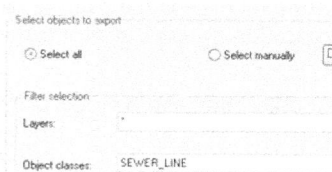

3. Select object attributes, as shown in the following illustration. The attributes that you want to export can be based on object properties, such as Layer or Color, Block Attributes, Object Data, or Link Templates.

   Alternatively, you can use the properties of an Object Classification so that all of the other attributes are grouped together.

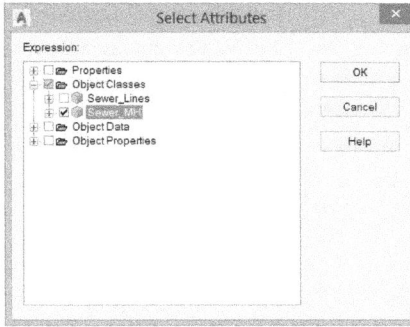

4. Select geometry types.

   Since some export types can accept mixed geometries, such as SDF or Oracle, you can choose which geometry types are stored in the file. Point, Line, or Polygons and combinations of these types are available to choose from, as shown in the following illustration.

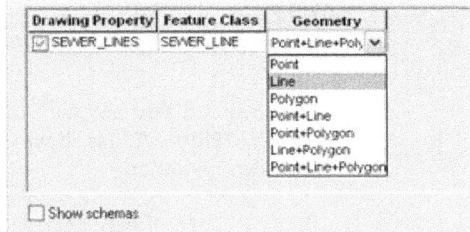

5. Perform coordinate conversion.

   For the last step, you might want to perform a coordinate conversion when exporting your data. Some third-party software systems might require more common coordinate systems, so you might want to convert your coordinate system into a Latitude/Longitude coordinate system, as shown in the following illustration.

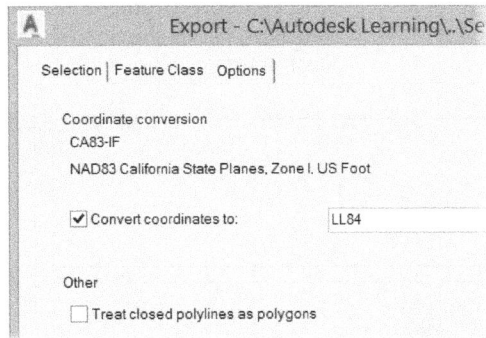

Exercise: Import an ArcView ShapeFile

In this exercise, you will import an ArcView ShapeFile. The ShapeFile uses a California State Plane Zone I, NAD27 coordinate system, and the current drawing uses a California State Plane Zone I, NAD83 coordinate system. You will perform a coordinate conversion during the import.

You will also create an object data table to store attribute information from the ShapeFile, and you place the imported objects on an existing WATERVALVES layer, as shown in the following illustration.

You will use the ShapeFile's column called TYPE to choose which kind of BLOCK will be used for each point. The drawing already contains BLOCKs named AIR RELIEF, BLCWOFF, CAP, UNK, and VALVE that match the TYPE column.

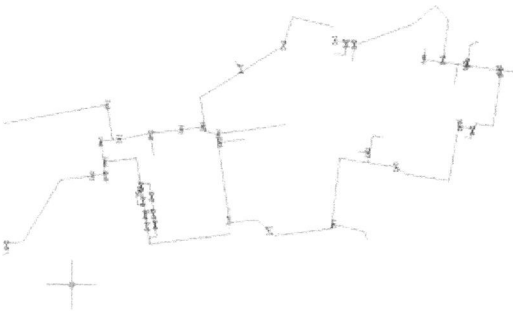

1. Open ...\5-Importing and Exporting Data\Redding_Water.dwg.

2. On the Home ribbon, under Data, click Import From Files, as shown in the following illustration.

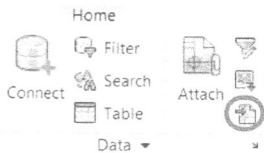

3. In the Import Location dialog box:
   - For Files of Type, verify that ESRI Shapefile (*.shp) is selected.
   - Browse to the ...\ Data\SHP folder.
   - Click Valves.shp, as shown in the following illustration.
   - Click OK.

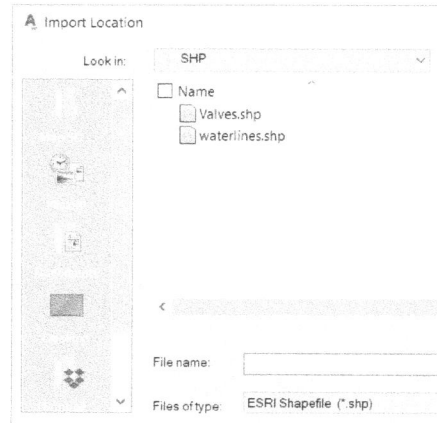

4. In the Import dialog box, for Drawing Layer, select WATERVALVES, as shown in the following illustration.

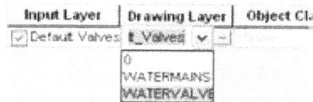

5. In the Input Coordinate System, note CA-I, which is derived from the associated SHP files Valves.prj file, as shown in the following illustration.

6. Under Data:

- Click into the cell under the Data heading to display the ellipses (...).
- Click the ellipses (...) to display the Attribute Data dialog box, as shown in the following illustration.

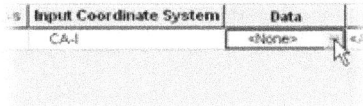

Input Coordinate System	Data
CA-I	<None>

7. In the Attribute Data dialog box:

- Toggle on Create Object Data.
- For Object Data Table to Use, click the drop-down list arrow and select Valves from the tables list, as shown in the following illustration.
- Click OK.

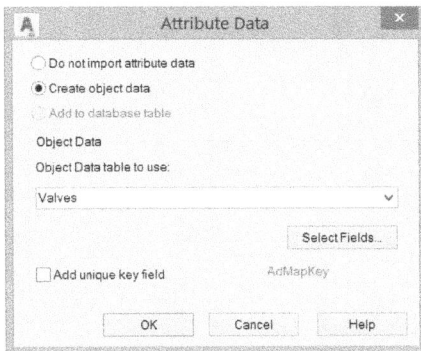

8. Under Points, click ellipses (...), as shown in the following illustration.

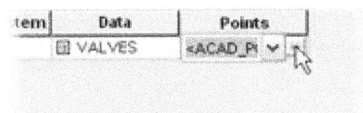

Item	Data	Points
	VALVES	<ACAD_P...

9. In the Point Mapping dialog box:

- Click Get Block Name from Data.
- Choose TYPE, as shown in the following illustration.
- Click OK.

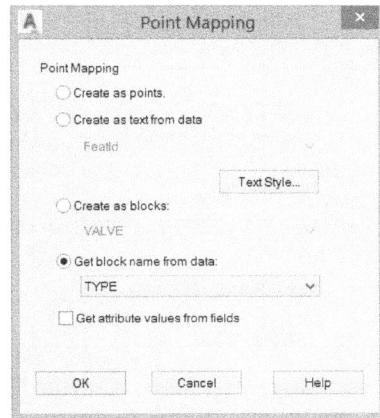

10. In the Import dialog box, click OK. Review the properties of one or more of the imported objects. Note the object data values in the Properties Palette, as shown in the following illustration.

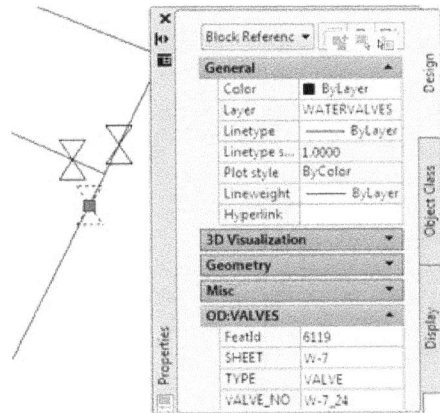

11. Save and close the drawing.

Exercise: Export an Autodesk SDF File

In this exercise, you will export an Autodesk SDF 3.0 file, as shown in the following illustration. The SDF file is stored in a WGS 84 Latitude-Longitude coordinate system, and the current drawing uses a California State Plane Zone I, NAD83 coordinate system. You will perform a coordinate conversion during the export.

You will also export the two object classes and associated attribute data that is associated to the Sewer Line and Sewer Maintenance Hole classes. These object classes will become individual feature classes in the SDF file. The SDF file can then be attached as feature data.

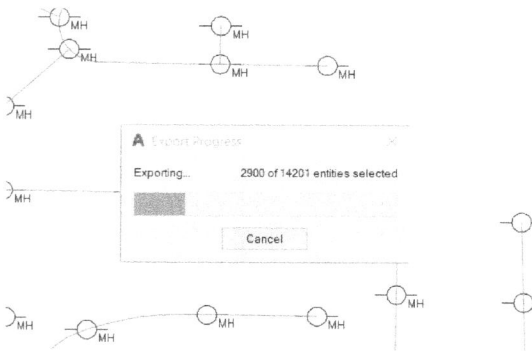

The completed exercise

1. Open ...\5-Importing and Exporting Data \Redding_Sewer_Export.dwg.

2. On the Output ribbon, under Map Data Transfer, click DWG to SDF, as shown in the following illustration.

3. In the Export Location dialog box:

    ▪ For Files of Type, verify that Autodesk SDF (*.sdf) is selected.
    ▪ Navigate to the *Data\For-Export* folder.
    ▪ For File Name, enter **Sewer**, as shown in the following illustration.
    ▪ Click OK.

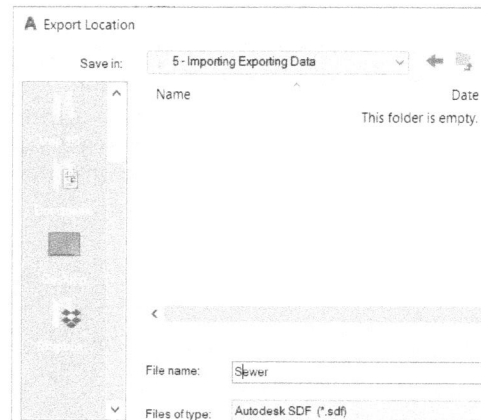

4. In the Export dialog box, under Filter selection, click the Select Object Classes button ( ) to open the Select Object Classes dialog box, as shown in the following illustration.

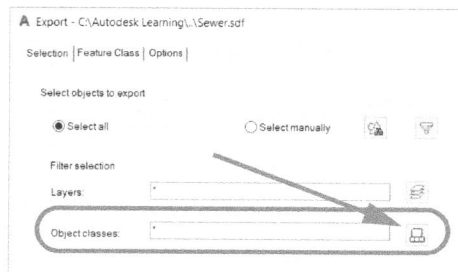

5. Select SEWER_LINE and SEWER_MH, as shown in the following illustration.

Click Select.

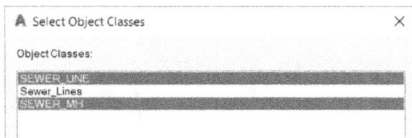

6. Click the Feature Class tab.

- Under Object to Feature Class Mapping, select Create Multiple Classes Based on Drawing Object.
- For Drawing Object to Use, select Object Class, as shown in the following illustration.
- Click Select Attributes.

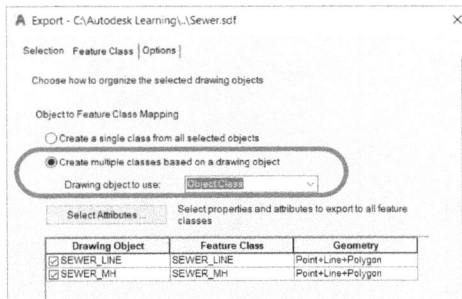

7. In the Select Attributes dialog box:

- Expand Object Classes.
- Toggle on the SEWER_LINE and SEWER_MH, as shown in the following illustration.
- Click OK.

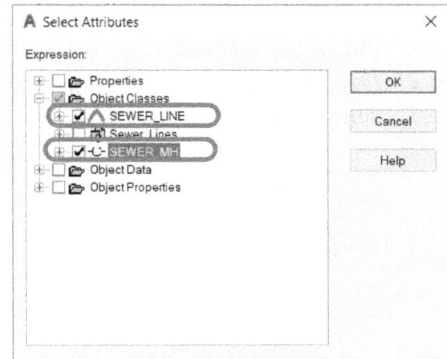

8. In the Feature Class tab:

- For the SEWER_LINE Geometry, select LINE.
- For the SEWER_MH Geometry, select POINT, as shown in the following illustration.

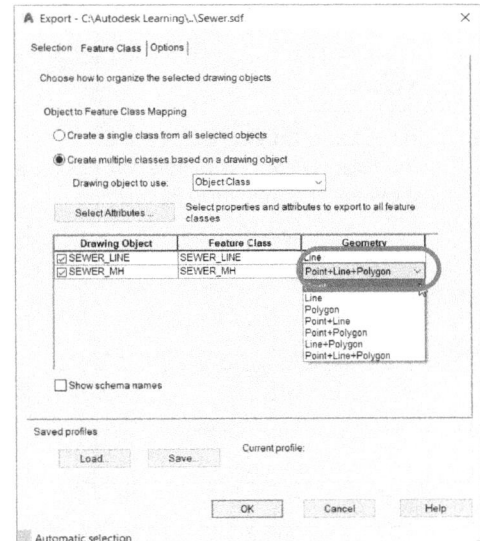

9. In the Export dialog box, click the Options tab.

10. Under Coordinate Conversion:

 - Check Convert Coordinates To.
 - Enter **LL84**, as shown in the following illustration.

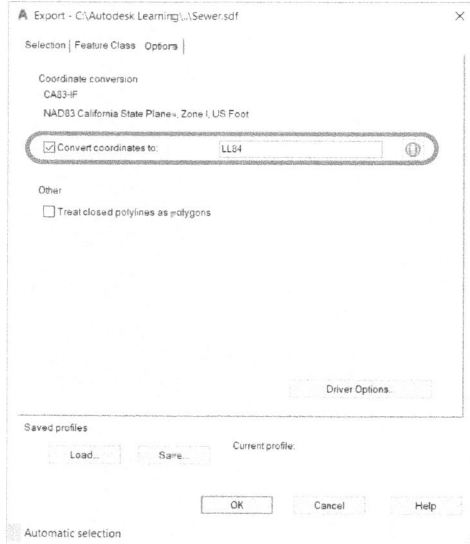

11. In the Export dialog box, click OK.
The Export Progress dialog box opens, as shown in the following illustration.

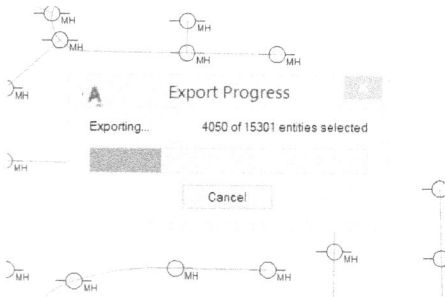

12. Save and close the drawing.

Chapter Summary

Having completed this chapter, you can:

- Import an ArcView Shape file and export an Autodesk SDF file.

Establishing a Geospatial Environment

The lessons in this chapter describe working with the SDF format, and feature sources, such as shape files and ODBC points.

Feature sources can be both raster and vector. Raster feature sources can be images, such as air photographs or digital elevation models (DEMs). Vector data includes formats, such as SDF, SHP, and Oracle Spatial. Using feature sources in your drawing is a powerful way to display and use GIS data without the need to import or export external formats.

Objectives

After completing this chapter, you will be able to:

- Connect to a feature source.
- Use Geospatial Coordinate Systems.
- Work with point data.
- Use filters to limit geospatial data that displays in the map.

Lesson: Connecting to a Feature Source

Overview

This lesson explains the use and definition of a feature source in the AutoCAD® Map 3D software. You learn how this new method of connecting to data, as shown in the following illustration, with feature sources is vastly superior to attaching drawings or using Link Templates to retrieve data.

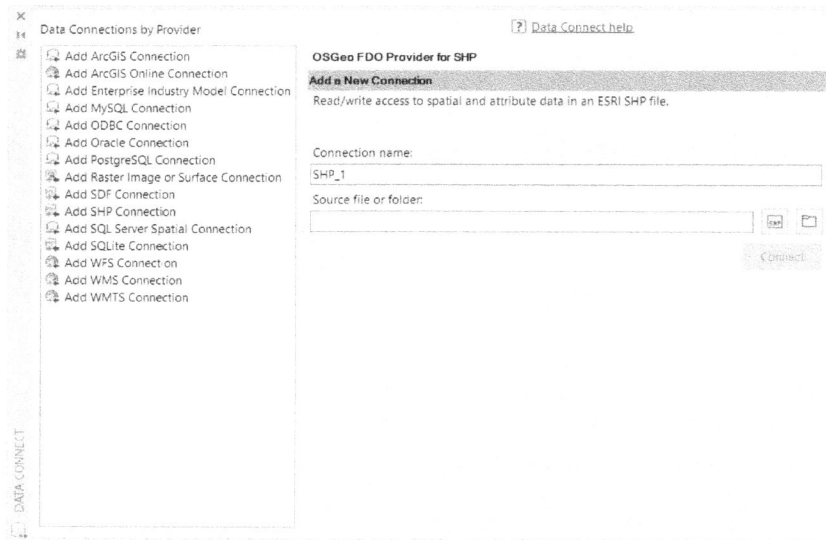

Objectives

After completing this lesson, you will be able to:

- Describe a feature source.
- Decide when to use feature sources.
- Explain the process of connecting to a feature source.
- Connect to a feature source.

About Feature Sources

A feature source is any source of spatial data that has been connected by means of feature data objects (FDOs). An FDO enables you to connect directly to SDF and raster data and databases that contain spatial data. No import or export is required to use the spatial data that resides in the original feature source.

Feature sources render features on the screen very rapidly. You can create maps far more efficiently by moving your drawing into a feature source, such as SDF.

The three main types of feature sources are:

- File-based raster and vector.
- Database vector and ODBC.
- OpenGIS raster and vector.

Definition of Feature Sources

A feature source connects to a geographic datastore of GIS features using an FDO provider, enabling you to query, edit, add, delete, and thematically render those features in the Display Manager. Each feature source can be a connection to either file-based or database datastores.

A feature source is similar to a data source. A feature source connects to geographic features (i.e., parcel polygons and attributes) but a data source only connects to attribute data (i.e., parcel ownership and zoning). A list of FDO Providers is shown in the following illustration.

File-Based Feature Sources

For file-based feature sources, you can use SHP and SDF for vector information, as shown in the following illustration. Many file-based raster feature sources are available, including ECW, MR SID, TIFF, and JPEG. Another type of file-based feature source is the digital elevation model (DEM).

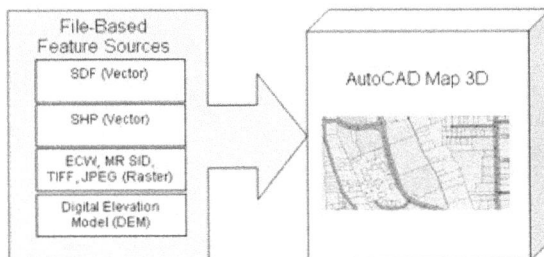

Database Feature Sources

The two types of database feature sources are:

- Points only from X, Y, and Z columns.
- Vectors: Points, lines, and polygons.

The point type of feature source can be provided by the ODBC feature source.

Oracle Spatial, ArcSDE, and, now SQL Server and MySQL provide a full-vector feature source containing points, lines, and polygons, as shown in the following illustration.

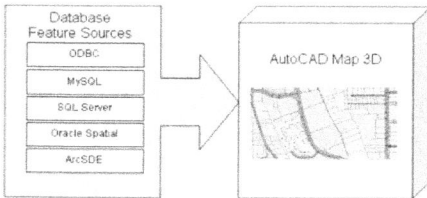

The **OSGeo FDO Provider for SQL Server Spatial** is available with SQL Server 2008 or newer and uses the spatial columns native to SQL Server.

OpenGIS Feature Sources

OpenGIS feature sources include the Web Map Service (WMS), a raster-based feature source that returns images, such as PNG, as data. The Web Feature Service (WFS) returns full-vector feature sources from external sites. These OpenGIS feature sources require a URL to find the server (such as Autodesk MapGuide® Enterprise) that provides the WFS or WMS, as shown in the following illustration.

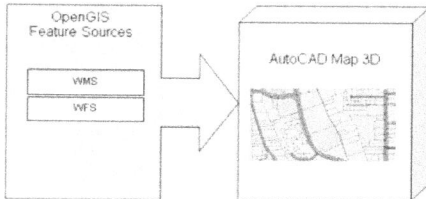

Examples of Feature Source Uses

Feature sources can be used to connect to contour lines stored in an SDF file, as shown in the following illustration.

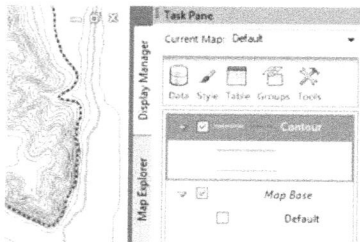

A number of image types, such as MR SID, can be placed on a layer in Display Manager, as shown in the following illustration.

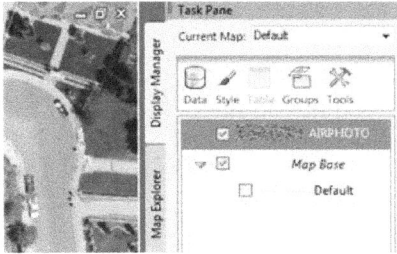

Digital elevation models, such as a DEM from the USGS, can be connected, as shown in the following illustration.

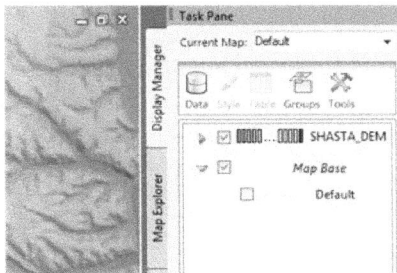

Autodesk Connector for ArcGIS

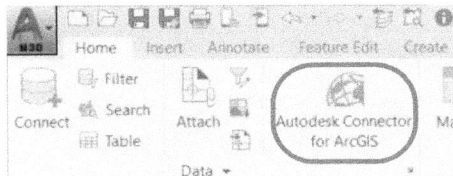

For ESRI (R) ArcGIS Online and Enterprise portals, you can connect directly to these sources using your ESRI ArcGIS login information. You require ESRI ArcGIS login credentials to enter the portal.

Inside the portal, you can navigate to your project site by entering an address, location name, or longitudinal and latitudinal coordinates.

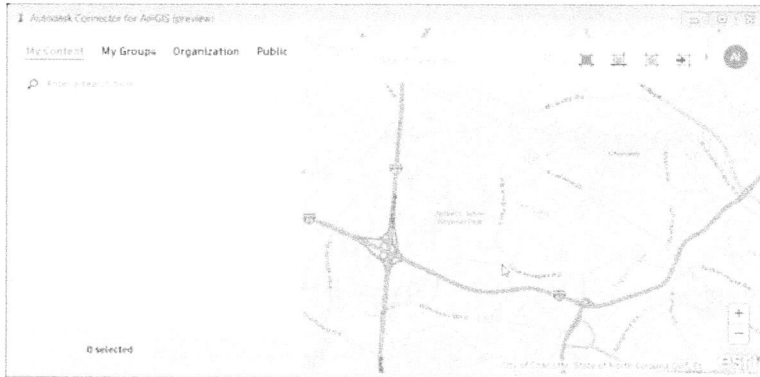

From there, you can browse through available datasets contained within your organization's ArcGIS Online content to be included with your project.

You can select the entire area to import or select a region either by rectangle or polygon. Then, you can select the available content you want to reference. If you have the proper login credentials, you can even update the GIS information in the source.

When to Use a Feature Source

You can use feature sources with DWG™ format to provide a hybrid environment of DWG layers and feature sources. For example, a road network can be stored in SQL Server while the sidewalk edges are stored in DWG format. You can then combine both layers of information to produce a map.

Guidelines for Connection to Feature Sources

The following guidelines can help you in choosing to use feature sources.

Feature Source Use Guidelines:

Data Sharing

A feature source is a file or database that stores your graphical data with the attribute data. In DWG files, attributes are usually connected to graphics with link templates, object data, or block attributes. If you need to share this information constantly with others outside of your immediate department, you might want to convert your data into a feature source, such as SDF or SHP.

File-based feature sources can be transferred easily and maintained in the Map environment without being converted back into DWG.

High Performance

Some DWG files can become very large and tax your operating system. Traditionally, the only way to access such a large DWG was to query to pull a subset of the data. Feature sources increase performance by an order of magnitude. You can move to a file-based geodatabase, such as an SDF file, to increase performance.

Central GIS Connectivity

If you use GIS databases, such as Oracle Spatial or ArcSDE, you can use feature sources in the AutoCAD Map 3D software to maintain the data. You can use Autodesk FDO providers to connect directly with many GIS databases without translating or batch converting data from one format to another.

SQL Server Spatial Support

If you currently use DWG™ to store graphical information and either Object Data or SQL Server to store attribute data, you can move to a central GIS repository using feature sources. The FDO provider for SQL Server enables you to store all the graphics in the SQL Server as graphical entities. In this way, you can store GIS data in SQL Server.

Cartographic Tools

Using feature sources, you can stylize data based on its attributes. Theming, hatching, coloring, and symbology are easier using feature sources than using the AutoCAD® layers and linestyles. The cartographic tools available to data drawn from a feature source are far superior to those used for stylizing DWG objects.

Rapid Publishing To Autodesk Infrastructure Map Server

You use a wizard to migrate data stored in feature sources to the Autodesk Infrastructure Map Server. All stylization that was done to your features or drawing objects also migrates. You can publish one drawing at a time or multiple drawings at once by loading them into Infrastructure Studio first.

OpenGIS Conformity

Web Feature Services (WFS) and Web Mapping Services (WMS) can be added to your map as feature sources. WFS, a vector-based feature source, can be updated. WMS is raster-based and read-only.

About Feature Layers

Connecting to feature sources is the first part in displaying geospatial data in a map. Once the feature sources are connected, you can then add the layer to the map, as shown in the following illustration.

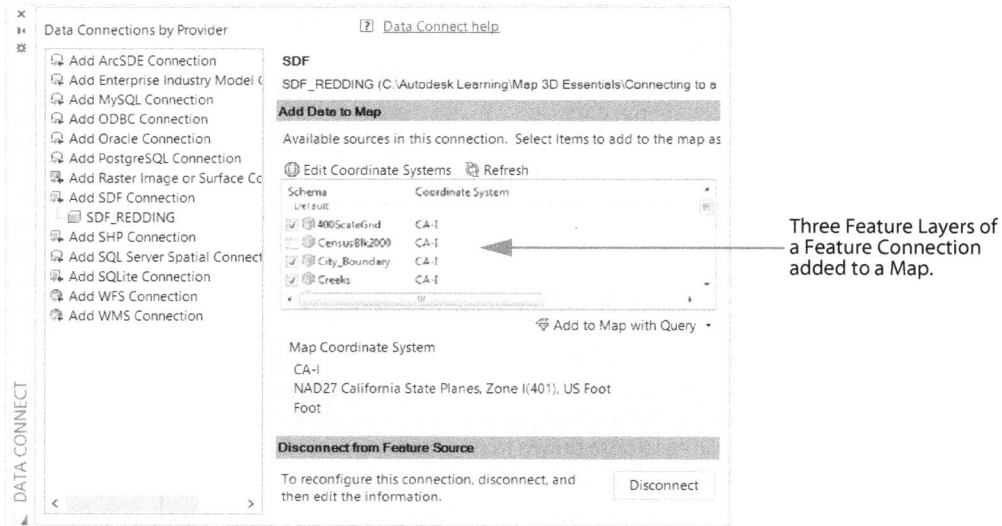

Three Feature Layers of a Feature Connection added to a Map.

Definition of Feature Layers

A feature layer is a layer in Display Manager containing features from a feature source, such as SDF, SHP, Oracle, or Raster. A feature source can contain many types of feature data. Each can be added as a layer to the map. If the feature source is connected but not added to the map, it can be seen in the Map Explorer but not in the Display Manager. Once added to the map, it can then be stylized. The example in the following illustration shows the SDF_WATER Feature Source Connected without a Feature Layer in Display Manager.

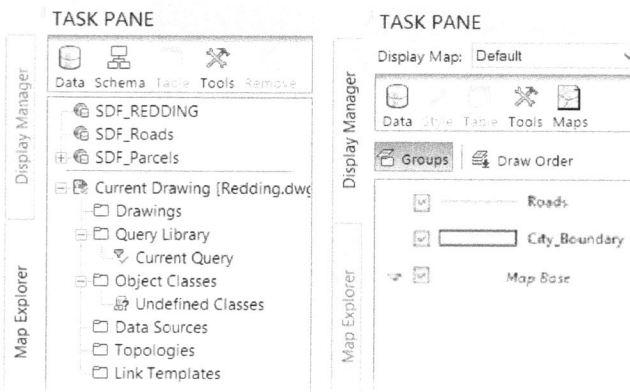

A feature layer is similar to a query of an attached drawing in Map Explorer. The feature source is similar to the attached drawing and the feature layer is similar to the query of that attached drawing.

> If you remove a feature layer from the Display Manager, the feature source is still connected.

Example of a Feature Layer

A good example of a feature layer is a Sewer Main layer that is drawn from an *UTILITIES.SDF* file. The SDF file contains the Sewer Main, Sewer Valves, and Sewer Holes, but only the Sewer Main is drawn as a feature layer.

Process of Connecting to a Feature Source

Feature Source Types

The process of connecting to a feature source varies according to its type. The five types of feature sources are:

- File-based vector
- File-based raster
- Database
- OpenGIS vector (WFS)
- OpenGIS raster (WMS)

Process: Connecting to a Feature Source

1. To use a database feature source, ensure that the client for that FDO data provider is installed. For example, to connect to an ODBC database, create the ODBC connection in the Control Panel, as shown in the following illustration.

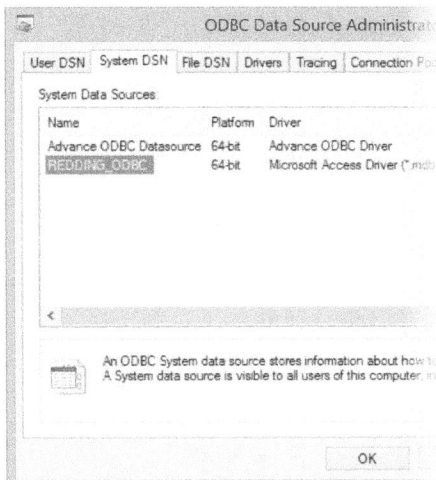

2. To add data, choose either a feature source or drawing object. Having chosen the feature source as the layer, you then choose the type of feature source to be added to the map.

    Choosing a file-based feature source prompts a request to browse to that file. Otherwise, enter the configuration of the database. For Raster and SHP files, you choose either the folder containing the files or the file itself, as shown in the following illustration.

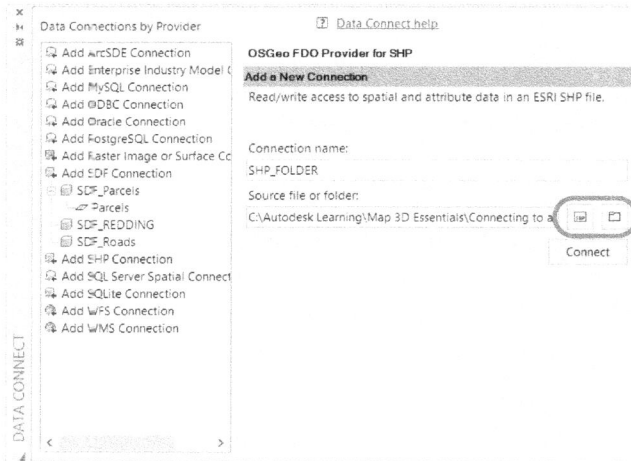

3. Choose the FDO provider type:

    -   File-based, such as SDF, SHP, or Raster.
    -   Database, such as Oracle, SQL Server, MySQL, ArcSDE, or ODBC.
    -   Web-based, such as WFS or WMS OpenGIS.

4. Depending on the feature source, either set the filename or set the server name or connection to the datastore.

    If required, select the coordinate system of the feature source and add the feature source as a layer, as shown in the following illustration.

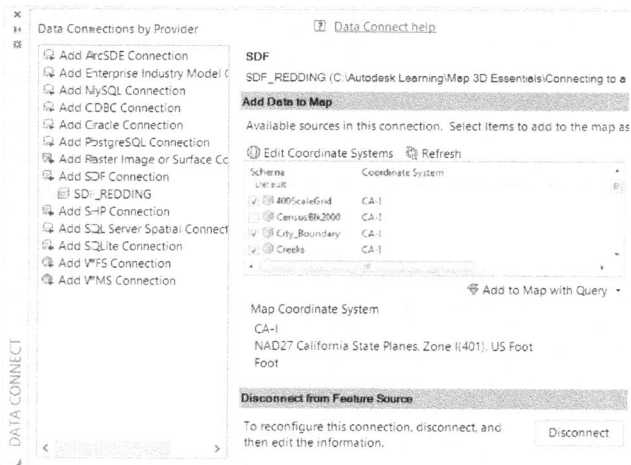

5. Once the feature source is added, it is visible in the Display Manager and Map Explorer, as shown in the following illustration.

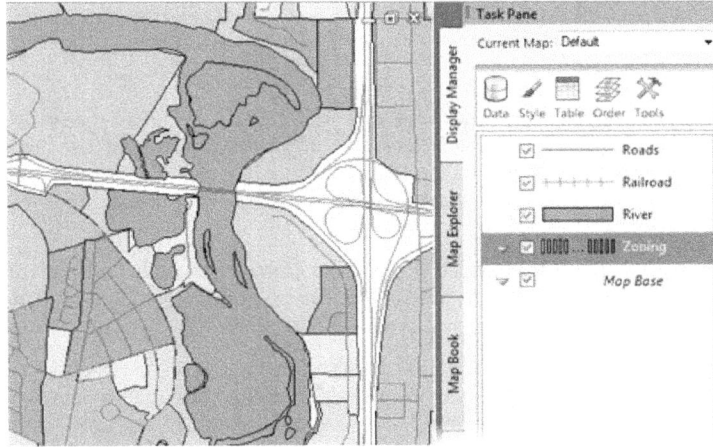

Lesson: Using Coordinate Systems

Overview

Global coordinate systems are a method of representing all or part of the curved surface of the earth on a flat plane. Many mapping systems use different coordinate systems. You must be able to assign the correct coordinate systems to these drawings to use them in a single environment. The AutoCAD Map 3D software can convert objects from source drawings to the global coordinate system of the current drawing.

The most important aspect of this feature is that you can combine drawings with differing coordinate systems into a single coordinate system. In this lesson, you learn to apply coordinate systems in the AutoCAD Map 3D software, as shown in the following illustration.

In this lesson, you explore how geospatial data connected to a map can be assigned a coordinate system and how the current map enables the re-projection of the attached geospatial data. Since geospatial feature data can be set to any number of coordinate systems, you learn how to manage the global coordinate system to which all the connected feature sources conform. In this lesson, you learn that both raster feature sources, such as aerial photographs, and vector feature sources, such as SDF files, dynamically re-project in your drawing file.

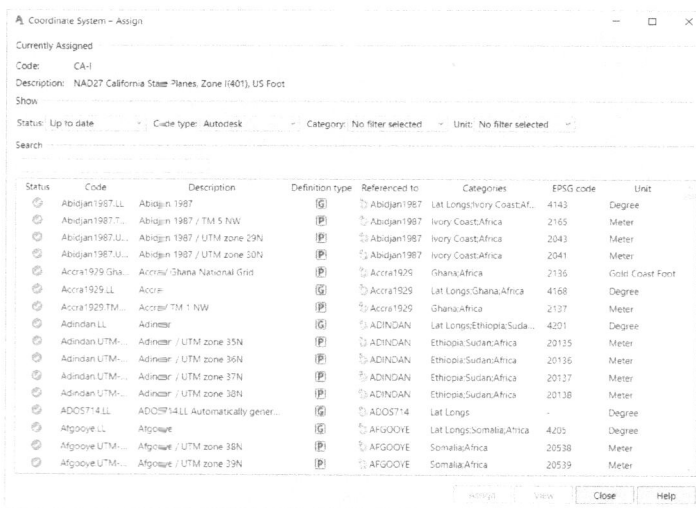

Objectives

After completing this lesson, you will be able to:

- Describe the concept of coordinate systems.
- Explain how the AutoCAD Map 3D software applies coordinate systems to drawings.
- Explain how to override and assign geospatial coordinate systems.
- Dynamically re-project vector and raster data.

About Coordinate Systems

If all maps were created with the same coordinate system, you would not need to convert or transform mapping objects from one drawing to another. Using the AutoCAD Map 3D software to perform coordinate conversions and transformations does not require that you understand the projection systems or why different coordinate systems are used, but a background in these topics can be helpful.

Coordinate Systems Defined

A global coordinate system incorporates angular spherical coordinates representing latitude and longitude into the AutoCAD Map 3D Cartesian coordinate system and accounts for the curvature of the earth's surface with a projection. The global coordinate system includes the map origin, projection system, and units.

Because projection systems usually distort maps as they get farther away from the meridian of the system, no single system is suitable for all areas of the globe. To increase accuracy, many larger states and countries use more than one zone or coordinate system definition for their areas. For example, the state of California has six zones arranged in east to west bands. India and its neighboring countries use eight zones.

Key Terms

Term	Definition
Projection	The mathematical model used to transform the curved surface of the earth to a planar representation.
Datum	Horizontal and vertical locations relative to a specific location.
Local parameters	Components that include the projection origin, scale factor, units of measure, and displacements (False Eastings and False Northings).
Coordinate system	A projection, ellipsoid, and local parameters.

Coordinate System Example

In the following illustration the same point on a map is expressed using two different coordinate systems. If you were working with two maps, one using the UTM system, and another using latitude-longitude, you would need to transform one into the other to see their geometry displayed in a single coordinate environment.

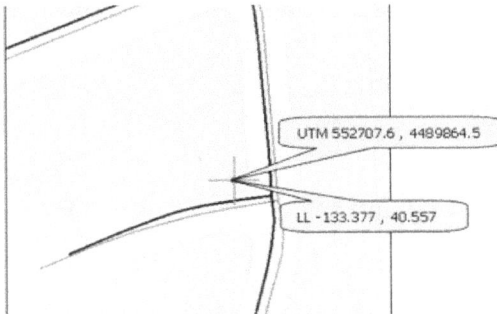

UTM 552707.6 , 4489864.5

LL - 133.377 , 40.557

About Geospatial Coordinate Systems

The current DWG is used as the base coordinate system for any new features being added to the map. Any new Geospatial data dynamically re-projects to match the DWG current coordinate system. This permits multiple coordinate systems from multiple sources to be accommodated in a single map.

Importance must be put on assigning the correct coordinate system to the map and to the geospatial data. Usually, the geospatial data already has a coordinate system assigned but in the cases where the coordinate system might not be assigned in the file, you can set the coordinate system to the geospatial data, as shown in the following illustration.

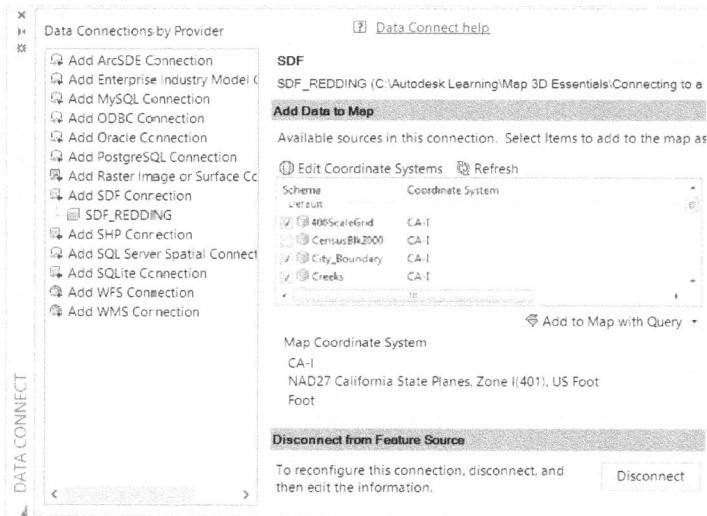

SDF and Map with Different Coordinate Systems
seen in Data Connect Dialog Box

Assigning coordinate systems to geospatial data is similar to assigning coordinate systems to source DWGs. Unlike DWGs that require that the source objects be re-queried into a project drawing, geospatial data is dynamically re-projected in the map.

Example of Assigning Geospatial Coordinate Systems

You often need to assign the coordinate system during the connection to a SHP file; otherwise, the data might display in the wrong location. For example, a ROADS.SHP file and its associated ROADS.SHX and ROADS.DBF files are available, but not ROADS.PRJ. You must assign the coordinate system to the SHP file manually when connecting.

Override Coordinate System Process

Sometimes the Geospatial data might have an incorrect coordinate system assigned or the coordinate system does not completely match the names of the coordinate systems in the AutoCAD Map 3D software. You can override the coordinate system when connecting to the geospatial data in these cases. The coordinate system can be overridden for any Geospatial data including Raster, SDF, or WFS, as shown in the following illustration.

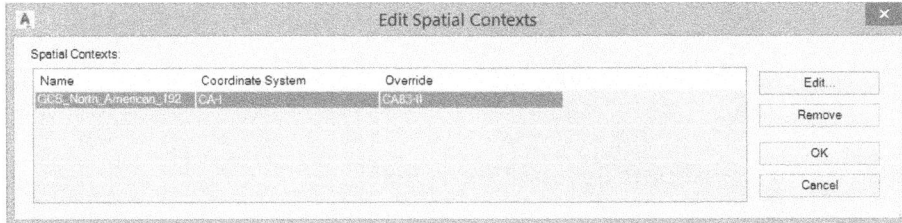

> **Oracle Spatial Coordinate System Override**
> With Oracle Spatial, the coordinate systems are assigned by Spatial Reference ID (SRID). For example, UTM Zone 10, NAD 83, Meters, is recorded in Oracle as SRID 82212. You might want to override the coordinate system in the AutoCAD Map 3D software to UTM83-10 to ensure that the correct coordinate system is assigned.

Process: Override Coordinate System

The following steps demonstrate how to override the coordinate system when connecting to geospatial data.

1. Connect to geospatial data, as shown in the following illustration.

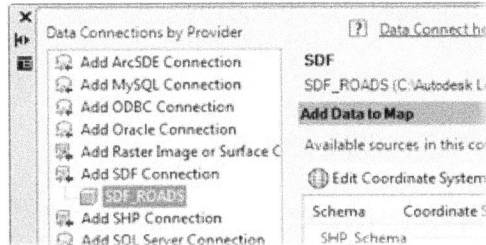

2. Edit the coordinate system during connection, as shown in the following illustration.

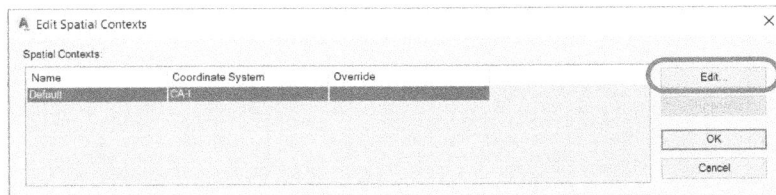

3. Choose Coordinate System Override, as shown in the following illustration.

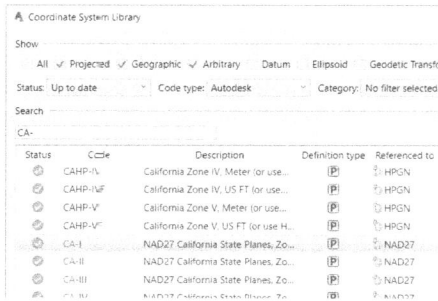

Guidelines for Coordinate System Overrides

Changing a coordinate system to one different from that assigned can be problematic and might have unexpected results. To avoid problems:

- Ensure that the coordinate system is correct. Follow up with the creators of the data.
- Research the coordinate system that is assigned to the geospatial data. You might find that a number of coordinate systems in the AutoCAD Map 3D software match.
- Ensure that you assign the coordinate system of the current map (DWG) before connecting to geospatial data.
- Create a new coordinate system if none match the existing one in the geospatial file. Do not assign an incorrect coordinate system.

Define Coordinate Systems

There are times when a project requires a local coordinate system be created or the coordinate system required is not available. AutoCAD Map 3D provides tools for CAD operators to create custom coordinate systems by enabling you to create the following:

- Coordinate System Definition
- Datum Definition
- Ellipsoid Definition
- Geodetic Transformation Definition
- Geodetic Transformation Path Definition

To create a coordinate system, on the Map Setup tab, under Coordinate System, select Create Coordinate System, as shown in the following illustration. It is recommended that you become familiar with Coordinate Systems before attempting to create your own.

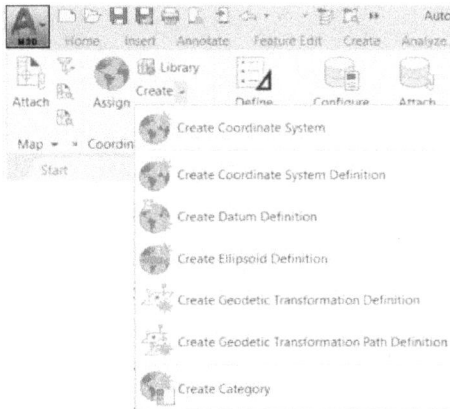

Online Maps Service

Once a coordinate zone is assigned to a drawing (as outlined in the following section), you are able to access the **Online Maps Service**.

This service is only available if you have an Autodesk account and you are signed in. To sign in, go to the upper right area of the Map 3D application

The online maps are geolocated, meaning they have coordinates so they "know where they belong". Since the Map 3D drawing is set up with a coordinate zone, it also knows where it belongs. The Online Maps Service will access maps in various styles and dynamically reference them into your drawing.

Map Styles

In the Map drop-down list in the Online Maps panel, there are four choices for map styles.

- **Map Aerial:** Displays the map as a satellite image.
- **Map Road**: Displays the map as a vector image similar to road maps.
- **Map Hybrid**: Displays the map as a satellite image with the vector data shown over top.
- **Map Off**: Displays no map.

If the maps are displayed in multiple viewports, then each viewport can have a different map style.

Capture Online Maps

Online maps are only temporary by default. They will not remain with the drawing when it is reopened and you cannot plot them. They need to be captured in order for you to plot them or save them with the drawing.

To capture an image, there are two choices:

- **Capture Area:** to be used in the Modelspace, where you define a rectangle for the area of capture.
- **Capture Viewport:** you select a viewport in a layout. The viewport must be active (in Modelspace mode through the viewport). Even if the viewport is an irregular shape, the captured area will be rectangular to the extents of the viewport shape.

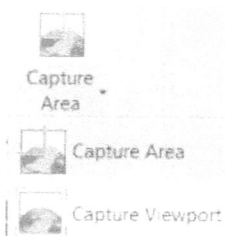

The captured online map will be placed on the current layer. Prior to capturing the map, make an appropriate layer current.

Once an area of an online map is captured, it will remain in the drawing. It can be turned off through its layer. By clicking on the boundary of the captured map, a context sensitive ribbon is displayed:

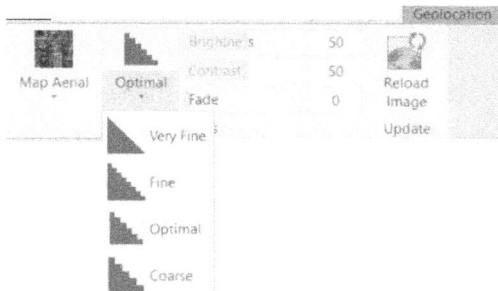

You can control the following:

- Change the map style (Aerial/Road Hybrid/Off).
- Change the resolution of the map. The options are Coarse, Optimal, Fine, and Very Fine.
- Control the brightness, contrast, or fade amount.
- Reload (update) the map.

You need to be logged in to your Autodesk account to make any of these changes to the captured map.

Once the map is captured, a copyright notice is added to it as shown below.

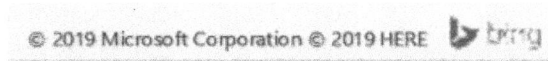

Exercise: Re-project Geospatial Data

In this exercise, you will add a roads layer and a raster layer (that are both in the California State Plane coordinate system) into a map that is in the UTM 83 coordinate system. You will then re-project the data into a latitude and longitude coordinate system dynamically, as shown in the following illustration.

I ▾ 🔒   550910.7982, 4489278.7355, 0.0000   MODEL   ▦   ▾ ⁺ ∟ ⨀

1. Open ...\6-Geospatial Environment\ Redding-Coordinates.dwg.

2. On the Map Setup ribbon, under Coordinate Systems, click Assign, as shown in the following illustration.

3. In the Assign Global Coordinate System dialog box:

   ▪ Note that the current coordinate system is UTM83-10, as shown in the following illustration.

   ▪ Click Close.

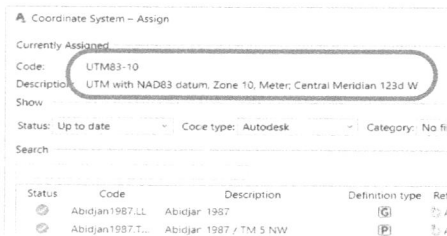

4. In Display Manager, click Data>Connect to Data.

5. In the Data Connect window:

   ▪ Under Data Connection By Provider, click Add SDF Connection.

   ▪ For Connection Name, enter **SDF_ROADS**.

   ▪ For source file, click the Browse icon (🔲).

6. In the Open dialog box:

   ▪ Browse to ...\Data\SDF\.

   ▪ Select Roads.sdf.

   ▪ Click Open.

7. Click Connect.

8. Under Schema:

   ▪ Ensure Roads is checked.

   ▪ Note that the coordinate system is CA-I, as shown in the following illustration.

   ▪ Click Add to Map.

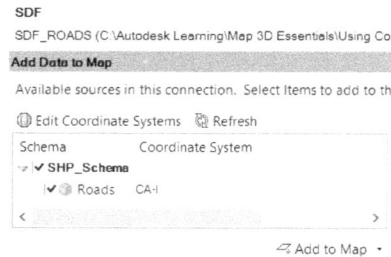

9. In the Data Connect window:

   ▪ Click Add Raster Image or Surface Connection.

   ▪ For Connection Name, enter **Raster_AirPhoto**.

   ▪ For Source file for folder, click the single file Browse icon (🖼).

10. In the Open dialog box:
    - Browse to ...\Data\Images\.
    - Select AirPhoto.sid.
    - Click Open.

11. Click Connect.

12. Under Schema, select SID and ensure that AirPhoto.sid is checked.

13. Click the Edit Coordinate Systems tab.

14. In the Edit Spatial Contexts dialog box:
    - Click Default.
    - Click Edit.

15. In the Select Coordinate System dialog box:
    - Under Category, select USA, California.
    - Under Coordinate Systems in Category, click CA-I, as shown in the following illustration.
    - Click Select.

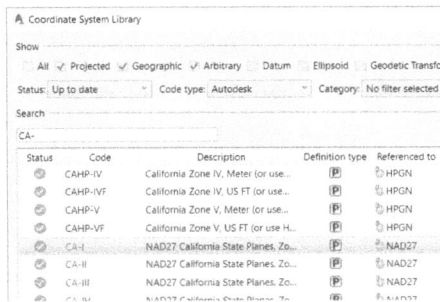

16. In the Edit Spatial Contexts dialog box, click OK.

17. In the Data Connect window, click Add to Map.

18. Close the Data Connect dialog box.

    The Roads and AirPhoto layers are now re-projected from California State Plane into UTM83-10, as shown in the following illustration.

19. On the Map Setup ribbon, under Coordinate Systems, click Assign, as shown in the following illustration.

20. In the Assign Global Coordinate System dialog box:
    - Under Search, enter **LL**.
    - Select the coordinate system with a code of LL and a Description of No datum, Latitude-Longitude; Degrees -180 to +180.
    - Click Assign.

21. Note that the coordinates at the bottom of the window are now in latitude and longitude and the Roads and AirPhoto layers are dynamically re-projected, as shown in the following illustration.

22. Close the drawing without saving.

Lesson: Working with Point Data

Overview

In this lesson, you learn about point data and how to use it. Point data is derived from ODBC and is an effective way to display points stored in a database, as shown in the following illustration.

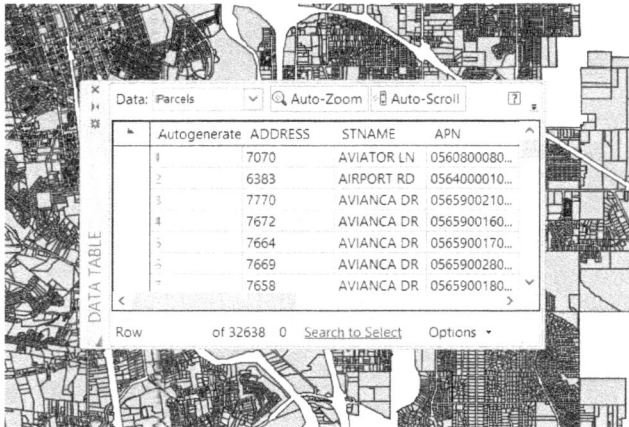

Objectives

After completing this lesson, you will be able to:

- Explain ODBC point data.
- Describe how ODBC point data can be used.
- Attach and stylize an ODBC point source.

About Point Data

The ODBC provider connects to databases that contain points. An ODBC database typically specifies points by latitude and longitude columns or by any coordinate system applied to X and Y coordinates, as shown in the following illustration. The Z value can be expressed in any units as well.

Definition of ODBC Point Data

ODBC point data is used to place symbols or points on a map. Each point usually has X and Y coordinates defined in a Cartesian grid. Sometimes, the Z value (elevation) is also stored. Following are some further definitions for ODBC point sources:

Coordinate System

X, Y, and Z point data are usually assigned a coordinate system, such as UTM or State Plane. When the points are brought in from ODBC, you can apply a different system to project the point data as a data source.

Styles

Although X, Y, and Z values can be shown on a map when connected, ODBC databases do not store feature styles. You can define features when you configure a data source.

Application Programming Interface (API)

The Feature Data Objects (FDO) API provides access to data in a data store. A provider is a specific implementation of the API, such as the FDO provider for ODBC that enables access to an ODBC-based data store, as shown in the following illustration.

Example of ODBC Sources

Points collected on a GPS are a good example of point data. They can be collected in UTM and have elevations reco⁻ded as well. Many GPS software applications move points from the GPS into a database, such as Microsoft Access. Using an FDO provider for ODBC, these points can be shown in the Display Manager. The following illustration shows GPS Waypoints from ODBC Connection.

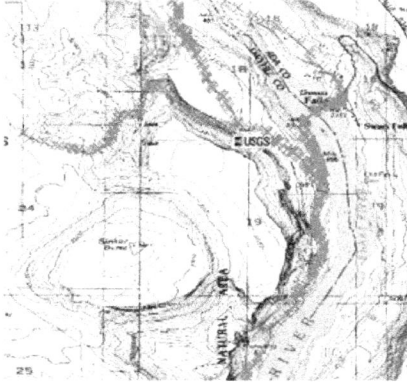

Guidelines for Point Data

If you capture physical assets in the field using a global positioning system (GPS), store the ODBC point data in a database as X, Y, and Z columns.

X, Y, and Z coordinates are kept up-to-date on a real-time basis by some applications. Each time features are refreshed, the latest locations are reflected. For example, if you store the real-time location of buses in a city in a Microsoft Access database, you can point your map to the database to view those bus locations, as shown in the following illustration.

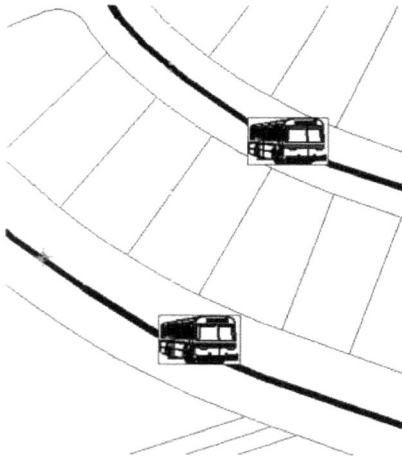

Guidelines for Using ODBC Point Data

The following guidelines help ensure that your ODBC points can be optimally viewed and managed:

Coordinate Systems

Although you can assign point data from ODBC to another coordinate system, performance is increased if the data is collected in the same coordinate system as your map. For example, if your map is currently in California State Plane Zone 1 South, Feet, your point data is rendered more quickly if it is collected and stored in that coordinate system.

Formats

Using ODBC points ensures that points are generic and accessible to all systems. Although points can be stored in other formats (such as SDF, SHP, Oracle, ArcSDE, etc.) and are accessible by FDO providers, those point types are proprietary and exist in the data stores.

Indexing

Place an index in the database from which you want to retrieve ODBC points. Doing so increases performance when the points are used for any application.

> Even with database indexing, ODBC points do not perform as well as other FDO feature sources because the indexing is strictly nonspatial in the ODBC database.
>
> If you have a 64 bit operating system and have MS Office 365 installed, you will not be able to install the required 64 bit ODBC driver successfully because the installed MS Office 365 will cause it to fail. You MUST install the ODBC driver first. Consult with your IT department to assist you with this if need be.
>
> For more information, consult the Autodesk Knowledge Network on this issue.

Example of Using ODBC Points

A good example of ODBC point utilization is a municipal inventory of assets in the field, such as park benches. Over time, park benches wear out, get damaged, or are stolen and a city must go into the field and perform an inventory of them. With the aid of a GPS unit, this can be done rapidly.

The X and Y coordinates of all of the park benches can be stored in Microsoft SQL Server on the network. An ODBC connection to that database enables users to attach that ODBC feature source for an updated layer of the city's park benches, as shown in the following illustration.

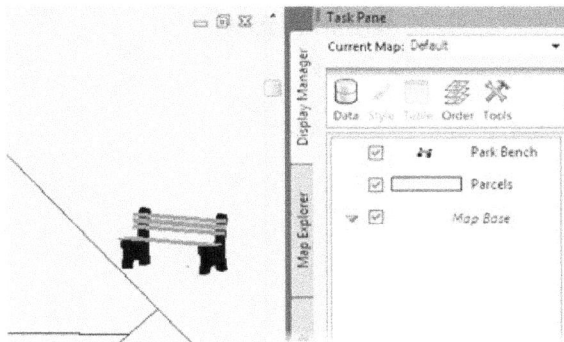

Exercise: Attach an ODBC Point Source

In this exercise, you will create an ODBC connection to a Microsoft Access database. You will use this connection to create an ODBC feature source that is going to generate a hydrants layer from the X and Y columns in the database, as shown in the following illustration.

1. In Microsoft Windows, click Start>Run.

2. For Open, enter **odbcad32**, as shown in the following illustration.

   ▪ Click OK.

   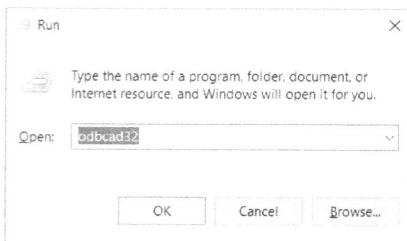

3. In the ODBC Data Source Administrator dialog box, click System DSN tab. (**Note:** If you do not have Administrative rights on your computer, try the same steps on the User DSN tab.)

4. Click Add.

5. In the Create New Data Source dialog box, under Name, select Microsoft Access Driver (*.mdb, *.accdb), as shown in the following illustration.

   ▪ Click Finish.

   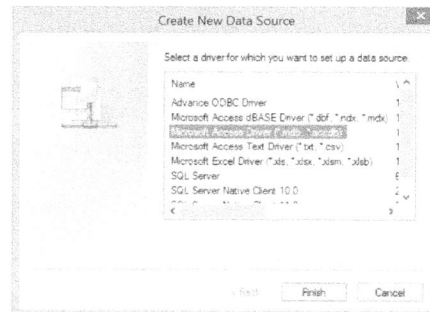

6. In the ODBC Microsoft Access Setup dialog box, for Data Source Name, enter **REDDING_ODBC**.

   ▪ Click Select.

7. Browse to ...*Data\Databases* and select REDDING_HYDRANTS.mdb, as shown in the following illustration.

8. Click OK.

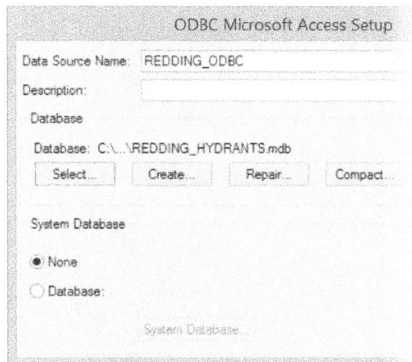

9. Click OK to complete the ODBC setup.

- To close the ODBC Data Source Administrator dialog box, click OK, as shown in the following illustration.

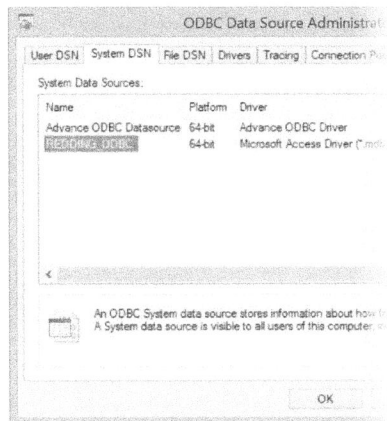

The REDDING_ODBC data source is now set up for all users on your computer. You use that ODBC database to create a new layer.

10. Open ...\ *6-Geospatial Environment\ Redding-Points.dwg*.

11. In Display Manager, click Data>Connect to Data, as shown in the following illustration.

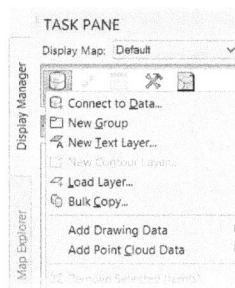

12. In the Data Connect window, for Data Connections by Provider, click Add ODBC Connection, as shown in the following illustration.

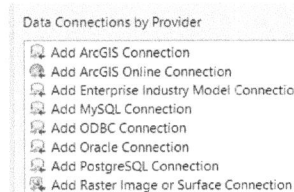

13. Under Add a New Connection:

- For Connection Name, enter **ODBC_HYDRANTS**.
- For Source Type, select Data Source Name (DSN).
- For Source, browse to REDDING_ODBC and then click Select, as shown in the following illustration.
- Click Test Connection.

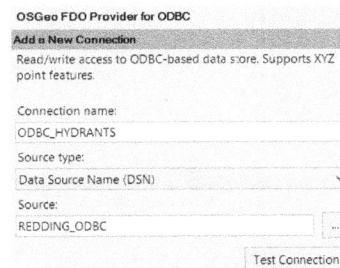

14. In the User Name & Password dialog box, click Login and then click Connect.

15. Under Add Data to Map:

- Click the Edit Coordinate Systems tab.
- Click the Default spatial context.
- Click Edit, as shown in the following illustration.

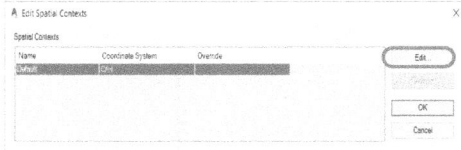

16. In the Select Coordinate System dialog box:

- For Category, select Lat Longs.
- For Coordinate System in Category, select LL, No Datum, Latitude-Longitude; Degrees -180 to +180.
- Click Select.

17. In the Edit Spatial Contexts dialog box, click OK.

18. Under Add Data to Map:

- For X, select LON.
- For Y, select LAT.
- For Z, select <none>, as shown in the following illustration.

ODBC

ODBC_HYDRANTS (REDDING_ODBC)

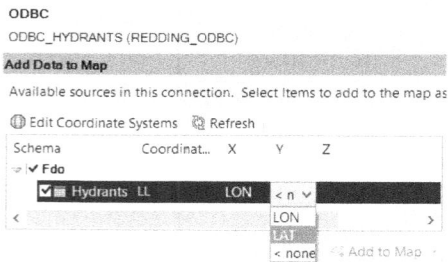

19. Click Add to Map.

20. Close the Data Connect dialog box. Your drawing should look similar to the following illustration.

21. Save and close the drawing.

Lesson: Query Features on Connect

Overview

In this lesson, you use the query on connect method to filter geospatial data that is queried into your map. By filtering geospatial data before viewing information in a map, you can increase performance, answer questions, or limit information before export. You use the Add to Map with Query, as shown in the following illustration, and Query to Filter Data tools to filter geospatial data when connecting.

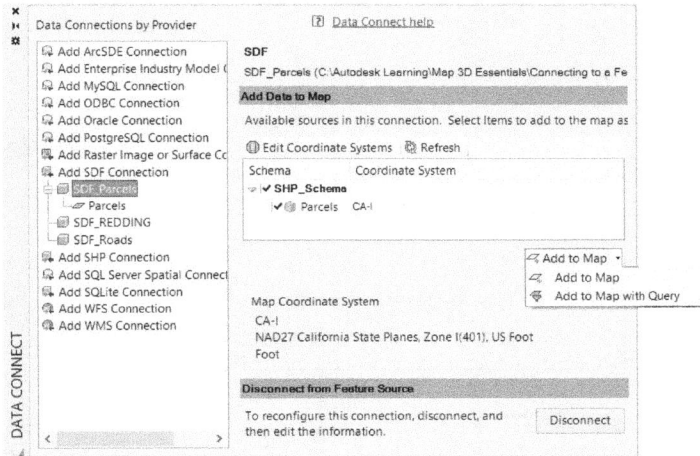

Objectives

After completing this lesson, you will be able to:

- Describe the concept of attribute and spatial filtering the feature source with a query.
- Explain the uses and reasons for filtering spatial and attribute data.
- Query using an attribute filter.
- Query using a spatial filter.

About Filtering Feature Sources

You can filter geospatial feature sources in two distinct ways. The first is an attribute-based query by which you can filter the spatial data that displays on your map. Alternatively, you can filter data spatially by locating a region on a map to crop the data when it is rendered on your map. As you connect to geospatial feature sources, you can filter the data visible in a map by creating a query, as shown in the following illustration. These queries can show a subset of the data in the original feature source. The Create Query dialog box is used to create filter statements that can be a combination of conditions using the available functions. Logical operators, such as AND, OR, and NOT can be used to string multiple conditions together.

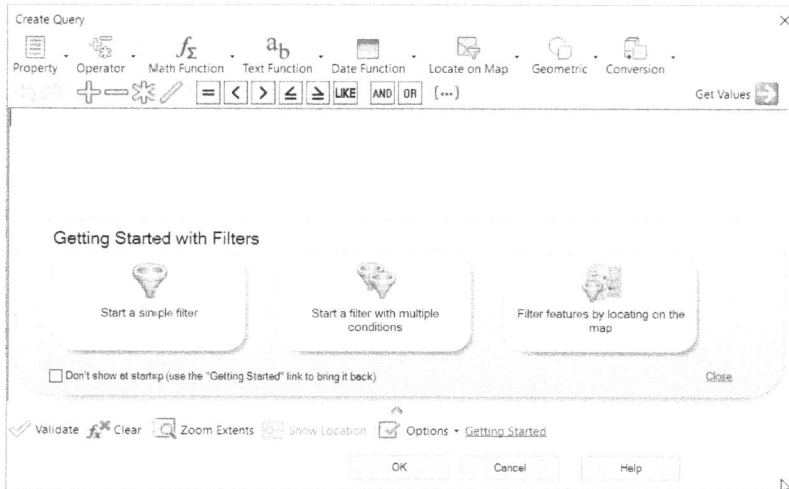

Attribute Filtering

In each vector-based geospatial feature, there are a set of attributes or properties that can be used to create a series of conditions to filter the features that display in your map. The properties, regardless of type, such as string, numeric, or date types, can be used to filter the features you want to see. In the Create Query window, you have a series of operators and functions that you can use to create very complex queries, as shown in the following illustration.

Filtering Feature Data Based on Attributes

Using a query to filter attribute data of features is similar to using Define Query of Attached Drawing(s). The attribute data of a source drawing consists of object data and link template information whereas feature sources include their own attribute data.

> You can modify or create a new query by right-clicking on the Feature layer in Display Manager and choosing Query to Filter Data.

Spatial Filtering

You spatially filter a feature source layer so that only some of the features display in your map. To spatially filter the layer, define a query condition or set of conditions that specify which features you want.

In the Create Query or Modify Query dialog box, the Locate On Map enables you to filter features that are in a polygon, rectangle, or circle. These polygonal objects can be drawn dynamically or already exist in the map.

Also, in the Locate On Map tool, you can choose to spatially filter based on touching any part of a circle, fence, point, polygon, or rectangle, as shown in the following illustration. Again, you can choose to draw these linear features on the map or choose preexisting objects. These spatial filters can be combined into a number of conditions.

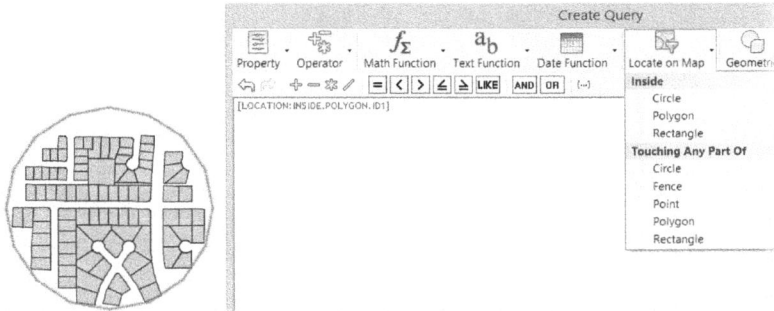

Example of a Spatial Filter for a Feature Source

A local utility stores all of the parcels for nine counties in Oracle Spatial. To view the parcels and water mains that fall within the city limits, a spatial filter can be used to choose the city limit polygon and query those features that fall within it.

When to Use Filtering with Feature Sources

Guidelines for Filtering Feature Sources

The following guidelines will describe how and when to use the spatial and attribute filters for feature sources:

- Large feature sources should be filtered to increase performance.
- Multiple feature sources can be simultaneously filtered spatially but not based on attribute. For example, a folder of SHP files can be queried based on location using the common filter.
- Smaller feature sources, such as city limits, should be connected to your map before you filter other data to provide a reference on which to base your spatial filters.

- Wildcards (%) should be used with caution when applied to your attribute filters as you might query a large amount of data.
- Extremely complex filters, especially when combining attribute and spatial conditions, might take a longer time to process.
- Spatial and Attribute Filters do not function with raster feature sources.
- Sub-sets of Feature Sources can be exported to SDF using filters. For example, a water main stored in Oracle Spatial can be filtered by "Abandoned" and saved as SDF using Export Layer Data to SDF.

Although you can filter a feature source after the features are connected, it is always recommended that you filter during the Data Connect process. This increases map performance because you limit the amount of data before viewing it in the map.

Example of a Common Filter for Multiple Feature Sources

Connecting to multiple features simultaneously can take some time to render in a map because, for example, all of the SHP files are stored in one folder. However, you can reduce the amount of data loaded into a map. When connecting to feature sources, Add to Map With Query and the Create Query dialog box enable you to use the Common Filter in conjunction with the Locate on Map spatial filter, as shown in the following illustration.

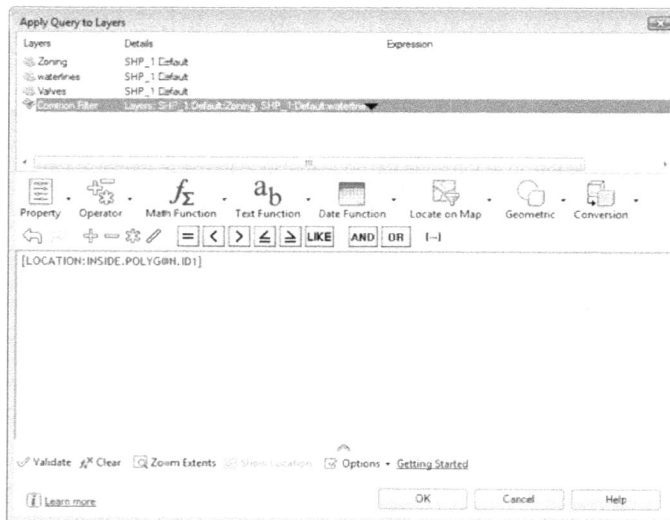

Exercise: Use an Attribute Filter with an SDF

In this exercise, you will connect to an SDF file that contains parcel polygons. You will filter the parcels so that only the features that are on a street called "Brittany Drive" display in the map, as shown in the following illustration.

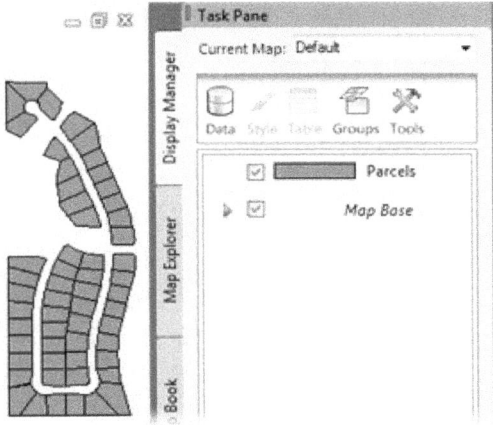

1. Open ...\ *6-Geospatial Environment\Redding-QueryFeatures.dwg*.

2. In Display Manager, click Data>Connect to Data.

3. In the Data Connect window:
   - Click Add SDF Connection.
   - For Connection Name, enter **SDF_PARCELS_BRITTANY_DRIVE**.
   - For Source File, click the Browse icon ( ).

4. In the Open dialog box:
   - Browse to ....\ *Data\SDF*.
   - Click Parcels.sdf.
   - Click Open.

5. Click Connect.

6. Under Schema, ensure that the Parcels are checked.

7. On the Add to Map:
   - Click the down arrow.
   - Select Add to Map with Query, as shown in the following illustration.

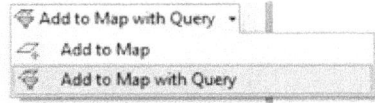

8. In the Create Query dialog box, click Property>STNAME, as shown in the following illustration.

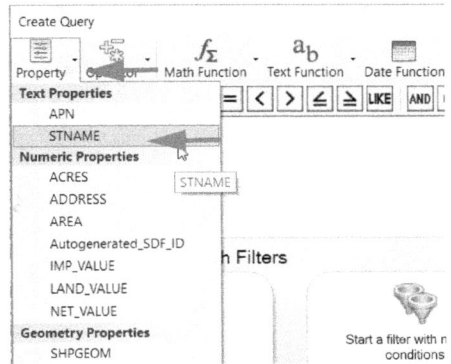

9. Click = (Equal To), as shown in the following illustration.

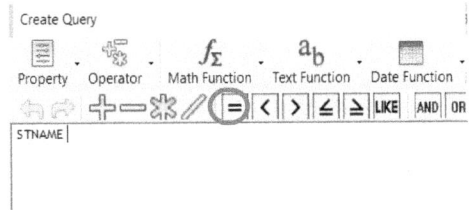

10. Click Get Values.

- Under Select a Property to Retrieve Its Values, select STNAME.
- Under Filter the List of Values, enter **BRIT**.
- Click the green arrow button.
- Select BRITTANY DR.
- Click Insert Value, as shown in the following illustration.

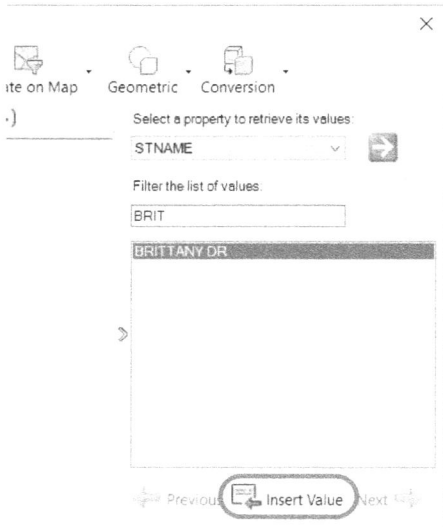

11. In the Create Query dialog box, click OK, as shown in the following illustration.

12. Note that only the parcels on Brittany Drive display as shown in the following illustration.

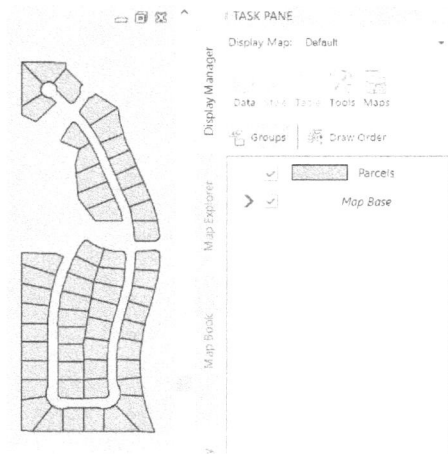

13. Save and close the drawing.

Chapter Summary

Having completed this chapter, you can:

- Connect to a feature source.
- Use Geospatial Coordinate Systems.
- Work with point data.
- Use the Attribute and Spatial filters to limit the geospatial data that displays in the map.

Editing Features

The lessons in this chapter cover the processes of editing features displayed in the drawing area and saving them back to the original feature sources, and converting DWG™ objects to features. The techniques of Merging and Splitting features are also covered in these lessons.

Objectives

After completing this chapter, you will be able to:

- Edit feature attributes and geometry.
- Move data between DWG objects and FDO features.
- Use geospatial split and merge tools, along with associated settings, to split a polygon and merge a polyline along with associated attributes.
- Use the Map to AutoCAD wizard to convert FDO objects to drawing objects for editing purposes.

Lesson: Editing Feature Attributes and Geometry

Overview

Feature sources are connected to and queried by using FDO providers. This lesson covers the process of editing features displayed in the drawing area and saving them back to the original feature sources, as shown in the following illustration.

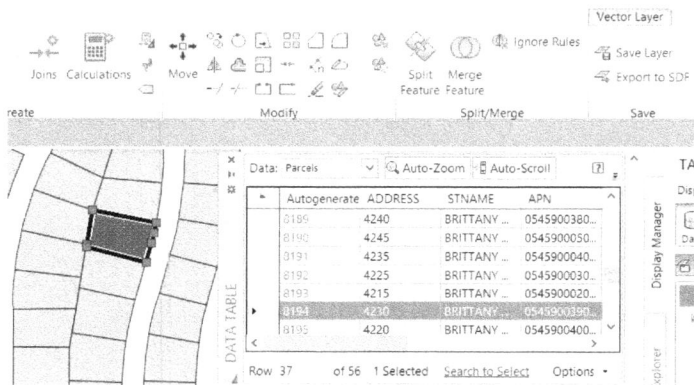

Data Grid and Vector Layer ribbon

Objectives

After completing this lesson, you will be able to:

- Explain the typical data formats that are used for editable feature sources.
- Explain the process of editing the geometry of a feature source.
- Describe the process of editing the attributes of a feature source.
- Edit geometry and attributes.

Typical Data Formats

You can view feature sources from a number of FDO providers. Some FDO providers enable you to keep your data current by editing feature geometries and attributes without having to convert them to an AutoCAD® format and then export them back out to the original format.

Editable Feature Sources

Editable feature sources enable attribute and graphic creation, modification, and deletion. Other feature sources are either read-only or do not contain any vector-based features that can be edited.

The following feature sources support full editing:

- ArcSDE
- Enterprise Industry Model
- MySQL
- ODBC
- Oracle Geometries
- PostgreSQL
- SDF
- SHP
- SQL Server
- SQL Server Spatial
- SQLite

> OpenGIS formats (WMS and WFS) are read-only and cannot be edited.

Example of an Editable Feature Source

An example of a feature source that is completely editable (including its attributes and geometry) is the OSGeo SDF provider. When you add an SDF file as a layer, its attribute data can be added and its geometry modified.

Editing Geometry

You can query a feature from a feature source and edit its geometry, as shown in the following illustration.

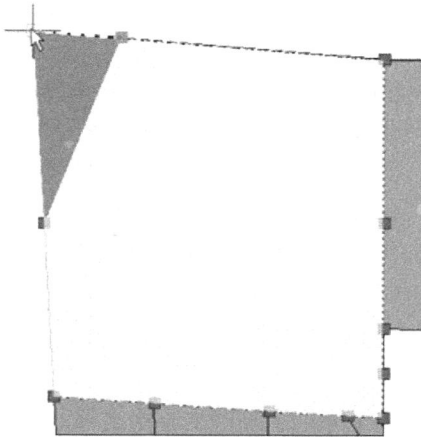

Example of editing features
from an SDF feature source

Editing Geometry

You can draw features very quickly and select them, but you cannot edit them until they are temporarily converted into drawing objects.

The process of temporarily converting features into drawing objects is called checking out. When you have modified the drawing objects, you can check them back in to the original feature source.

New drawing objects can be converted into features using the New Feature from Geometry tool.

Process: Editing Features

1.   Verify that the feature source displays in the Display Manager, as shown in the following illustration.

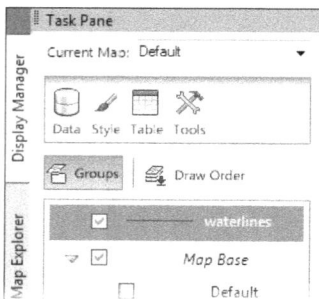

---

2. If the Check Out Edits Automatically option is not enabled, on the Feature Edit ribbon, on the Edit Set panel, click Check Out to make a feature editable, as shown in the following illustration.

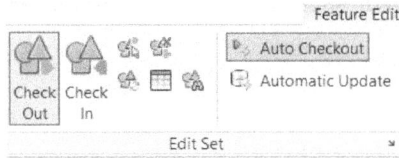

3. Use grips or any standard AutoCAD tools to modify the feature, as shown in the following illustration.

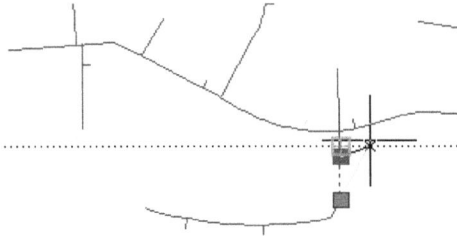

4. When you have modified the feature, on the Feature Edit ribbon, on the Edit Set panel, click Check In to submit the changes back to the feature source, as shown in the following illustration.

> You do not have to use Check In or Check Out if you have enabled Automatic Update or Auto Checkout in the Edit set panel on the Feature Edit ribbon.

Feature Editing Options

The automatic check-in and check-out of FDO Features can be set using the Feature Editing Options settings found by clicking the down arrow of the Edit Set panel, as shown in the following illustration.

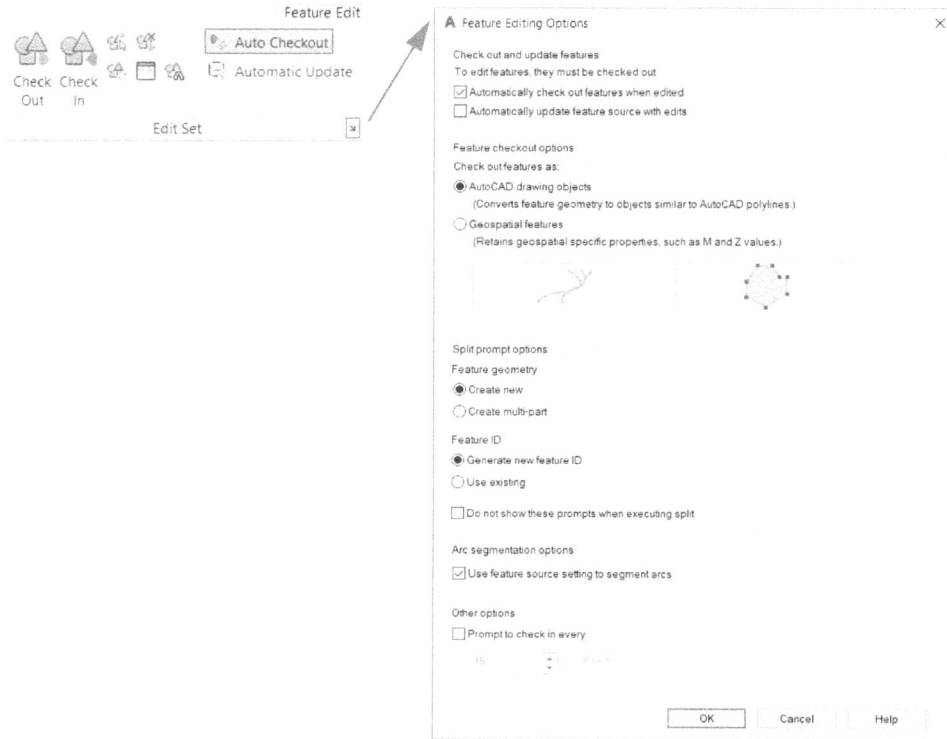

Process: Creating Features

1. Ensure that the feature source displays in the Display Manager, as shown in the following illustration.

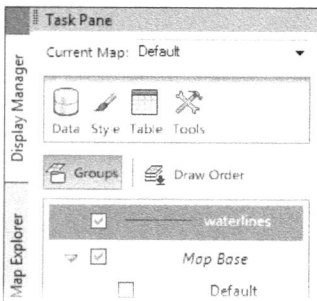

2. Using the AutoCAD drawing tools, create a new drawing object, as shown in the following illustration.

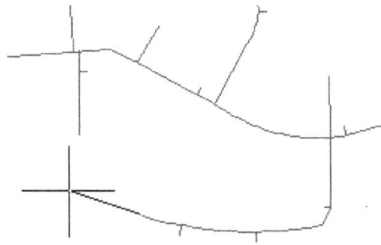

3. When you have created a drawing object, on the Create ribbon, click Create from Geometry, as shown in the following illustration.

4. Enter the new attribute data into the Data Table for the new feature, as shown in the following illustration.

5. Modify the new feature, if required. To submit the feature back to the feature source, on the Feature Edit ribbon, on the Edit Set panel, click Check In, as shown in the following illustration.

Guidelines for Editing Features

- For best performance, check out only those features that you want to edit.
- Although hundreds of coordinate systems are recognized, you might get a warning that the coordinate system for a feature source is not recognized. If so, do not mix objects from this feature source with other objects or they are not located correctly in your map.
- If for security reasons, you have read-only access to a feature source on your network, adding new features, or modifying existing ones, might result in an error.
- Some feature sources, such as ArcSDE and Oracle feature classes with a geodetic coordinate system, do not support curved geometry. When you add a curved object to one of these feature sources, the curved object is tessellated as a polyline using the default tolerance settings. To change the way such an object is tessellated, either change the tessellation settings (click Setup>Autodesk Map Options>Save Back) or recreate the object using a polyline.
- Ensure that the drawing objects you create using New Feature from Geometry match the features in the feature source. For example, if your SHP file contains rivers (lines), points that you draw do not upload correctly into the SHP file.

Editing Attributes

You can modify feature attributes using the Data Table, as shown in the following illustration.

Editing Feature Attributes

You can edit feature attributes using the Data Table. Similar to the way the Data View enables you to view attached databases with link templates, data tables enable you to view any attached data source attribute information, as shown in the following illustration.

Editing in the Data Table

- The Data Table can be docked or floating and shown with transparency.
- By selecting objects in the Data Table, you can automatically zoom to objects on the screen.
- Selecting features in the graphic area can automatically scroll to records in the Data Table.
- Attributes can be filtered with the Filter button in the Data Table.
- You can edit a feature attribute by selecting the record in the Data Table. The update is committed when the record is no longer highlighted.
- New attributes can be added in the Data Table.

Process: Editing Feature Attributes with Data Grid

1. In the Data Table, ensure that the layer or feature class is selected in the Data drop-down list, as shown in the following illustration.

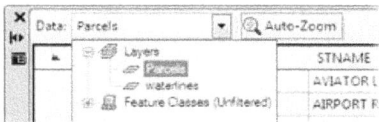

2. If Auto-Zoom is active in the Data Table, you can select a record and its corresponding feature is highlighted and zoomed to, as shown in the following illustration.

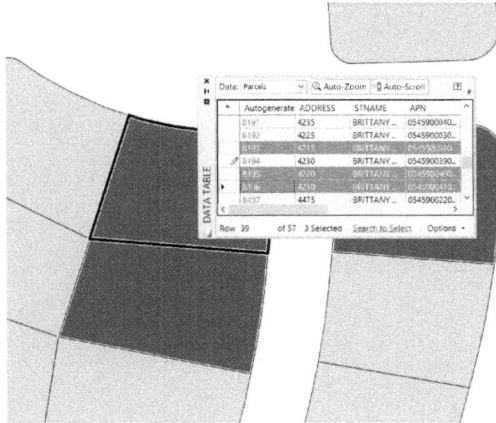

3. Select the record and column that you want to edit. Enter a change to the attribute value, as shown in the following illustration.

Guidelines

- The Data Table can be used for some data validation because it supports FDO data rules for feature sources. FDO data validation is recommended.
- Enter only values that match the data type of the feature attribute you are editing. For example, PARCEL_ID, an integer column, does not accept a value of "ABC123".
- Ensure robust security for your data sources by limiting the number of people who can update live databases.
- SHP and SDF files are file-based feature sources, so be wary when multiple people are editing the data in the file as there is limited concurrence control.

Exercise: Edit Geometry and Attributes

In this exercise, you will use Data Grid to view the attribute information associated with an SDF feature source and to edit that information. You will also modify the geometry of a Parcel SDF and a Waterline SHP by checking the features out for editing, modifying them using AutoCAD grips, and confirming the edits by checking them back in. When complete it should look like that shown in the following illustration.

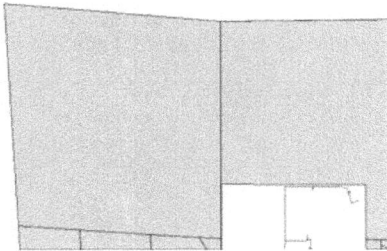

1. Open ...\7-Editing Features\Editing Feature Attributes and Geometry\Redding-Edit.dwg.

2. In Windows Explorer:
   - Browse to ...\Data\SDF, as shown in the following illustration.
   - Drag and drop Parcels.sdf and waterlines.shp files into the Display Manager.

   Note: If it does not work, ensure that Groups is highlighted, rather than Draw Order.

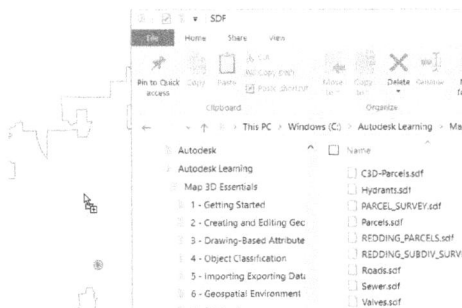

3. Click View ribbon>Views panel>Named Views.

4. In the View Manager dialog box:
   - Expand Model Views.
   - Select PARCEL_EDIT, as shown in the following illustration.
   - Click Set Current.
   - Click OK.

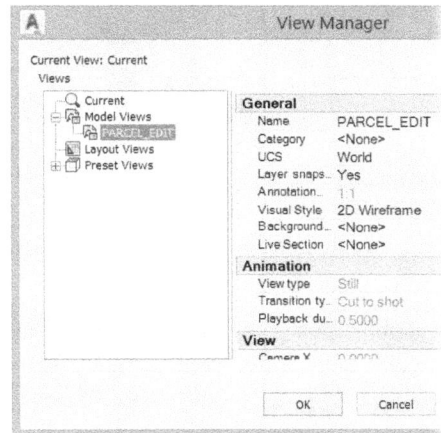

5. On the Feature Edit ribbon, under Edit Set, click the diagonal arrow (Feature Editing Options), as shown in the following illustration.

6. In the Feature Editing Options dialog box:
   - Unselect Automatically Check Out Features When Edited, as shown in the following illustration.
   - Click OK.

7. In the Drawing Editor, highlight the large parcel, as shown in the following illustration.

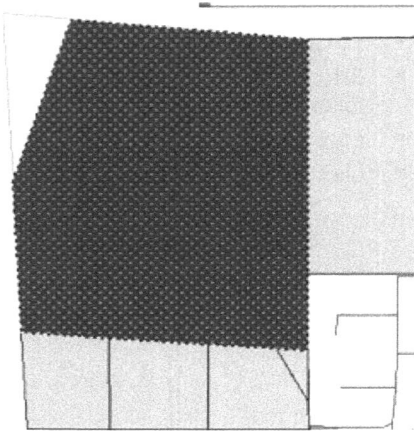

8. On the Feature Edit ribbon, under Edit Set, click Check Out.

9. Right-click on the selected parcel and select Show Data Table, as shown in the following illustration.

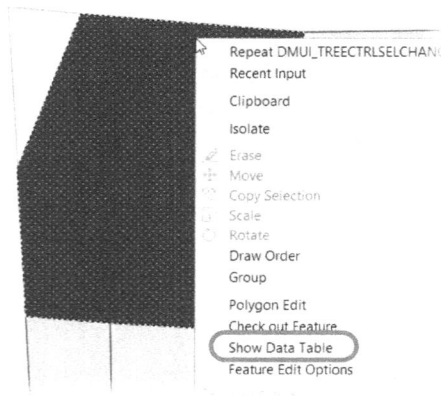

10. In the Data Table, the 12450 RANDOLPH record is selected, as shown in the following illustration.

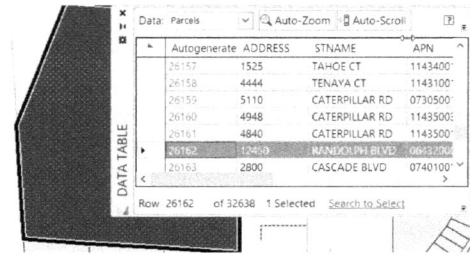

11. In the Data Table pane:
   - Click that record in the STNAME column.
   - Change RANDOLPH BLVD to RANDOLPH RD, as shown in the following illustration.

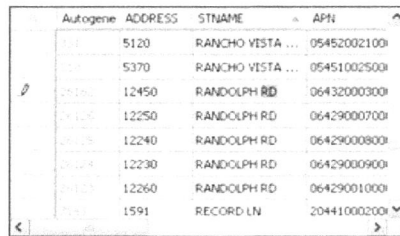

12. Close the Data Table.

13. In the drawing editor:
   - Click the topmost grip of the selected parcel.
   - Stretch the line and snap it to the edge of the city boundary, as shown in the following illustration.

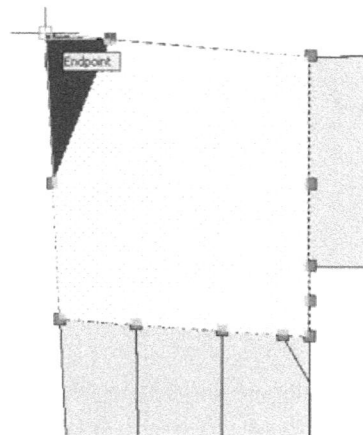

14. On the Feature Edit ribbon, under Edit Set, select Check In, as shown in the following illustration.

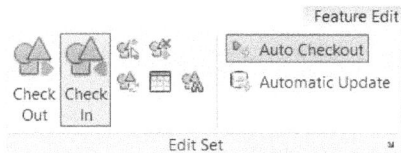

The parcel feature is now saved back to the SDF feature source, as shown in the following illustration.

15. On the Feature Edit ribbon, under Edit Set, click the diagonal arrow (Feature Editing Options), as shown in the following illustration.

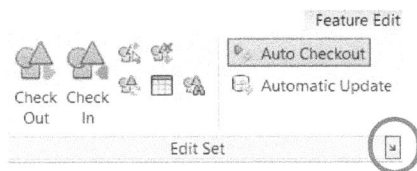

16. In the Feature Editing Options dialog box:

- Select Automatically Check Out Features When Edited, as shown in the following illustration.
- Click OK.

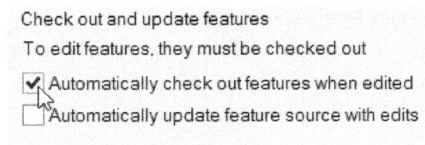

17. Highlight the waterline, as shown in the following illustration.

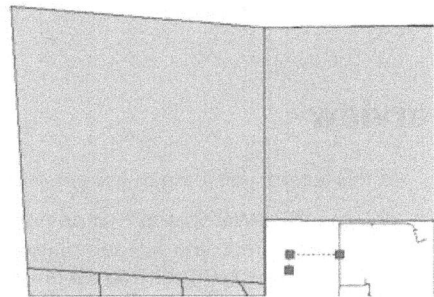

18. Press <Delete>, as shown in the following illustration.

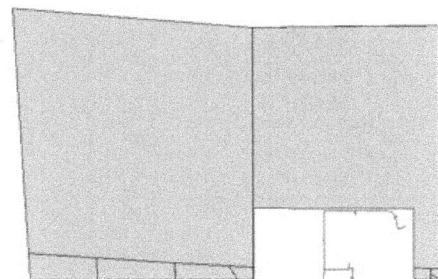

19. On the Feature Edit ribbon, click Check In. The waterline deleted feature is now saved back to the SDF feature source, as shown in the following illustration.

20. Save and close the drawing.

Lesson: Moving Data Between DWG Objects and FDO Features

Overview

In this lesson, you learn to use existing DWG objects to create FDO features.

You can use DWG objects that do not have any attribute data attached and those that have block attributes, object data, link templates, or object classifications. The following illustration shows how to use the New Features from Geometry tool.

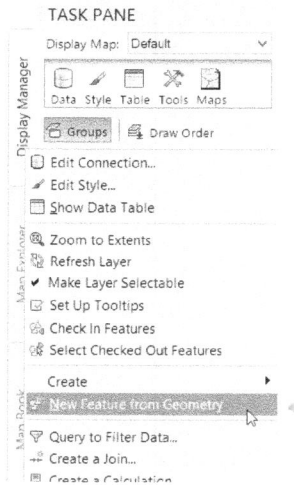

Objectives

After completing this lesson, you will be able to:

- Describe how to use existing DWG objects as geometry for FDO features.
- Describe how to export DWG objects to FDO features so that the attached data is maintained.
- Review the process for exporting DWG objects to FDO features.
- Convert DWG objects into FDO features.

About Creating Features from Geometry

The Create from Geometry tool, as shown in the following illustration, enables you to use DWG objects as graphics in any vector-based FDO feature source (SDF, SHP, Oracle, SQL Server, MySQL, or ArcSDE). Since the DWG objects are migrated as geometry, no tabular information, such as block attributes, object data, or link template connections is attached. Also, since most FDO feature sources support multiple feature types, such as a multipolygon and islands, the New Feature from Geometry tool enables you to select multiple objects to act as a single object, before prompting you to enter data in the data window. This New Feature tool does not enable bulk selection, so you must add objects individually. After selecting one object, you enter its attribute information in the Data Table and then select the next object.

Example of Creating Features from Geometry

Engineering departments often receive information in DWG format. The New Feature from Geometry tool enables the simple input of that new data into a system that is stored in an FDO feature source, such as SQL Server.

For example, the water mains are stored in SQL Server and maintained by the utilities department. A new set of water mains has to be brought into the GIS using DWG information from an outside engineering firm. The New Feature from Geometry tool enables each water main to be selected and its associated attribute information to be entered in Data Table for each main that is brought into the system, as shown in the following illustration.

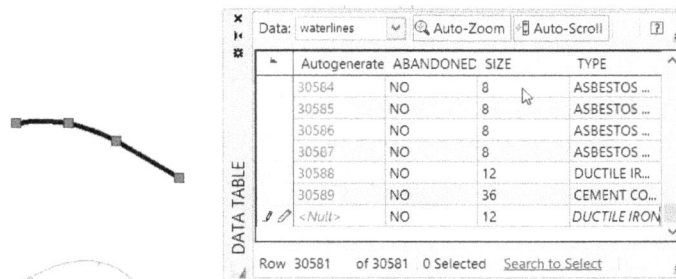

This is an example of the New Features from Geometry tool being used to select a polyline on the Water Main layer and add attributes.

Once the features are checked in, the attributes and graphics are saved to the FDO feature source.

About Exporting Geometry to FDO Features

Using export tools is one method of retaining block attributes, object data, and link template information when moving DWG objects to FDO features. Two key export tools are Convert DWG to FDO Connection (Oracle) and Convert DWG to Autodesk SDF.

Whether you use Oracle or SDF, you can export your DWG objects by layer. Each layer becomes a feature class in the SDF data store. It is recommended that you use object classification before moving any data to Oracle or SDF to retain all of the information. These classes are created in the SDF or Oracle if the feature class has not been already created in the data store.

If you are not certain that the object classes match the destination data store or if you only want to move certain fields, export to SDF, as shown in the following illustration. You can then use bulk copy and match the fields you want to move to the new data store.

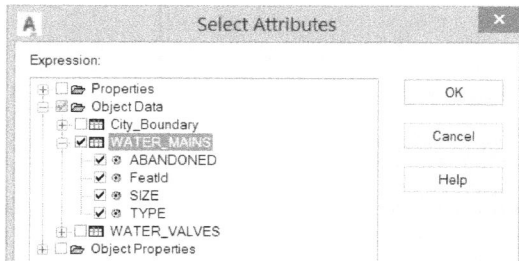

Example of Exporting Geometry to FDO Features

Many organizations move their data to FDO feature sources to take advantage of the functionality in the AutoCAD Map 3D software, such as stylizing and buffering features.

An engineering firm plans to move hundreds of DWG files to FDO feature sources. Each DWG file represents a feature: one DWG is the water mains and another is the water valves. Each DWG also has a link template connection to a Microsoft Access database that contains all of the attribute information. The firm has decided to move all of the data into Oracle Spatial.

To facilitate this move, each DWG is converted to an SDF file, which includes the Microsoft Access data. When the bulk copy has been performed to load the SDF into Oracle, the Microsoft Access database and the DWG are no longer required because all of the data is in Oracle.

The following illustration demonstrates how the valve blocks and their associated link template data can be exported into an SDF file. Then *Valves.sdf* can be merged with an existing SDF, such as water.sdf that contains all of the water features, or it can be brought into Oracle Spatial. Either way, the Bulk Copy tool is used.

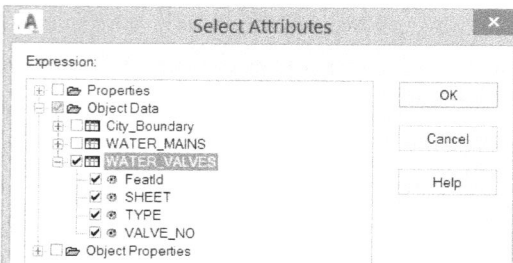

Process of Exporting Geometry to FDO

If you want to keep attribute information, such as block attributes, link template connections, object data, or object classification, you must export your DWG objects into a feature source. The key feature sources are SDF data stores and Oracle Spatial.

Process: Exporting DWG Objects

The following steps and illustration show the flow of exporting DWG objects to FDO feature sources.

- Ensure that the objects have associated data available. For example, if using link templates, ensure that the database is attached.
- Choose the type of FDO export: SDF or Oracle.
- Filter the data you want to export. Usually this is done by layer.
- Choose the object attributes you want to export, such as block attributes or link template information.
- Choose the feature class name. Unless the DWG objects are classified, each feature class is exported individually.
- Use Bulk Copy to move the new SDF into another master SDF or other large FDO data store, such as Oracle.

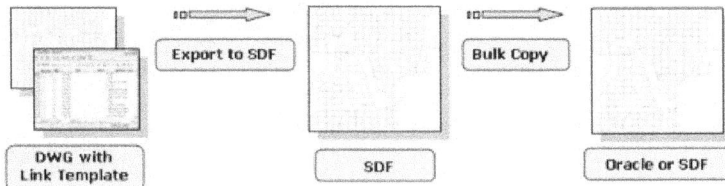

Alternative Workflow

If the DWG attributes (i.e., Object Data or Link Template columns) match the existing FDO data store, you can directly append the existing data, as shown in the following illustration.

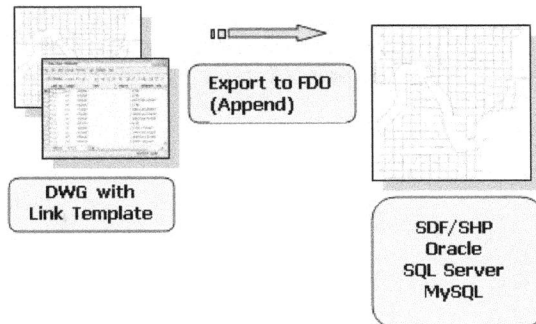

All DWG objects should be classified before being exported to SDF or any other FDO feature source.

Exercise: Convert DWG Objects into FDO Features

In this exercise, you will move waterlines and water valves stored in a DWG into an SDF file. The waterlines are polylines with object data attached. The water valves are blocks with object data attached.

The object data will be retained for the waterlines by exporting the objects into an SDF. Because the water valves will be directly converted into FDO features, the object data will be lost and be entered manually instead. The completed exercise will look like that shown in the following illustration.

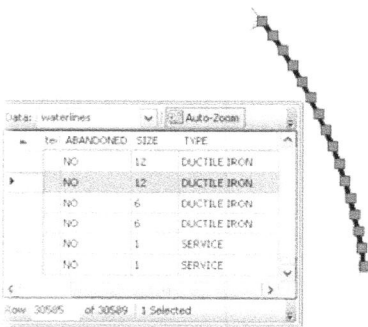

1. Open ...\7-Editing Features\Moving Data Between DWG and FDO Features\Redding-Moving.dwg.

2. In Display Manager:
   - Ensure that the valves and waterlines are connected, as shown in the following illustration.
   - SDF_VALVES should point to ...\Data\SDF\Valves.sdf.
   - SDF_WATER should point to ...\Data\SDF\waterlines.sdf.

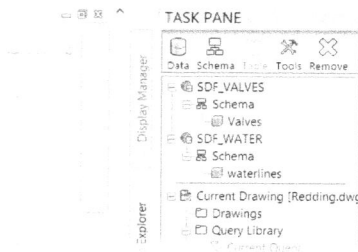

3. On the View tab, under Views, select NEW-WATERPIPES, as shown in the following illustration, then zoom to the lower end of the blue waterline.

4. In the Display Manager, right-click on Valves and select New Feature from Geometry, as shown in the following illustration.

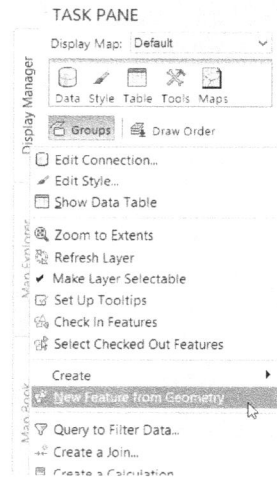

5. Select the last valve at the end of the blue line, as shown in the following illustration, and press <Enter>.

6. Choose Yes to erase the valve after operating.

7. The Data Table dialog box opens:

- Scroll to the bottom of the list.
- For SHEET, enter **X-15**.
- For TYPE, enter **BLOWOFF**, as shown in the following illustration.
- Do not enter a **VALVE_NO**.

	Autogenerate	SHEET	TYPE	VALVE_NO
	13115	T-13	BLOWOFF	T-13_73
	13116	V-13	BLOWOFF	V-13_78
	13117	V-13	BLOWOFF	V-13_79
	13118	-C-1	BLOWOFF	-C-1_17
	13119	P-3	BLOWOFF	P-3_126
	13120	C-1	BLOWOFF	C-1_99
	<Null>	X-15	BLOWOFF	<Null>

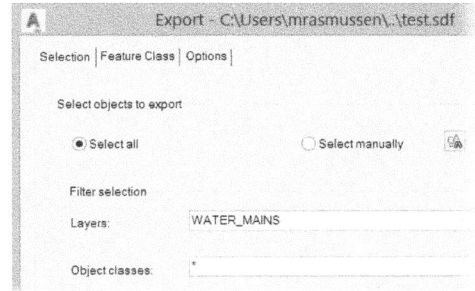

Data: Valves · Auto-Zoom · Auto-Scroll

DATA TABLE

Row 13116 of 13116 0 Selected Search to Select

8. Repeat Steps 4 through 8 for the remaining four valves, panning as required.

- For SHEET, enter **X-15**.
- For TYPE, enter **VALVE**.

9. In the Display Manager, right-click on Valves and select Check In Features.

10. The water pipes contain object data that you want to retain.

- On the Output ribbon, under Map Data Transfer, select DWG to SDF, as shown in the following illustration.

Current Map to DWG
As Image
To FDO
Connection DWG to SDF
Map Data Transfer

11. In the Export Location dialog box:

- Browse to the ...*Data\SDF* folder.
- For File Name, select waterlines.sdf.
- Click OK

12. In the Existing File dialog box, click Append.

13. In the Export dialog box:

- On the Selection tab, under Filter selection, for Layers, enter **WATER_MAINS**, as shown in the following illustration, or select the layer by clicking on the Layer Select Icon.

Export - C:\Users\mrasmussen\..\test.sdf

Selection | Feature Class | Options

Select objects to export

● Select all   ○ Select manually

Filter selection

Layers: WATER_MAINS

Object classes: *

14. In the Export dialog box:

- On the Feature Class tab, click Select Attributes.
- In the Select Attributes dialog box, check the WATER_MAINS object data table, as shown in the following illustration.
- Click OK.

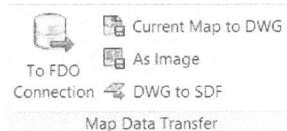

Select Attributes

Expression:

Properties
Object Data
City_Boundary
WATER_MAINS
ABANDONED
Featid
SIZE
TYPE
WATER_VALVES
Object Properties

OK
Cancel
Help

15. In the Export dialog box:

- On the Options tab, click OK to export the SDF file.

16. In the Display Manager, right-click on waterlines and select Refresh Layer.

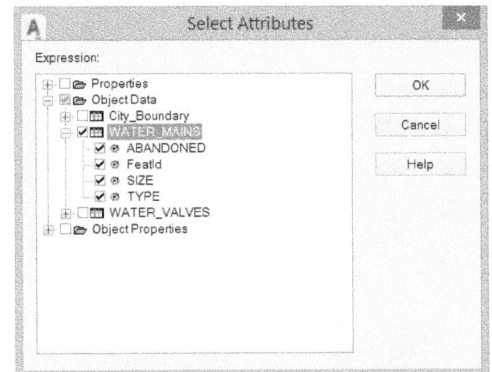

17. In the Display Manager:

- Select the waterlines layer.
- Click Table.

18. Select one of the new waterlines and note that the object data has been successfully moved into the SDF file, as shown in the following illustration.

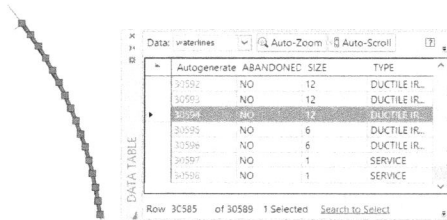

19. Save and close the drawing.

Lesson: Merging and Splitting Features

Overview

In this lesson, you learn how to use the Split and Merge tools for geospatial data. Using these tools ensures that you retain attribute information when you spatially change geospatial information. You explore these two techniques to modify and create new features in your map, as shown in the following illustration.

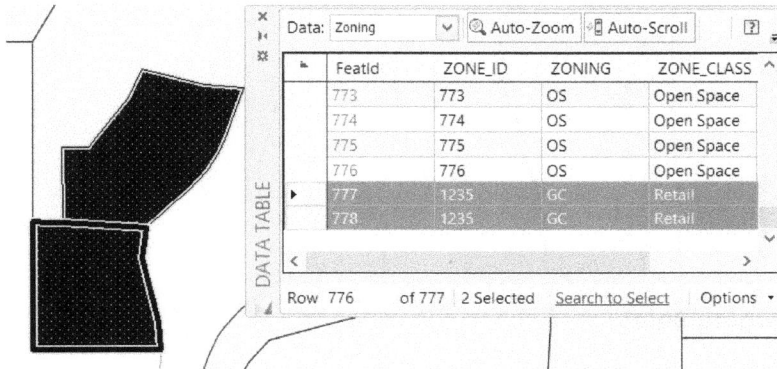

Objectives

After completing this lesson, you will be able to:

- Explain the concept of merging features.
- Explain the concept of splitting features.
- Split a zoning area.
- Merge a waterline.

About Merging Geospatial Features

You can select any number of connected or touching features and merge them into a single feature. Attributes are combined according to the rules established in advance for the Merge command. The Data Table opens to show the newly-created feature so that you can see how the attributes have been assigned.

Typically, when merging multiple geospatial features, you would lose the attribute data that is contained in the features. With the Merge tools, you can retain this information, as shown in the following illustration.

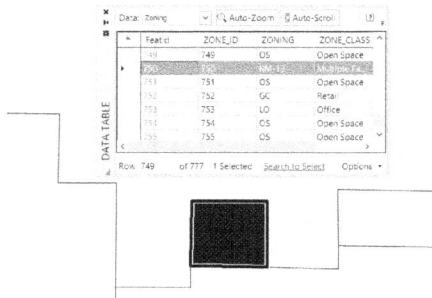

Geospatial Merging Rules

The following rules are used when determining what the attribute fields should be set to when the features are merged together. These rules change depending on whether the fields are strings or numerical.

- **Concatenation (string only) -** Concatenates the property values together separated by the text in the Separator Text field. For example: "STEEL - PVC"
- **Empty -** Sets the property value to blank for the merged feature.
- **Expression (string only) -** Enables you to specify an expression using the Merge Rule Expression builder.
- **First Selected (default for string) -** Sets the property value to that of the first selected feature in the merge.
- **Last Selected -** Sets the property value to that of the last selected feature in the merge.
- **Average (numeric only) -** Averages the property values from the merged features.
- **Calculation (numeric only) -** Sets the property value based on a custom calculation specified in the Expression field.
- **Maximum (numeric only) -** Sets the property value to that of the maximum property value of the merged features.
- **Median (numeric only) -** Sets the property value to that of the median property value of the merged features.
- **Minimum (numeric only) -** Sets the property value to that of the minimum property value of the merged features.
- **Standard Deviation (numeric only) -** Sets the property value to that of the minimum property value of the merged features.
- **Sum (default for numeric) -** Sets the property value to the sum of property values of the merged features.

Merge rules for numeric field, as shown in the following illustration.

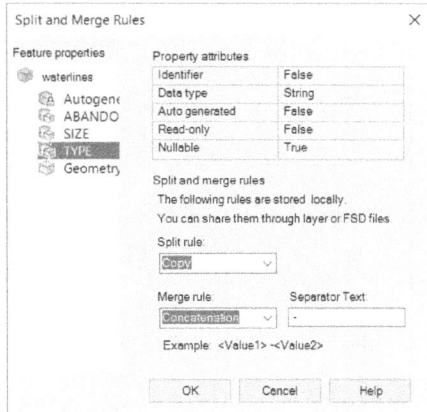

Example of Merging Features

If you merge two parcels that contain square footage attributes (3,000 square feet and 5,000 square feet), you can set the area column to sum the area of the two parcels (8,000 square feet).

About Splitting Geospatial Features

To split a geospatial feature into two parts, you can use the Split tool. The resulting feature property values are determined by the rules you specify in the Split and Merge Rules dialog box.

When you split a feature, as shown in the following illustration, you can draw or select a line or polygon to split the feature. You can specify whether the result is a new feature or a multipart feature. A multipart feature is a single feature that contains non-contiguous parts but has a single attribute in the data table, such as a non-continuous line or polygon. Typically, when splitting geospatial features, you would lose the attribute data that is contained in the feature. With the Split tools, you can retain this information.

You can also specify whether the new feature uses the existing feature ID or a new one.

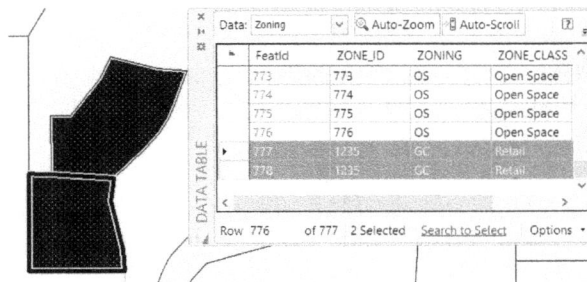

Geospatial Splitting Rules

The following rules are used when determining what the attribute fields should be set to when the features are split apart, as shown in the following illustration. These rules change depending on whether the fields are strings or numerical.

- **Copy (default) -** Copies the property values to each new feature.
- **Empty -** Sets the property values to "empty" or a default for new features. Keeps the original values for the selected feature.
- **Expression (string only) -** Enables you to specify an expression using the Split Rule Expression builder.
- **Calculation (numeric only) -** Enables you to specify a numeric expression using the Split Rule Expression builder.
- **Divide (numeric only) -** Divides the property values equally into each new feature.
- **Proportional (numeric only) -** Distributes the property values proportionally into each new feature based on the numeric value specified in the Based On field. Usually based on the Area or Length of each new object.

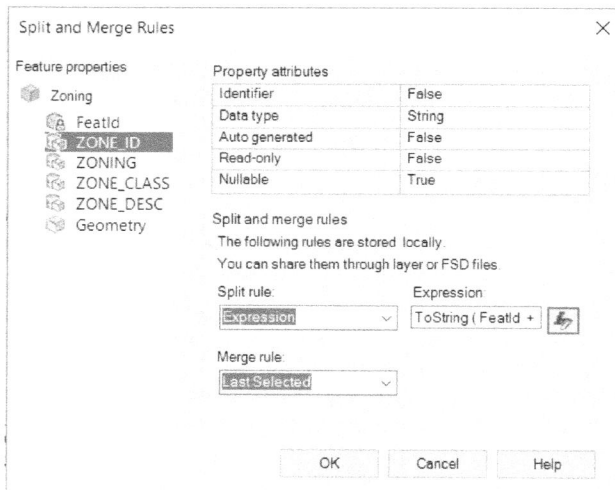

Example of Splitting Features

You can split a road with a recorded length of 200 feet as a numeric attribute by setting it to automatically be a proportion of the lengths of two new features, such as 30 feet and 170 feet.

Exercise: Split a Zoning Feature

In this exercise, you will split a zoning polygon in which default settings determine how the fields are handled, as shown in the following illustration. Also by default, all fields are copied in both polygons, except for FeatId which is defined as an autonumber. You will change the settings for the column ZONE_ID so that it becomes the current FeatId plus 1,000. Since ZONE_ID is a text field, you will use a ToString function after you add 1,000 to the FeatId value.

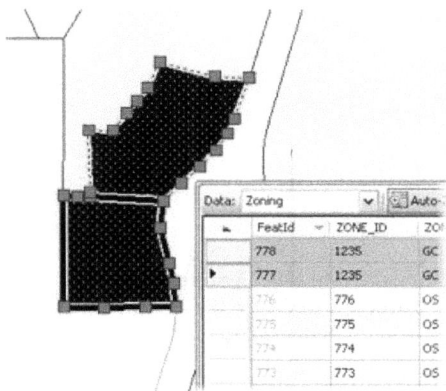

1. Open ...\7-Editing Features\Merging and Splitting Features\ReddingZoningSplit.dwg.

2. In Display Manager, ensure that the Zoning layer is available.
    - If it is not available, in Data Connect, click SDF_Zoning.
    - For the source file, browse to ...\Data\SDF\Zoning.sdf.
    - Click Connect.

3. On the View ribbon, under Views, select Zoning Split, as shown in the following illustration.

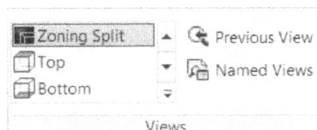

4. In Display Manager:
    - Select Zoning.
    - Click Table.

5. In the Data Table dialog box, click Options> Set Split and Merge Rules, as shown in the following illustration.

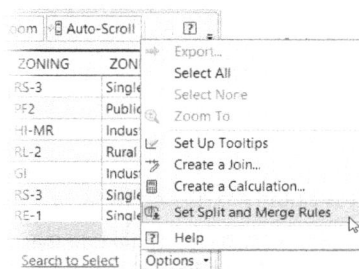

6. In the Split and Merge Rules dialog box:
    - Select ZONE_ID.
    - Under Split and Merge Rules, for Split Rule, click Expression.
    - Click the Expression icon ( ).

7. In the Split Rule Expression: ZONE_ID dialog box:
    - Select Property>FeatId.
    - Click Add (the Plus Symbol (+)).
    - For Value, enter **1000**.
    - Highlight the FeatId + 1000 expression.
    - Click Conversion>ToString.
    - Delete the [Optional Format] and the comma.
    - Click OK.

Optionally, you can just enter **ToString(FeatId + 1000)**, as shown in the following illustration.

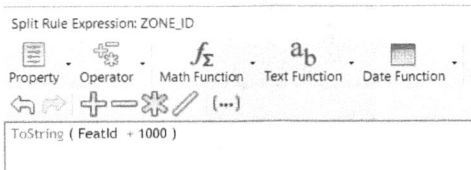

8. In the Split and Merge Rules dialog box, click OK, as shown in the following illustration.

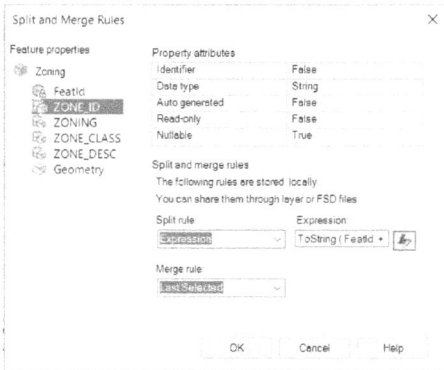

9. Close the Data Table dialog box.

10. On the Feature Edit tab, under Edit Set, select Check Out, as shown in the following illustration.

11. Select the Zoning polygon in the middle of the map, as shown in the following illustration.

■ Press <Enter>.

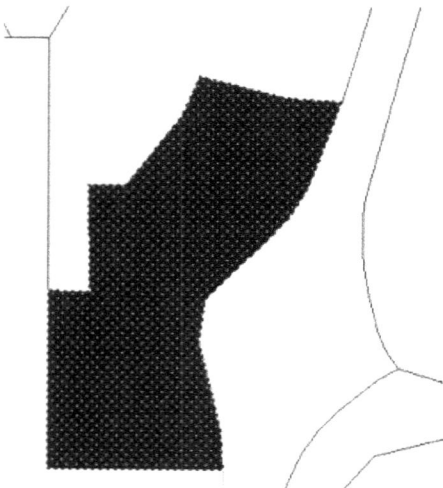

12. On the Vector Layer Contextual tab, under Split/Merge, select Split Feature, as shown in the following illustration.

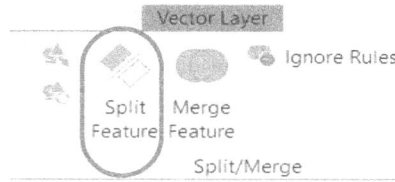

13. For Create New or Multipart, right-click and select New, as shown in the following illustration.

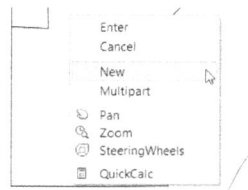

■ For Generate New Feature ID or Use Existing, click New in the Command Line, as shown in the following illustration.

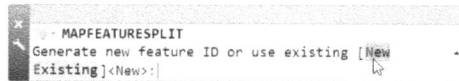

■ For Would You Like to Draw or Select the Line for Split? click Draw in the Command Line, as shown in the following illustration.

■ Draw a horizontal line across the Zoning polygon, as shown in the following illustration.

■ Press <Enter>.

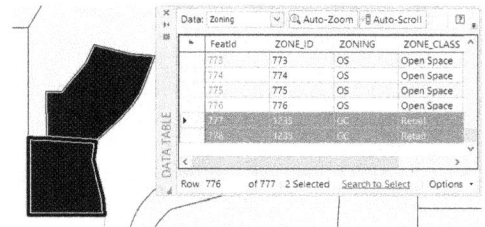

17. Save and close the drawing.

14. In the Data Table dialog box, note that ZONE_ID is the current FeatID plus 1,000, as shown in the following illustration.

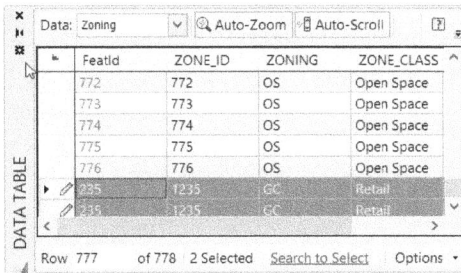

15. On the Feature Edit tab, under Edit Set, select Check In, as shown in the following illustration.

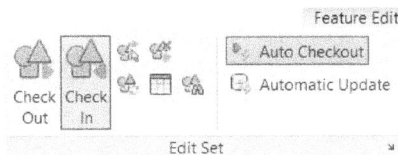

16. Note that there are two new FeatIds in the Data Table dialog box, as shown in the following illustration.

Exercise: Merge Waterline Features

In this exercise, you will set the Merge rules for merging multiple geospatial features. You will ensure that the TYPE of waterline will be a concatenation of the two pipe types. The other fields will use the default First Selected value. Once the rules are set, you will merge two separate waterlines into one pipe, as shown in the following illustration.

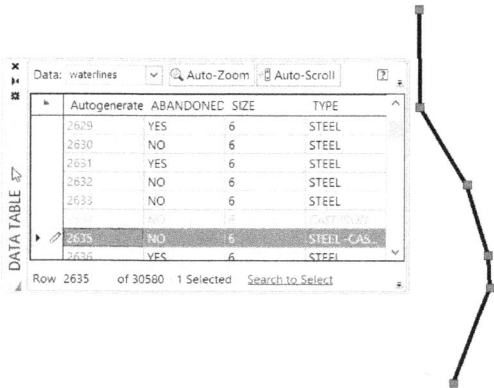

1. Open ...\7-Editing Features\Merging and Splitting Features\ReddingWaterline Merge.dwg.

2. In Display Manager, ensure that the Waterlines layer is available.

   - If it is not available, in Data Connect, click SDF_WATERLINES.
   - For the source file, browse to ...\Data\SDF\Waterlines.sdf.
   - Click Connect.

3. On the View tab, under Views, select Waterline Merge, as shown in the following illustration.

4. In Display Manager:

   - Select Waterlines.
   - Select Table.

5. In the Data Table dialog box, select Options>Set Split and Merge Rules, as shown in the following illustration.

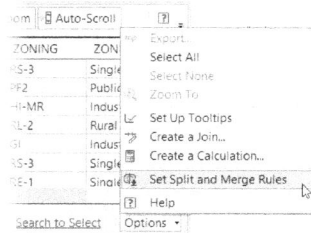

6. In the Split and Merge Rules dialog box:

   - Under Feature Properties, click TYPE.
   - For Merge Rule, select Concatenation.
   - For Separator Text, enter -, as shown in the following illustration.
   - Click OK.

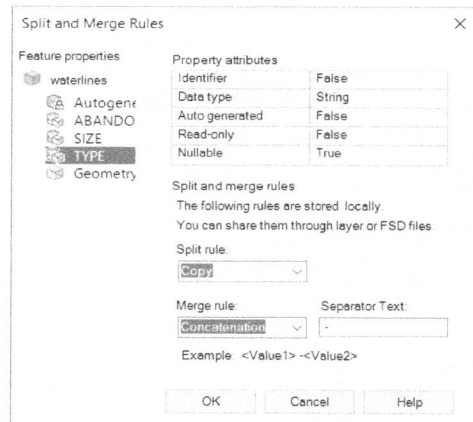

7. Close the Data Table palette.

8. On the Feature Edit tab, under Edit Set, select Check Out, as shown in the following illustration.

9. Select the two waterline segments, as shown in the following illustration.

- Press <Enter>.

10. On the Vector Layer Contextual tab, under Split/Merge, select Merge Feature, as shown in the following illustration.

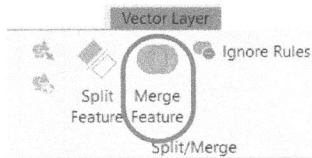

11. For Specify Feature ID for Use, click Select.

- Select the lower waterline segment.
- Press <Enter>.

12. In the Data Table window, note that the TYPE is now concatenated to STEEL - CAST IRON, as shown in the following illustration.

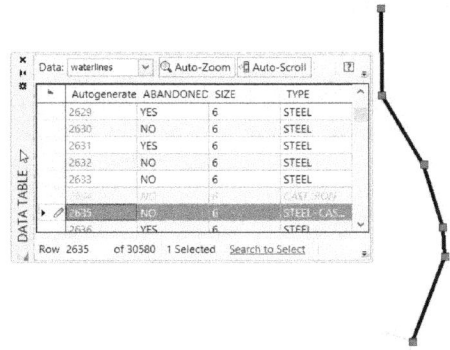

13. On the Data tab, under Edit Set, select Check In Features, as shown in the following illustration.

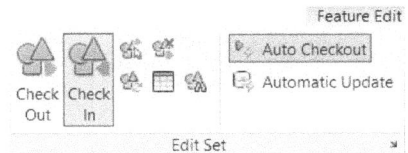

14. Save and close ReddingWaterlineMerge.dwg.

Lesson: Enhanced Data Exchange

Overview

Many organizations need to share their data with other organizations that do not have the AutoCAD Map 3D software but still need to see objects in the same way they are being displayed with the FDO feature stylization engine. In this case, the enhanced Map to DWG command enables you to share your data without losing the cartographic style in the AutoCAD Map 3D file, as shown in the following illustration.

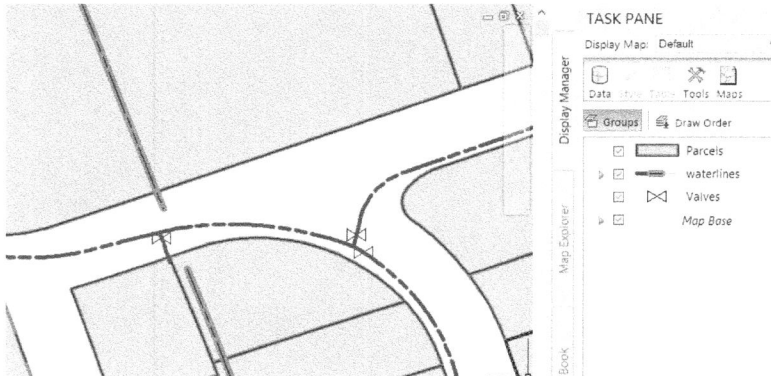

Objectives

After completing this lesson, you will be able to:

- Share FDO data with AutoCAD users that do not have the AutoCAD Map 3D software.
- Turn polygon fills into hatches.
- Turn points into AutoCAD blocks.

About Map to DWG Wizard

In Chapter 5, you learned how to import other file formats into the AutoCAD Map 3D software, such as ESRI Shape files. When using the Import command, the objects in the Shape file were physically converted to AutoCAD entities with the option of creating object data from the database file connected to it. Unfortunately, the objects do not take on a specific look unless they were imported to a layer on which properties had been set up.

Enhanced data exchange provides more functionality for sharing data between the AutoCAD software and other GIS systems. Save Current Map to AutoCAD creates a new drawing file with the FDO objects converted to AutoCAD drawing entities. When using the Map to AutoCAD command, each FDO object becomes its own entity while keeping the style currently being used in the map. Conversion templates can be used to specify which blocks, hatch patterns, and linetypes to use in the new drawing file. The conversion template can also help you automate the layers that are to be used for various objects. Some styling is lost in translation but each FDO object becomes one entity. Therefore, a complex line style becomes multiple polylines as shown in the following illustration.

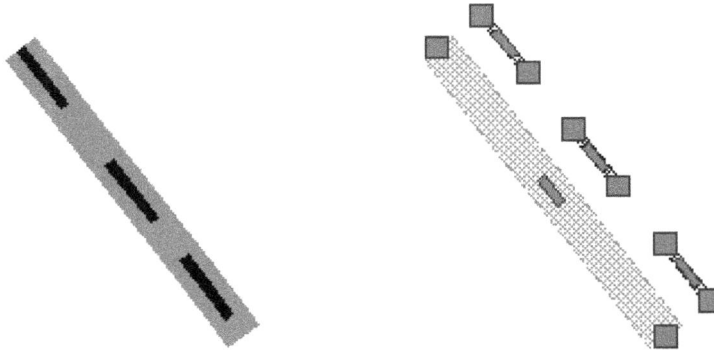

Process: Save Current Map to AutoCAD

1. Open the AutoCAD Map 3D file, which contains multiple FDO layers that have been styled in different ways.

2. On the Output tab, select Save Current Map to AutoCAD, as shown in the following illustration.

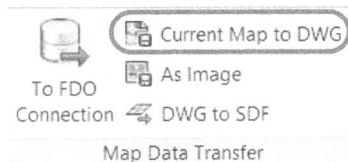

3. Browse for the file location and enter the drawing filename. Click Save.

Exercise: Save Current Map to AutoCAD

In this exercise, you will open a drawing with multiple geospatial features then save it to an AutoCAD drawing format to share with others, as shown in the following illustration.

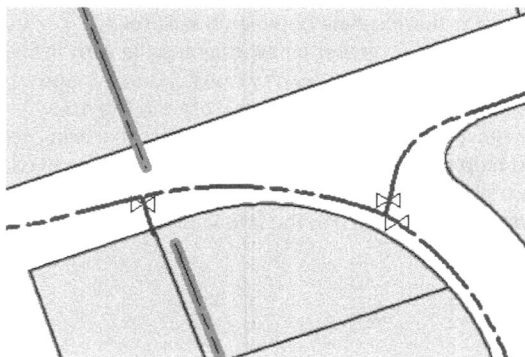

1. Open ...\7-Editing Features\Moving Data Between DWG and FDO Features\Redding-DWG.dwg.

2. On the Output tab, under the Map Data Transfer panel, select Current Map to DWG, as shown in the following illustration.

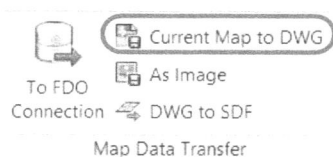

3. Specify the file location by browsing to ...\7-Editing Features\Moving Data Between DWG and FDO Features\Redding-EditDrawing.dwg.

   ▪ Click Save.

4. Open the drawing you just created (...\7-Editing Features\Moving Data Between DWG and FDO Features\Redding-EditDrawing.dwg).

5. Select a line to see that it is one entity and then select a hatch pattern. Press <Esc>.

6. Save and close the drawing.

Chapter Summary

Having completed this chapter, you can:

- Edit feature attributes and geometry.
- Move data between DWG objects and FDO features.
- Use geospatial Split and Merge tools, along with associated settings, to split a polygon and merge a polyline along with associated attributes.
- Use the Map to AutoCAD wizard to convert FDO objects to drawing objects for editing purposes.

Raster Images

The AutoCAD® Map 3D software has extensive image-handling capabilities that increase productivity in a wide variety of applications. This chapter introduces the main features of these capabilities.

Objectives

After completing this chapter, you will be able to:

- Insert raster images.
- Connect to a raster feature source.
- Modify raster image properties and behavior.
- Attach and stylize a DEM.
- Create contour lines from a DEM.

Lesson: Inserting Raster Images

Overview

This lesson covers the use of raster images in the AutoCAD Map 3D environment. The AutoCAD® software has supported the use of raster images for some time now, but the AutoCAD Map 3D software enhances this capability by including the ability to read georeferencing data. This locates the raster image in its correct place on the earth, thereby correlating it to all other georeferenced data in a map. The correlation information is stored in correlation files, most of which are separate from the image files themselves.

The following illustration shows a raster image of an aerial photo correlated to a contour map of the same location.

Objectives

After completing this lesson, you will be able to:

- Describe what raster data is compared to vector data.
- Insert a raster image.

About Raster Data

The term raster data refers to data files that most commonly represent images, such as photographs or other graphics. These can be aerial photographs, pictures from a digital camera, or files produced by a wide range of digital graphics applications. A scanned hard copy document can produce a raster image that resembles a line drawing or even a text document.

Raster files store information about individual components known as pixels or bits, in a regular array of data. For this reason, raster files are sometimes called bitmaps. The raster file specifies the location and color of each component. The number of components involved is based on a quality known as resolution or density. A 100 x 100 square of raster data contains 10,000 individual components.

Raster files come in a wide variety of formats, each with its own specifications and file extension. Some common raster image formats are .bmp, .jpg, .gif, .tif, .tga, and .png. These are all supported by the AutoCAD Map 3D software.

To insert an ECW or SID file, you must first download the free Raster Object Enabler from the Autodesk website.

Raster Data Types

The amount of information per component is referred to as depth. The following list describes some of the raster data types and their respective attributes:

- In a simple binary file, each pixel is either black or white. This is a common way to represent a line drawing. Binary images are the simplest type of raster files and are the smallest file size.
- When each pixel represents a shade of gray, the image is referred to as grayscale and resembles a black-and-white photograph. It stores more information per pixel than a binary file and has a larger file size.
- Next, in terms of depth or complexity (and file size), is a color image. The color depths available are known as 8 bit, 16 bit, and 32 bit. Each increased level of color depth provides a more realistic image. The higher the resolution and color depth, the more realistic the image is, but the file size grows geometrically in the process.

The key difference between a raster and vector file of a line is that in the vector file the line can be accessed and edited as an individual entity, while in a raster file the line is actually a collection of all of the pixels that represent it.

Raster Data Management

The AutoCAD Map 3D software uses the Image Manager to provide information to the user about the raster images that are associated with a particular drawing. Raster files do not become part of a drawing created in the AutoCAD Map 3D software, but rather are attached to the drawing, similar to an external reference created in the AutoCAD software. The drawing stores the location and size of the raster file, but not the raster data itself.

The following illustration shows how a raster image is listed in the Image Management dialog box.

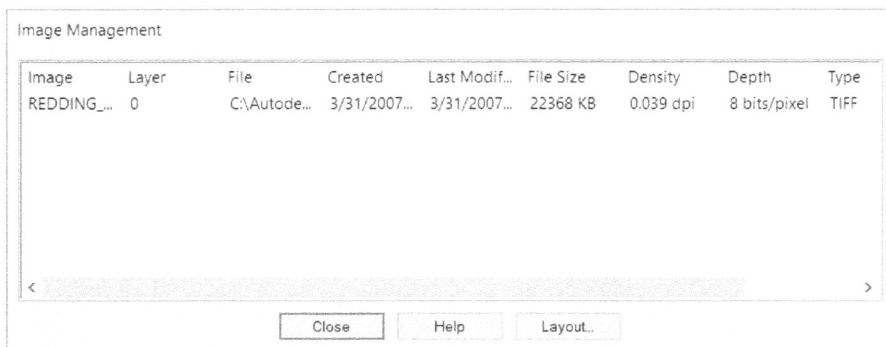

Image	Layer	File	Created	Last Modif...	File Size	Density	Depth	Type
REDDING_...	0	C:\Autode...	3/31/2007...	3/31/2007...	22368 KB	0.039 dpi	8 bits/pixel	TIFF

Image Management

Close   Help   Layout...

Key Points

- Raster files are also referred to as pixel-based, or bitmap, images.
- The number of pixels per square inch is called resolution.
- The amount of information stored in each pixel is known as depth.

Some Common Examples

The most commonly used raster images in the mapping world are aerial photographs. These are typically ortho-rectified to remove distortion, and georeferenced so they can be placed in maps at the correct locations. Other raster images might include scanned documents, such as old deeds or property plans. Digital photos or other graphics can also be incorporated into sets of plans.

Exercise: Inserting Raster Images

In this exercise, you will insert a digital raster graphic (DRG) image of Redding, California, into an existing drawing, as shown in the following illustration.

1. Open ...\8-Raster Images\CITY.dwg.

2. On the Insert tab, Image panel, click Image, as shown in the following illustration.

3. In the Insert Image dialog box:

   - For Files of Type, select Tagged Image File Format (*.tif, *.tiff).
   - Browse to ...\ Data\Images. REDDING_DRG.tif.
   - Click Information. A preview of the image is shown, as are the image type, size, depth, and other data.
   - Note that the Modify Correlation box is checked, as shown in the following illustration.
   - Click Open.

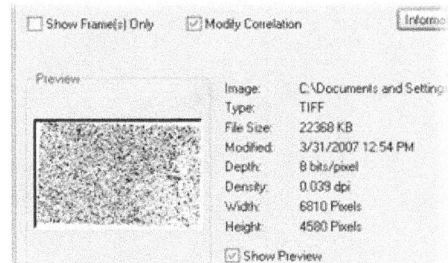

4. In the Image Correlation dialog box:

   - Note that on the Source tab, the Correlation Source is a World file. This is the REDDING_DRG.tfw file that stores the correlation data for this image.
   - Note that under Insertion Values, the Insertion Point X and Y coordinates have been adjusted by the World file, as shown in the following illustration.
   - Click OK.

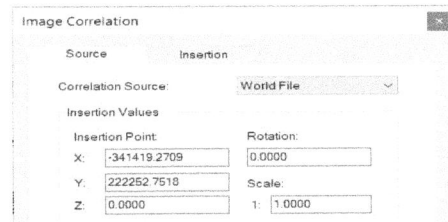

The image is placed in the correct location in the drawing.

5. Save and close the drawing.

Lesson: Modifying Inserted Raster Image Properties and Behavior

Overview

Raster files are referenced by a drawing, but are not part of a drawing file. You can make changes in the display of a raster image in the AutoCAD Map 3D software without changing the raster file itself. You might want to clip the display of the image, leaving part of it visible, or adjust the brightness, contrast, or fade values to enhance the overall readability of the map.

The following illustration shows a drawing with a raster image that has been clipped to only display a specific area:

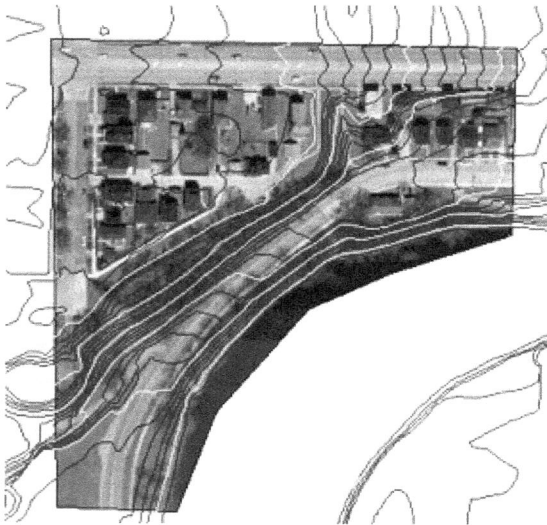

Objectives

After completing this lesson, you will be able to:

- Describe common image manipulation requirements.
- Change image properties.

About Inserted Image Properties

You can make some property changes to the display of raster images in the AutoCAD Map 3D software. These changes are stored in the drawing. However, the actual raster image file is not edited in this process. Display changes that can be performed include draw order and clipping. You can also adjust the brightness, contrast, and fade values of an image.

The following illustration shows the Image Adjust dialog box.

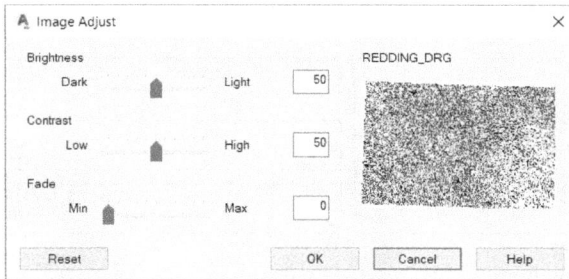

Tips for Modifying Raster Images

Some tips for modifying raster images include:

- To make adjustments to an image, select it and use the shortcut menu.
- To select an image, you must toggle on its frame. To do this, click View menu>Imaging Tools>Toggle Frames.
- To activate the clipping feature that has been applied to an image, use the ON and OFF options in the Image Clipping command. To delete an image clipping, use the Delete option in the Clip command.

Example

If an aerial photograph covers a large part of a town map and you only want to display the part where a new construction project is proposed, you can clip the image to only include that area. If an image overpowers the linework in a drawing, you can adjust the brightness or fade values to suit.

Exercise: Change Inserted Image Properties

In this exercise, you will change some of the properties of an image that has already been inserted into a drawing. The following illustration shows an image with its brightness value lowered.

1. Open ...\8-Raster Images\CITY-Modify.dwg. Note that the image displayed in the drawing obscures the linework that occupies the same area.

2. In the Modelspace:
   - Select the image frame.
   - Right-click on Draw Order>Send to Back, as shown in the following illustration.

   The linework is now visible on top of the image.

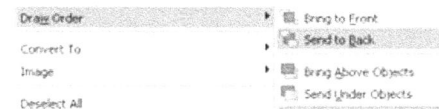

3. In the Modelspace:
   - Select the image frame.
   - In the contextual Image tab, move the sliders for Brightness, Contrast, and Fade, as shown in the following illustration.

4. In the Modelspace:
   - Select the image frame.
   - Right-click on Image, select Image> Adjust.

5. In the Image Adjust dialog box:
   - Click Reset. Brightness, Contrast, and Fade are set back to their original values of 50, 50, and 0, as shown in the following illustration.
   - Click OK.

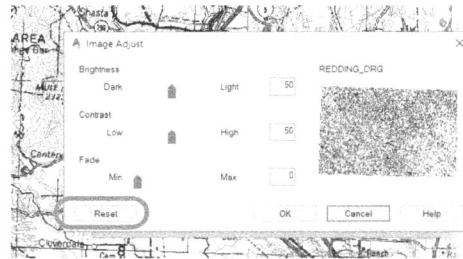

6. In the Modelspace:
   - Select the image frame.
   - In the contextual Image ribbon, on the Clipping panel, click Create Clipping Boundary.

7. At the command line:
   - Press <Enter> to accept the default for a rectangular boundary.
   - Click points in opposite corners on the screen to create the rectangle for the clipped image.

   The clipped image displays, as shown in the following illustration.

8. Save and close the drawing.

Lesson: Connecting to Raster Images

Overview

This lesson covers connecting to raster images in the AutoCAD Map 3D environment. Similar to inserting raster images, connecting to an image enables you to read the georeferencing data that locates the raster image in its correct place on the earth. Raster feature sources can be images, such as aerial photographs or digital elevation models (DEMs). Connecting to the raster feature source rather than inserting a raster image is advantageous because it greatly increases performance. When zooming and panning in the drawing, only the part of the image in the current view regenerates if it is connected as a feature source, which saves time. Another advantage is that the Raster enabler is not required for connecting to ECW and SID files.

The process of connecting to a raster image is similar to the process of connecting to other FDO data. The key difference is that as images are connected to the drawing, multiple images can be combined into one layer creating one seamless background image, as shown in the following illustration.

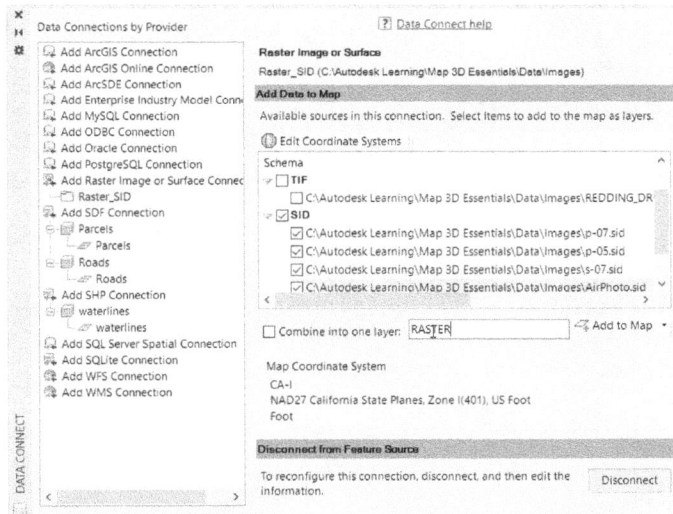

Objectives

After completing this lesson, you will be able to:

- Connect to a raster image.

Key Points

- Raster files can also be connected to using FDO Raster Feature Sources.
- ECW and SID Files can be added to the map without the Raster Enabler using the FDO Raster Feature Sources.

Exercise: Connect to a Raster Feature Source

In this exercise, you will create a new layer in Display Manager using four MR SID files as a feature source for a single layer. You will also change the display order of the raster layer, as shown in the following illustration.

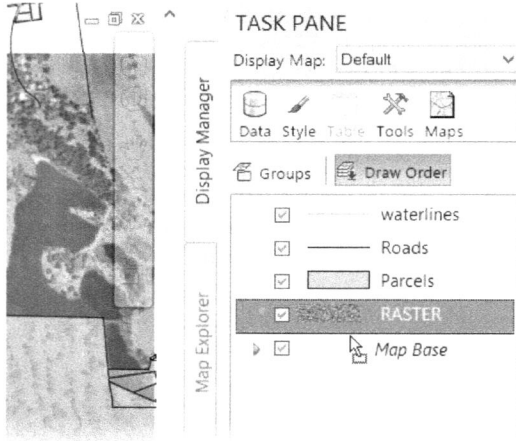

1. Open ...\8-Raster\Images\ Redding-connect.dwg.

2. Verify that Display Manager is selected in the Task Pane.

3. Click Data>Connect to Data, as shown in the following illustration.

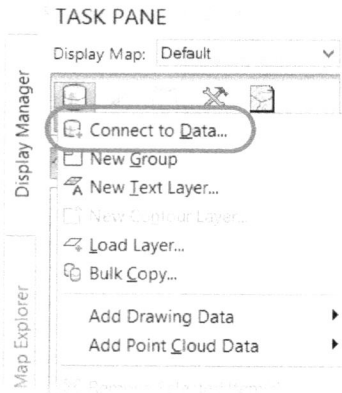

4. In the Data Connect window:
   - Click Add Raster Image or Surface Connection.
   - For Connection Name, enter **Raster_SID**.
   - For Source Folder, click the Folder icon, as shown in the following illustration, and browse to ...\Data\Images.
   - Click Connect.

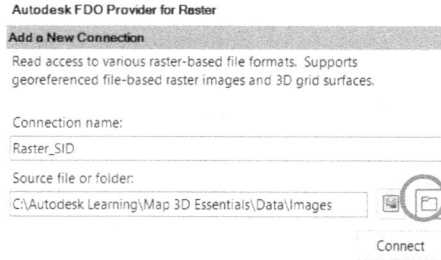

5. In the Add Data to Map area:
   - Check the p-05.sid, p-07.sid, s-05.sid, and s-07.sid files.
   - Do not check the **DEM** or **TIF** categories.
   - Check Combine Into One Layer.
   - For the Layer name, enter **RASTER**, as shown in the following illustration.
   - Click Add to Map.

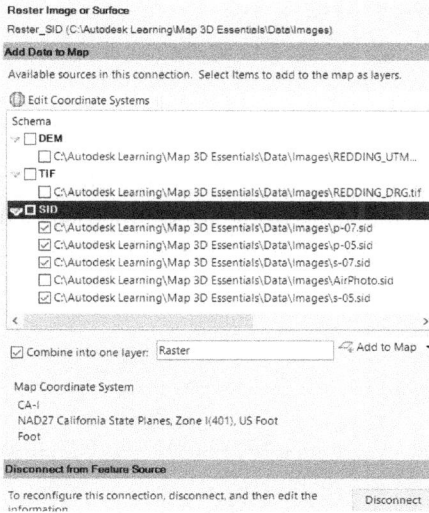

Raster Image or Surface

Raster_SID (C:\Autodesk Learning\Map 3D Essentials\Data\Images)

Add Data to Map

Available sources in this connection. Select items to add to the map as layers.

🔲 Edit Coordinate Systems

Schema

- ▾ ☐ DEM
  - ☐ C:\Autodesk Learning\Map 3D Essentials\Data\Images\REDDING_UTM...
- ▾ ☐ TIF
  - ☐ C:\Autodesk Learning\Map 3D Essentials\Data\Images\REDDING_DRG.tif
- ▾ ☐ SID
  - ☑ C:\Autodesk Learning\Map 3D Essentials\Data\Images\p-07.sid
  - ☑ C:\Autodesk Learning\Map 3D Essentials\Data\Images\p-05.sid
  - ☑ C:\Autodesk Learning\Map 3D Essentials\Data\Images\s-07.sid
  - ☐ C:\Autodesk Learning\Map 3D Essentials\Data\Images\AirPhoto.sid
  - ☑ C:\Autodesk Learning\Map 3D Essentials\Data\Images\s-05.sid

☑ Combine into one layer: Raster   🔷 Add to Map ▾

Map Coordinate System

CA-I
NAD27 California State Planes, Zone I(401), US Foot
Foot

Disconnect from Feature Source

To reconfigure this connection, disconnect, and then edit the information   Disconnect

6. Close the Data Connect window, as shown in the following illustration.

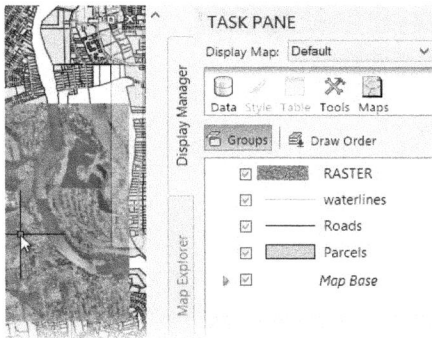

7. Select the Image layer, click Draw Order, as shown in the following illustration.

8. Drag the Raster layer below the Parcels layer, as shown in the following illustration.

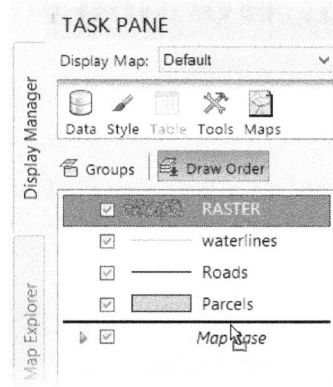

9. Save and close the drawing.

Lesson: Working with DEM Files

Overview

In this lesson, you learn what a DEM file is and when to use a DEM in your map. DEM files have a high visual impact on any map and are a useful visualization tool, as shown in the following illustration.

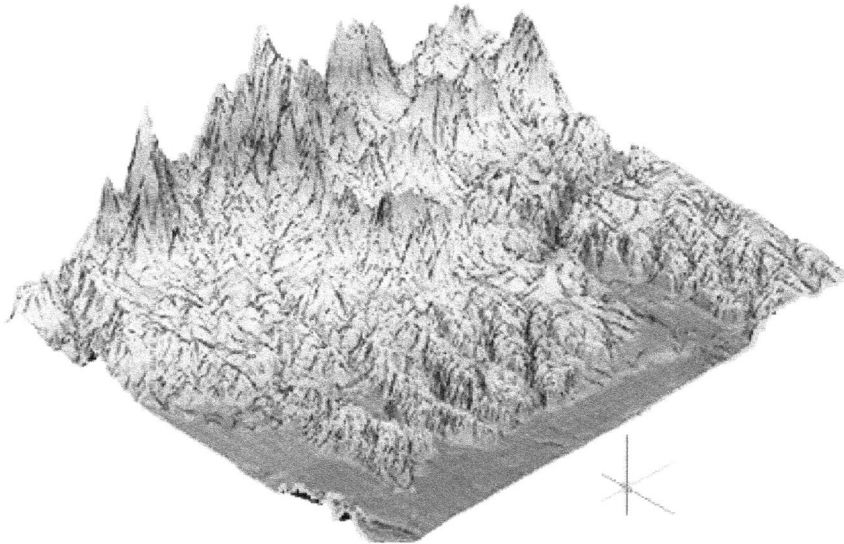

Objectives

After completing this lesson, you will be able to:

- Describe a DEM.
- Explain when to use DEM data.
- Explain how to create contour lines.
- Attach and stylize a DEM.
- Create contour lines from a DEM.

About DEM

Digital elevation model (DEM) files are commonly used for 3D visualization of the Earth's surfaces, as shown in the following illustration.

Definition of DEM

A DEM file contains elevation data for certain points on the earth, as shown in the following illustration. Some DEMs are raster data with each grid cell having an elevation value. Most DEMs use UTM (Universal Transverse Mercator) coordinates (meters) for the projection, and have specific data associated with them. Elevations are usually in meters.

Depending on the resolution or scale at which the data was collected to create the DEM, the size of the files can vary. For example, each cell in a U.S. Geological Survey (USGS) 7.5-minute DEM is a 30 x 30 meter grid cell. This file would be much larger than that of the 1:250,000 scale of a 90 x 90 meter grid cell.

Some DEM files are created from LIDAR (light detection and ranging), which is similar to radar. A LIDAR system beams light in pulses or continuously to a target (i.e., Earth) that reflects a small portion of the light back to the receivers. If the LIDAR files are converted into a DEM, it might be extremely accurate as LIDAR returns millions, if not billions, of points.

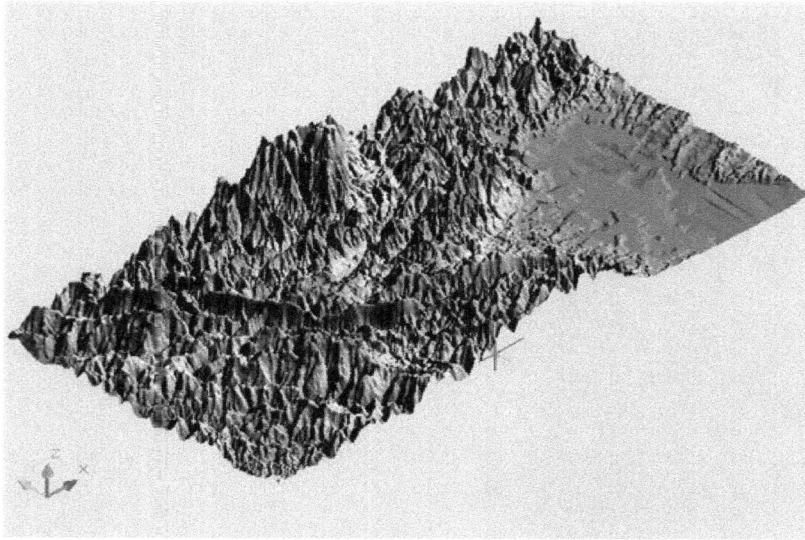

DEM Formats

The AutoCAD Map 3D software supports the following formats natively:

- DEM from USGS
- DTED (Digital Terrain Elevation Data)
- GeoTIFF (with elevations)
- ESRI Grid (GRD and ADF)

> Spatial Data Transfer Standard (SDTS) is used to transfer spatial data with little potential for information loss. DEMs that are in SDTS require some translation before use.

> DEM files can be created, edited, and merged using the AutoCAD Raster Design.

Example of Using a DEM

You can use DEMs for hill shading to render 2D maps with color or grayscale from a specific light source to highlight terrain.

With the Sunproperties command, you can change the position of the sun to create shading for any time and date, and at any latitude. You might even want to put the sun at a strange angle, such as northeast, to more easily see terrain that might not be obvious in a traditional setting.

When to Use DEM Data

Guidelines for Using DEM Feature Sources

You can use DEM data for visualization. There are many options for stylizing DEM files, including basing a DEM theme on its height, aspect, or slope.

Aspect

You can color code a DEM based on aspect (the direction each side of a hill faces). For example, you might choose to color the north-facing hills dark blue and the south-facing hills yellow.

Slope

Stylizing DEMs based on slope (or steepness) creates hill shading to determine the relief of the landscape.

Draping

Two-dimensional feature sources can be draped over a DEM to show the landscape with layers, such as parcels, roads, rivers, or aerial photographs, as shown in the following illustration.

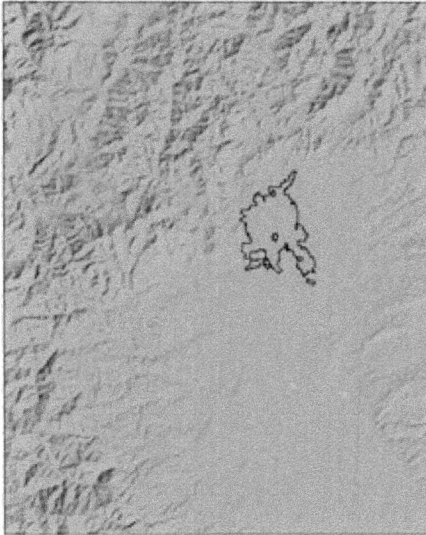

Guidelines for Using DEM Files

Draping

DEM files, by themselves, are visually impressive. However, without other data draped over them, their context might be lost. For example, when roads are draped over a DEM, its location is easily understood. Feature sources in your map are automatically draped over the DEM layer.

Editing

A DEM is considered raster data and is strictly a visual aid to your map. Although slope, aspect, and elevation can be visualized, the data cannot be edited like other vector feature sources, such as SDF.

Scale

The scale of the DEM affects rendering performance. For example, a 7.5-minute DEM with a 30-meter block is appropriate for viewing at the 1:25,000 scale. A smaller-scale DEM, such as the 1-minute DEM, would be appropriate for the 1:250,000 scale. Although you can render large DEMs well, select the correct DEM for the scale you are using.

Coordinates

Although a DEM's coordinate system might be projected to a map's coordinate system, as with other raster files, the best results are achieved when both use the same coordinate system.

> Unlike *.dem*, GRID, and DTED files, GeoTIFF files might not have elevations stored in them. If you use a GeoTIFF as a DEM, ensure that elevations are stored in the file.

DEM Themes

You can base a theme for your DEM on height, slope, or aspect, as shown in the following illustration. You cannot create a theme for a raster feature source that is not a DEM.

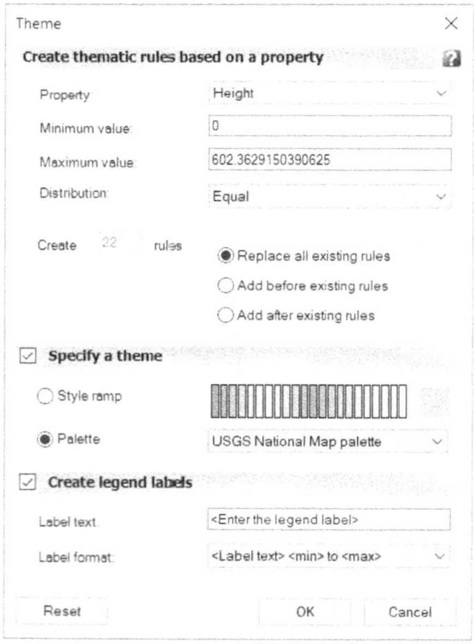

Exaggeration

In using the Exaggeration tool on the elevations of your DEM, be careful or you might misrepresent the actual elevations of the terrain, as shown in the following illustration.

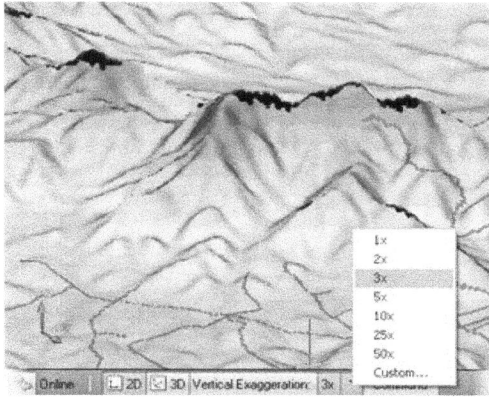

As with all forms of GIS data, be sure you know the source, accuracy, coordinate system, and quality of a DEM before adding it to your map.

An Example of DEM Use

Visualizing a surrounding landscape in three dimensions can be very useful when creating your maps or making land use decisions. A good example of this would be the use of a DEM to visualize obstructions (such as a building) to a view from a particular location, as shown in the following illustration.

How to Create Contours

Contour lines are interpolated lines. Each line connects points of equal elevation on the surface. They are used to visualize, usually in 2D topographic maps, hills, valleys, and landscapes. With contour lines, each line connects points of equal elevation on the surface.

A contour line can also be used to visualize any value. For example, if the DEM file stores point locations of temperatures, slopes, or even criminal activity, the lines can be created to represent these values. The generic term for contour lines that represent any value is isoline.

You add contour lines to surface layers in Display Manager, as shown in the following illustration.

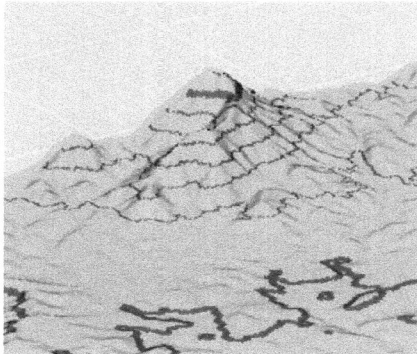

Types of Contours

Contours are created as SDF files from the 3D Raster layer. You can create the following two types of contour SDF files:

- **Contour Lines -** Lines contain elevation values, as shown in the following illustration.

■ **Contour Polygons -** Polygon contains the elevation value, as shown in the following illustration.

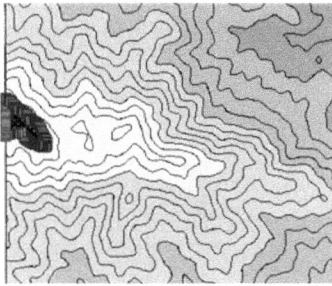

Process: Creating Contours

The contour lines or polygons require a source DEM or 3D Raster file to extract the elevation values. The following procedure demonstrates how to create a contour SDF file.

1. Ensure that the DEM is connected to your drawing and that it displays as a layer in Display Manager, as shown in the following illustration.

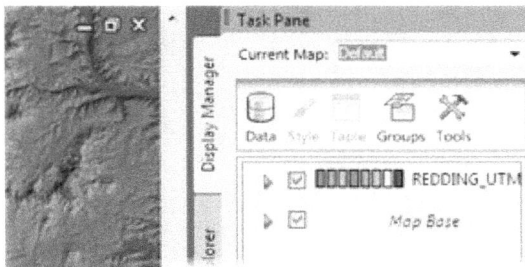

2. Right-click on the 3D Raster layer and click Create Contour Layer, as shown in the following illustration.

3. The SDF file is attached and stylized. You can change the style of the contour lines to suit your requirements. Ensure that the correct interval is selected, such as 10 feet or meters. Select the type of contour you want to create: polygon or polyline, as shown in the following illustration.

4. Name your SDF file something descriptive, such as *10mContours.sdf*, as shown in the following illustration.

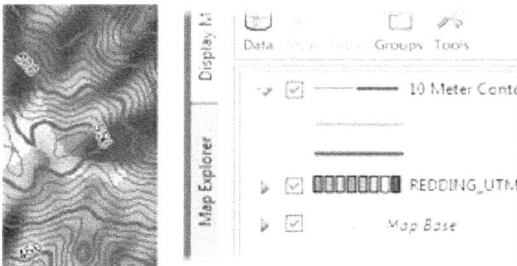

Exercise: Attach and Stylize a DEM

In this exercise, you will attach and stylize a DEM file from the USGS. You will also attach a ROADS SDF file to drape over the DEM Surface, as shown in the following illustration.

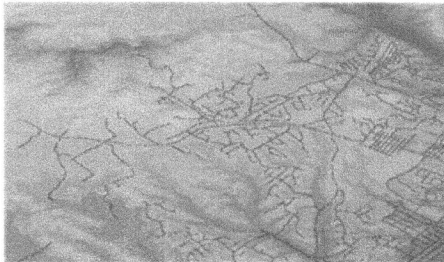

1. In the ...\8-Raster Images folder, open Redding-DEM.dwg.

2. In Display Manager, click Data>Connect to Data, as shown in the following illustration.

3. In the Data Connect window, under Data Connections by Provider, click Add Raster Image or Surface Connection.

4. Under Autodesk FDO Provider for Raster:

   - For Connection Name, enter **Raster_DEM**.
   - For Source file or folder, use the Browse icon to select ...\Data\Images\ REDDING_UTM27-10.DEM.
   - Click Connect.

5. In the Add Data to Map area:

   - Ensure REDDING_UTM27-10.DEM is selected, as shown in the following illustration.
   - Click Add to Map.

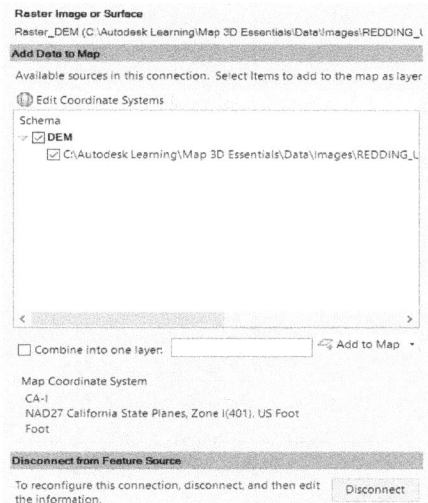

6. Once the DEM displays, close the Data Connect dialog box.

7. Zoom to the extents of your map, as shown in the following illustration.

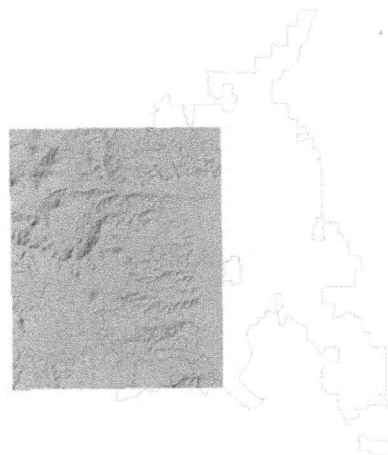

8. In Display Manager, highlight the REDDING_UTM27-10 layer. Click Style.

9. In the Style Editor dialog box, under Raster Style for 0 - Infinity Scale Range, select Theme in the drop-down list, as shown in the following illustration.

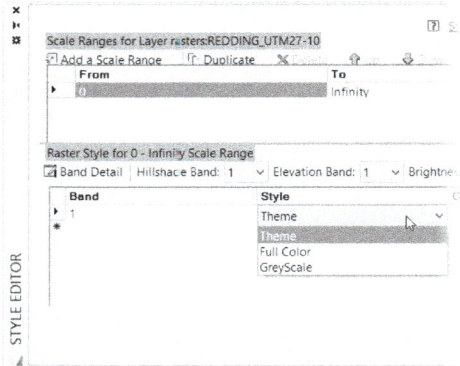

10. In the Theme dialog box:
- Under Specify Theme, click Palette.
- For Palette, select USGS National Map palette, as shown in the following illustration.
- Click OK.

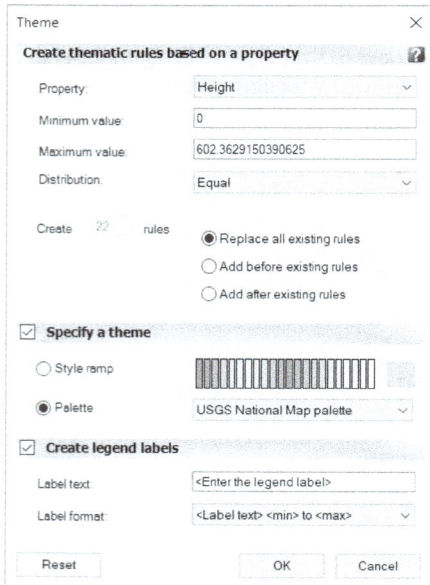

11. In the Style Editor window, click Apply.

12. Close the Style Editor window, as shown in the following illustration.

13. To use 3DOrbit mode, at the command line, enter **3do**.

14. Orbit and zoom in to a similar position as shown in the following illustration.

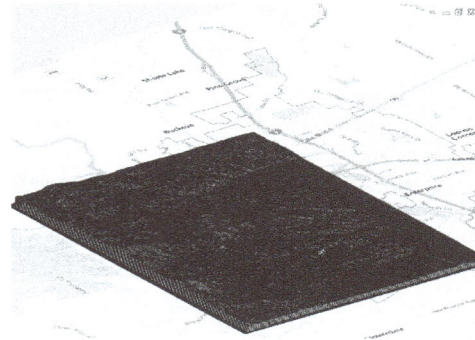

15. While still in 3DOrbit mode, right-click over the Modelspace>Visual Styles>Realistic.

16. To exit 3DOrbit mode, press <Esc>.

17. To toggle off the edges to see the 3D DEM more effectively, at the command line:

- Enter **vsedges**.
- Enter **0**.

The DEM now displays without edges, as shown in the following illustration.

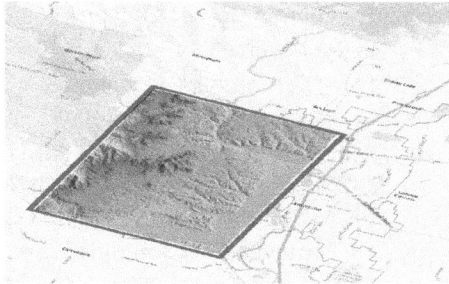

18. In Windows Explorer:

- Browse to the ...*Data\SDF* folder
- Drag and drop Roads.sdf into the Modelspace.

19. Change the color of the Roads to red through the Style Editor, as shown in the following illustration.

20. Zoom into the map to see that the Roads layer is automatically draped over the DEM, as shown in the following illustration.

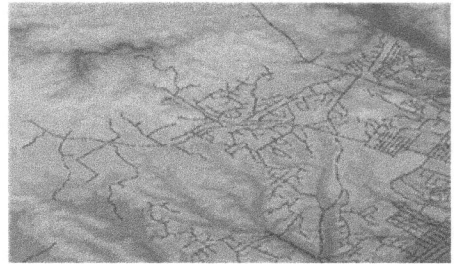

21. Save and close the drawing.

Exercise: Create Contour Lines from a DEM

In this exercise, you will attach a DEM file and create a new Contour Line SDF file based on the elevation data stored in the DEM, as shown in the following illustration.

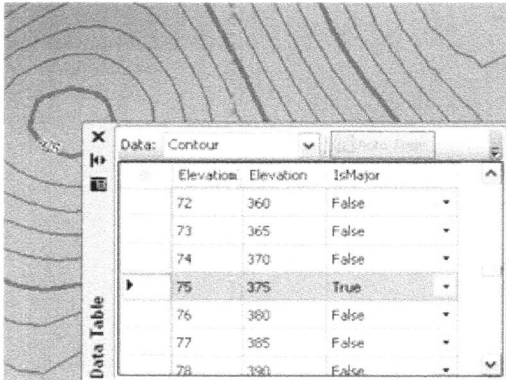

1. In ...\8-Raster Images, open Redding-DEM-contours.dwg.

2. In Display Manager, right-click on the REDDING_UTM27-10>Create Contour Layer, as shown in the following illustration.

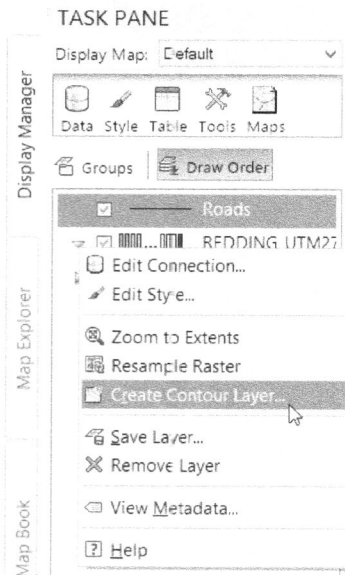

3. In the Generate Contour dialog box, do the following, as shown in the following illustration:

   - For New Contour Layer Name, enter **REDDING 5m Contour**.
   - For Contour Elevation Interval, enter **5**.
   - Select Meters.
   - For Major Contour Every, enter **5**.
   - Check Label the Elevation.
   - For Create Contours as, select Polyline.
   - For Save Contours into Filename, browse to ...\8-Raster Images\.
   - For Filename, enter **5mContour.sdf**.
   - Click Save, then click OK.

4. In Display Manager:

    - Select the REDDING 5m Contour layer.
    - Click Table.

Attributes for 5mContour.sdf contain elevation information and an IsMajor flag for theming major contours, as shown in the preceding illustration.

5. Save and close the drawing.

Chapter Summary

Having completed this chapter, you can:

- Insert raster images.
- Connect to the raster feature source.
- Modify raster image properties and behavior.
- Attach and stylize a DEM.
- Create contour lines from a DEM.

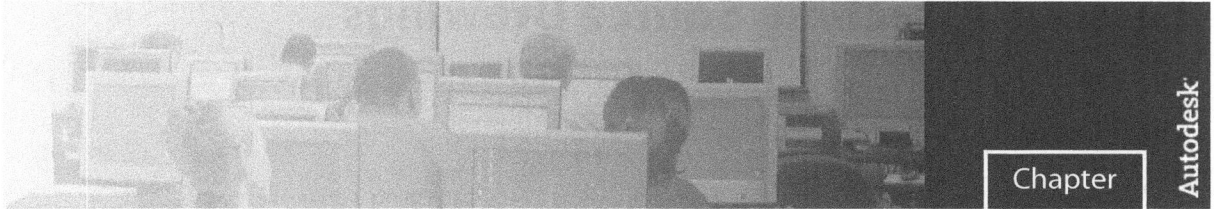

Source Drawings

Most mapping systems, even those that cover small geographic areas, can consist of overwhelming amounts of data. This data can be in the form of drawings, databases, images, spreadsheets, etc.

With the AutoCAD® Map 3D software, you can attach multiple drawing files without opening them and loading them into memory. The AutoCAD Map 3D software accesses attached source drawings at the object level, and only for specific purposes defined by the user. A user of the AutoCAD Map 3D software can attach drawings and work with subsets of objects in those drawings to edit, analyze, report, convert coordinate systems, and create new drawings from existing data. The AutoCAD Map 3D software combines large numbers of source drawings into a single, cohesive mapping system.

Objectives

After completing this chapter, you will be able to:

- Attach multiple source drawings to a current drawing.
- Work in a single environment with drawings that use different coordinate systems.

Lesson: Attaching Source Drawings

Overview

In this lesson, you learn how to attach source drawings after establishing a drive alias to create a multiple-drawing environment, as shown in the following illustration. Once the source drawings are attached, several functions and tools become available, including views, queries, coordinate conversions, and reports.

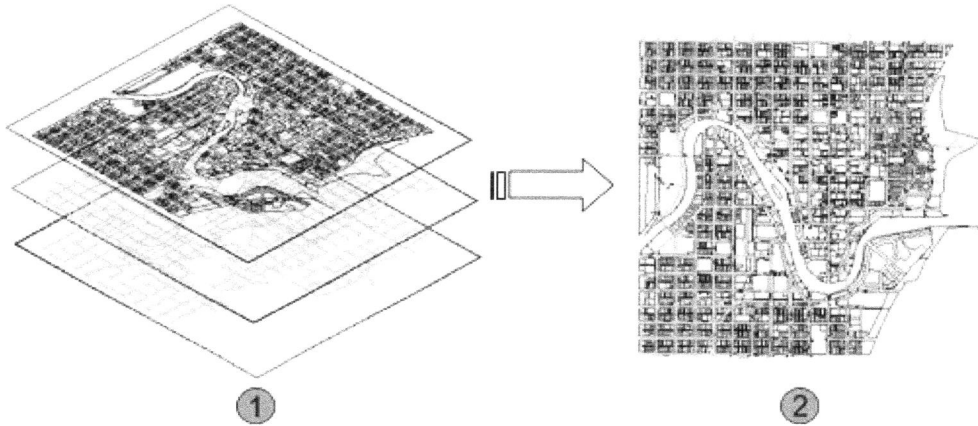

▦ Source drawings

▦ Current drawing

Objectives

After completing this lesson, you will be able to:

- Describe how source drawings are accessed at the object level.
- Explain how source drawings should be organized.
- Explain how a drive alias is used in the multiple-file environment.
- List the definitions saved in a current drawing.
- Describe Quick View.
- Create a drive alias.
- Attach source drawings to a current drawing.

Accessing Drawings at the Object Level

Mapping systems usually consist of large amounts of data and geometry. Source drawings are drawing files that are attached to a current drawing but are not loaded into memory until a request is made through queries. Being able to access this data from multiple drawings simultaneously at the object level improves performance while making all of the data available in a single environment.

The following illustration shows how a multiple-drawing environment enables you to work with a set of objects from multiple drawings.

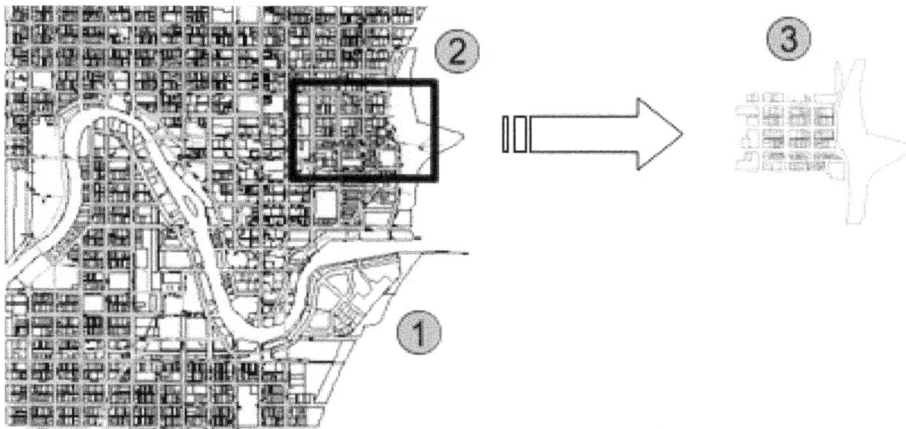

1. Parcels, sewer, and storm drain system source drawings.

2. The area of interest you want to work with.

3. The result of a query to retrieve only the lot boundaries within the area of interest.

Source Drawing Behavior

When you open a drawing file that was created in the AutoCAD Map 3D software, the entire drawing is read into memory. Attaching drawings as sources in a current drawing that was created in the AutoCAD Map 3D software is a fundamentally different approach to drawing objects. When a drawing is attached, instead of opening the drawing and loading its data into memory, the objects become available in the current drawing.

When multiple drawings are attached, each object in those drawings responds to queries, views, and editing as a single mapping system. This mapping environment can incorporate drawings from multiple departments, industries, disciplines, or individuals.

The following illustration shows multiple drawing files attached as source drawings to a current drawing.

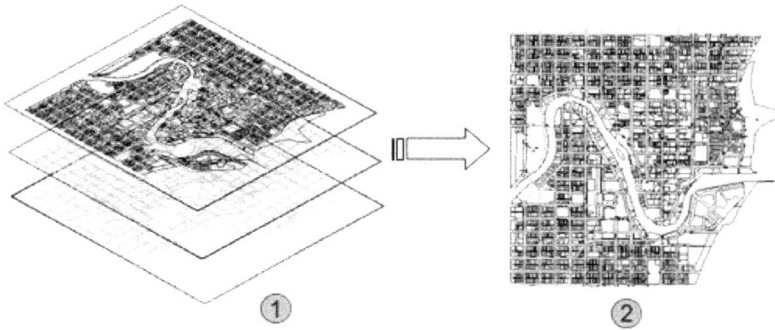

▣ Parcel, sewer, and storm drain source drawings.

▣ The current drawing to which all three source drawings are attached.

How Objects Are Accessed

To create a mapping system, attach source drawings to your current drawing. You can then access the objects in these source drawings in the following ways:

- **Queries -** Tools that retrieve objects from source drawings into the current drawing. By combining query types with Boolean functions, you can compose a very sophisticated query to retrieve a wide range or very specific set of objects. For example, display all the drainage pipes over 500mm in diameter within a range of 400 meters from property parcel #PP-4509 that have not been inspected since 1959.
- **Quick View -** Any attached source drawings can be selected to be included in a Quick View. Quick View creates a temporary display of all of the objects in the drawings.
- **Save-Back -** You can edit queried objects and place them in a save set, where they are locked to prevent other users from editing them until they are saved back to the source drawings. This functionality enables multiple users to access different objects in the same drawings with editing rights and manages locking at the object level.

Source Drawings Are Like Database Tables

You use databases to manage, categorize, and filter data to meet specific requirements. You can consider drawing files as database tables. Each object in the drawing is like a record in a table with a specific value, such as layer, color, start and end points, object type, etc. Source drawings make up the database environment by acting like tables with records, and the AutoCAD Map 3D software provides DBMS-like tools to categorize and filter the data.

How Source Drawings Are Used

You can access several drawings simultaneously. The current drawing defines the set of source drawings, eliminating the need to attach each drawing every time you open the current drawing. All objects in each source drawing are available to the current drawing.

A current drawing can access multiple source drawings, as shown in the following illustration.

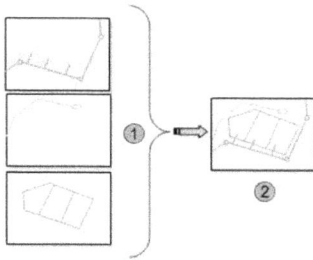

| 1 | Source drawings |
| 2 | Current drawing |

Multiple users can access the same set of drawings simultaneously, as shown in the following illustration.

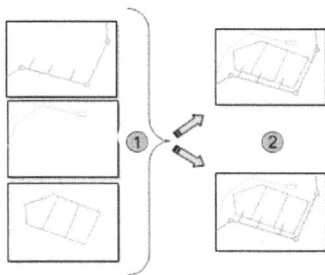

| 1 | Source drawings |
| 2 | Current drawing |

Multiple users can edit the same drawing simultaneously using object locking to edit different objects in the drawing, as shown in the following illustration.

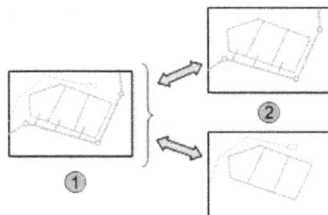

| 1 | Source drawings |
| 2 | Current drawing |

Source Drawing Organization

When you begin to work with source drawings, it is important to recognize the difference between a single-drawing environment and a multiple-drawing environment. Attaching source drawings creates a multiple-drawing file environment, in which each drawing is an important working component of the total set of drawings.

Tiled and Coincident Source Drawings

If you are working with an existing set of drawings, it is likely these drawings are organized as either tiled or coincident, as shown in the following illustration. Tiled drawings generally contain all of the data and geometry for a specific area. Coincident drawings contain a specific type of data and geometry for all areas.

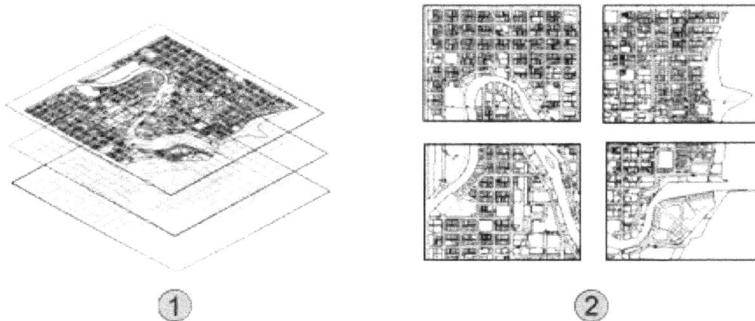

1 Coincident drawings

2 Tiled drawings

Tiled drawings act like pages in a Map Book. Coincident drawings act like drawing layers. Even if they have multiple layers in them, coincident drawings are organized to document a specific type of information.

Multiple Coordinate Systems

When you work with multiple source drawings that do not use the same coordinate system, you need to be able to convert them to the system used in the current drawing. Sometimes a coordinate system has not been used and the mistake is not recognized because the drawings are never combined in a single environment. By using the tools in the AutoCAD Map 3D software, you can combine different coordinate systems into a single, cohesive system.

In the following illustration, a single point is represented by two different coordinate systems. Both are legitimate descriptions of the same location. If two source drawings use different coordinate systems, you cannot geographically integrate them in a single environment without using a method to convert them.

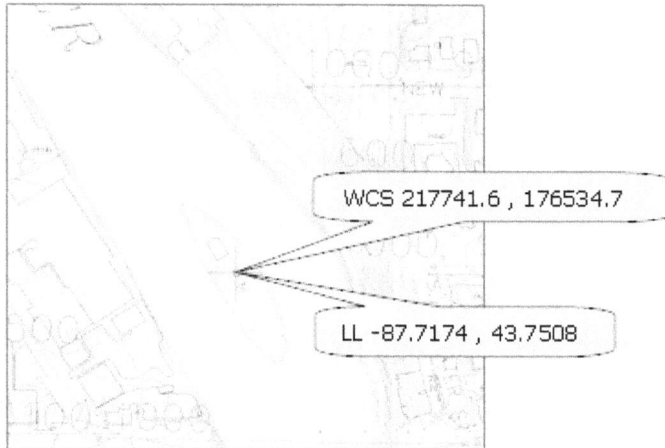

Layer and Block Definition Standards

When you organize source drawings into a single environment for the first time, it is not uncommon to uncover deviations from layering and block definition standards. If sewer lines in one drawing are on a layer named Lines and in another drawing on a layer named Sewer Lines, this might not cause a problem as individual drawings. However, when you try to access these objects from your current drawing, you have to create multiple query definitions to access all of the objects you are interested in, and you might not be sure you are in fact, accessing all the objects you require.

The need to adhere to standards across all source drawings becomes more pronounced when you combine them into a single environment.

Examples of Source Drawing Organization

Tiled drawings are a legacy organization style to answer the need for smaller drawing-file sizes, as shown in the following illustration. One of the problems with tiled drawings is that they force objects to break at boundaries. This organization makes it difficult to create system wide topology models and attach data to objects that cross these boundaries. If your drawings are organized as tiles for Map Book plotting, you can use the Book Plot tool in the AutoCAD Map 3D software to produce Map Books regardless of file organization.

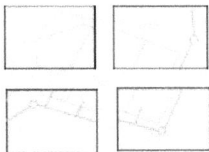

Using coincident drawings is a better method of organization, as shown in the following illustration. Similar to layers, coincident drawings enable access to continuous objects regardless of Map Book boundaries. If the geographic area and file size are too large to open these drawings directly, you can attach them as source drawings and easily access all of the objects and data they contain.

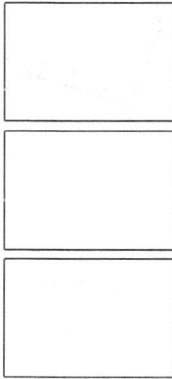

About the Drive Alias and Source Drawings

The AutoCAD Map 3D current drawing acts as the management tool for attached source drawings. When you are setting up a current/source drawing relationship, it is important to understand how current drawings, source drawings, and the drive alias work together to create the multiple-drawing environment.

In this case, four source drawings are attached to a current drawing, as shown in the following illustration. The current drawing uses the alias as a definition for the location of the four source drawings.

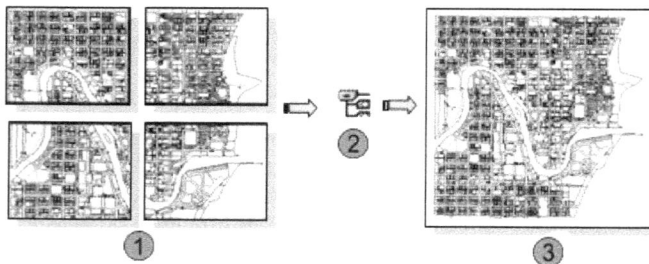

1. Source drawings

2. Drive alias

3. Current drawing

The Drive Alias Defined

The drive alias is a user-defined name that points to a directory. The directory can be on the local machine or a network drive. All source drawings are attached through an alias, as shown in the following illustration. An alias is not saved in the drawing, but instead as a system setting in the AutoCAD Map 3D software.

The following illustration shows how a drive alias points to a specific directory. All drawings in this directory are available to be attached to the current drawing through this alias.

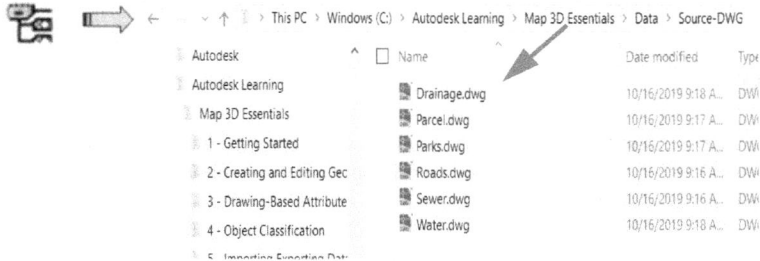

The default alias of the AutoCAD Map 3D software is C = C:. In this case, C is the alias, and the directory it references is the root directory on the C:\ drive.

Examples of How an Alias is Used

If a current drawing has been set up with a large number of source drawings and you need to move it to another computer, instead of reattaching all of the drawings, copy the current drawing to the new computer and only update the alias.

An alias is also typically used when network drives are defined differently. For example, one computer might point to a network drive as drive F:, and another computer might point to the same drive as K:. You can define an alias with the same name for both computers, pointing to the same location, so you can share current drawings that have source drawings attached.

About Settings Saved in the Source Drawing

The persistence of settings is an important aspect of the AutoCAD Map 3D current/source drawing relationship. Once you have set up a current drawing and attached source drawings, you can save the current drawing and reopen it with all of the definitions still present.

Definition of Settings Saved in the Source Drawing

Drawing Set

The attachment to source drawings and their settings is saved in the current drawing file. When the drawing is reopened, depending on the option settings, the AutoCAD Map 3D software maintains the link to the source drawings and reactivates them.

Drive Alias

A drive alias is saved on the local computer as part of the AutoCAD Map 3D software system. When you move a current drawing from one computer to another, the drive alias is not included as part of the drawing.

> Settings and definitions that are saved in a current drawing include query libraries, display maps, current queries, etc. Because this lesson focuses on source drawings, the information presented does not address all of the definitions in a current drawing.

About Quick View

Attached drawing files are not displayed in the current drawing until a query or Quick View is performed, as shown in the following illustration. Quick View provides a fast and convenient method of viewing and confirming source drawings.

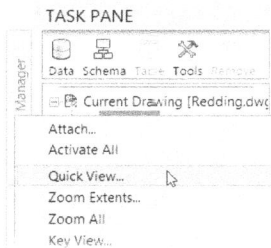

Quick View Defined

Using Quick View, you can view source drawings as a preview object in the current drawing. You can view multiple source drawings at the same time, and each drawing displays in its entirety. When you perform a quick view, the objects in the source drawing are not affected in any way. You can remove the preview object generated for quick view from the screen by entering the Redraw command.

Attributes of Quick Views

- Quick View produces a Preview object in the AutoCAD Map 3D software in the current drawing. Individual objects in the Quick View are not selectable.
- Preview mode does not show objects on layers that are Off or Frozen.
- Quick View can be set to not interpret blocks in the source drawings, but rather to display them as points.

Example of Quick View

Typically, one of the first things you do after attaching source drawings is to perform a Quick View to verify the presence of the source drawings and to confirm they are located correctly.

Lesson: Working with Coordinate Systems

Overview

As with feature data sources, the AutoCAD objects can be re-projected to ensure that all objects in the drawing are being shown in the same location no matter which coordinate system they were originally drawn in. In the following illustration, the lots are in a state plane coordinate system and the contours reside in a latitude-longitude coordinate system. Despite the differing coordinate systems, the AutoCAD Map 3D software enables all objects to assume the same coordinates.

Objectives

After completing this lesson, you will be able to:

- Decide how to use coordinate conversion for specific purposes.
- Convert drawing coordinates.

How Coordinate Conversion Works

Introduction to the Coordinate Conversion Process

The AutoCAD Map 3D software uses the source drawing and current drawing relationship to perform coordinate conversion.

- You can apply a coordinate system to a single current drawing.
- You can apply coordinate systems to source drawings. Before assigning a coordinate system to source drawings, they must be detached or deactivated from an open current drawing. As with assigning coordinate systems to current drawings, the assignment does not change any coordinate values for the objects in the drawing, but rather defines what coordinate system the existing objects represent.
- When a draw query is performed from a source drawing that has a different coordinate system than the current drawing, the objects are transformed into the current drawing coordinate system. This is the only time the actual coordinates of objects are changed. If they are saved back to the source drawing, the transformation is reversed to the original coordinate system.

Process: Converting Coordinates

The following is an overview of how objects are handled by the AutoCAD Map 3D software during a coordinate conversion.

1. A coordinate system is assigned to the current drawing. The parcel drawing coordinates are in a UTM coordinate system. The following illustration shows the coordinates of the parcel edge.

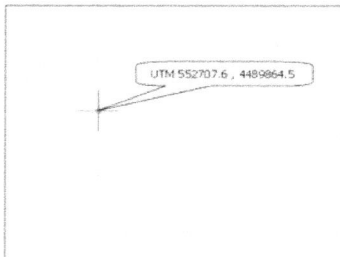

2. A coordinate system is assigned to a source drawing. If the source drawing is currently attached and active in the current drawing, it must be detached or deactivated before assigning the coordinate system. This drawing is of the road and water mains for the same area as the parcel drawing, but has been created using latitude-longitude coordinates. The following illustration shows the latitude-longitude coordinates of the same parcel edge.

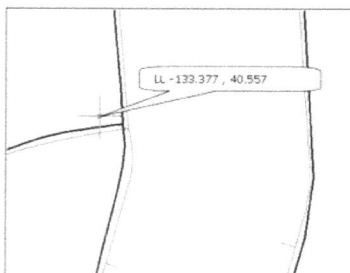

3. The source drawing is attached to the current drawing, and a draw query is performed. The objects in the source drawing adopt the coordinate system of the current drawing, as shown in the following illustration.

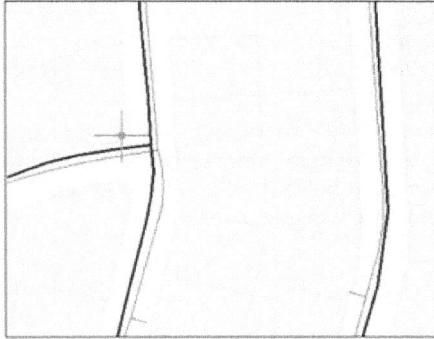

Process: Converting Coordinates Permanently

The steps below list the process to permanently convert coordinates of an existing drawing.

- Start a new drawing. Assign the target coordinate system.
- Assign the existing coordinate system to the drawing you want to convert.
- Attach the drawing to the new, empty current drawing.
- Draw query all objects from the existing drawing into the empty drawing.
- Detach the source drawing (that contains the objects in the old coordinate system).
- Save the current drawing as a new drawing or save it over the old drawing. The coordinates are now permanently converted.

When to Use Coordinate Conversion

Converting objects from one coordinate system to another is only done when you must access drawings that use different coordinate systems. In most cases, the drawings you need to convert have been created by different agencies that must conform to specific coordinate system standards.

There are two main considerations when converting coordinate systems. You can convert the objects permanently, or temporarily convert them and leave them in their original coordinate system when you have finished working on the drawing.

Guidelines for Coordinate Conversion

The following considerations might affect your use of coordinate conversion:

- If your office or agency only works with one coordinate system and does not access any outside data or have any requirement to produce data for access outside your office, you might not need to apply global coordinate systems to any of your drawings. However, this scenario is very uncommon since most mapping systems use several sources of data.

- When you work with drawings that are part of your mapping system but owned by another department and in a different coordinate system, you might be required to access the data and yet maintain its original coordinate system. In this case, assigning the coordinate system to the drawing as a source drawing and converting the objects into the current drawing without permanently changing them is the correct approach.

- If you have been given a drawing that is in a different coordinate system than your mapping system and you do not have to give the drawing back, you should permanently convert the objects into your own system.

- If you work in an office or agency that uses a standard coordinate system, you must still be able to identify the coordinate system in use in a particular map before you can assign it to that coordinate system in the AutoCAD Map 3D software. It is strongly recommended that you not accept a map without a full description of the coordinate system in use.

Exercise: Create a Drive Alias

In this exercise, you will create a drive alias called MAP_3D, as shown in the following illustration, which references the Map 3D directory and all of the lesson directories that it contains. The alias is persistent on your computer and is available for any other lessons using the AutoCAD Map 3D software.

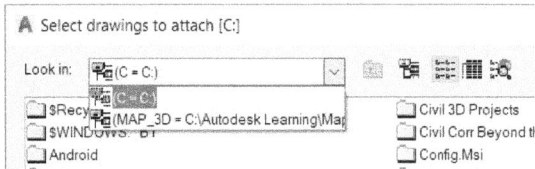

1. Start a new blank drawing.

2. In Map Explorer, click Data>Attach Source Drawings, as shown in the following illustration.

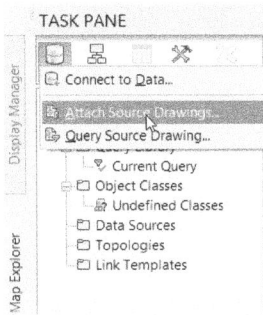

3. In the Select Drawings to Attach dialog box, click Create/Edit Aliases, as shown in the following illustration.

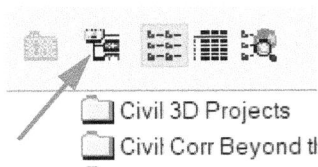

4. In the Drive Alias Administration dialog box:
    - Under Drive Alias Details, for Drive Alias, enter **MAP_3D**.
    - Click Browse.

5. In the Choose Directory dialog box:
    - Navigate to *C:\Autodesk Learning\Map 3D Essentials*.
    - Click OK.

6. In the Drive Alias Administration dialog box:
    - Click Add, as shown in the following illustration.
    - Click Close.

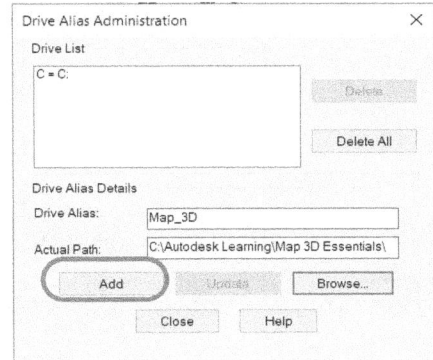

7. Click OK to close the Select Drawing To Attach dialog box.

Exercise: Attach Source Drawings

In this exercise, you will start a new drawing and attach the drainage, sewer, and parcel maps for the city of Redding. You will perform a drawing extents and a Quick View of the three maps, as shown in the following illustration.

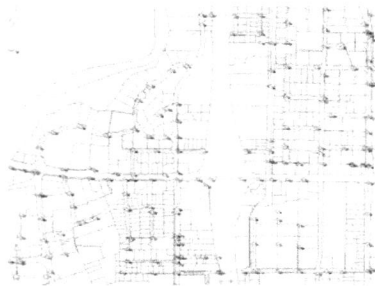

The completed exercise

1. Open ...\9-Source Drawings\Redding.dwg.

2. In Map Explorer, click Data>Attach Source Drawings.

3. In the Select Drawings to Attach dialog box, for Look In, select the MAP_3D alias from the list, as shown in the following illustration.

   Note: If you did not complete the exercise Create a Drive Alias, you need to do so at this time.

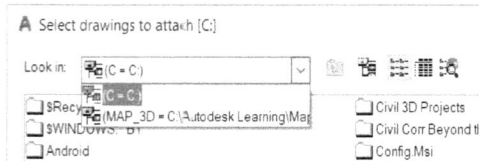

4. In the Select Drawing To Attach dialog box:
   - Navigate to ...\Data\Source-DWG.
   - Press <Ctrl> and select Parcel, Sewer, and Drainage, as shown in the following illustration.
   - Click Add.
   - Click OK.

5. In Map Explorer, right-click on Drawings> Quick View, as shown in the following illustration.

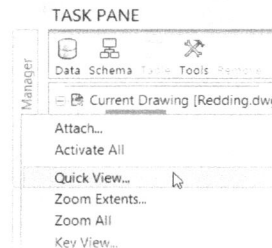

6. In the Quick View Drawings dialog box:
   - Confirm that all three drawings are highlighted.
   - Ensure that Zoom to the Extents of Selected Drawings is checked, as shown in the following illustration.
   - Click OK.

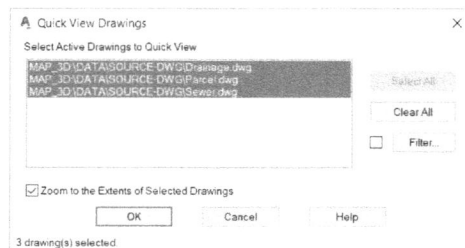

7. Save the drawing. The completed exercise should look similar to that shown in the following illustration.

8. Save and close the drawing.

Chapter Summary

Having completed this chapter, you can:

- Attach multiple source drawings to a current drawing.
- Work in a single environment with drawings that use different coordinate systems.

Source Drawing Queries

This chapter introduces concepts and techniques required for working with queried data. You learn to perform simple queries using conditions and to display the results of a query in different ways. This chapter also presents two advanced query techniques: combined query types and property alteration. You can combine location, property, object data, and SQL conditions to form compound criteria queries. Property alteration can help you create thematic maps for presenting themes from retrieved data in unlimited ways.

Objectives

After completing this chapter, you will be able to:

- Create and execute property and location queries from source drawings.
- Define queries from source drawings based on attached data.
- Define queries from source drawings based on multiple criteria.
- Alter the properties of objects during a query.
- Create and use queries from the Query Library.
- Edit objects from multiple source drawings from a single environment.

Lesson: Define Property and Location Queries

Overview

In this lesson, you learn how to perform simple location and property condition queries and how to display the results of a query in different ways. A query is a tool that you use to retrieve objects from source drawings. You define the query to select specific information from drawings.

The following illustration shows how a location and property query can retrieve a subset of objects.

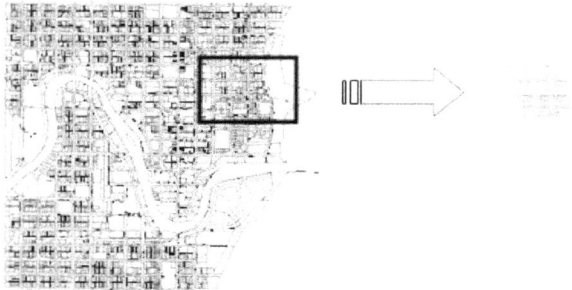

Objectives

After completing this lesson, you will be able to:

- Describe the concepts of property and location queries.
- Describe location condition queries.
- Describe property condition queries.
- Explain the process of executing queries.
- Define and execute a property and location query.

About Queries

Digital maps often contain large amounts of graphical information. Using queries, you can access specific data from multiple source drawings and create maps that are specific to your purpose.

Queries Defined

A query is a request for specific information. You use queries to get drawing objects and linked textual information from source drawings. For example, a query can request information from a drawing for all water pipes within a 200-yard radius of a specific point. The result is a map showing a circular area containing lines that represent all of the pipes in the specified area. Queries can be based on location, object properties, or attribute data. You can define new queries, save the definition, and run saved queries in the future. The ability to query from multiple drawings is an important feature of the AutoCAD® Map 3D software.

A query is like a filter that enables you to only retrieve the data you need from the source drawings.

Key Terms

Term	Definition
Query	A set of criteria that specifies the retrieval of objects or records from source drawings to the current drawing.
Query type	A condition that you specify to retrieve selected objects.
Location condition	Retrieval based on the location of objects in the source drawings.
Property condition	Retrieval based on standard properties, such as color, linetype, layer, etc.

Query Modes

Along with the condition, a query also contains an action, referred to as a mode, which specifies how the retrieved objects are handled. The following three query modes control the display of objects retrieved by a query.

Mode	Definition
Preview Mode	A query executed in Preview mode does not create objects in the current drawing, but shows the objects as a temporary image. The image remains until you redraw your display, so you can use the Realtime PAN and ZOOM commands to view the queried objects.
Draw Mode	When a query is executed in Draw mode, objects retrieved are copied into the current drawing.
Report Mode	Used to produce a list of objects in source drawings. Information, such as the insertion points, start and end points, object data values, and SQL values, can be included in the report.

An Example of the Use of Queries

By performing different types of queries, organizations can use a single set of digital maps for many different purposes.

Suppose a government agency wants to perform road maintenance analysis from a set of objects that reside in regional maps. The agency can query to retrieve the specified roads. Other agencies can use the same regional maps to perform agricultural irrigation studies or to track population data.

The following illustration shows three maps which were created from the same set of source drawings. These maps can be saved as new maps, or used as a temporary way to view data.

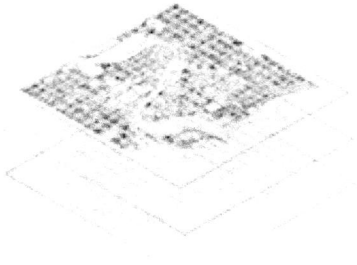

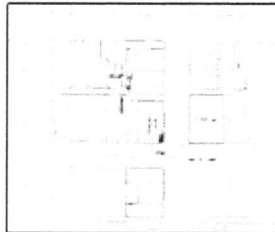

About Location Conditions

You use location queries to retrieve objects from source drawings based on location criteria. You can set location conditions based on boundaries, buffer distances, existing objects, crossing criteria, and many other criteria. All location conditions are based on coordinates, defined by at least one condition.

The following illustration shows the results of a crossing circle location condition. The parcels are part of the current drawing and all other geometry has been queried from attached source drawings.

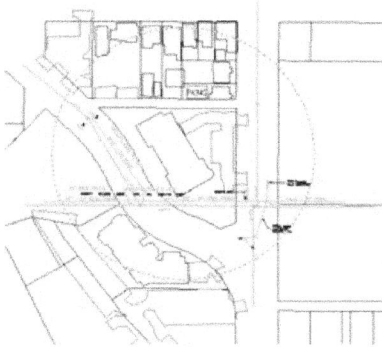

The following table contains a partial list of the location conditions used in a query.

Condition	Definition
Buffer Fence	Retrieves objects within a specific distance of a polyline that you define.
Fence	Retrieves objects that cross a polyline (fence) that you define.
Point	Retrieves all closed polygons that include the selected point.
Polygon Mode	References a polygon that you draw in the current drawing.
Polyline	You select an existing closed polyline in the current drawing as the boundary.

Boundary Types

Two selection types apply to the boundary types for location queries:

- **Inside -** Selects objects that are completely within the selection boundary.
- **Crossing -** Selects objects that are inside or crossing the boundary.

Example of a Location Condition

The following illustration shows a current drawing of lots and street center lines. Attached are source drawings that contain sewer and storm drain information. By using a buffer fence for a street segment, you can retrieve all information about sewers and storm drains around the street in question.

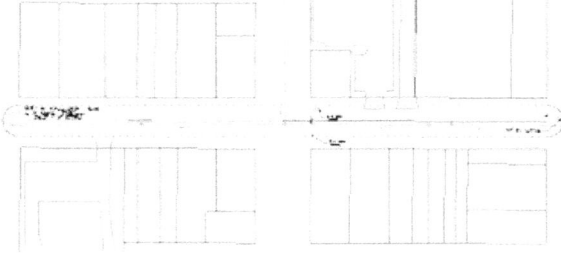

In some cases, objects in source drawings might be linked to database records with geographic coordinates included as part of their definitions. To query based on this information, you perform a SQL query. The location conditions in the AutoCAD Map 3D software only consider the coordinates that are defined by the source drawing.

About Property Conditions

You can use properties as query conditions. All objects in the AutoCAD® software and the AutoCAD Map 3D software have properties associated with them, as shown in the following illustration. These properties include layer, color, etc.

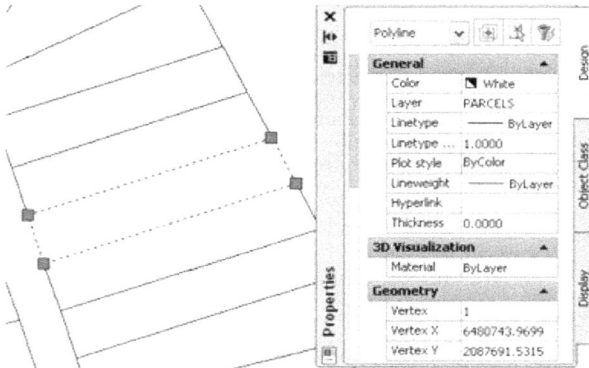

Property Conditions Defined

Property conditions use object properties, such as layer, elevation, and linetype, to retrieve objects from source drawings. For example, you can retrieve closed polylines with a specified area or retrieve text of a given value.

In the Property Condition dialog box, you can select an object property to use to retrieve objects from source drawings, as shown in the following illustration.

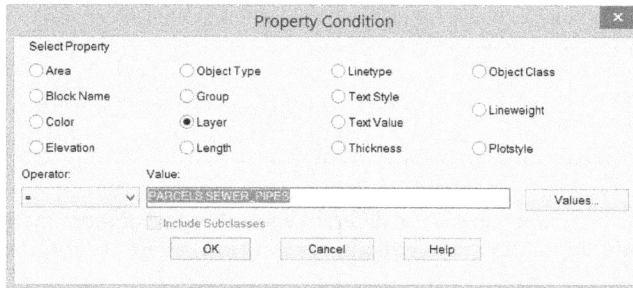

Types of Properties

The following list describes the properties that you use most frequently in a mapping environment. For more information about properties, see the AutoCAD Map 3D Help.

Property	Definition
Layer	Retrieves all objects on a specified layer or list of layers.
Block Name	Retrieves all blocks matching the block name.
Object Type	Retrieves all objects of a specific type, such as all polylines.
Text Value	Retrieves any text strings that match a specific value.

Examples of Property Queries

You can structure a property query to retrieve information like the following:

- Elevation greater than 4,000.
- Polygons with an area less than 150.
- Text value equal to Main Street.
- Layers equal to "SOIL."

> Location coordinates are also considered a property of an object in the AutoCAD software. To base a query on the location of objects, you use a location condition.

About Data Queries

When you asscciate data with drawing objects in the AutoCAD Map 3D software, you can query based on those linked attributes, as shown in the following illustration, to identify sets of objects that correspond to specific criteria. Although several different types of data can be associated with drawing objec:s, the process of performing data queries is similar in all cases.

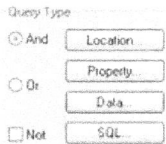

Types of Data Queries

Data can be associated with drawing objects in several different ways. While all of these methods support querying, each has its own terminology and options, resulting in a variety of data query types.

The following illustration of the Data Condition dialog box shows the types of data that can be queried.

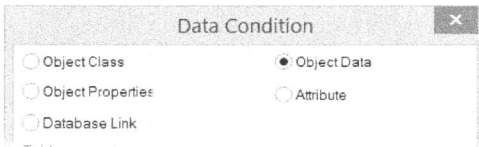

When you select Data as the Query Type from the Define Query of Attached Drawing(s) dialog box, the Data Condition dialog box displays five options. They are as follows:

Condition	Definition
Object Class	A special classification for data that can be assigned directly to objects in the AutoCAD Map 3D software.
Object Data	An option for data stored in tables that are internal to the drawing in the AutoCAD Map 3D software.
Object Properties	Refers to data stored in all of the AutoCAD normal and custom objects. When using this data type, it is recommended that you check the box to include all subclasses.
Attribute Data	A special type of data stored in the AutoCAD blocks.
Database Link	An option that searches the Key Field of external database tables with records that are linked to drawing objects.

To search all of the data available in external database tables with records linked to drawing objects, use an SQL Query Type.

Features of Query Types

Following are some important features of the different types of data queries:

- Object data is stored in tables in the drawing. This function is unique to the AutoCAD Map 3D software.
- Database queries can only analyze the data in the key field of attached database records, while SQL queries can analyze the data in any field of the database.
- If the source drawing that is attached to the drawing you are querying from has a database attached to it, the database connection must be established in the current drawing.

Example

A drawing contains a large number of lines and polylines representing all of the sewer pipes in a city. Data about the sewer pipes, such as pipe diameter, material, installation date, and contractor, has been associated with the drawing objects. Through a data query, all of the pipes that were installed before a certain date or by a certain contractor can be easily identified.

The Process of Executing Queries

Objects that are queried from source drawings (depending on the query mode) can be displayed as a preview, be drawn into the current drawing as copies of the originals, or have information about them sent to a report. Before executing queries in draw mode, it is important to understand how to manage these objects once they are in the current drawing.

Draw Mode Queries

Objects that you retrieve using a draw mode query are copied into the current drawing, including any layer definitions that are associated with the objects. If you are working in a current drawing that does not include the layer definitions of the objects queried and you do not want the new definitions, you can close the drawing without saving.

When you query objects using draw mode and you save the current drawing, all queried objects become native to the current drawing and their association to the originals in the source drawing is lost.

Guidelines for the Draw Query

The draw query is typically used to create a new map or to use a base map.

- **Creating a new map -** If you are creating a new map from multiple drawings and you want the objects to remain resident in the new map, you can draw query the objects and save the drawing.
- **Using a base map -** Often a base map is used as a current drawing. These current drawings typically include source drawing attachments and some simple geometry to navigate the geographic area. When objects from source drawings are queried using the draw mode, they are not meant to be included as permanent objects. After the tasks have been performed, this map can be closed without saving. Any objects or layer definitions created during the draw query are not saved.

Compound Queries

You can combine multiple filtering parameters into a single query to return more specific results. Any of the four query types can be used in any combination. For example, by indicating only a specific geographic area in combination with specific data values, a very specific subset of objects is returned.

You can combine parameters to apply filters to retrieve successively smaller sets of objects, or augment an initially retrieved set by successive query conditions. The interface in the AutoCAD Map 3D software enables you to build very specific conditions without mastering the intricacies of writing SQL statements manually.

About Compound Queries

Compound queries are based on multiple filtering criteria and you can use them to procure a more specific set of results. Location, property, data, and SQL query types can be combined into a single query. The multiple parameters are combined with AND, OR, and NOT operators that determine how they interact with each other.

Key Points About Compound Queries

- Compound queries are automatically written as SQL statements by the AutoCAD Map 3D software.
- Most real-world analysis involves the use of compound queries.

Example

You can retrieve all of the sewer pipes that were installed in the northeastern quadrant of a town before 1998, except for those made of PVC material.

Guidelines for Building Compound Queries

You build compound queries in the Define Query of Attached Drawing(s) dialog box. Each part of the compound query is built individually, and each additional part must specify an operator to determine how it interacts with the other parts.

Guidelines

- When constructing a compound query, think about the set of objects you are trying to retrieve and what uniquely identifies them.
- It might help to think about the compound query in plain spoken terms first. For example, "I am looking for all of the objects that are either completely within, or partially pass through, this area only (Location, crossing), and are on this specific layer in the AutoCAD software (Property, AND operator). However, from that set, I want to remove those that have this data associated with them (Data, AND NOT operator)".
- Always execute the query in Preview mode initially to see how well the query worked.

Compound Query Operators

When multiple query types are combined into a single compound query, the relationship between the query types must be defined with AND, OR, and NOT operators.

- **AND -** Retrieves data where objects must meet both conditions to be included. This choice is a radio button.
- **OR -** Retrieves data that matches either one condition or another. This choice is a radio button.
- **NOT -** A check box that is combined with either an AND or an OR operator. An AND NOT operator removes objects from an initial selection set. An OR NOT operator adds objects to an initial selection set.

Exercise: Define a Property and Location Query

In this exercise, you will define and execute a query to retrieve all sewer system and parcel information from a number of source drawings. You will then define a location query, as shown in the following illustration, to retrieve all objects from source drawings in a crossing circle.

1. Open ...\10-Source Drawing Queries\Define Property and Location Queries\ Redding-Define.dwg.

2. In Map Explorer, verify that the Parcel, Drainage, and Sewer drawings are attached and activated, as shown in the following illustration.

Note: If you did not complete the exercise Create a Drive AI as in the previous chapter, you need to do so at this time to get rid of the error.

3. In Map Explorer, click Data>Query Source Drawing, as shown in the following illustration.

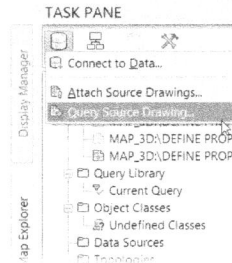

4. In the Define Query of Attached Drawing(s) dialog box, under Query Type, click Property, as shown in the following illustration.

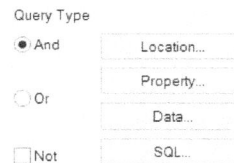

5. In the Property Condition dialog box:
   - Under Select Property, select Layer.
   - Click Values.

6. In the Select dialog box:
   - Select the PARCELS and SEWER_PIPES layers, as shown in the following illustration.
   - Click OK.

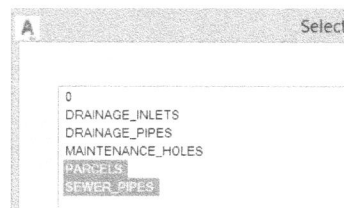

7. In the Property Condition dialog box:

- Under Value, verify that all of the layers are listed, as shown in the following illustration.
- Click OK.

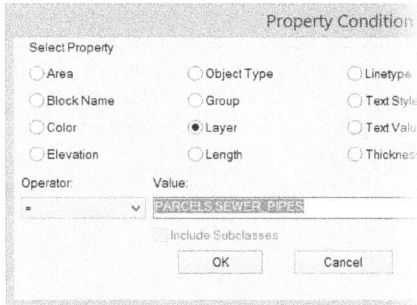

8. In the Define Query of Attached Drawing(s) dialog box, under Query Mode, verify that Preview is selected, as shown in the following illustration.

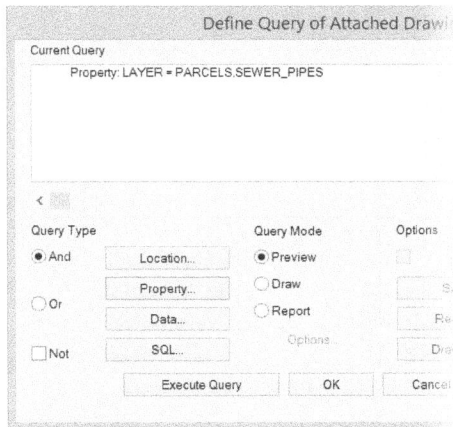

9. Click Execute Query.

The executed query retrieves all objects on the selected layers and displays them as a preview object, as shown in the following illustration.

10. On the View ribbon, under Views, select PARCELS, as shown in the following illustration.

11. In Map Explorer, click Data>Query Source Drawing.

12. In the Define Query of Attached Drawing(s) dialog box:

- Click Clear Query to delete the previous query.
- Click Location.

13. In the Location Condition dialog box:

- Click Circle.
- Under Selection Type, verify that Crossing is selected, as shown in the following illustration.
- Click Define <.

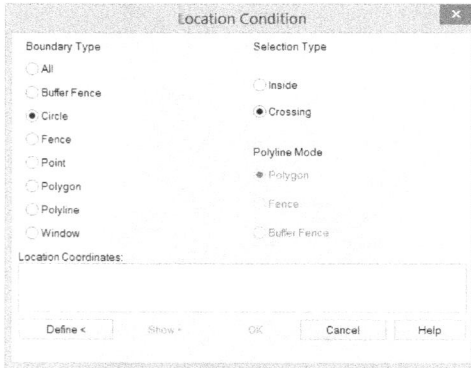

14. Click in the center of the lot. Drag the circle, as shown in the following illustration.

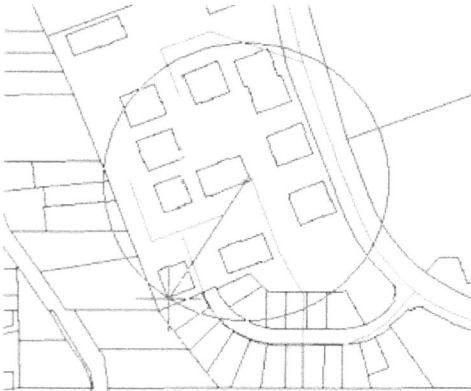

15. In the Define Query of Attached Drawing(s) dialog box:

- Under Query Mode, select Draw.
- Click Execute Query.

All objects inside and crossing the defined circle are queried into the Redding drawing. Because the query was executed as a Draw query, the objects are now resident in the Redding drawing and can be edited or analyzed, as shown in the following illustration.

16. Save and close the drawing.

Lesson: Altering Properties During Queries

Overview

Altering properties during queries is a flexible and efficient method for changing the properties of objects that are queried from source drawings. You can create properties that represent the underlying data that is associated with each object. The result is commonly used to theme a map. However, it is recommended that you use the Display Manager for thematic mapping, rather than property alteration. The Display Manager provides robust thematic-mapping capabilities without changing the actual properties of the objects.

You can also mass edit objects during a query using property alteration. You can define a query of objects and simultaneously change the properties of those objects. This ability is especially important when you are working with multiple drawings.

In this lesson, you learn how to use property alteration, as shown in the following illustration, to alter objects from multiple drawings and to automate tedious tasks.

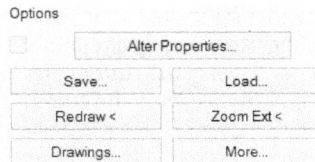

Objectives

After completing this lesson, you will be able to:

- Describe property alteration.
- Describe the process for altering properties.
- Decide when to use property alteration.
- Alter properties during a query.

About Property Alteration

Property alteration can quickly change the properties of objects from source drawings, and this function can be used to edit entire sets of objects simultaneously or to serve as a method of thematic display.

You use property alteration during the execution of queries from source drawings to change the properties of the objects as they are queried into the current drawing. Using object properties, such as color, linetype, text, and hatch patterns, you can modify the queried objects without affecting the source drawing data. Property alteration is only applied in draw mode. You can edit entire sets of objects simultaneously and display maps according to theme.

Creating Expressions

Expressions that you specify in a property alteration can be a constant value, such as the number one (1) or the color red. They can also be more advanced, using dot variables, object data variables, or AutoLISP expressions.

Using Object Data as a Range

In the following illustration, a source drawing contains objects with object data attached. One of the fields in the object data table is for pipe material. When you define the property alteration, each material that is found in the object data table is used to create a new layer in the current drawing. Each object with the matching material value is placed on the corresponding layer in the current drawing.

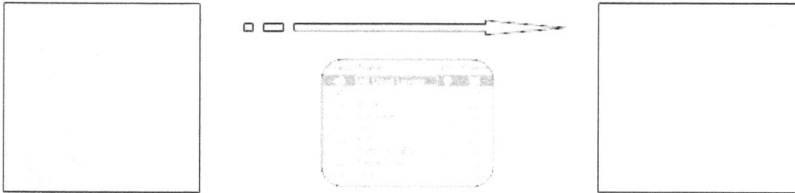

About Range Tables

You use a range table to specify a set of actions when the AutoCAD Map 3D software receives specific values for retrieved data. The range table does not specify the type of property alteration, but supplies the values for the property alteration. A range table can be the basis for different types of property alteration. The OTHERWISE operator applies to all retrieved data values that are not included in the other expressions.

Example of Using Property Alteration

Property alteration can be used to establish a layer standard. Suppose you have several drawings with the same block insertions. Over time, the blocks have been inserted on incorrect layers. You can attach each drawing as a source drawing, define a query that retrieves the blocks, and at the same time alter their layer definitions to a new or existing layer. Once the blocks are on the correct layer, you can save them back to the original drawings.

> Saving objects back to source drawings is covered in another lesson.

Process for Altering Properties

If you are working in a single drawing, you cannot use property alteration. If you are working in a single drawing, and the objects you want to alter can be selected using standard selection tools (such as Quick Select, manual selection, or layer management), property alteration is not required.

You use property alteration when you need to define a set of objects to be altered, and the only method to identify and select them is through a query. This can be the case when the objects reside in multiple drawings, or the objects you need to select cannot be selected using standard selection tools (for example, all storm drain lines with an object data diameter value of 36, within 500 feet of a specific location). In this case, the only method of selecting these objects is through a query.

Process: Property Alteration

The following steps and illustration show the flow of a property alteration.

- Open an existing current drawing or start a new current drawing.
- Attach source drawings that contain the objects you want to alter.
- Define a query to retrieve the objects you want to alter.
- Define a property alteration for the queried objects.
- Execute the query in Draw mode.

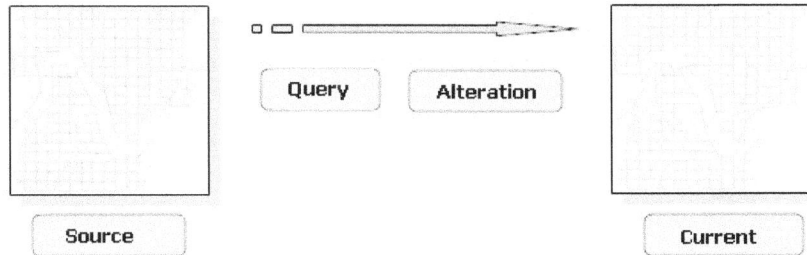

Property alteration is only enabled during a Draw mode query.

Property Alteration Components

When you want to perform a property alteration, the following components must be available:

- A current drawing.
- Source drawings.
- A query to define the objects retrieved.
- An alteration definition.

Guidelines for Property Alteration

The two main reasons to use property alteration are mass editing of objects and thematic display of objects. This section covers how to use property alteration as a mass editing tool.

Considerations for Altering Properties

Consider the following issues when you are using property alteration.

- **Familiarity with data** - You should be familiar with the data that you intend to alter. In some cases, the objects come from multiple source drawings. If you save the alterations back to the source drawings, it is important to understand how the changes affect the source drawings.

- **Permanent changes** - Sometimes all you need is a temporary view of altered properties. However, when you save altered objects, the changes are permanent.

- **Applying the correct alteration** - Some objects do not respond to the alteration that has been defined. For example, hatches are not applied to text objects that are part of the query.

- **Query definition** - Be sure to define the query in such a way that only the objects that you want to alter are retrieved. You can define the query and execute it as a preview to ensure that the query retrieves the required objects.

Property Alteration or Display Manager?

In deciding whether to use property alteration or the Display Manager, consider the following points:

- Property alteration can only be used as a draw query.

- Property alteration changes the actual properties of the objects in the current drawing. The objects in the source drawing retain the original properties unless the altered objects are saved back.

- The Display Manager changes the display properties of objects, not the actual properties.

- The Display Manager does not require you to have a source-current drawing relationship or to use a query. It can alter the display of objects from in a drawing.

Example of Property Alteration

Several drawings exist for a storm drain system. Each drawing uses a limited number of object types: polylines for the storm drain lines and blocks for inlets and manholes. Layer standards have not been well enforced and each drawing has different layer names for the same object types. You want to conform the storm drain lines to the layer standards.

1. Start a new drawing and define the target layer for the storm drain lines, as shown in the following illustration.

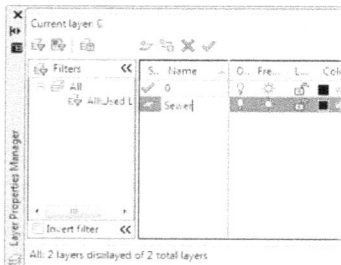

2. Attach the drawings that contain the storm drain lines that do not conform to the layer standards, as shown in the following illustration.

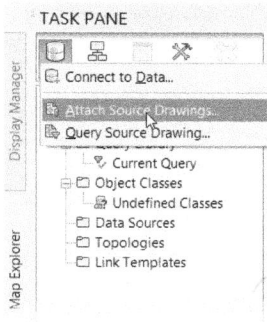

3. Define a property query that retrieves all of the polyline object types. Preview the query to confirm that the correct objects are defined, as shown in the following illustration.

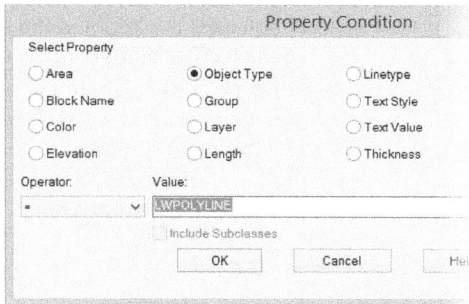

4. Define a layer alteration, as shown in the following illustration, that places the storm drain lines on the correct layer in the current drawing. Execute the query.

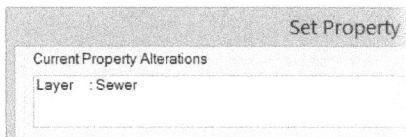

Exercise: Alter Properties During a Query

In this exercise, you will create a query to retrieve all sewer lines from a source drawing. During the query, you will define an altered property that creates new layers for pipe materials and places each sewer line on the layer corresponding to its material, as shown in the following illustration.

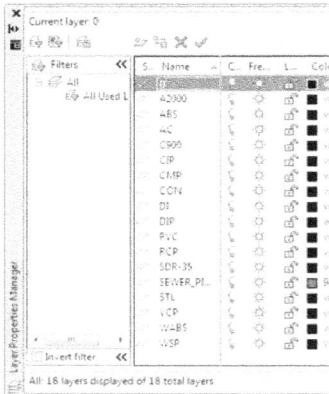

1. Start a new drawing.

2. In Map Explorer, click Data>Attach Source Drawings, as shown in the following illustration.

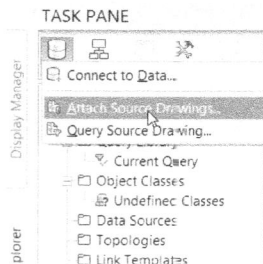

3. In the Select Drawing(s) to Attach dialog box:

   - Under Look In, select the MAP_3D alias.
   - Navigate to the *Data\Source-DWG* folder.
   - Select the Sewer drawing, as shown in the following illustration.
   - Click Add.
   - Click OK.

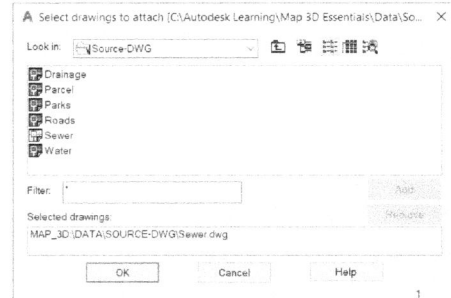

4. In Map Explorer, right-click on Drawings and select Quick View.

5. In the Quick View Drawings dialog box:

   - Verify that the Zoom to the Extents of Selected Drawings check box is selected.
   - Click OK. After completing this step, your drawing should look as shown in the following illustration.

The next few steps define the query to retrieve the objects you want to alter.

6. In Map Explorer, click Data>Query Source Drawing.

7. In the Define Query of Attached Drawing(s) dialog box, under Query Type, click Property.

8. In the Property Condition dialog box:
   - Click Layer.
   - Click Values.

9. In the Select dialog box:
   - Select SEWER_PIPES, as shown in the following illustration.
   - Click OK.

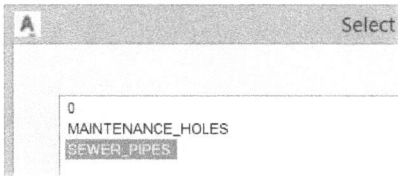

10. In the Property Condition dialog box, click OK, as shown in the following illustration.

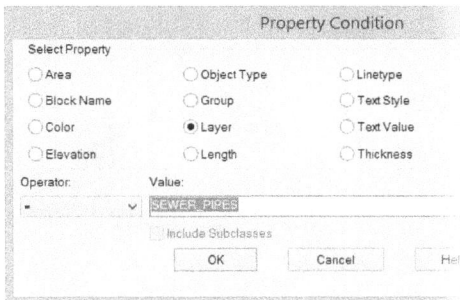

Now the query is defined. In the next steps, you define how the objects will be altered.

11. In the Define Query of Attached Drawing(s) dialog box, under Options, click Alter Properties, as shown in the following illustration.

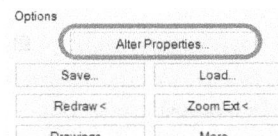

12. In the Set Property Alterations dialog box:
   - Select Layer, as shown in the following illustration.
   - Click Expression.

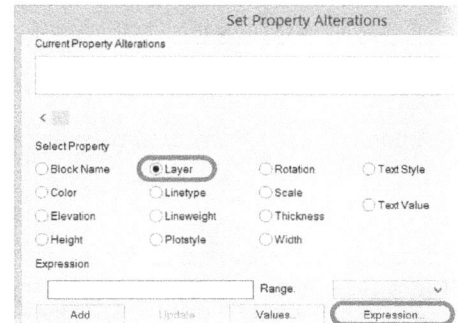

13. In the Property Alteration Expression dialog box:
   - Expand Object Data and the SEWER_PIPES table.
   - Select PIPETYPE, as shown in the following illustration.
   - Click OK.

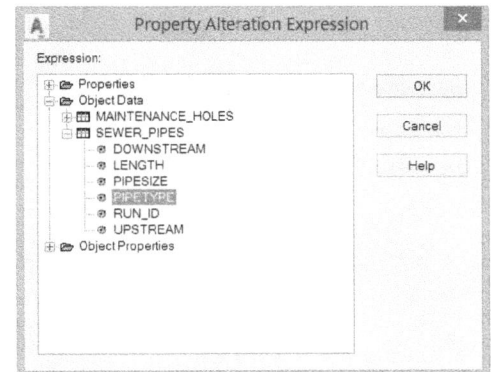

14. In the Set Property Alterations dialog box:
   - Under Expression, click Add, as shown in the following illustration.
   - Click OK.

15. In the Define Query of Attached Drawing(s) dialog box:

- Under Query Mode, select Draw.
- Verify that Alter Properties is checked, as shown in the following illustration.
- Click Execute Query.

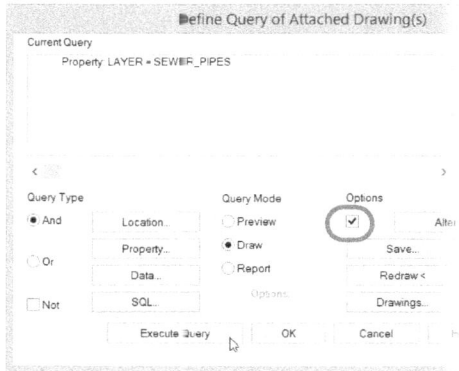

Objects on the SEWER_PIPES layer are queried into the current drawing. Layers for each value in the PIPETYPE object data field are created, and individual objects are placed on the correct layer according to their value.

16. On the Home tab>AutoCAD Layers panel click Layer Properties, as shown in the following illustration.

17. Open the Layer Properties Manager to verify the new layers that are named after PIPETYPE, as shown in the following illustration.

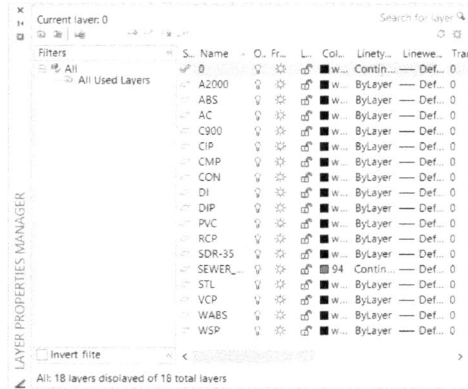

18. To only display the ABS layer, in the Layer Properties Manager palette:

- Freeze all layers except the 0 layer and the ABS layer.
- Close the Layer Properties Manager palette. The drawing should look as shown in the following illustration.

19. Save and close the drawing.

Lesson: Using the Query Library

Overview

Saved queries are a powerful method of automating common tasks when you are working in a system of multiple drawings, users, and needs. This lesson covers saving and managing queries, as shown in the following illustration.

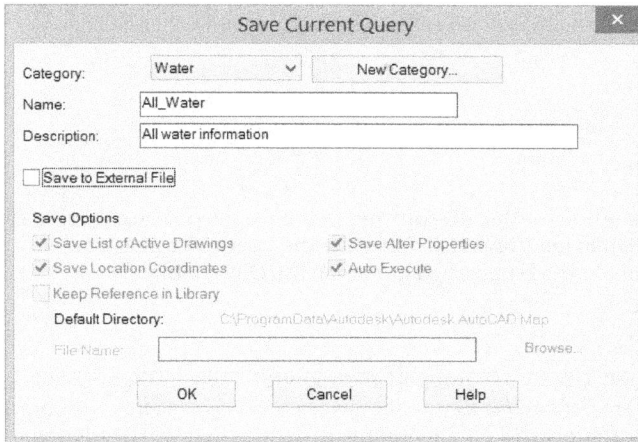

Objectives

After completing this lesson, you will be able to:

- Describe the Query Library and explain saved queries.
- List the differences between internal and external saved queries.
- Decide how to use the Query Library and saved queries.
- Save and run a saved query.

About the Query Library and Saved Queries

In a mapping system, you often repeat the same analysis and data manipulation tasks. By using saved queries, as shown in the following illustration, you can easily define and repeat common tasks in the mapping system.

Saved Queries Definition

When you define a query in the AutoCAD Map 3D software, you have the option of saving all of the settings for that query. You can then load, revise, and execute the query. You give a name and description to every query for use in the list of saved queries in the Query Library.

Query Library Categories

Queries that you save in the Query Library are grouped in categories. These categories are especially important when many queries are defined for a current drawing. When you search the library to find a saved query you can filter by category to limit the number of queries that you need·to search.

Saved Query Formats

You can save a query in two formats:

Format	Definition
Internal	Saves the current query definition with the current drawing. This method stores the query in an internal format, which you can modify in the current drawing using the Define Query dialog box.
External	Saves the query to a file. You can edit the file with a text editor to add other expressions or AutoLISP statements. You can then load the query and run it in the current drawing or other drawings.

Example of Using Saved Queries

Mapping systems commonly display a certain type of data to a specific user. For example, if a current drawing uses parcel objects as a base map and all infrastructure is saved in drawings that are attached to the current drawing, you can define a query to only retrieve the objects that you work with regularly. You can save the query, and instead of redefining the query each time you need access to the data in the source drawings, you can simply execute the saved query.

Internal and External Queries

Internal and external saved queries behave differently, but both can be referenced in the Query Library.

Internal Queries

These are some of the features of an internal query:

- You can run internal queries from the workspace and the Query Library.
- When you save an internal query, some options are not available, such as not saving location conditions, reattaching source drawings, or autoexecute.
- Internal queries cannot be shared from one current drawing to another.

External Queries

These are some of the features of an external query:

- External queries can be referenced in the Query Library, but you cannot run them directly from the Query Library.
- You can save external queries to a common network location so that multiple users can access them.
- When you save an external query you can set options, such as redefining location conditions at the time of execution, reattaching source drawings at the time of execution, etc.
- The QRY file that is generated when you save an external query is in LISP format and is easily modified, as shown in the following illustration.

What the Query Library Can Do

In the Query Library, you can do the following tasks:

- Delete or rename queries.
- Organize queries into categories.
- Create, rename, or delete groups.
- Change the external reference (directory and query filename).
- Execute a query.

Guidelines for Using the Query Library

Using saved queries and the Query Library can increase an individual user's efficiency and productivity. When applied to a mapping system that includes multiple users and drawings, saved queries and the Query Library require more planning before they are implemented.

In the following illustration, two different drawings have queries saved as internal queries, which are only available to the drawings in which they reside. However, the external queries are available to both drawings.

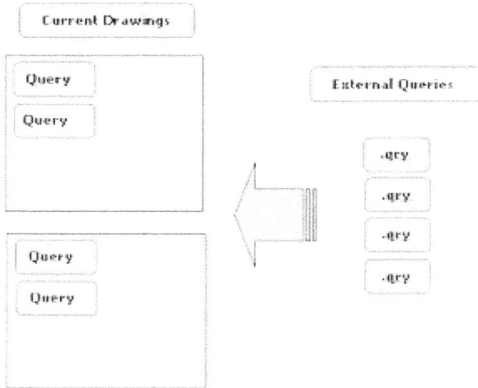

Designing a Saved Query System

When you are designing a mapping system that uses saved queries and the Query Library, follow these guidelines:

- If your mapping system includes multiple users who are accessing the same source drawings from different current drawings, use a system of external queries to give access to the same queries from a single location.

- If you use queries that include both location and property conditions, and the location conditions need to be defined each time the query is executed, use external queries. For example, suppose a query always retrieves all storm drain information but only in a crossing circle. By using an external query, you can select the circle location each time it is executed.

- If you want to run saved queries directly from the Query Library or workspace and you do not need to distribute queries to other users, use internal queries.

> Queries and Query Libraries that are stored in a source drawing are not accessible for use in the current drawing.

Exercise: Save and Run a Saved Query

In this exercise, you will define a property query to retrieve all water system data. You will then save the query as an internal query and execute it from the Query Library, as shown in the following illustration.

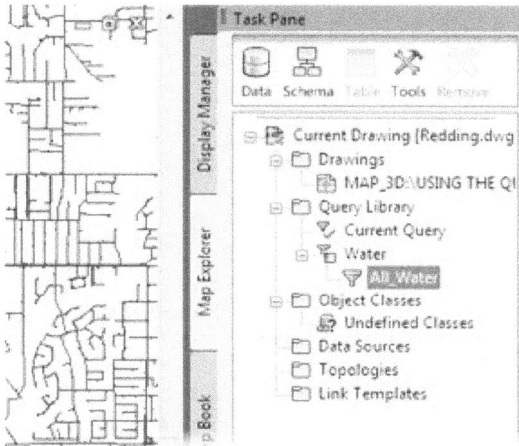

1. Open ...\10-Source-Drawing Queries\Using the QueryLibrary\ Redding-Query.dwg.

2. Verify that the water drawing is attached and active.

3. In the Display Manager, double-click Current Query.

4. In the Define Query of Attached Drawing(s) dialog box, under Query Type, click Property.

5. In the Property Condition dialog box:
   - Select Layer.
   - Click Values.

6. In the Select dialog box:
   - Select all layers that begin with WATER_, as shown in the following illustration.
   - Click OK.

7. In the Property Condition dialog box, click OK, as shown in the following illustration.

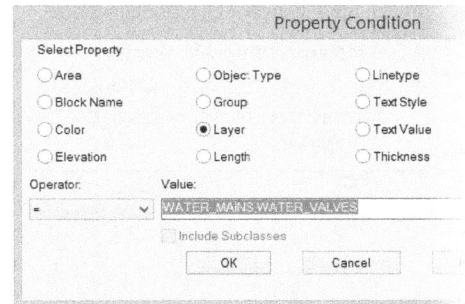

8. In the Define Query of Attached Drawing(s) dialog box:
   - Under Query Mode, select Draw.
   - Under Options, click Save, as shown in the following illustration.

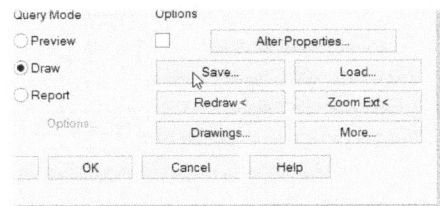

9. In the Save Current Query dialog box, click New Category, as shown in the following illustration.

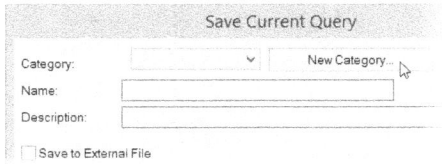

10. In the Define New Category dialog box:
    - For New Category Name, enter **Water**, as shown in the following illustration.
    - Click OK.

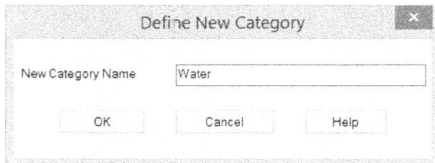

11. In the Save Current Query dialog box:
    - For Name, enter **All_Water**.
    - For Description, enter **All water infrastructure**, as shown in the following illustration.
    - Click OK.

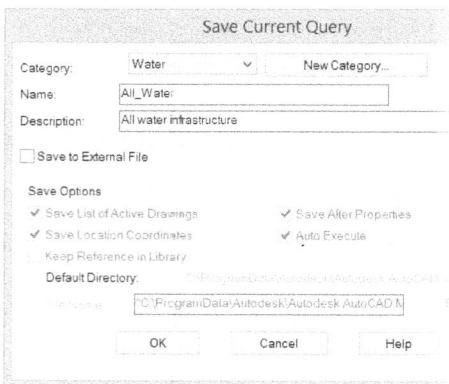

12. In the Define Query of Attached Drawing(s) dialog box, click OK, as shown in the following illustration.

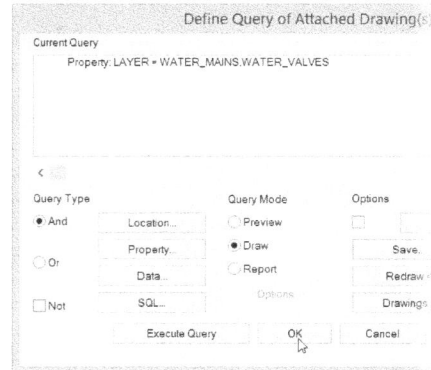

The new query is saved and added to the workspace but not executed.

13. In the Map Explorer:
    - Expand the new Water category.
    - Double-click the All_Water query, as shown in the following illustration.

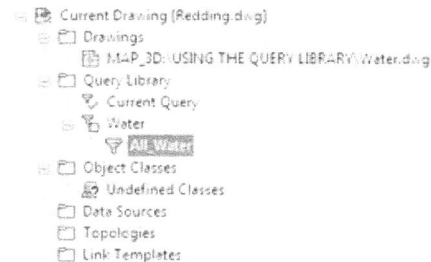

14. In the Define Query of Attached Drawing(s) dialog box:

- Click Zoom Ext <.
- In the Zoom Drawing Extents dialog box, click OK.
- Click Execute Query, as shown in the following illustration.

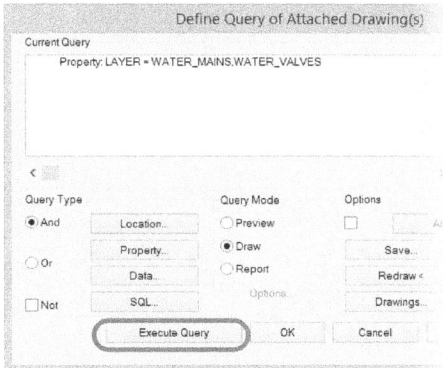

15. The following illustration shows what the drawing should look like.

Save and close Redding.dwg.

16. Save and close the drawing.

Lesson: Save Back to Queried Drawings

Overview

With the AutoCAD Map 3D software, multiple users can view and query objects in the same file on a network at the same time. When you edit objects retrieved by a query, the objects are locked in the source drawing until you commit the changes you have made to the source drawing by a process called save back. Once you have edited and saved them, the objects are unlocked and again available to all users.

In this lesson, you learn how to save back objects to the source drawing, as shown in the following illustration.

Objectives

After completing this lesson, you will be able to:

- Explain the concepts of editing source drawing objects and save back.
- List the process of editing objects from source drawings and save back.
- Decide how to set user rights and establish a multiple-drawing edit environment.
- Save queried and new objects to source drawings.

About Editing Source Drawing Objects

One of the most powerful aspects of working in a multiple-drawing environment is the ability to access drawings at the object level and to edit them. When you edit objects that have been queried from source drawings, the AutoCAD Map 3D software uses a system of object locking and transacting to enable your edits.

About Save Back

Save back refers to the process of querying objects from source drawings, editing them, and saving them back to the original source drawing. Save back also refers to creating new objects in a current drawing and saving them back to a source drawing based on criteria that you set.

Using Editing Options

You can use any editing command to edit retrieved objects. The AutoCAD Map 3D software is notified whenever you make a change to a drawing object.

You can do the following:

- **Add new objects** - You use the Add Objects to Save Set option to prepare all new objects in the current drawing for saving to source drawings.
- **Modify retrieved objects** - When you modify objects, they are flagged so that those objects can be saved back to the original drawing.
- **Delete objects** - The objects are recorded as deleted and removed from the source drawing as part of the save back operation.

Saving Back

You can identify the set of objects to be saved back and the method for saving them. Two types of objects can be saved back:

Object	Save back method
Queried objects that were edited	Queried objects can only be saved back to their original source drawings
Newly created objects added to the save set	You can save objects back using a combination of the Area, Layer, Selective, and None options in the Save Objects to Source Drawings dialog box.

Example of Using Save Back

You work for the public works department of a local government agency that uses several drawings to map the public infrastructure. Although multiple users access each of the maps based on these source drawings, by using save back, you can query precisely the data that you need, edit it, and save it back to the source drawing without disrupting the other users.

Editing Process

When you create or edit objects, you should add them to the save set. This ensures that your edits are saved back and in a multiuser environment, locks the objects so that other users cannot edit the same objects. You can select additional objects to include in the save set at any time.

Background Process

When you edit a queried object, the AutoCAD Map 3D software is notified that a change has occurred and responds with a prompt to add objects to a save set. If you agree to add the objects to the save set, the editing process starts. When you have finished editing, the changes are contained in a save set. If you do not add an object to the save set, your changes to that object are not included. While you are editing in the AutoCAD Map 3D software, object locks are placed on all of the objects in the save set. Drawing locks are placed on the affected source drawings to prevent other users from editing those files.

The following illustration shows how save back works when multiple users access the same object in the same source drawing.

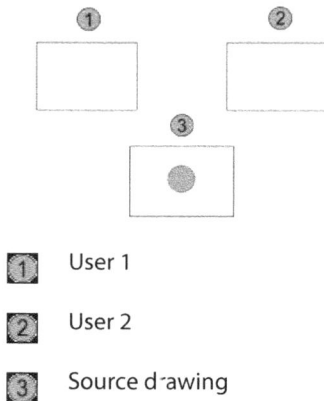

①	User 1
②	User 2
③	Source drawing

Two users attach the same drawing as a source drawing, as shown in the following illustration.

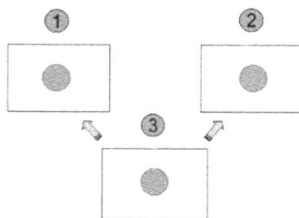

Both users draw query the object into their respective current drawings, as shown in the following illustration.

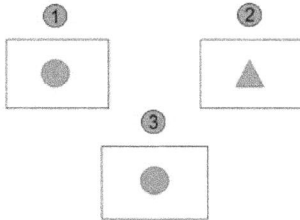

User 2 edits the object and adds it to the save set, as shown in the following illustration. This locks the object in the source drawing. User1 cannot edit the object at this time.

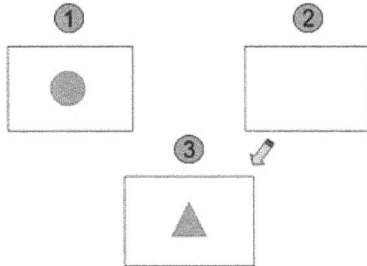

User 2 saves the edit back to the source drawing. This unlocks the object.

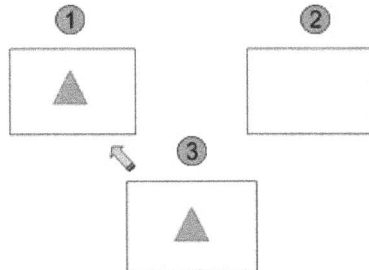

User 1 attempts to edit the object and is prompted to re-query the object for the latest version, as shown in the following illustration.

Process: Using Save Back

The following steps outline the process for saving back a queried object from a source drawing.

1. Define a query to retrieve the objects to edit and any other objects that are required to complete the task, as shown in the following illustration.

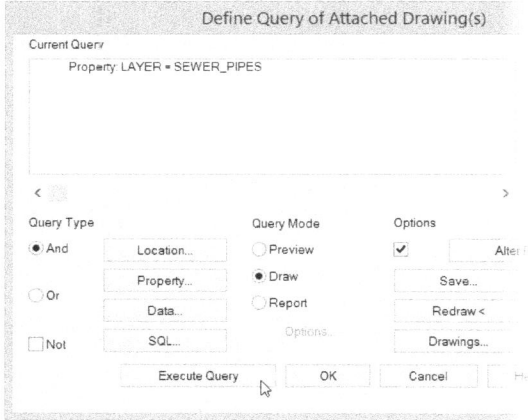

2. Edit the queried object and add it to the save set, as shown in the following illustration.

3. Save the edited object back to the source drawing, as shown in the following illustration.

Key Steps

The following steps outline the editing process in the AutoCAD Map 3D software.

- Open a drawing and attach the source drawings to be edited.
- Use one or more queries to retrieve data from the drawings.
- Use any command to modify a queried object.
- Save changes back to source drawings.

Canceling Edits

You can cancel save back in the following ways:

- On the Home tab, under Data, select Remove Objects from Save Set.
- In the Drawing Maintenance dialog box, select the required drawings. Select User List. Select the required objects. Click Remove Locks.
- Quit the current drawing. All changes that you have made in this editing session, or since the last save back operation in the Autodesk Map 3D software are undone. All locks are removed from the locked objects and source drawings.
- Detach the source drawings.

Setting Up a Multiple-Drawing Edit Environment

In a network environment, the AutoCAD Map 3D software provides object locking and operating system file locking. When you use a system such as this, there are recommended guidelines to help you incorporate this feature effectively.

Restrictions in the Multiple-User Environment

The following examples describe how the AutoCAD Map 3D software and the AutoCAD software respond when users try to work on the same file.

- Users of the AutoCAD Map 3D software and the AutoCAD software cannot work on the same drawing at the same time.
- If a user of the AutoCAD Map 3D software activates a drawing, users of the AutoCAD software cannot open, insert, or externally reference that drawing. If a user of the AutoCAD software tries to open that drawing, a warning message displays.
- If a user of the AutoCAD software opens a drawing, a user of the AutoCAD Map 3D software cannot attach that drawing. If a user of the AutoCAD Map 3D software tries to attach that drawing, a warning message displays.

Enabling Multiple-User Access

To enable multiple users to work on the same drawings at the same time, set the following options in the Options dialog box, Multi-User tab:

- Select the Force User Login option so that the AutoCAD Map 3D software can identify the users responsible for locked objects.
- Select the Enable Object Locking option to prevent users from editing the same objects at the same time.

Save Back Options

When you edit queried objects and add them to the save set, or add new objects to the save set, the following save back options are available.

Option	Definition
Area	The object is saved to the source drawing with the matching drawing extents. If the object lies inside the extents of more than one drawing, the first drawing encountered in the list of attached drawings (the drawing set) is the destination for the object. The object does not need to be inside the extents, it just needs to touch the extents to be included. The source drawing extents are updated when objects are saved to the source drawings.
Layer	The object is saved to the first drawing in the drawing set that contains the object's layer.
Selective	Specify the drawing to which selected objects are to be saved back. Specify the objects for each drawing.
None	The previous choices are saved.

Guidelines for Saving Back

The following list describes some considerations when you are saving objects to source drawings. Each option of the save back criteria functions in a chronological order.

- If Layer is first, objects are placed in the drawings based on the first drawing with a specific layer.
- If Area is first, objects are saved back based on their location.
- If Selective is first, you specify which objects are to be saved in each drawing.

Example of Save Back

If you change the layer of a selected object, you can save the object back to the original drawing or to a drawing that contains the new layer. You can specify the order in which the save back options are going to be performed.

If you organize drawings by layer, you can save back using the Layer option, so that you can correct errors where objects have been placed on the wrong layer.

If you organize drawings by area (for example, by tiling drawings), then Area is the best method.

The key feature in the save back procedure is that you save back in one step or incrementally.

Exercise: Save Queried and New Objects to Source Drawing

In this exercise, you will query objects from source drawings, edit those objects, and add them to the save set. You will also create new objects and add them to the save set. When you are finished editing, you will save all of the objects back to the source drawings, as shown in the following illustration.

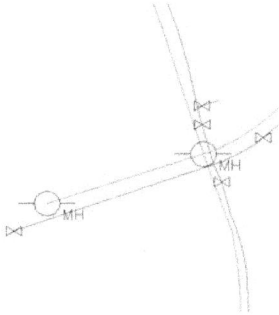

1. Open ...\10-Source Drawing Queries\Save Back to Queried Drawings\Redding-Start.dwg.

   - Verify that the Zoning, Water, and Sewer drawings are attached and active.

2. In Map Explorer, right-click on Drawings and select Quick View.

3. In the Quick View Drawings dialog box:

   - Verify that the Zoom to the Extents of Selected Drawings check box is selected.
   - Click OK. The following illustration shows what the drawing should look like.

4. On the View tab, under Views, select the Edit view.

5. In Map Explorer:

   - Click Data.
   - Select Query Source Drawing.

6. In the Define Query of Attached Drawing(s) dialog box, click Location.

7. In the Location Condition dialog box:

   - Select Circle.
   - Under Selection Type, verify that Crossing is selected, as shown in the following illustration.
   - Click Define.

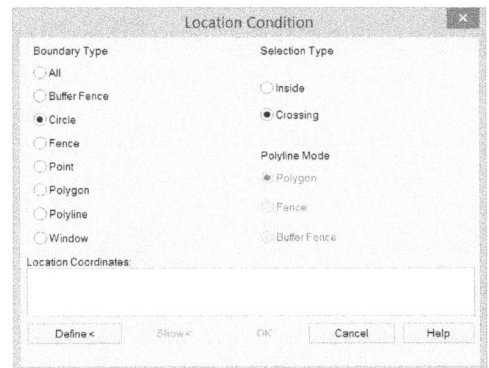

8. Define a circle, as shown in the following illustration.

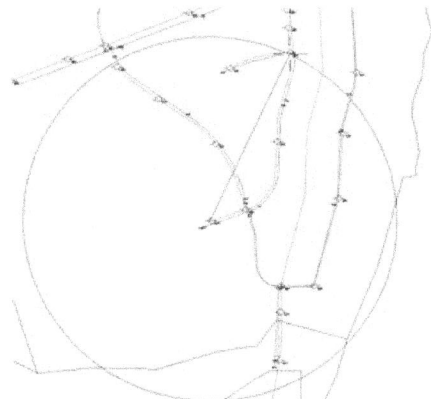

9. In the Define Query of Attached Drawing(s) dialog box:
    - Under Query Mode, select Draw, as shown in the following illustration.
    - Click Execute Query.

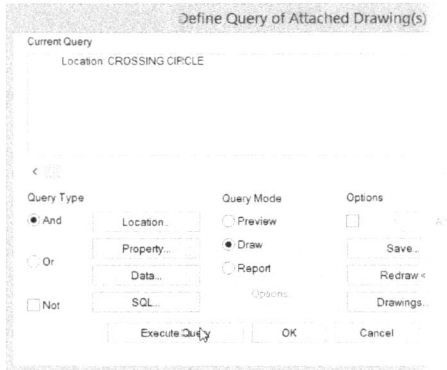

10. The resulting query should look, as shown in the following illustration.

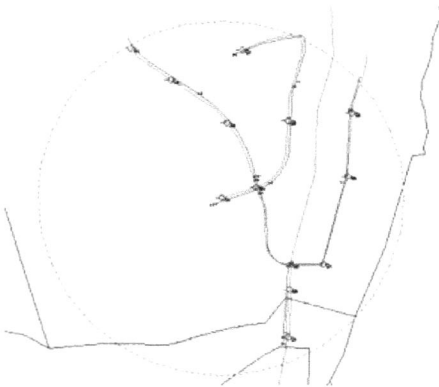

The objects are now in the current drawing and in the source drawings. In the next steps, you will edit the objects and set the save back criteria.

11. In the Modelspace:
    - Select the short waterline, as shown in the following illustration.
    - Press <Delete>.

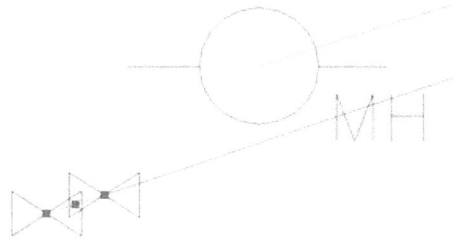

12. In the Confirm Save Back dialog box, click Yes, as shown in the following illustration. The objects are erased and their status is saved in the save set.

13. Select the Water Valve, as shown in the following illustration.
    - Press <Delete>.

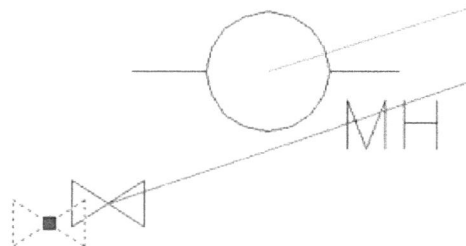

14. In the Confirm Save Back dialog box, click Yes, as shown in the following illustration. The objects are erased and their status is saved in the save set.

15. On the Home tab:
    - Under AutoCAD Layers, select the Layer dropdown.
    - Select WATER_MAINS to make it the current layer, as shown in the following illustration.

    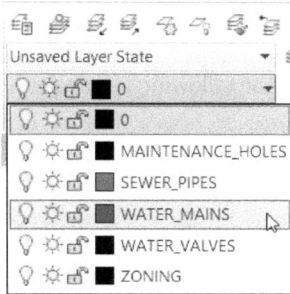

16. At the command line:
    - Enter **LINE**.
    - Press <Enter>.
    - Draw a new Water Main perpendicular to the Water Main, at the Valve, as shown in the following illustration.

    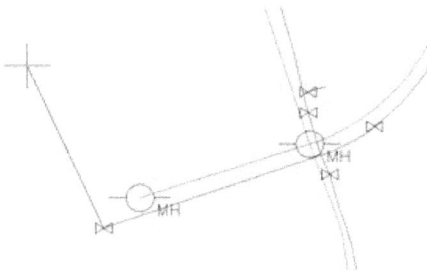

17. Set the WATER_VALVES layer current, as shown in the following illustration.

    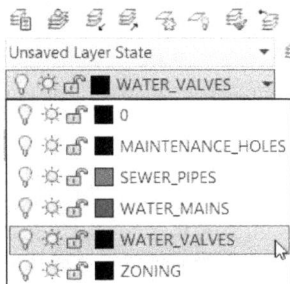

18. On the Insert tab, under Block, select Insert, as shown in the following illustration.

    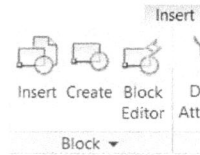

19. In the Insert dialog box:
    - For Name, select VALVE.
    - Under Scale, for both X and Y values, enter **20**, as shown in the following illustration.
    - Click OK.

    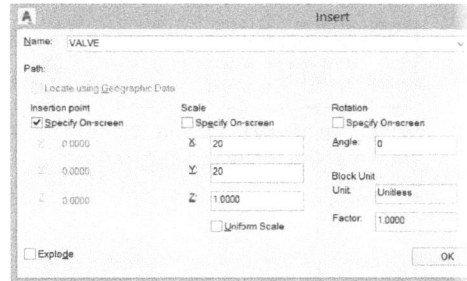

20. Insert the VALVE block at the end point of the waterline, as shown in the following illustration.

    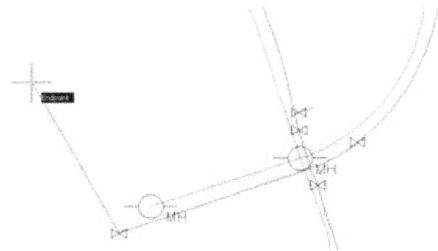

21. On the Home tab, under the Data down arrow, select Add to Save Set, as shown in the following illustration.

22. In the Command Line, click Select, as shown in the following illustration, to select objects.

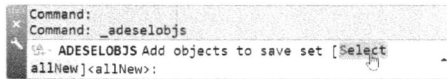

23. Select the new VALVE and Water Main, as shown in the following illustration.

- Press <Enter>.

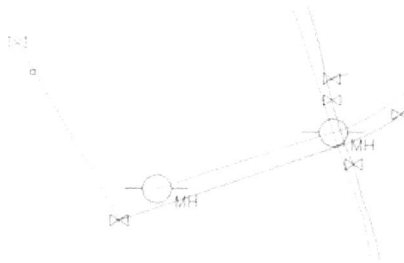

24. On the Home tab, under the expanded Data panel, select Save to Source, as shown in the following illustration.

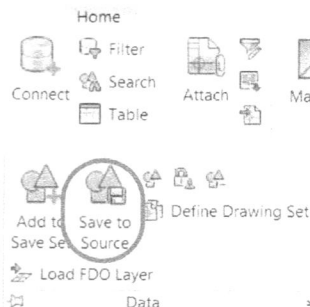

25. In the Save Objects to Source Drawings dialog box:

- Under Status, verify that there are two queried objects, two objects set for deletion, and two newly created objects in the save set.
- Under Save Order for Newly Created Objects, for the first field, select Layer.
- For the second field, select None, as shown in the following illustration.
- Click OK.

26. Ensure that the queried and new objects are removed from the current drawing and saved back to the source drawings based on their layers. The drawing should look, as shown in the following illustration.

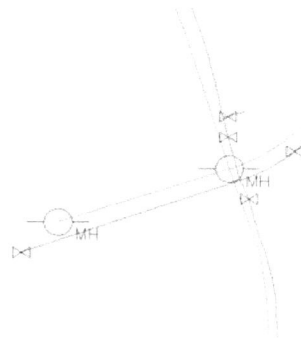

27. Close the drawing without saving any changes. The edited objects in the Water drawing have already been saved. You can run the query again to view the newly created water main and valve.

Chapter Summary

Having completed this chapter, you can:

- Create and execute property and location queries from source drawings.
- Define queries from source drawings based on attached data.
- Define queries from source drawings based on multiple criteria.
- Alter the properties of objects during a query.
- Create and use queries from the Query Library.
- Edit objects from multiple source drawings from a single environment.

Stylizing

The Display Manager is a tool to create, edit, and manage styles that are applied to objects. Styles can be applied to as many elements as required, and styles can be combined to produce effects, such as displaying roads as black with a dotted yellow line down the middle.

Styles also provide the ability to change the display order and to specify different styles for different view scales. The Properties palette in the AutoCAD® software is used to edit all of the properties in the Display Manager. One of the most important aspects of the Display Manager is that it changes how objects display, rather than their properties.

The stylizing tools for feature sources enable you to simply and effectively produce maps with your available GIS data.

Objectives

After completing this chapter, you will be able to:

- Describe the Display Manager.
- Stylize features.
- Create a thematic map.

Lesson: About the Display Manager

Overview

The Display Manager provides a powerful tool to display the AutoCAD® Map 3D objects, as shown in the following illustration. In this lesson, you learn the concepts and principles of the Display Manager and explore how it is used. This lesson provides an overview of the feature without going into technical procedures or exercises.

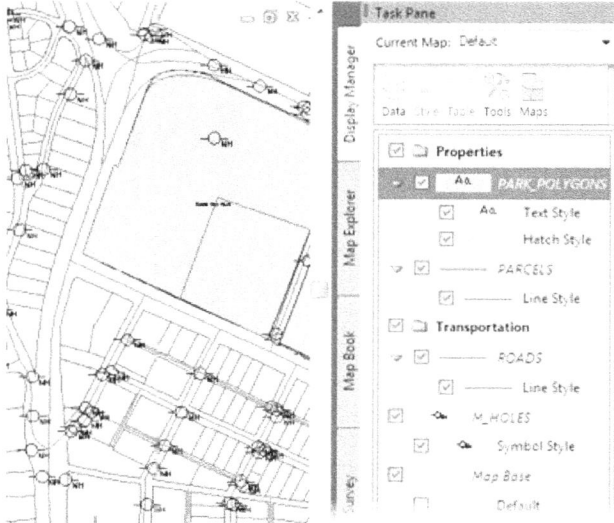

Objectives

After completing this lesson, you will be able to:

- Describe a display map.
- Define the Display Manager.
- Describe how the Display Manager interprets data.
- Describe how display maps are applied.

About Display Maps

Display Maps introduce a fundamentally different approach to displaying the AutoCAD Map 3D objects. The central point of this approach is that several display maps can be created in a single drawing. By using the Display Manager, you can create any number of display maps in a single drawing.

In the following illustration, the objects on the left display using their native properties. A subset of the same objects displays on the right, using definitions established using the Display Manager.

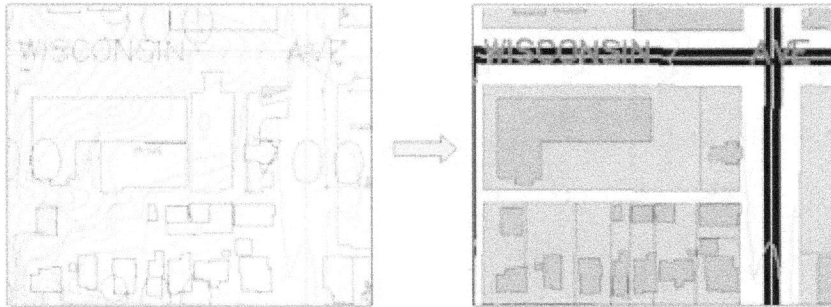

Display Maps Defined

With Display Maps, you can present drawings with very different appearances without affecting the actual properties of objects in the drawings. You create Display Maps using display definitions that you can also manage.

Example of a Display Map

The display map, as shown in the following illustration, uses a theme style to highlight and identify sewer lines installed by a specific contractor. The display of the objects has been altered, but the object properties remain intact. Any work that is required on the objects can be done while viewing them using an altered display state.

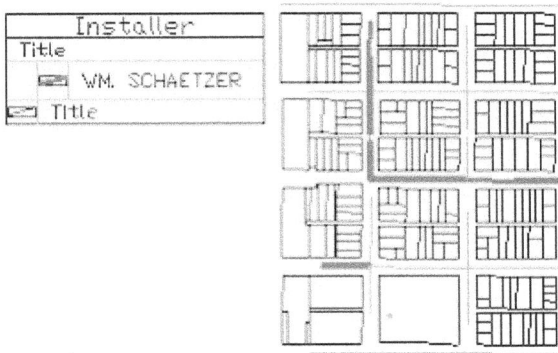

About the Display Manager

You use the Display Manager tools to define display maps, as shown in the following illustration.

Display Manager Tools

The following lists the high-level tools used to define display maps.

Display Manager

This tab of the Task pane, as shown in the following illustration, is the central management tool for creating and editing display maps. The elements of the display map are listed. You can toggle stylization on and off, create additional display maps, create thematic legends, define display properties, define map scale thresholds, etc.

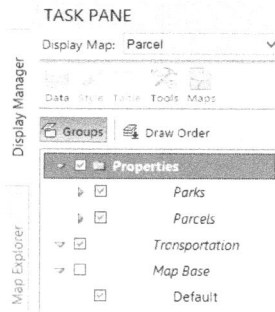

Display Library

The Display Library is a management tool for drawing object styles. From the library, you can use styles in multiple display maps and apply them as reference styles in a group of elements, as shown in the following illustration.

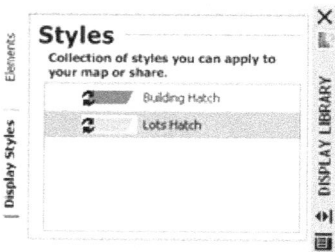

Properties Palette

The Display Manager uses the Properties palette to define styles for drawing objects but not features, as shown in the following illustration.

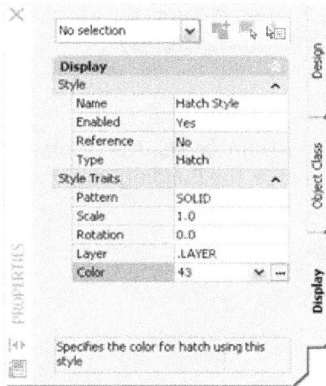

Compare Thresholds

Scale-dependent maps display different data depending on the zoom level of the map. When you create maps that are scale threshold dependent, you do much of the work in the Display Manager and in the Thresholds area, as shown on the left in the following illustration. In the Compare Thresholds dialog box, you can view the behavior of a single element at different scales. Each time you change the view scale, the elements are modified to represent the map at that threshold, as shown on the right in the following illustration.

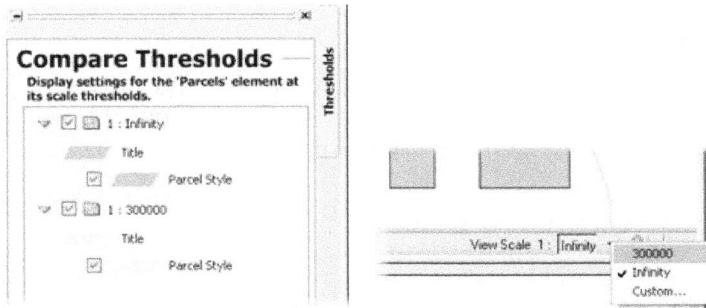

How the Display Manager Looks at Data

Before creating a display map, it is helpful to understand how display maps view the AutoCAD Map 3D data. When you create a display map, you define elements in the Display Manager. An element is a definition of a type of data. You can create elements for layers, queries, feature classes, raster objects, and topologies. You can assign styles to an element to define how objects display.

Element Definition

In the following illustration, the drawing on the left is open with several layers. The Display Manager only looks at layers that have been included as elements, in this case, the Buildings and Index layers. The map on the right only displays these two elements.

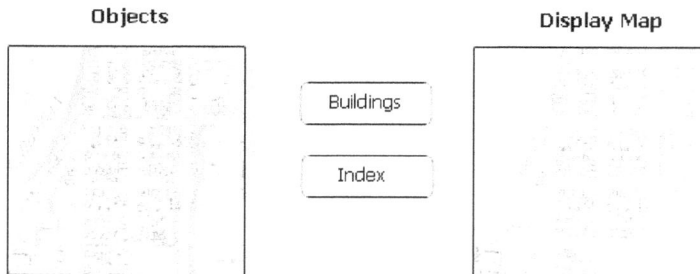

Display maps are like Feature Alteration

A display map behaves similar to the Feature Alteration tool during a query, with two exceptions. The object properties are not changed in any way and you are not limited to queries from source drawings.

Example Display Map

The display map in the following illustration shows how a complex drawing of a storm drain system displays with the lines highlighted and the text de-emphasized. In this case, all of the objects are on the same layer and a query element has been used to define the text.

How Display Maps Are Used

The purpose of a display map is to display map objects using a specified display definition. You can use display maps for many reasons, including exhibits, visualization, and analysis, and to verify data as it is entered.

Visualization

When you work in a map with dense geometry, you can create a display map to highlight certain layers or groups of objects, as shown in the following illustration.

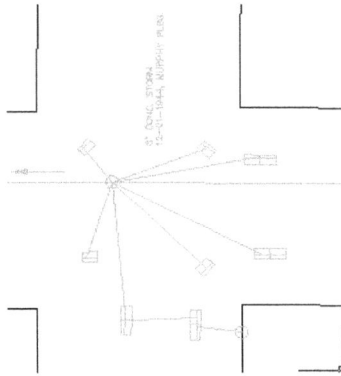

Exhibits

You can create maps with high-impact display definitions to exhibit different characteristics, as shown in the following illustration.

Analysis

By using thematic elements and styles, you can generate a display map that clearly presents the underlying data in the geometry, as shown in the following illustration.

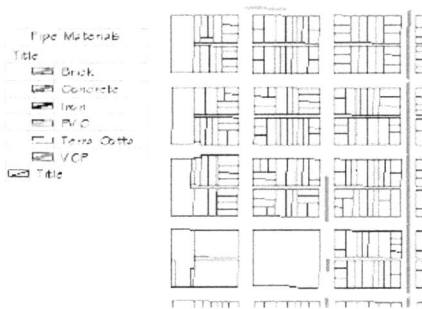

Assist Data Input

When you enter data or make changes to a large number of objects in a drawing, it can be difficult to keep track of the changes that you make. By creating an element that uses the layer you are working on, with a style that denotes the changes you are making, you can easily update the map and cause objects you have edited to be displayed differently, as shown in the following illustration.

Example: Using a Display Map to Review Data Input

The building footprints for the city are not closed polylines, but they need to be. Because there are hundreds of building footprints, it is difficult to keep track of which ones are complete. You can create an element that has a hatch property and update the map frequently while you are making the changes. The completed closed polygons display with a hatch, as shown in the following illustration.

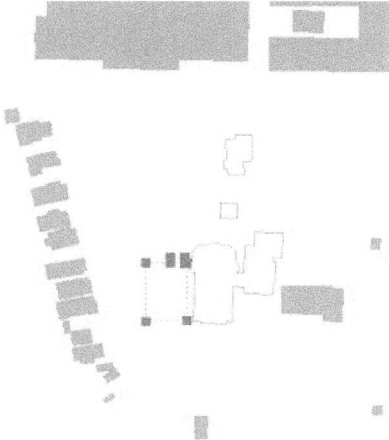

Exercise: Create a Display Map from Existing Drawings and Add Elements

In this exercise, you will create a new display map, with elements, in an existing drawing. The elements focus on road centerlines, parcel outlines, park points, and park outlines, as shown in the following illustration. The display map draws from geometry in an attached drawing. Styles are not applied. This exercise can be considered preparation for a fully stylized map.

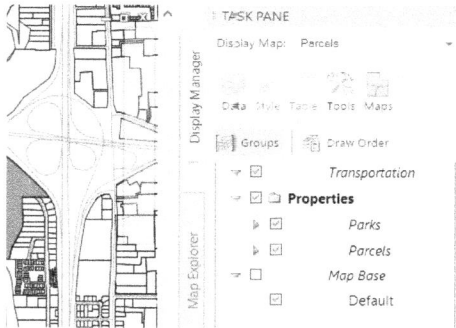

1. Open ...\11-Stylizing\Creating Display Maps\ Redding-Maps.dwg.

2. In Map Explorer:

    - Review the layers.
    - Confirm that the ...\11-Stylizing\Creating Display Maps\Parcel.dwg, Roads.dwg, and Parks.dwg files are attached and active In Map Explorer.

3. Click the Display Manager tab.

    Clear the Map Base checkbox to toggle that element off, as shown in the following illustration. All geometry is removed from the screen, leaving only the Online Map visible. Leave the Map Base element toggled off for this exercise.

4. To create a new Display Map, click on Maps, and select New, as shown in the following illustration.

    - Enter **Parcel** for the name.
    - Click OK.

    Note: If the Map Base toggles back on, repeat Step 3.

5. Click Data>Add Drawing Data>Query Source Drawing, as shown in the following illustration.

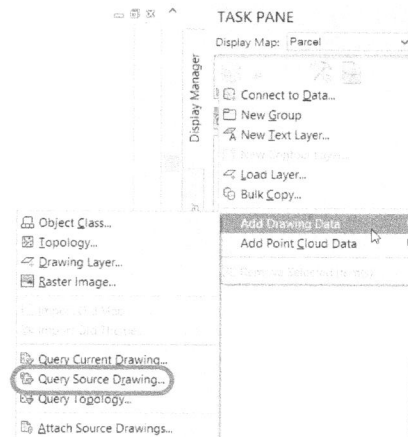

6. In the Define Query of Attached Drawing(s) dialog box, under Query Type, click Property, as shown in the following illustration.

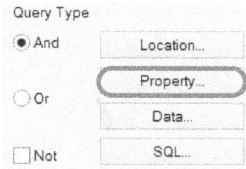

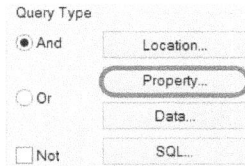

Query Type

- ● And — Location...
- ○ Or — Property... *(circled)*
- Data...
- □ Not — SQL...

7. In the Property Condition dialog box:
- Under Select Property, select Layer.
- Click Values.

8. In the Select dialog box:
- Select the PARK_POLYGONS and PARKS layers.
- Click OK.

9. Click OK to close the Property Condition dialog box, as shown in the following illustration.

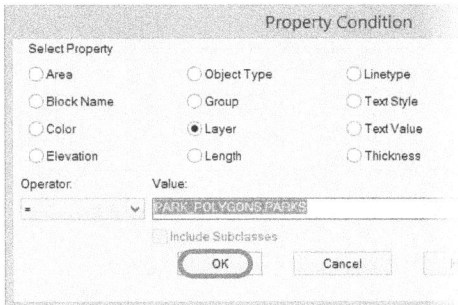

Property Condition

Select Property

- ○ Area — ○ Object Type — ○ Linetype
- ○ Block Name — ○ Group — ○ Text Style
- ○ Color — ● Layer — ○ Text Value
- ○ Elevation — ○ Length — ○ Thickness

Operator: = | Value: PARK_POLYGONS,PARKS

□ Include Subclasses

OK | Cancel

10. Click OK to close the Define Query of Attached Drawing(s) dialog box.

11. In the Display Manager:
- Right-click on the Attached Drawings Element.
- Click Rename.
- For the Layer name, enter **Parks**, as shown in the following illustration.

Parks
Map Base
Default

12. Click Data>Add Drawing Data>Query Source Drawing.

13. In the Define Query of Attached Drawing(s) dialog box, under Query Type, click Property, as shown in the following illustration.

Query Type

- ● And — Location...
- ○ Or — Property... *(circled)*
- Data...
- □ Not — SQL...

14. In the Property Condition dialog box:
- Under Select Property, select Layer.
- Click Values.

15. In the Select dialog box:
- Select the PARCELS layer.
- Click OK.

16. Click OK to close the Property Condition dialog box.

17. Click OK to close the Define Query of Attached Drawing(s) dialog box, as shown in the following illustration.

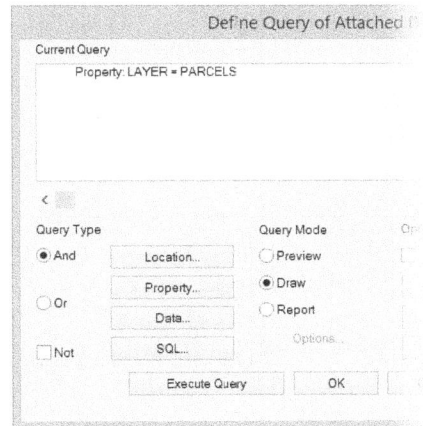

Define Query of Attached

Current Query

Property: LAYER = PARCELS

<

Query Type | Query Mode
- ● And — Location... — ○ Preview
- Property... — ● Draw
- ○ Or — Data... — ○ Report
- Options...
- □ Not — SQL...

Execute Query | OK

18. In the Display Manager:
- Right-click on the Attached Drawings Element.
- Click Rename.
- For name, enter **Parcels**.

19. Click Data>Add Drawing Data>Query Source Drawing.

20. In the Define Query of Attached Drawing(s) dialog box, under Query Type, click Property.

21. In the Property Condition dialog box:

- Under Select Property, select Layer.
- Click Values.

22. In the Select dialog box:

- Select the ROADS layer.
- Click OK.

23. Click OK to close the Property Condition dialog box.

24. Click OK to close the Define Query of Attached Drawing(s) dialog box.

25. In the Display Manager:

- Right-click on the Attached Drawings Element.
- Click Rename.
- For name, enter **Transportation**, as shown in the following illustration.

26. In the Display Manager:

- Click Data>New Group.
- Right-click on Untitled Group.
- Click Rename.
- For name, enter **Properties**.

27. Highlight the Parcels and Parks layers and drag them into the new Properties group, as shown in the following illustration.

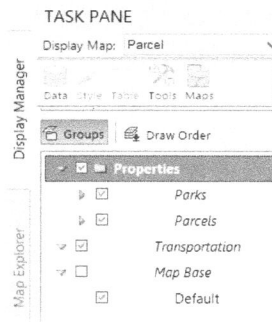

28. In Display Manager, drag the Transportation layer above the Properties group, as shown in the following illustration. Be careful not to drag it into the Properties group, but above it.

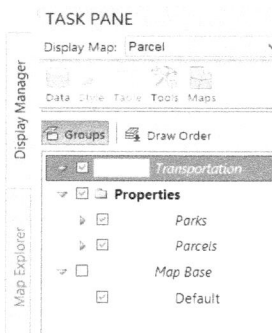

29. Save and close the drawing.

Note: You will receive a warning about the association of objects in the current and source drawings. This does not affect the map and is normal.

Exercise: Add Styles to Display Map Elements

You can apply styles to elements at any time. This exercise starts with several elements defined in a drawing, focusing on parks, roads, and parcels for the city of Redding. You will apply Entity, Hatch, and Text styles to produce a map that is attractive and that offers a concise display of data. Some elements require multiple styles, as shown in the following illustration.

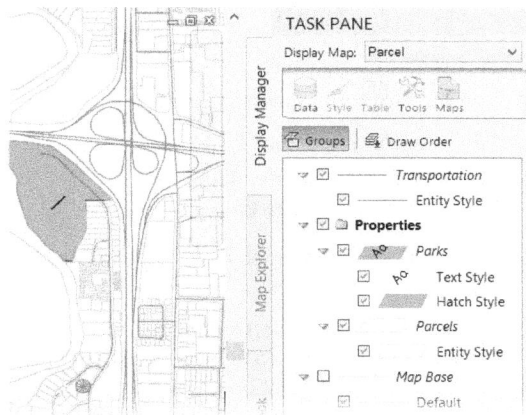

1. Continue working on the previous drawing or open ...\11-Stylizing\Creating Display Maps\ Redding-Maps2.dwg.

2. In Map Explorer:
   - Review the layers.
   - Confirm that the ...\Data\Source-DWG\ Parcel.dwg, Roads.dwg, and Parks.dwg files are attached and active.

3. In Display Manager, review the elements that have been defined, as shown in the following illustration.

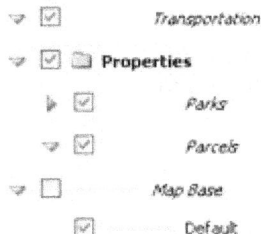

4. In Display Manager:
   - Click the Parks element to select it.
   - Click the triangle pointer to fully expand the Parks element, as shown in the following illustration.

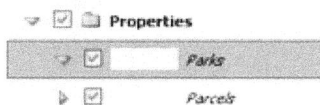

   - Right-click on the Parks layer.
   - Click Add Style>Hatch, as shown in the following illustration.

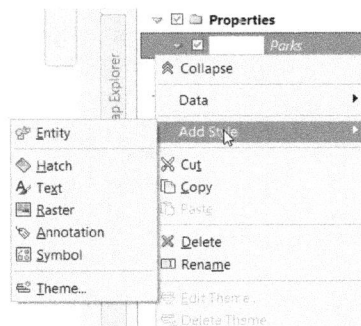

5. Under Parks, right-click on Hatch Style> Properties, as shown in the following illustration.

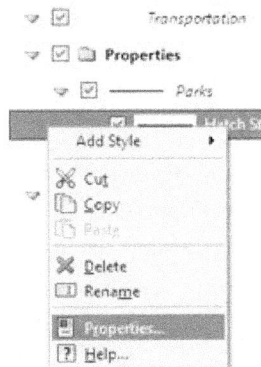

6. On the Display tab in the Properties palette, under Style Traits:

- For Pattern, leave as Solid.
- For Color, change the value to Green, as shown in the following illustration.

The new style properties display on the screen. Leave the Properties palette displayed for the next steps.

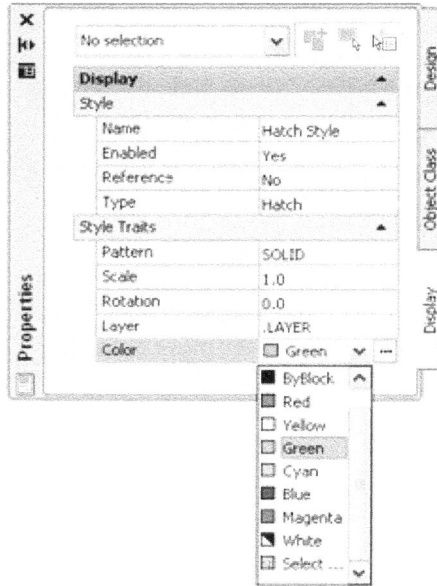

7. In the Display Manager, right-click on Parks> Add Style>Text.

8. Under Parks, right-click on Text style> Properties.

9. In the Properties palette, under Style Traits, for Value, click the Browse icon.

10. In the Expression Chooser dialog box:

- Expand to Object Data>PARKS.
- Select NAME, as shown in the following illustration.
- Click OK.

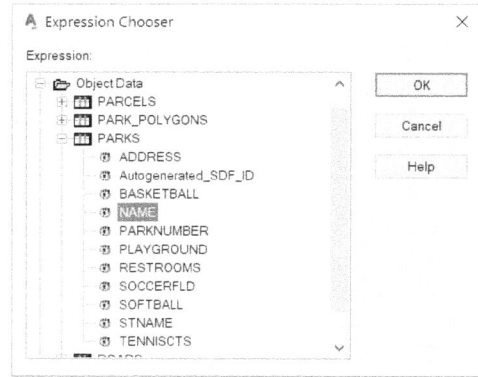

11. In the Properties palette, under Style Traits:

- For Height, enter **10**.
- For Rotation, enter **45**.
- For Color, choose White.

12. In the Display Manager, right-click on Parks> Properties.

13. In the Properties palette, change the Thumbnail Preview to Polygon, as shown in the following illustration.

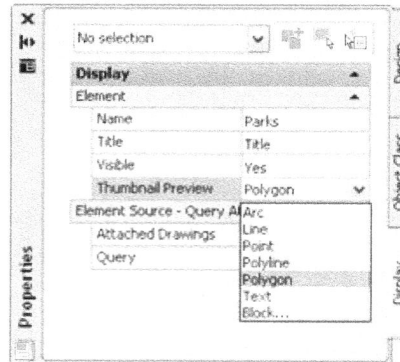

14. Right-click on Transportation>Add Style> Entity.

15. In the Display Manager, under Transportation, right-click on Entity style> Properties.

16. In the Properties palette:

- Under Style Traits, for Color, choose Red.
- Close the Properties Palette.

The display map should look as shown in the following illustration.

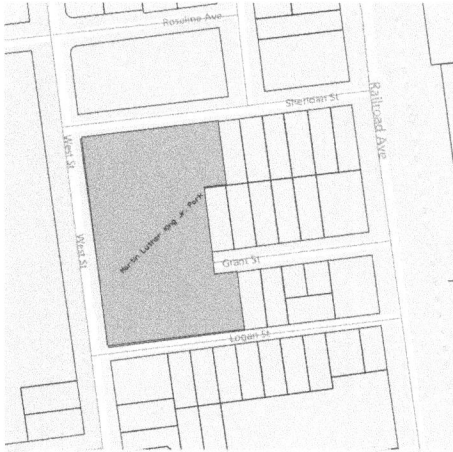

17. In the Display Manager:

- Right-click on the Parcels>Add Style> Entity.
- Right-click on Entity style>Properties.

18. In the Properties palette, for color, select Dark Gray, as shown in the following illustration.

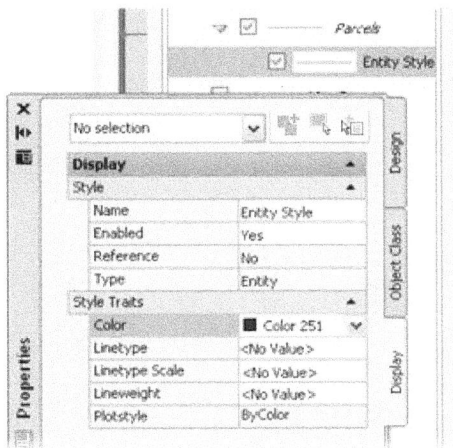

19. In Display Manager, right-click on Parcels> Properties.

20. In the Properties palette, change the Thumbnail Preview to Polygon.

21. In the Display Manager, right-click beneath the layer list>Update. The view should update as shown in the following illustration.

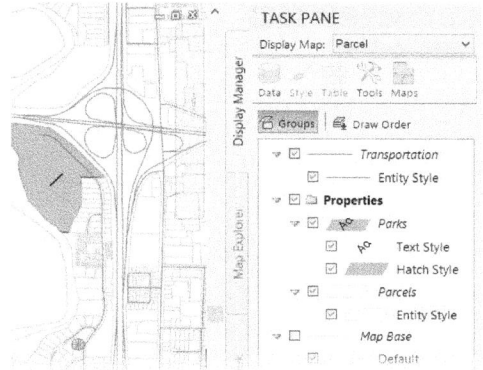

22. Save and close the drawing.

Note: You will receive a warning about the association of objects in the current and source drawings. This does not affect the map and is normal.

Lesson: Stylizing FDO Features

Overview

In this lesson, you learn how to stylize features, as shown in the following illustration. Features are objects stored in external files and databases. You can display and edit them in your map and then save the changes back to the original source.

Objectives

After completing this lesson, you will be able to:

- Describe feature stylization.
- Describe the available feature styles.
- Apply styles to features.

About Feature Stylization

Feature stylization determines the graphical representation of connected feature sources. When you connect a feature source and add it as a layer in Display Manager, you can stylize the layer, as shown in the following illustration.

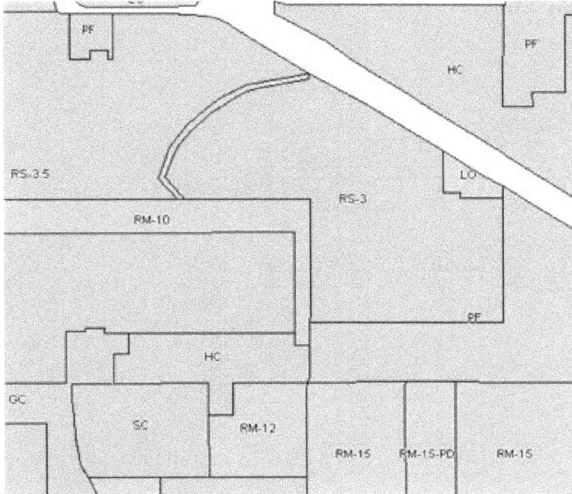

Feature Stylization

You stylize features through Display Manager. Scale Ranges, Labels, and Styles can be modified in the Display Manager. The Style dialog box contains cartographic tools, such as area and symbol styles. New styles can stack symbols, giving you the flexibility of cartographic stylization, as shown in the following illustration.

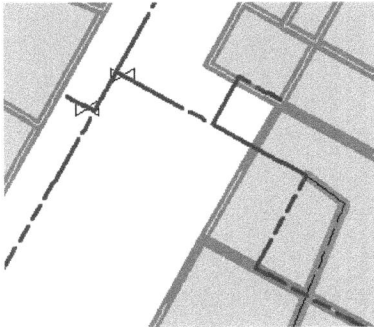

Scale Ranges

You can specify the scale ranges at which a feature is visible, set the line color, and add labels. To specify styles for a layer, you define a style for a scale range. The default scale range is 0-infinity. As you define the styles for how data should display at various scales, you can add narrower scale ranges. For example, you can create one scale range that displays roads with detailed theming when you zoom in, and create a second scale range that displays roads as simple lines when you zoom out, as shown in the following illustration.

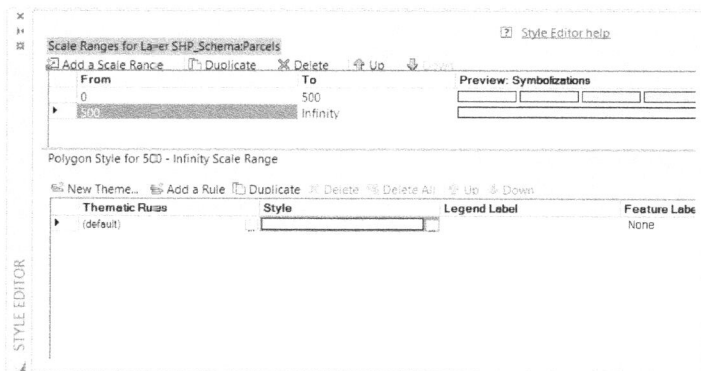

Labels

You can use various scales and any feature property for labels. Most features have attribute information that you can use as a label, as shown in the following illustration. For example, a Roads.sdf file might have its street name stored in a column called ST_NAME.

When creating dynamic labels using the Style Editor, you can edit individual labels by double-clicking on them and selecting the edit converted text in the toolbar, as shown in the following illustration.

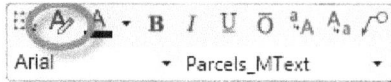

Alternatively, you can convert all of the labels, or only those in the current view to annotative text or Mtext. Once a label has been edited, a new layer is created in the Display Manager to show the edits. Alternatively, MText can be turned into FDO text so that it can be kept in an external database or data store.

This is done in the Annotate tab, under the Map Annotation panel. Select Label to Text or Mtext to Text layer and use the Mtext to Text Layer command. The Create Text Layer dialog box, as shown in the following illustration, opens containing various options, such as selecting the source text and selecting the destination file.

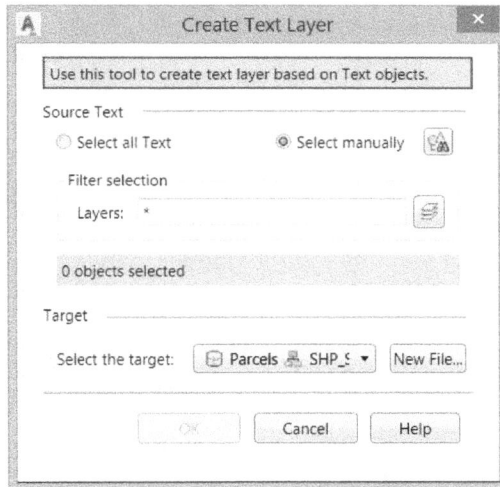

Themes

You can style a feature source layer by applying a theme based on any of the columns in the feature data. For example, the *Parcels.sdf* file can be thematically colored based on the property value, as shown in the following illustration.

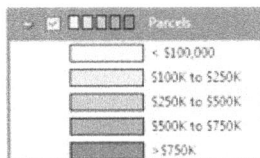

Example of Feature Stylization

A municipal planner might want to view a map in which areas are color-coded, based on zoning designations, as shown in the following illustration. The planner would connect directly to Zoning.shp as a feature source using the FDO provider for SHP.

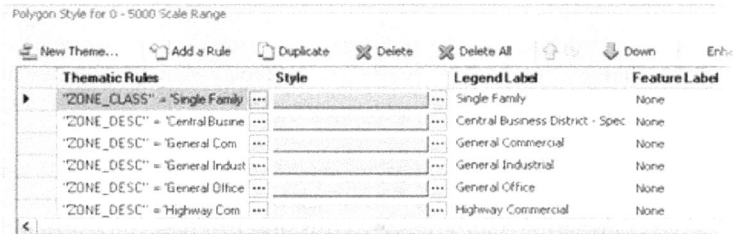

From the Display Manager, the planner would then use the Style dialog box to apply a theme based on zoning designations to the area, as shown in the following illustration.

Available Feature Styles

You can apply feature styles to almost all of the available feature sources. Stylization is inherent in some data sources, such as OpenGIS WMS (raster) and DWF™ features.

Feature data objects can be stylized in the following ways:

- Polygon styles
- Line styles
- Point styles
- Raster 2D
- Raster 3D

Stylizing Polygonal Areas

Using the Style Polygon dialog box, you can style areas with a fill style and color and a background color. You can specify the edge line style, color, and thickness, as shown in the following illustration. For a solid, filled polygon, you can set the foreground transparency and color. However, if you want a pattern fill, you can set the colors for both the foreground and background by adding multiple fills. The edge or border of the polygon can be set by choosing the linetype, thickness, and color. You can also set multiple borders as shown in the following illustration.

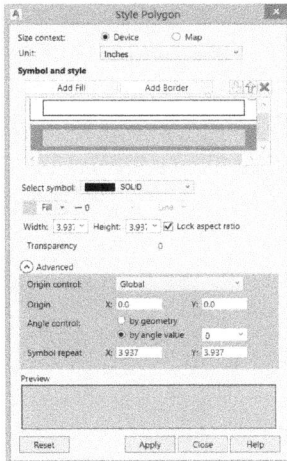

Stylizing Lines

You can style line features by adjusting thickness, color, and pattern. You can style each line as a single line or combine several line styles to create a new composite line style. For example, to create a highway style, place a thick black line under a thin, dashed, yellow line, as shown in the following illustration.

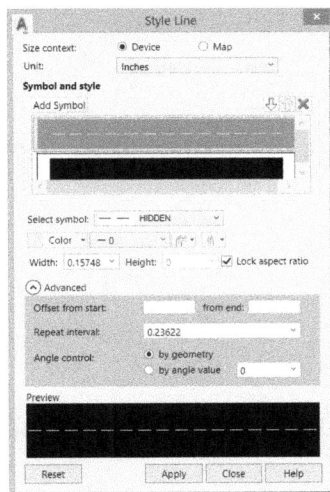

Stylizing Points

You can use symbols to stylize point features to represent and display the points, as shown in the following illustration. A number of predefined symbols are part of this style. The Symbol browse button enables you to browse through the AutoCAD® DWGs that can be used as symbols.

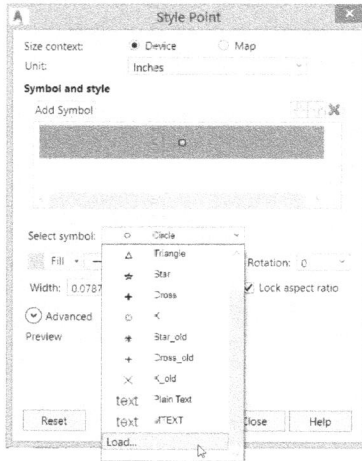

Define Symbols

You can use any AutoCAD linework to create symbols for use in stylizing drawings. Symbols can be edited directly with AutoCAD's Block Editor and shared easily between drawings. To define a symbol, open a drawing that contains the objects you want to use for the symbol. On the Create ribbon, select Create Symbol from the Symbol panel. A dialog box opens, similar to creating blocks as shown in the following illustration. Enter a name for the symbol, select the objects to include, set the base point, and click OK. The symbol is then ready to use in a point style as required.

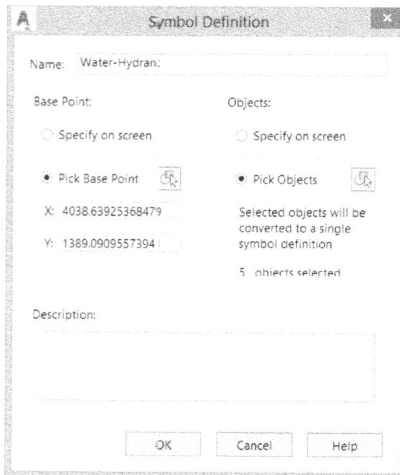

Exercise: Stylize FDO Features

In this exercise, you will connect to the Hydrants.sdf, Roads.sdf, and Parcels.sdf feature sources. Hydrants, a point layer, will be styled using a DWG Block of a fire hydrant. Roads, a line layer, will be stylized with simple line colors. Parcels, a polygon layer, will be stylized based on its land value, as shown in the following illustration.

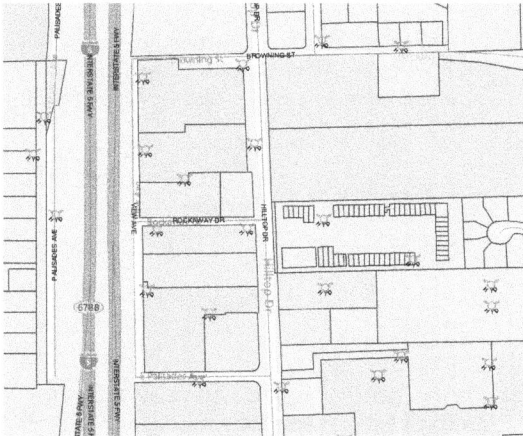

1. Open ...\11-Stylizing\Stylizing Features\Symbols.dwg.

2. On the Create tab>Symbol panel, click Create Symbol, as shown in the following illustration.

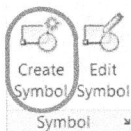

3. In the Symbol Definition dialog box:

   - Enter **Water-Hydrant** for the name.
   - Click Pick Objects and select the symbol at the bottom left of the drawing, as shown in the following illustration.
   - Specify the Base Point at the center of the circle.
   - Click OK.

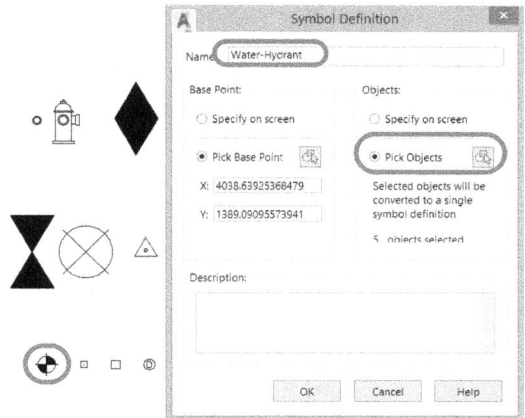

4. Close the block editor and the Symbols.dwg saving both on exit.

5. Open ...\11-Stylizing\Stylizing Features\ Redding-Style.dwg.

6. Verify that the Display Manager tab is selected in the Task Pane, as shown in the following illustration.

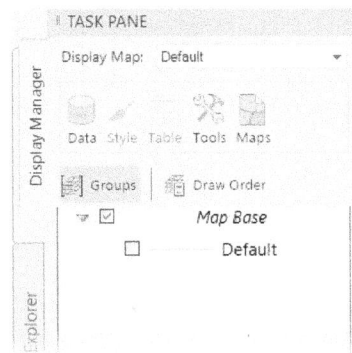

7. Using Windows Explorer, browse to ...\Data\SDF.

- Drag and drop Roads.sdf, Hydrants.sdf, and the Parcels.sdf into the Display Manager, as shown in the following illustration.

8. In the Display Manager, click Draw Order.

9. Drag the Roads layer above the Parcels layer and the Hydrants layer above the Roads layer, as shown in the following illustration.

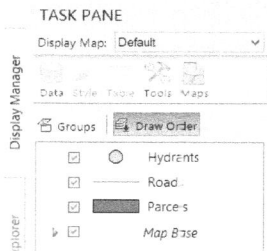

10. In the Display Manager:

- Select the Hydrants layer, as shown in the following illustration.
- Click Style.

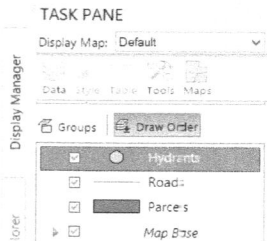

11. In the Style Editor pane:

- Under Scale Ranges for Layer Schema:Hydrants, for the To scale, enter **5000**, as shown in the following illustration.

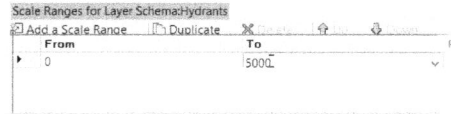

12. In the Style Editor pane, under Point Style for 0-5000 Scale Range, click the Style browse button, as shown in the following illustration.

13. In the Style Point dialog box, click the down arrow next to the Select symbol option, select Load..., as shown in the following illustration.

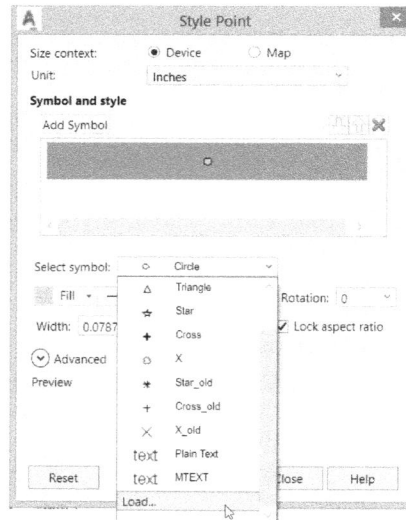

14. In the Select a Symbol dialog box, click Import. Browse to ...\11-Stylizing\Stylizing Features\Symbols-1.dwg. Click Open.

15. In the Select a Symbol dialog box:

- Select the WATER-HYDRANT symbol, as shown in the following illustration.
- Click Load.

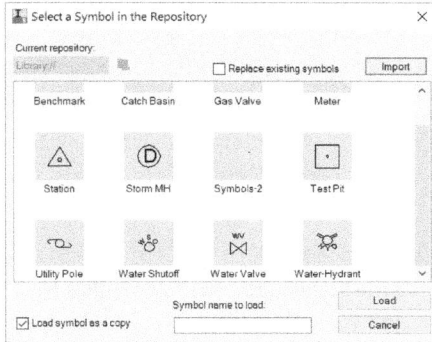

16. In the Style Point dialog box:

- For Units, select Inches.
- For Width, enter **0.2**, as shown in the following illustration.
- For Fill Color, select Use Default.
- For the Lineweight, select 0.
- For Edge Color, select red (255,0,0).
- Click Apply then Close.

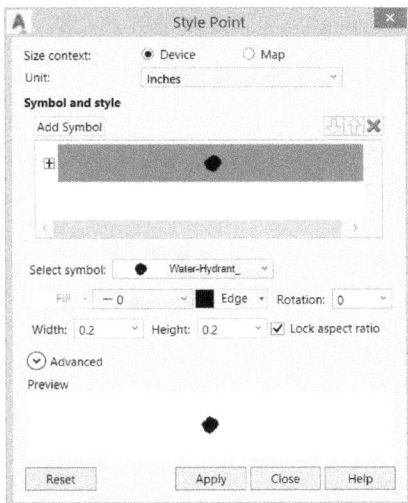

17. With the Style Editor pane still open, in the Display Manager, highlight the Roads layer.

18. In the Style Editor pane, under Scale Ranges, for the To range, enter **10000**, as shown in the following illustration.

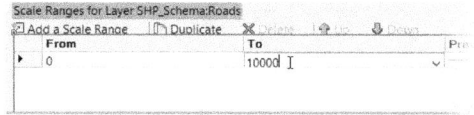

19. Under Line Style for 0-10000 Scale Range, under Style, click Browse, as shown in the following illustration.

20. In the Style Line dialog box:

- Change the color to red (255,0,0), as shown in the following illustration.
- Click Apply, then click Close.

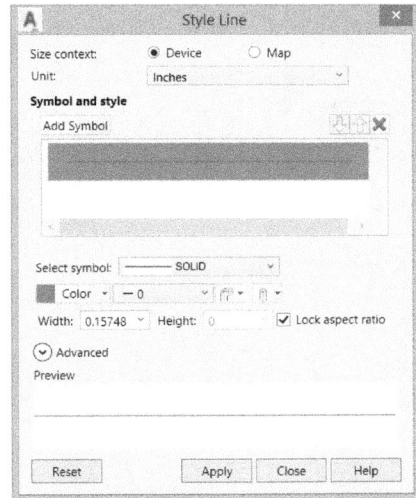

21. In the Style Editor pane, under Line Style for 0-10000 Scale Range, under Feature Label, click Browse, as shown in the following illustration.

Line Style for 0 - 10000 Scale Range

Thematic Rules	Style	Legend Label	Feature Label
(default)			None

22. In the Style Label dialog box:

- Click Add Label.
- For Text content, select ST_NAME.
- For Font, select Arial.
- For Units, select Inches.
- For Size, select 0.09.
- For Vertical Alignment, select Halfline, as shown in the following illustration.
- Click Apply, then click Close.

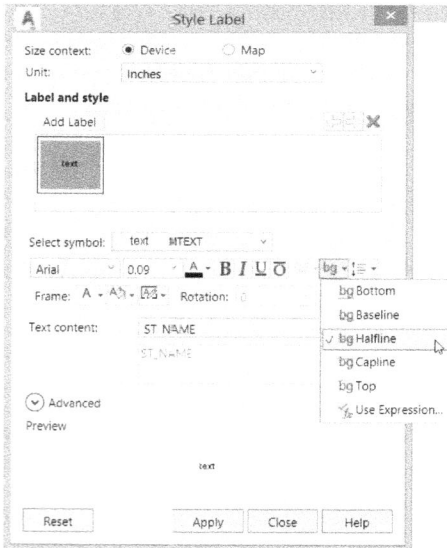

23. While the Style Editor pane is still open, highlight the Parcels in the Display Manager, as shown in the following illustration. If the Style Editor window is closed, click Style.

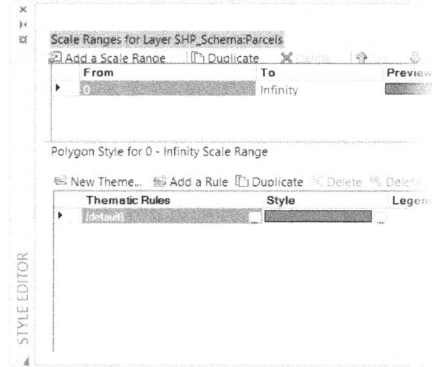

Scale Ranges for Layer SHP_Schema:Parcels

From	To	Preview
0	Infinity	

Polygon Style for 0 - Infinity Scale Range

Thematic Rules	Style	Legend
(default)		

24. In the Style Editor dialog box, click New Theme.

25. In the Theme Polygons dialog box:

- For Property, select LAND_VALUE.
- For Distribution, select Standard Deviation.
- Under Number of Rules, enter **5**, as shown in the following illustration.
- Next to Style range, click Browse.

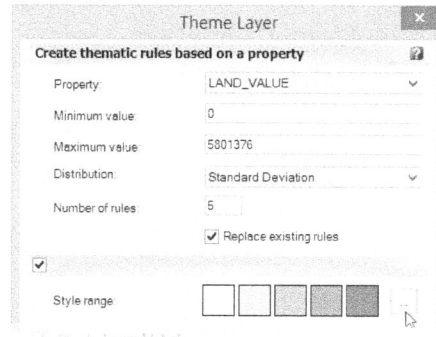

26. In the Style and Label Editor dialog box:

- For the Foreground color range, for the From color, choose more colors and select a light green (228,252,230).

- For the Foreground color range, for the To color, choose more colors and select a light red (254,206,205), as shown in the following illustration.

- Click OK.

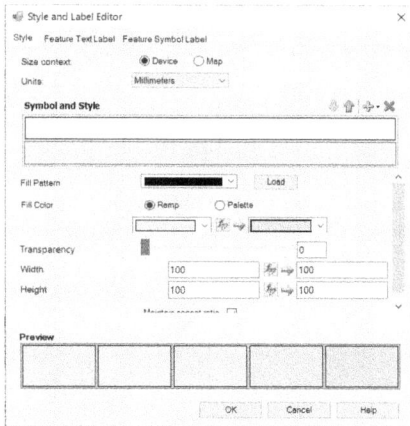

27. In the Theme Polygons dialog box, click OK, as shown in the following illustration.

28. Close the Style Editor pane.

29. Zoom in and out to see how your map changes depending on scale, as shown in the following illustration.

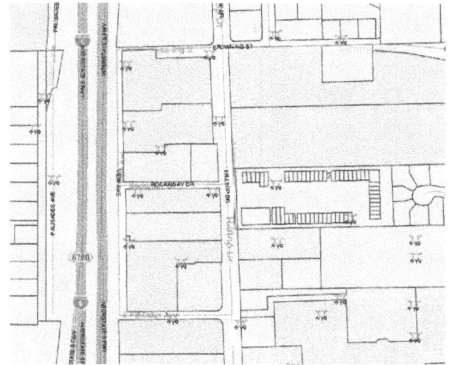

30. Save and close the drawing.

Exercise: Move Text Between a Drawing and an FDO Data Store

In this exercise, you will modify FDO labels by turning them into text. You will also take MText and turn it into an FDO layer, as shown in the following illustration.

1. Open ...\11-Stylizing\Text to FDO\ Redding-TXT-DFO.dwg.

2. Verify that the Display Manager tab is selected in the Task Pane, as shown in the following illustration.

3. On the View tab>Views panel, select the Modify-Text named view, as shown in the following illustration.

4. On the Home tab, under Online Map, turn the Online Map to Off.

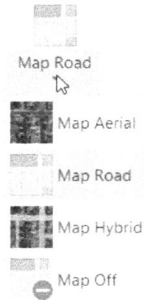

5. On the Annotate tab>Map Annotation panel, click Label to Text, as shown in the following illustration.

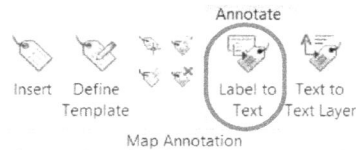

6. In the Convert Labels to Text dialog box:

   - For the feature layer, select Roads.
   - For the Selection scope, select Labels in the view window, as shown in the following illustration.
   - Leave all other settings set to the default.
   - Click OK.

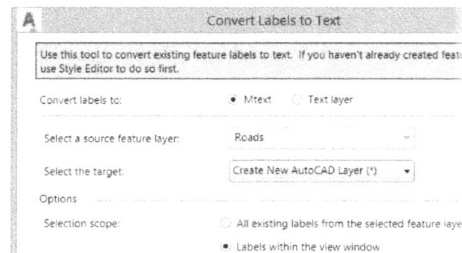

7. Note the new Roads_MText layer in the Display Manager.

---

8. Pan to another part of the drawing and note that the streets are no longer labeled outside the Modify-Text named view.

9. Return to the Modify-Text named view and double-click on one of the street labels. Note that it is now a multiline text object, which can be modified independent of all other street labels.

10. On the View tab>Views panel, select the APN-Labels named view, as shown in the following illustration.

11. On the Annotate tab>Map Annotation panel, select Mtext to Text Layer, as shown in the following illustration.

12. In the Create Text Layer dialog box:
    - For the Source text, choose Select all Text.
    - In the Filter selection, select the Parcels_MText layer.
    - For the Target, click New File….
    - Set the file format to .SDF.
    - Select the \Data\SDF folder.
    - Type PARCEL-LABEL for the File name.
    - Click Save.
    - Click OK to close the Create Text Layer dialog box.

13. Note the new Annotation layer in the Display Manager and the double labels in the view for the Parcel APNs.

14. Save and close the drawing.

Chapter Summary

Having completed this chapter, you can:

- Stylize drawing objects.
- Stylize features.
- Move text between the drawing and an FDO layer.

Plotting Maps

The final step in map creation is plotting the map. You can plot one sheet at a time or create a Map Book or atlas, which is a collection of maps of an area such as a city, as a series of contiguous sheets or pages. The AutoCAD® Map 3D software automates this process and provides the tools for generating Map Books easily.

Objectives

After completing this chapter, you will be able to:

- Prepare a layout sheet for review.
- Create a set of maps for a Map Book.

Lesson: Prepare a Layout Sheet for Review

Overview

In this lesson, you learn to set up a sheet for printing. When working with specific data sets, you might need to show it in various ways. For instance, you might need to show parcel information according to population on one sheet while showing it by land value on another sheet. Using multiple display maps helps you to accomplish this.

The following illustration shows a sheet layout with a north arrow and scale bar associated with the viewport of a display map.

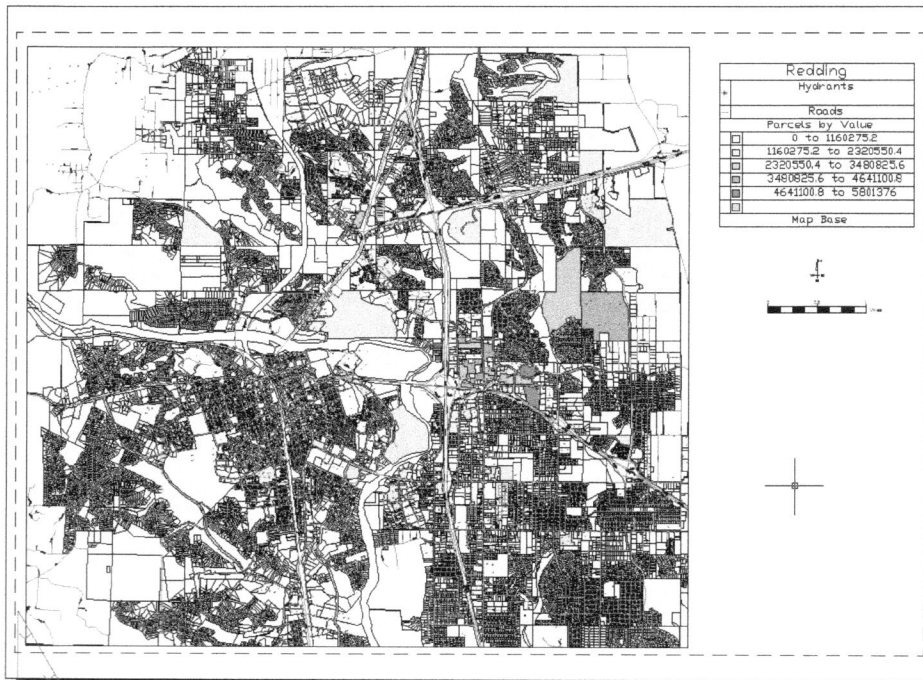

Objectives

After completing this lesson, you will be able to:

- Associate a display map to a viewport.
- Add a legend for the viewport.
- Add a dynamic scale bar.
- Add a dynamic north arrow.

About Display Maps

You can stylize maps using display maps. Multiple display maps can be created from information in a single drawing. Layers can be themed according to the data or scale at which they are being viewed. Once the required display maps have been created, they can be added to a layout for printing purposes.

Layouts

In the layouts, a display map can be assigned to a viewport and use its own background color. It can also be styled differently in each viewport with which it is associated. Templates can be used to create standards with the same layouts and display maps used multiple times. Therefore, the AutoCAD Map 3D software automatically looks for the data associated with a display map when creating a new drawing file. This saves time when setting up layouts and reusing frequently used data.

Process: Displaying Display Maps in Layouts

1. Create the display map or open a drawing in which one has already been created.

2. Switch to Paper Space.

3. Set up the sheet using the Sheet Manager.

4. On the Layout Tools tab, under the Viewports panel, select the type of viewport you want to create.

5. Draw the viewport in Paper Space. The current Model Space map displays in the new viewport.

6. Change the display map that displays by selecting the viewport in Paper Space. On the Layout Tools tab, under the Map Viewports panel, select Display Maps drop-down. Select the correct Display Map.

Legends

A legend helps viewers of the map understand what its symbols and colors represent. Each display map shown on a sheet layout should be accompanied by a legend. This process is automated for you. To add a legend, go to the Layout Tools tab. Under the Layout Elements panel, select Legend, as shown in the following illustration. The AutoCAD Map 3D software prompts you to select the viewport with which to associate the legend. Select an insertion point for the top left corner of the legend.

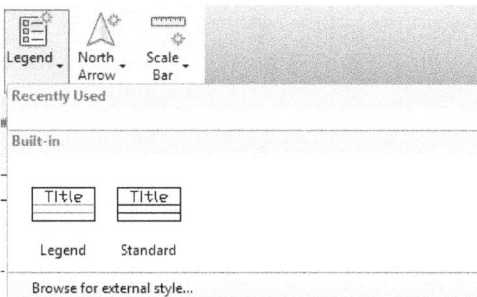

Dynamic Scale Bars

Scale bars help viewers of the map know how many units on the sheet represent a specified distance in the map. Any AutoCAD block can be used as a scale bar, but it is best to use a dynamic block so that as the map scale changes, the scale bar can dynamically change as well. A number of predefined scale bars are included with the software, as shown in the following illustration.

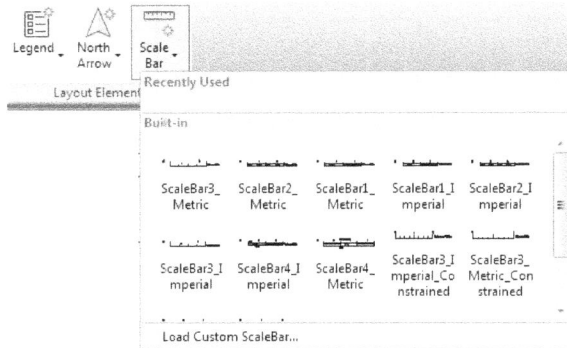

North Arrows

North arrows in a map help users to orient the map to the real world. Any AutoCAD block can be used as a north arrow, but a number of arrows are included with the software, as shown in the following illustration. Once added, the rotation of the map can be defined by rotating the north arrow in Paper Space.

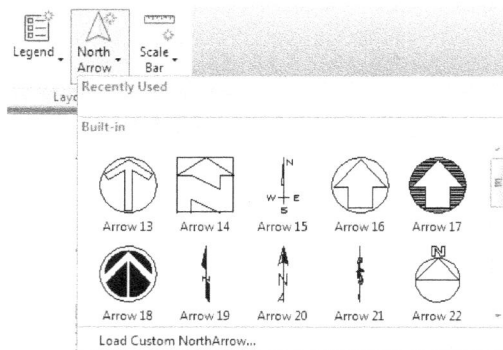

Exercise: Create a Layout for a Display Map

In this exercise, you will create a layout for a display map that has already been created. Then you will add a legend, north arrow, and scale bar. Finally, you will set the orientation of the map by rotating the north arrow. The following illustration shows the finished layout.

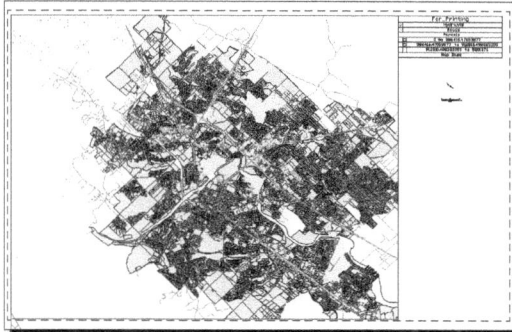

1. Open ...\12-Plotting Maps\Printing Display Maps\Redding-Display.dwg. The drawing contains a display map for the city of Redding and two layouts.

2. In the Display Manager, Ensure that Display Map: For_Printing is selected. Ensure that the following layers are connected and properly styled, as shown in the following illustration.

   ▪ Hydrants
   ▪ Roads
   ▪ Parcels

3. Switch to the DisplayMap Layout:

   ▪ Click the DisplayMap layout tab.
   ▪ Select the viewport rectangle on the page.
   ▪ Press <Delete>.
   ▪ Right-click on DisplayMap and select Page Setup Manager, as shown in the following illustration.

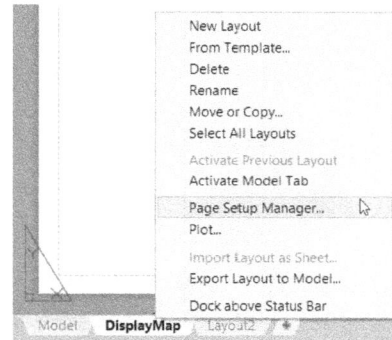

4. In the Page Setup Manager dialog box, click Modify.

5. In the Page Setup - DisplayMap dialog box:

   ▪ Under Printer/Plotter, for Name, select the DWF6 ePlot.pc3 plotter.

6. In the Page Setup - DisplayMap dialog box:

   ▪ Under Paper Size, select ARCH D (36.00 x 24.00 Inches), as shown in the following illustration.
   ▪ Click OK.
   ▪ Click Close.

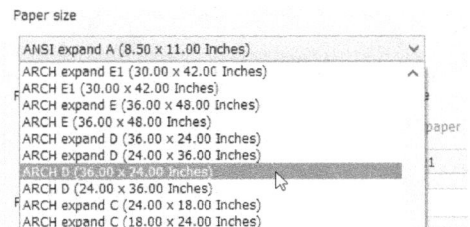

7. On the Layout Tools tab, under the Viewports panel, select Rectangular.

- Draw a viewport, as shown in the following illustration.

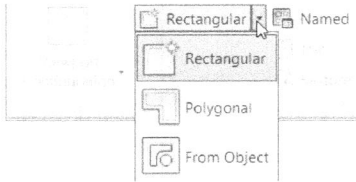

8. Select the Viewport you just drew:

- On the Layout Tools tab, under the Map Viewport panel, select Display Maps.
- Ensure that it is set to For_Printing, as shown in the following illustration.

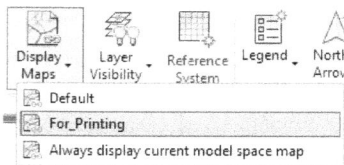

9. Select the Viewport you just drew again:

- On the Layout Tools tab, under the Layout Elements panel, click Legend>Standard.
- Place the legend to the right of the viewport, as shown in the following illustration.

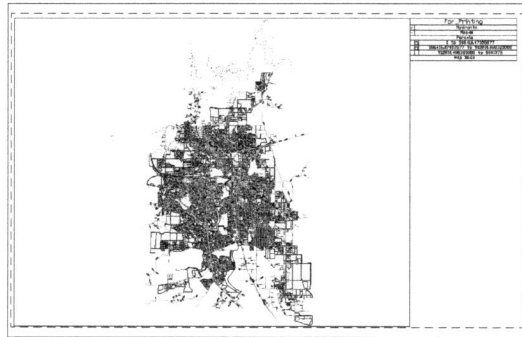

10. Select the Viewport you just drew again:

- Under the Layout Elements panel, select North Arrow>Arrow19.
- Place the arrow to the right of the viewport, just under the legend, as shown in the following illustration.

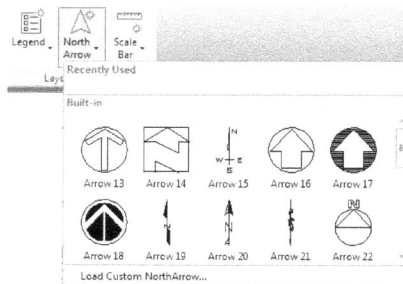

For_Printing
Hydrants
Roads
Parcels
0 to 386416.47053877
386416.47053877 to 912810.498325055
912810.498325055 to 5801376
Map Base

11. Select the Viewport you just drew again:

- Under the Layout Elements panel, select Scale Bar>ScaleBar4_Imperial, as shown in the following illustration.

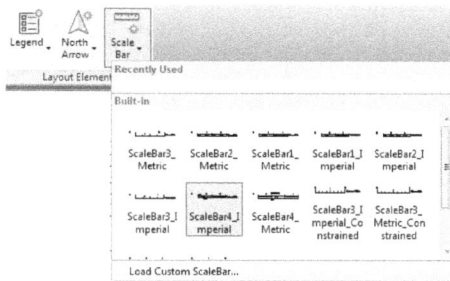

12. For the Scale Bar Properties:

- Set the units to Miles.
- Enter **.25** in the Scale bar division.
- Set the Scale ratio to 1:25000, as shown in the following illustration.
- Click OK.

13. Place the scale bar to the right of the viewport and below the north arrow, as shown in the following illustration.

- Note that the viewport scale changed as you placed the scale bar.

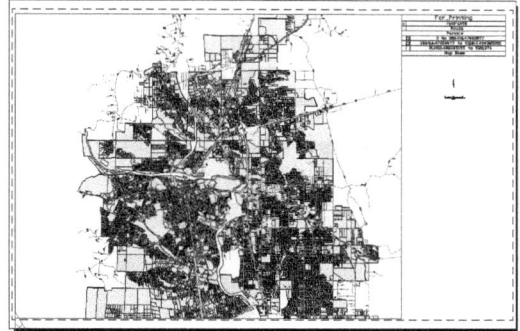

14. Select the north arrow, select the circular grip and rotate it 45 degrees, as shown in the following illustration.

- Note that the viewport rotation changed as you rotated the north arrow.

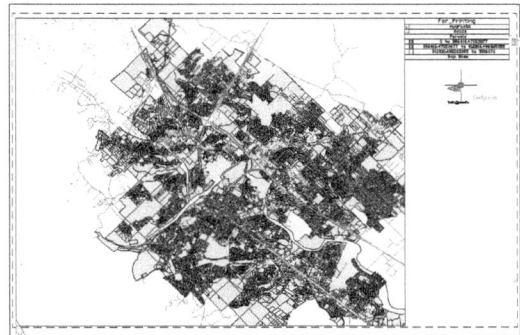

15. Save and close the drawing.

Lesson: Map Books

Overview

In this lesson, you learn to use Map Books to generate sets of sheets. When working with a map of a town or city, you often need to generate a set of sheets that covers the entire geographic area, with each sheet displaying a specific region. Typically, the individual sheets use the same scale and together form a tiled grid.

The following illustration shows the city of Redding laid out in a grid in which each area represents a sheet in a Map Book set.

Objectives

After completing this lesson, you will be able to:

- Describe what Map Books are, what they are used for, and what you need to generate them.
- Create a template for Map Books.
- Generate a Map Book.

About Map Books

A Map Book is a series of tiled layouts that are based on either the model space contents of a drawing or Map displays. One great benefit of using Map Books is that you can generate revised versions of the Map Book with extraordinary ease to reflect changes.

You save individual sheets in a Map Book as layouts in a drawing and reference them as sheet sets. Map Books can be published to either a multi-document DWF file or a plotter for hard copies.

To generate a Map Book from a specific drawing, you need a template created specifically for the task. The template is referenced by Map Book to create the layout of the sheets. Based on the main viewport established in the template, a grid for tiling the sheets in the drawing must be created. The template can be reused for various Map Books, but the grid is specific to an individual Map Book. The grid can be an entire set of rectangles with object data that was created in the AutoCAD Map 3D software attached to them that drives the naming of the sheets, or it can simply be a starting point that the AutoCAD Map 3D software uses to generate an automatically named grid of tiles.

The Map Book dialog box outlines a sequence of steps and settings for generating a Map Book. It is not a multidialog wizard, but rather a single dialog box with a navigation panel on the left side and details of each step on the right.

The following illustration shows the options for publishing a completed Map Book:

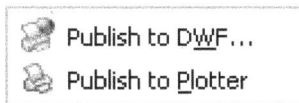

Requirements

The following is a list of the requirements for, and some key points about, generating a Map Book:

- A template in the AutoCAD software must be prepared and defined in the AutoCAD Map 3D software specifically for the purpose of generating Map Books. The template typically contains a layout with a title block, adjacent drawing navigation blocks, and main, key view, and legend viewports.
- A separate template is required for each layout design that uses a different size of sheet or another scale.
- For the drawing on which the Map Book is based, you must either create a grid or establish a starting point that matches the size of the main viewport in the template.
- The By Number tiling scheme with a 0% overlap of each tile is the safest choice. It actually reads the size of the main viewport in the template and multiplies by the scale factor set in the sheet template settings to set the grid sizes for the Map Book sheets. The only drawback in its use is that you cannot use a data-driven naming scheme.
- The percentage of overlap set under tiling scheme settings can produce viewports on the Map Book sheets that are not set to the scale factor specified in the sheet template settings.
- The By Area tiling scheme can also produce viewports on the Map Book sheets that are not set to the scale factor specified in the sheet template settings. If using By Area, be sure to specify an area size that matches the main viewport size in the template multiplied by the required scale factor.

- Using a Custom tiling scheme enables the use of a nonrectangular array of sheets and of a data-driven naming scheme. However, be sure the rectangles created in the drawing for selection are the correct size, based on the main viewport size in the template and the required scale factor. The viewport's themes still need to be rectangular as well.

- Grids and Graticules can be added to drawings for ease in labeling the map according to a defined coordinate system. There are four types of coordinate systems available for use: Latitude-Longitude, Military Grid Reference System, United States National Grid, and Current map coordinate system.

Example

Precise control of the viewport scaling on the generated Map Book sheets starts with the template, specifically the size of the main viewport. You choose a 10" x 10" square and in Map Book generation you set the scale factor to 100. If you want a regular tiled grid and choose to have the AutoCAD Map 3D software name the grids for you, either use a By Number tiling scheme (the AutoCAD Map 3D software creates correctly sized grids for you), or a By Area tiling scheme with an area divisible by 1000 in both directions. If you want an irregularly laid out grid, and/or want to specify the naming of the individual sheets, use a Custom tiling scheme but be sure the rectangles you create are 1000' x 1000' in size. In all cases, a 0% overlap is recommended.

Exercise: Create a Template for Map Books

In this exercise, a template file (* .DWT) in the AutoCAD software is created for Map Books. If you want to skip the creation of the template, go to the exercise Generate a Map Book, and use the Finished Map Book Template. The following illustration shows the finished template, ready to use to generate a Map Book.

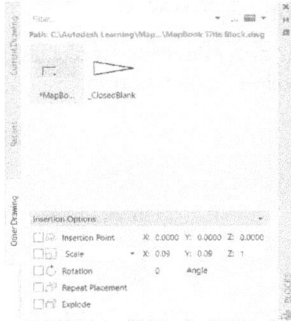

1. Create a new drawing using the default template.

2. In the Modelspace:
   - Right-click on Layout1>Rename.
   - Enter **MapBook**.
   - Right-click on Layout2>Delete, as shown in the following illustration.
   - Click OK.

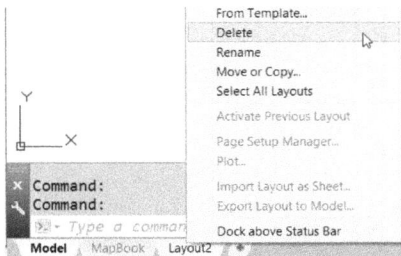

3. In the Modelspace:
   - Click the MapBook layout tab.
   - Click the viewport rectangle on the page.
   - Press <Delete>.
   - Right-click on Mapbook>Page Setup Manager, as shown in the following illustration.

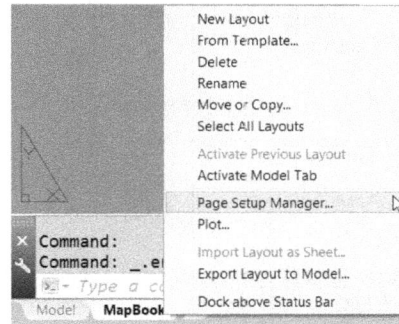

4. In the Page Setup Manager dialog box, click Modify.

5. In the Page Setup - Mapbook dialog box:
   - Under Printer/Plotter, for Name, select the DWF6 ePlot.pc3 plotter.
   - Click Properties.

6. In the Plotter Configuration Editor dialog box:
   - Under DWF6 ePlot pc3, select Custom Properties
   - Click Custom Properties, as shown in the following illustration.

7. In the DWF6 ePlot Properties dialog box:

- For Gradient Resolution, select 1200 dpi, as shown in the following illustration.
- Click OK.

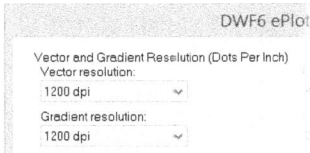

8. In the Plotter Configuration Editor dialog box, click OK.

9. In the Changes to a Printer Configuration File dialog box, click OK.

10. In the Page Setup - MapBook dialog box:

- Under Paper Size, select ARCH D (36.00 x 24.00 Inches), as shown in the following illustration.
- Click OK.

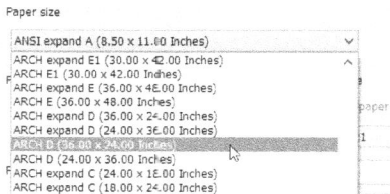

11. In the Page Setup Manager dialog box, click Close, as shown in the following illustration.

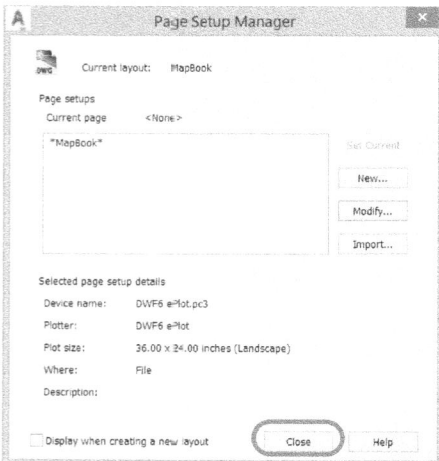

12. Click Save.

13. In the Save Drawing As dialog box:

- Change Files of Type to AutoCAD Drawing Template (*.DWT).
- Browse to ...\12-Plotting Maps\Map Books.
- For File Name, enter **Map Book Template**.
- Click Save.

14. In the Template Options dialog box:

- For Description, enter **For Map Books**, as shown in the following illustration.
- Click OK.

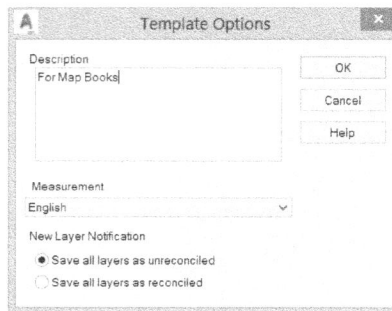

15. On the Insert tab, in the Block panel, click Insert, as shown in the following illustration.

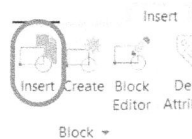

16. In the Blocks dialog box, Other Drawing tab:

- Click on the Ellipsis to browse to ...\12-Plotting Maps\Map Books\MapBook Title Block.dwg.
- Click on Open to insert the drawing.
- On the Insertion Options portion, clear all check boxes.
- Clear the Explode check box.
- For Scale, for X, enter **0.09**.
- For Scale, for Y, enter **0.09**.
- Click OK.

This will insert the title block unexploded, with an insertion point of 0,0,0, and a rotation angle of 0.

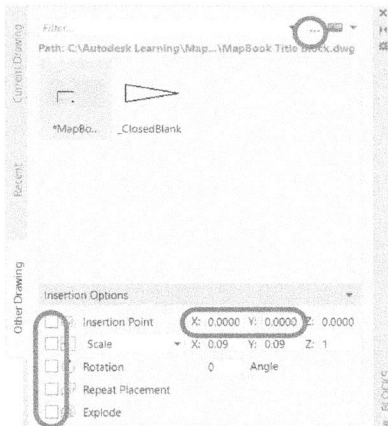

17. At the command line, to create a new viewport, enter **MV**.

- Snap to the corners of the rectangle inside the arrows to create a viewport that is exactly within the existing rectangle (which is exactly 18" x 14").
- To create another smaller viewport on the right side of the sheet, enter **MV**, as shown in the following illustration.

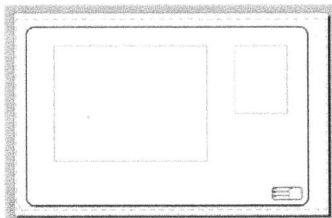

18. Select the first viewport (18" x 14"). On the Layout Tools tab, in the Map Viewports panel, click Reference System, as shown in the following illustration.

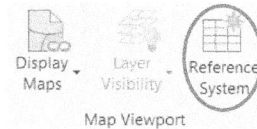

19. In the Create Reference System dialog box:

- Select Latitude-Longitude for the template.
- Set the Scale to 1000.
- Set the Precision at 0.1 Degree, as shown in the following illustration.
- Click OK.

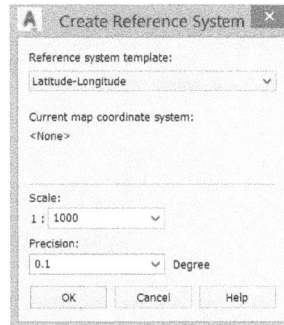

20. Click the Map Book tab of the Task Pane.

21. Click Tools>Identify Template Placeholders, as shown in the following illustration.

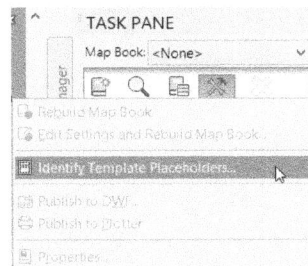

22. In the Identify Map Book Template Placeholders dialog box:

- Select Main Viewport and click Select Placeholder(s).
- Select the large viewport.
- Select Keyview Viewport and click Select Placeholder(s).
- Select the small viewport.
- Select Title Block and click Select Placeholder(s).
- Select the title block, as shown in the following illustration.
- Click Close.

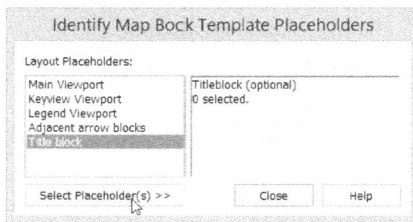

23. Click Save.

24. Close the drawing.

Exercise: Generate a Map Book

In this exercise, you will generate a Map Book. A template and a drawing containing a grid are already in place for you to choose.

The following illustration shows one completed sheet in the Map Book set with the two viewports:

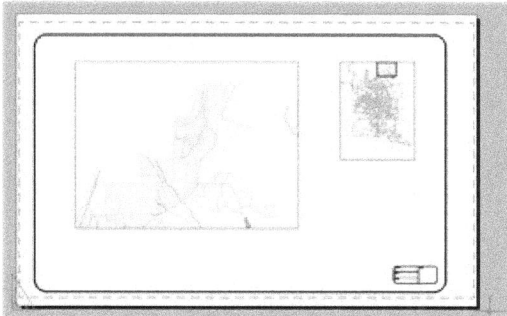

1. Open ...\12-Plotting Maps\Map Books\Map Book.dwg.

   The drawing contains a starting point for a grid of rectangles that are 18,000' wide by 14,000' high. It is designed to coincide with the Main viewport in Map Book Template.dwt that is 18" x 14", so that the individual Map Book sheets will display at a scale of 1" = 1,000'.

2. On the Map Book tab of the Task Pane, under New, select Map Book, as shown in the following illustration.

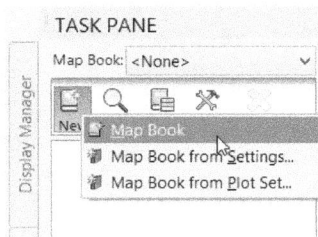

3. In the Create Map Book dialog box:
   - Under Source, select Model Space.
   - Under Model Space, for Map Book Name, enter **Redding 1000 Scale**, as shown in the following illustration.

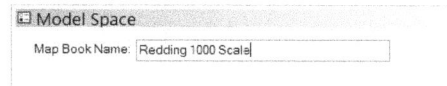

4. Under Sheet Template, click Settings.

5. In the Settings dialog box:
   - For Choose a Sheet Template, if you did the Create a Template for Map Books exercise, browse to ...\12-Plotting Maps\Map Books\Map Book Template.dwt. If you did not, browse to ...\12-Plotting Maps\Map Books\Completed Map Book Template.dwt.
   - Click Open.
   - For Choose a Layout, Mapbook is the only choice.
   - Under Layout Options, check Include a Title Block.
   - Select MapBook Title Block from the drop-down list.
   - Clear the Include Adjacent Sheet Links checkbox.
   - For Scale Factor, enter **1000**, as shown in the following illustration.

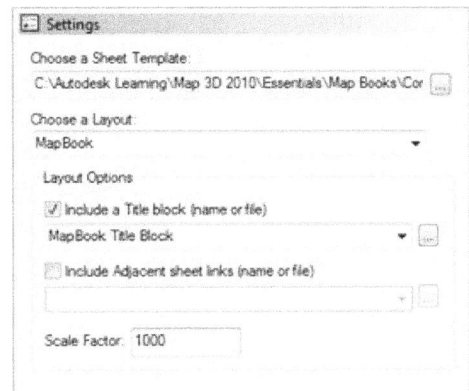

6. Under Tiling Scheme, select By Number.

- Under By Number, for Layer, enter **MAP_BOOK_GRID**.
- Click Pick Upper Left.
- Use a node csnap to select the point object at the upper-left corner of the map by the large red arrow.
- For Columns, enter **4**.
- For Rows, enter **7**.
- Set % Overlap of Each Tile to 0, as shown in the following illustration.

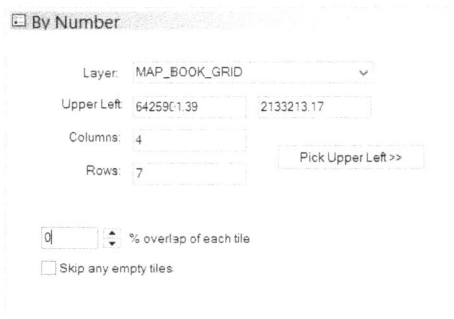

7. Under Naming Scheme, select Columns and Rows.

- Under Columns and Rows, for Begin With, select Columns.
- Under Columns, for Order From, select Left to Right.
- For Start With, select A.
- For Increment By, enter **1**.
- Under Rows, for Order From, select Top To Bottom.
- For Start With, select 1.
- For Increment By, enter **1**, as shown in the following illustration.

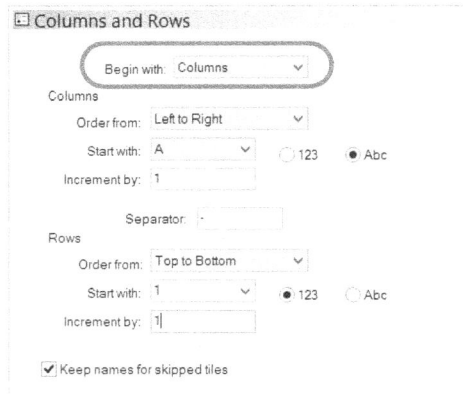

8. Under Key, select Layers.

- Under All Layers, select River, Roads.
- Click Add Layers for Map Key, as shown in the following illustration.

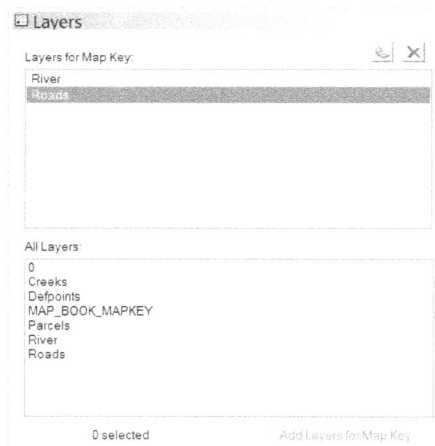

9. Under Legend, select None.

10. Under Sheet Set:

- Select Create New.
- Click Generate. The new layouts are created, as shown in the following illustration.

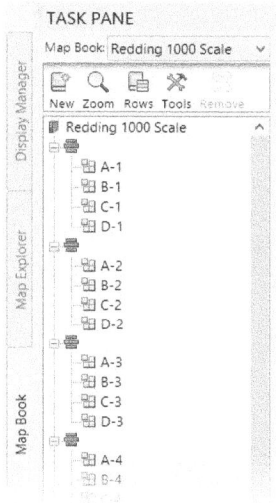

11. In the Model space, the Map Book grids display as shown in the following illustration.

12. Click on any Layout tab to view the completed sheet, as shown in the following illustration.

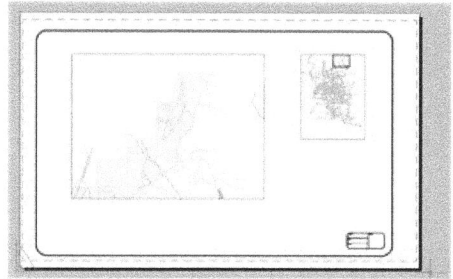

13. In the Map Book tab:

- Right-click on B-1>Zoom Tile, as shown in the following illustration, to zoom to that sheet in Model Space.
- Right-click on B-1>Zoom Layout to jump to that layout.

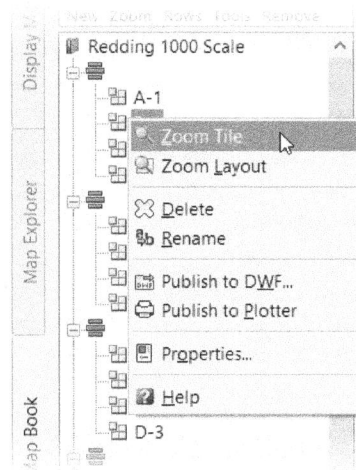

14. Erase the large red arrow pointing to the upper left corner of the map.

15. Save the drawing.

16. In the Map Book tab:

- Right-click on Redding 1000 Scale Map Book>Publish to DWF, as shown in the following illustration.

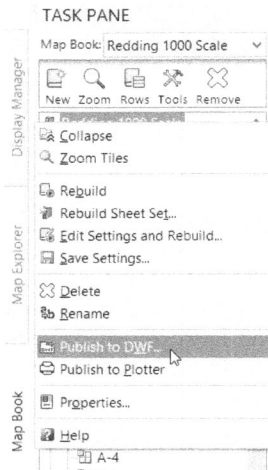

17. In the Select DWF File dialog box:

- Leave the name Redding 1000 Scale.dwf.
- Click Select.
- In the Sheet Set dialog box, click Yes.
- In the Select Sheet Set File dialog box, click Select.

When the publishing process is finished, double-click ...\12-Plotting Maps\Map Books\Redding 1000 Scale.dwf to view it in Autodesk Design Review.

18. Close the drawing.

Chapter Summary

Having completed this chapter, you can:

- Prepare a layout sheet for review.
- Create a set of maps for a Map Book.

Survey Data

The lessons in this chapter demonstrate how to load survey point data into your map. Survey Point data is often stored in text files and these files are loaded into your map and managed in the AutoCAD® Map 3D environment.

Objectives

After completing this chapter, you will be able to:

- Create a survey data store.
- Create and edit survey points.

Lesson: Creating Survey Data Stores

Overview

In this lesson, you create a survey data store that is based on an SDF file. The survey data store contains points that can be grouped by project or point group. You import data from an ASCII (text) file, as shown in the following illustration.

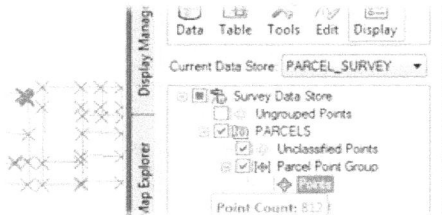

Objectives

After completing this lesson, you will be able to:

- Describe the concept of survey data stores.
- Explain the process of importing ASCII points into a survey data store.
- Create a parcel survey data store and import ASCII points.

About Survey Data Stores

The AutoCAD Map 3D software enables you to manage survey point data. Survey data is kept in a dedicated SDF data store. Unlike other SDF data stores, you cannot edit the schema or structure for a survey data store. In a survey data store, survey points are organized into projects and point groups, and unclassified points. Before you import any survey data, you must connect to or create a survey data store, as shown in the following illustration.

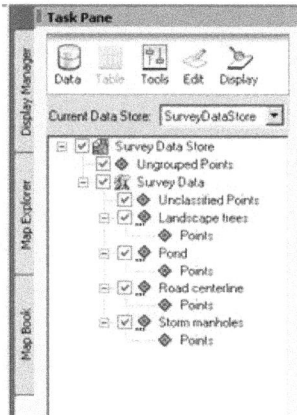

Survey Data Store Categories

In each survey data store, the points can be organized by project and point groups.

- Projects are the primary organizational group in a survey data store. Projects contain point groups.
- Point groups contain survey points. You can rename point groups or remove them from the survey data store. Any points that are not assigned to a point group display in the Unclassified Points group.

Example of Survey Data Store

Since survey data stores contain point collections, roads, parcel lines, and ponds can be defined by the survey locations that circumscribe these features. Often, tools such as Total Stations are used to survey an area. The resulting XYZ files can then be imported into a survey data store to draw the road edges.

Process of Importing ASCII Points

You can import survey point data in a variety of ASCII formats also known as text files.

The text files can be comma or tab delimited and are described using the following conventions:

- **P** is the point ID.
- **E** is the Easting value, X, or longitudinal values.
- **N** is the Northing value, Y or latitudinal values.
- **Z** is the elevation value.
- **D** is the description.

Process: Importing ASCII Points into a Survey Data Store

To add points to your survey data store, you can import ASCII, text-based point data. This data can be imported into a point group, project, or at the root of the data store. The following steps demonstrate how to perform the process of importing into a point group in a project.

1. Create a new survey data store, as shown in the following illustration.

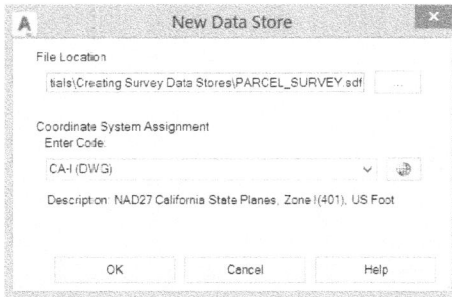

2. Create a new project in the data store, as shown in the following illustration.

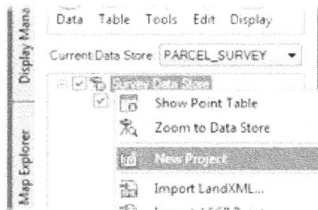

3. Create a new point group in the project, as shown in the following illustration.

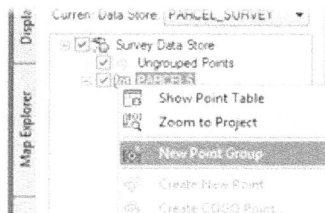

4. Import ASCII points into a new point group, as shown in the following illustration.

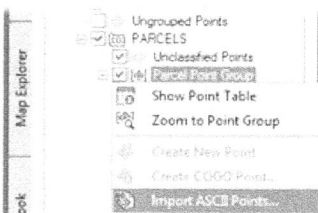

5. Choose an ASCII file and choose formatting, such as ENZ (comma delimited) and the Z-Units, as shown in the following illustration.

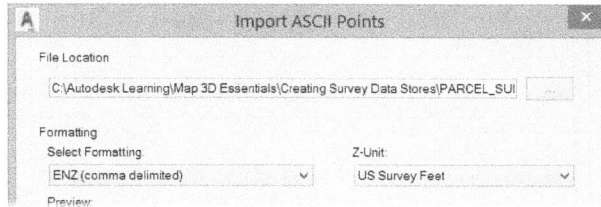

6. Ensure that the coordinate system is the same as the XYZ values contained in the text file, as shown in the following illustration.

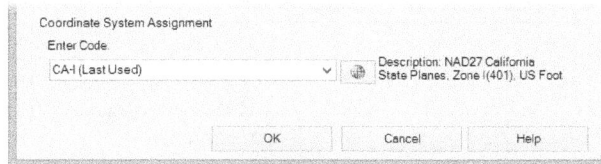

7. Points are then assigned to a point group in a project, as shown in the following illustration.

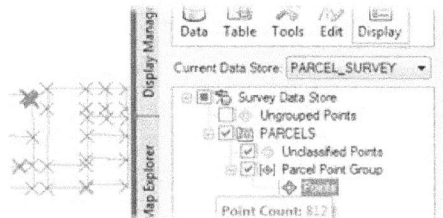

Exercise: Creating Parcel Survey Data Store

In this exercise, you will create a new survey data store that is contained in an empty SDF file. You will import a text file into your survey data store. The text file contains points with X, Y and Z values. These values are comma-delimited and represent ENZ or Easting, Northing, and Elevation, as shown in the following illustration.

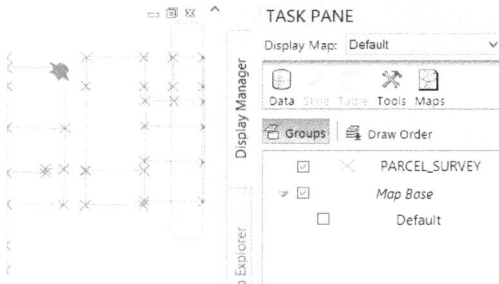

1. Open ...\13-Survey Data\Creating Survey Data Stores\PARCEL_OUTLINES.dwg.

2. On the Task Pane, click the Survey tab, as shown in the following illustration.

3. Under Data, select New Survey Data Store, as shown in the following illustration.

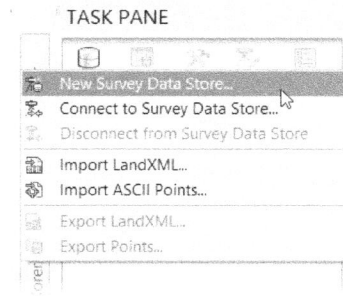

4. In the New Data Store file dialog box:
   - For File Location, click on the ellipses (...) to browse, as shown in the following illustration.
   - Browse to the ...\Data\SDF folder.
   - For File Name, enter **PARCEL_SURVEY**.
   - Click OK.
   - Click Yes to replace it.

5. For the Coordinate System Assignment, ensure that the code is set to CA-I (DWG), as shown in the following illustration.

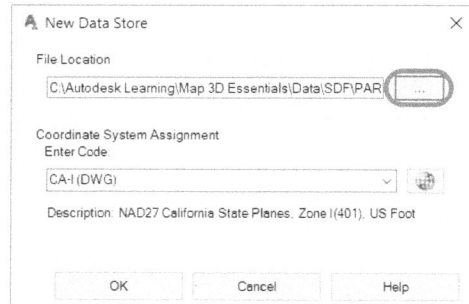

6. Click OK. Your screen should look as shown in the following illustration.

   Your drawing window may appear to go blank. If this happens, a Zoom Extents will restore it.

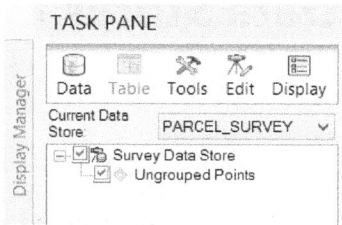

7. Click Data>Import ASCII Points, as shown in the following illustration.

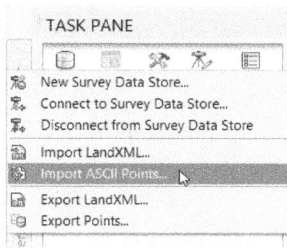

8. In the Import ASCII Points dialog box, for File Location, click the ellipses (...) for Browse.

9. In the Import ASCII File dialog box:

- Browse to the ...*Data\Database*\ folder.
- Select the PARCEL_SURVEY_CA-I_XYZ.txt file.
- Click OK.

10. In the Import ASCII Points dialog box, under Formatting:

- For Select Formatting, select ENZ (comma delimited), as shown in the following illustration.
- For Z-Unit, select US Survey Feet.

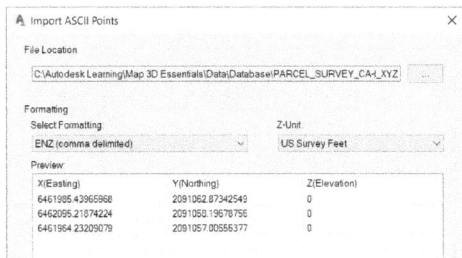

11. In the Import ASCII Points dialog box, under Coordinate System Assignment:

- For Enter Code, choose CA-I.
- Click OK. The points should display in the drawing window, as shown in the following illustration.

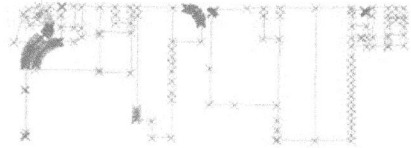

12. In the Survey task pane, toggle the data store off and on by checking the Ungrouped Points.

13. Click the Display Manager tab.

14. Note that the PARCEL_SURVEY Layer in the Display Manager, as shown in the following illustration.

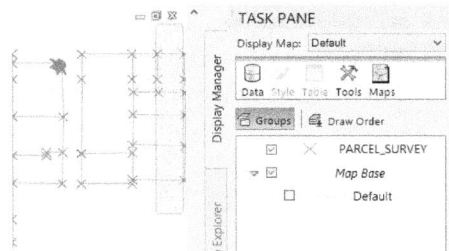

15. Save and close the drawing.

Lesson: Working with Survey Data Stores

Overview

In this lesson, you create and edit points in a survey data store. Survey points, which are stored in an SDF file, are created and edited in the Survey pane. COGO tools are used in this lesson to create new survey points, as shown in the following illustration.

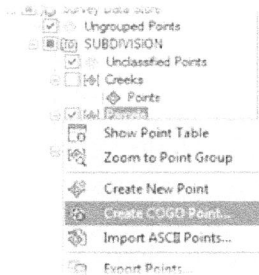

Objectives

After completing this lesson, you will be able to:

- Describe the survey point editing and creation tools.
- Describe the process of creating COGO survey points.
- Work with existing survey data stores.

About Creating and Editing Survey Points

To create or edit survey points, you must first click **Edit** on the Survey Task Pane tool strip. Unlike other types of SDF files, you can directly edit the survey points in the Edit mode, as shown in the following illustration. The changes are immediately made to the survey data store.

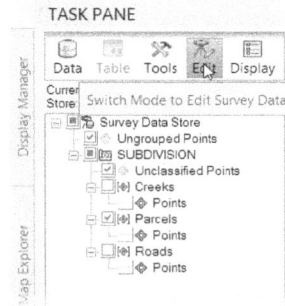

Creating New Survey Points

Survey points can be created in two ways:

- **Create New Point** - Draw a single point on the map.
- **Create COGO Point** - Use COGO Input tools to locate a point on the map, as shown in the following illustration.

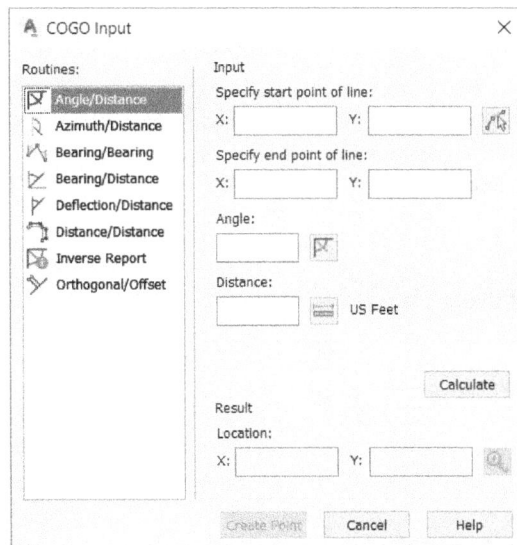

Editing Survey Point Attributes

The attributes of each survey point always use the same structure in the point. Attributes such as Latitude, Longitude, Easting, Northing, and Description are stored for each point.

These attributes can be edited in the Data Table window if the survey data store is editable, as shown in the following illustration.

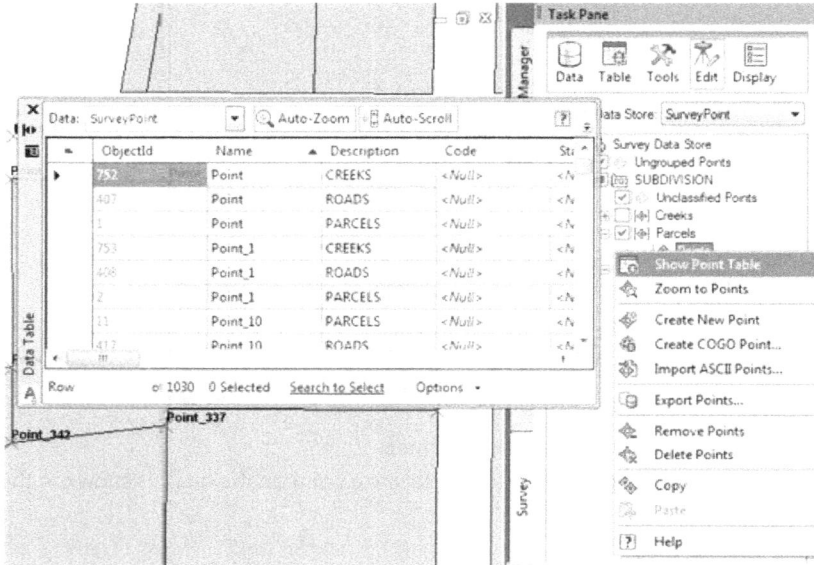

Survey Point Creation Example

Survey points are usually the basis for creating new geographic features on a map. Often, new survey points are recorded on survey notes and can then be manually entered into the survey data store. Using the new COGO Point tools, the survey technician can now enter the survey location using the Bearing/Distance tools.

Process of Creating COGO Survey Points

You can create new survey points in two ways: create a single point by drawing it on a map or use the COGO tools. You might want to draw a single point and then use in-line tools such as 'BD to trigger the COGO tools. However, built-in COGO tools enable you to draw your points without having to use the in-line tools. Unlike the in-line method, the COGO point creation tool enables you to preview your new point before drawing it.

Process: Creating COGO Survey Points

The following demonstrates the process of creating new COGO survey points in a survey point group.

1. Ensure that the survey data store is in Edit mode, as shown in the following illustration.

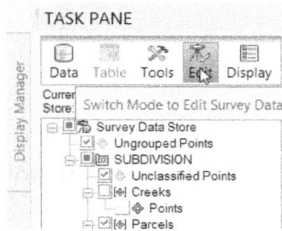

2. Choose the point group that you want to use to house the new points and select Create COGO Point, as shown in the following illustration.

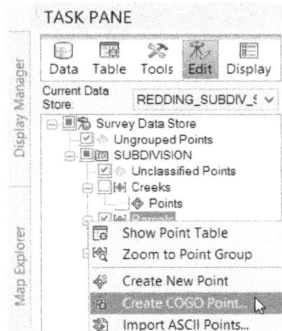

3. Choose the COGO routine you want to use, such as Bearing/Distance, as shown in the following illustration.

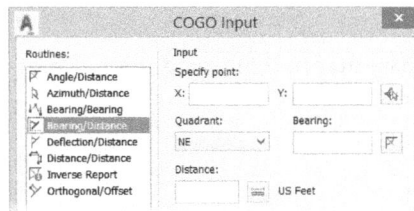

4. Choose the base point of the COGO location, as shown in the following illustration.

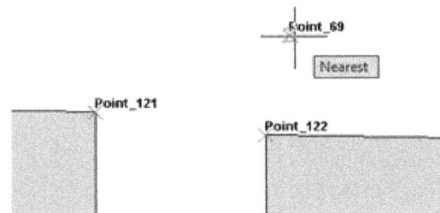

5. Enter the bearing or angle, as shown in the following illustration.

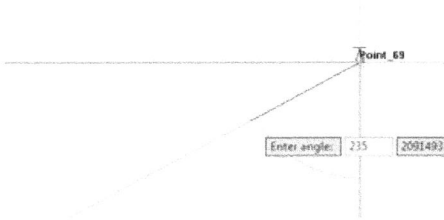

6. Define the distance you want to travel and preview the resulting point, as shown in the following illustration.

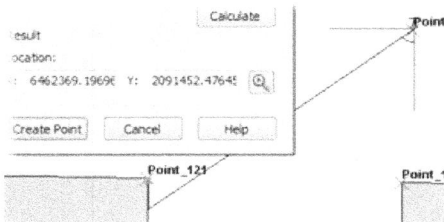

7. Once you have created the point, enter the attributes into the Data Table palette, as shown in the following illustration.

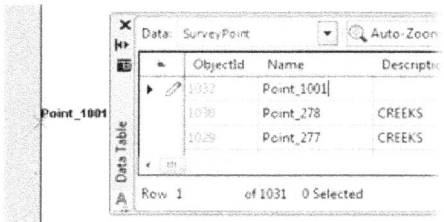

8. Complete the edits by putting the survey data store back into read-only mode, as shown in the following illustration.

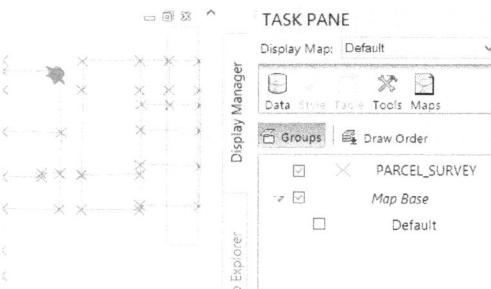

Exercise: Working with Survey Data Stores

In this exercise, you will attach a preexisting survey data store and a parcel SDF layer. You will use the COGO tools to create a new survey point that represents a point along the edge of a parcel polygon, as shown in the following illustration.

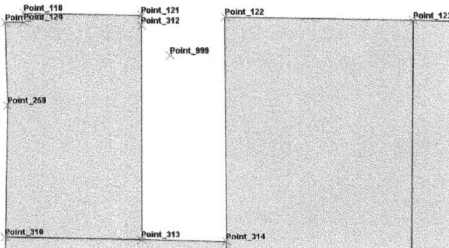

1. Open ...\13-Survey Data\Working With Survey Data Stores\REDDING_SUBDIV.dwg.

2. In the Task Pane, click the Survey tab.

3. Using Windows Explorer, browse to the ...\Data\SDF folder.

4. From Windows Explorer, drag and drop the REDDING_PARCELS.sdf file onto your map, as shown in the following illustration.

5. On the Survey tab:
   - Under Data, select Connect to Survey Data Store.
   - Browse to the ...\Data\SDF folder and select REDDING_SUBDIV_SURVEY.sdf.
   - Click OK.

6. On the View ribbon, under Views, select NEW PARCEL, as shown in the following illustration.

7. On the Task Pane, uncheck the Creeks and Roads point groups, as shown in the following illustration.

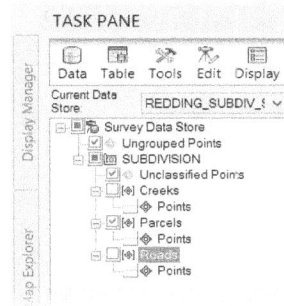

8. To toggle the Parcel layer off, in the Task Pane of the Survey tab, click Display.

9. Change the color of the Point Labels:
   - On the Display Manager tab, choose REDDING_SUBDIV_SURVEY.sdf, click Style to open the Style Editor.
   - Click on the Feature Label, as shown in the following illustration, to open the Style Label dialog box.

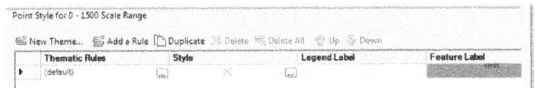

   - Change the color of the text to blue or a color that will show clearly on your Modelspace background. Close the Style Editor.

10. To make the points in the Parcel point group editable, select SUBDIVISION and click Edit on the Survey tab in the Task Pane, as shown in the following illustration.

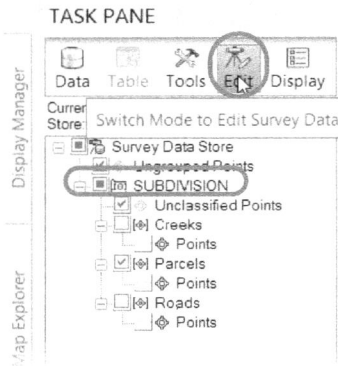

11. Right-click on the Parcels point group> Create COGO Point, as shown in the following illustration.

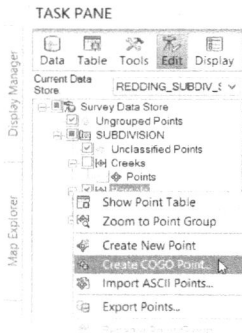

12. In the COGO Input dialog box:
    ▪ Under Routines, click Azimuth/Distance.
    ▪ Under Input, for Specify Point, click the Specify Point icon.
    ▪ Click Point_122 using the Node object snap, for the point location, as shown in the following illustration.

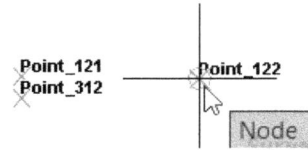

13. In the COGO Input dialog box:
    ▪ For Azimuth, enter **235**.
    ▪ For Distance, enter **60**.
    ▪ Click Calculate, to preview the new point location, as shown in the following illustration.

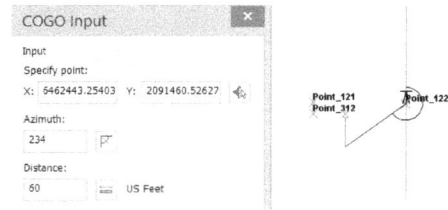

14. Click Create Point, as shown in the following illustration.

15. The Data Table displays with empty attributes for the new Survey Point.

- For Name, enter **Point_999**.
- For Description, enter **PARCELS**.

16. In the Task Pane, click Edit to commit the changes to the new point, as shown in the following illustration.

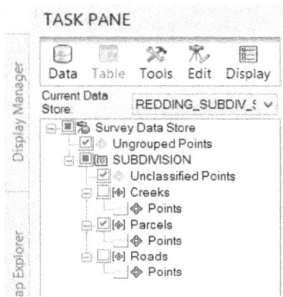

17. Click Display to view the Parcels layer, as shown in the following illustration.

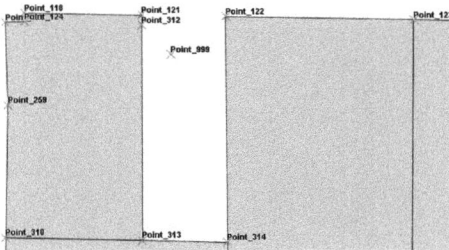

18. Save and close the drawing.

Chapter Summary

Having completed this chapter, you can:

- Create a survey data store.
- Create and edit survey points.

Industry Models

Industry Models are drawing files to which predefined databases are attached. They are used for modeling and managing infrastructure information. Specific industry model templates that are available in the AutoCAD Map 3D software, include electric, gas, survey, water, and wastewater. These templates have built in business rules, forms, and reporting framework along with dynamic symbolization.

Objectives

After completing this chapter, you will be able to:

- Open and edit an industry model.
- Start a new drawing from an industry model template.
- Import information from an FDO data source.

Lesson: Open, Edit, and Create an Industry Model

Overview

In this lesson, you learn what an industry model is, how to open and edit an industry model and how to use one of the six templates that ship with the AutoCAD Map 3D 2013 software to create a new industry model.

The following illustration shows a waste water industry model.

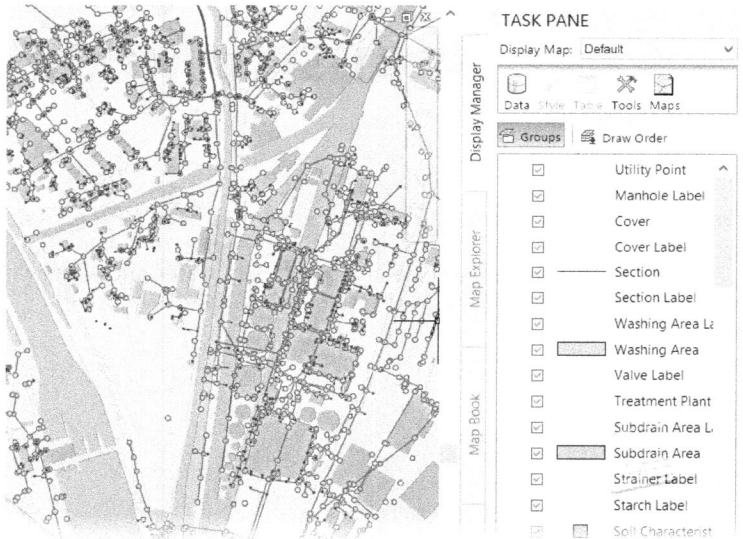

Objectives

After completing this lesson, you will be able to:

- Describe what an industry model is.
- Open an industry model.
- Edit an industry model.
- Start a new drawing from an industry model template.
- Import information into the industry model from an FDO data source.

About Industry Models

Before the AutoCAD Map 3D 2012 software, users needing to add rules and analysis reports to their data models required Autodesk® Topobase™ and a centralized Oracle database with an advanced schema that supports their industry. The AutoCAD Map 3D software will now enable them to keep their current setup of drawings and files while enabling them to add rules and relationships between objects and industry specific analysis reports. For example, using an electric industry model template that ships with the software, users can apply industry-specific standards and business process requirements to data as it is added to a model. Then they can run reports on voltage, phase, or load.

An Industry Model is a drawing file that contains:

- Industry-specific structure to help deal with water, wastewater, gas, electric, and land.
- Industry-specific symbology and styles.
- Industry-specific rules and workflows.
- Industry-specific forms and reports.
- Industry-specific analytic capabilities.

Industry Data Model drawings (.dwg) and templates (.dwt) contain a SQLite database file that has a classic Autodesk® Topobase™ table structure.

If you open a drawing with an industry model in it while you are in the Planning and Analysis Workspace, you will receive a warning message indicating that you should switch workspaces. If you click **Switch Workspace** in that message, as shown in the following illustration, the Maintenance workspace will become the current workspace.

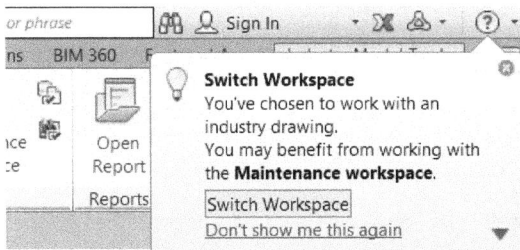

Display Models

The same base data can be used over and over in different types of maps while keeping the same graphical symbolization and representation of features. This is done with Display Models. Display models are useful because they are not bound to a specific schema. They are instead bound to a data structure which means that they can be shared by users and reused in different display models. Display Models are XML files that contain three components:

- Display Model files (.tbdm).
- Map definitions (tbdmmap).
- Layer definitions (layer).

Industry Model Explorer

The Industry Model Explorer becomes available once the workspace is changed to the Maintenance Workspace. This is where you can view industry models associated with the current project. There are different displays available in the Industry Model Explorer. The three main ones are listed below:

- **Industry Model Explorer** – Shows the data model structure with topologies, feature classes, and other objects (show by default).
- **Workflow Explorer** – Used for utility applications like Water, Wastewater, Gas, and Electric for viewing and processing industry model workflows.
- **Plot Explorer** – Used for plotting the active industry model and creating plot templates (Administrator must enable the Plot extension).

Importing Data into an Industry Model

Creating an industry model from scratch can be a tedious and expensive task. If the information for an industry model already exists in another format, it can be imported for use. Both drawing files and FDO data stores can be imported into an industry model. To do so, you follow a three step process:

1. Open or start a new industry model.

2. Map the incoming data to the industry model. On the Insert ribbon, under the Import panel, click Convert to Industry Model, as shown on the left in the following illustration. Then use the tools to Map the incoming data to the required industry model fields, as shown on the right in the following illustration.

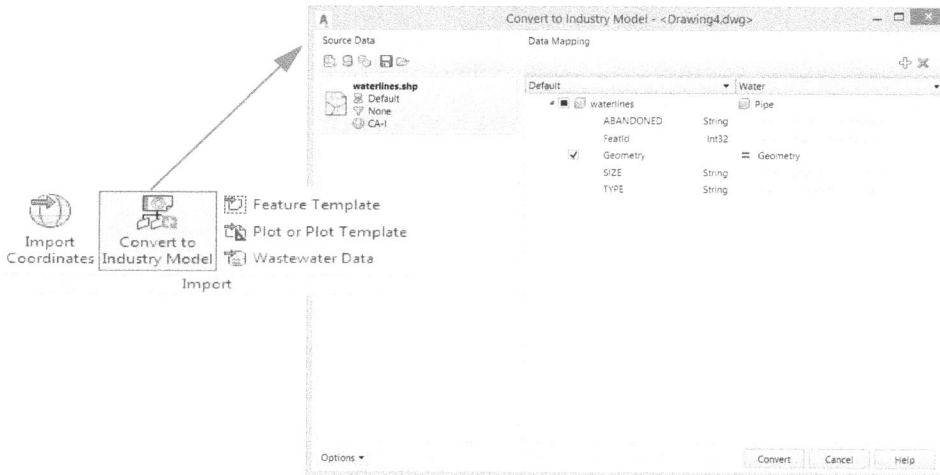

3. Convert the incoming data to the industry model by clicking **Convert** at the bottom of the Convert to Industry Model dialog box.

Exercise: Open and Edit an Industry Model

In this exercise, you will open a drawing containing an industry data model. Then new features will be added to it using workflows. The following illustration shows the finished industry model.

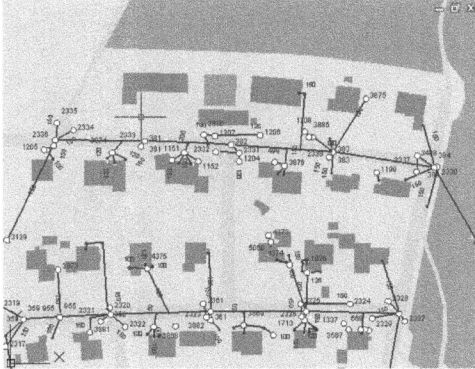

1. Open ...\14-Industry Models\ WasteWater_Industry_Model.dwg.

2. In the top right hand corner, a warning message will display from the communication center indicating you should switch workspaces, as shown in the following illustration.

   ▪ Ignore this message for now.

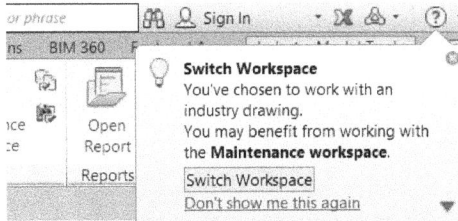

3. Note that the content sensitive ribbon that showed up in the Planning and Analysis workspace.

4. On the Display panel, click Connect to Data.

   ▪ Note that the data for the industry model resides in an SQLite Connection, as shown in the following illustration.

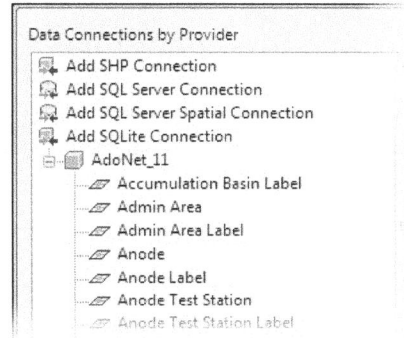

5. In the bottom right hand corner, select the workspace switching tool and change the workspace to the Maintenance Workspace, as shown in the following illustration.

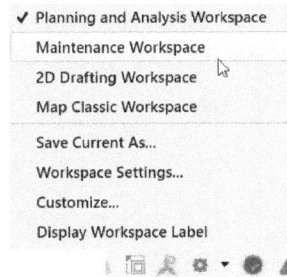

6. Note that the Industry Model Explorer panel that displays on the left.

7. On the View ribbon, in the Model Viewports panel, click Named, as shown in the following illustration.

8. Select EDIT from the Named Viewports tab, as shown in the following illustration, click OK.

9. In the Industry Model Explorer, click Workflow Explorer, as shown in the following illustration, to show the business workflows associated with this industry model.

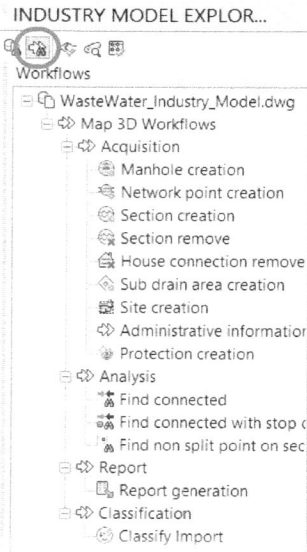

10. Under Acquisition, right-click on the Section Creation option and select Execute (or you can double-click), then:

- Select Yes to create intermediate points. Click OK.

- Digitize a section by picking the first and second points , as shown in the following illustration, then press <Enter>, then press <Esc> to finish.

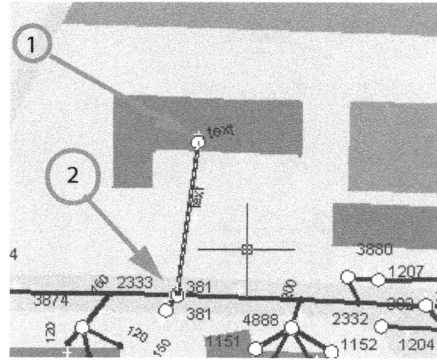

11. In the General tab, do the following. The list of fields is long, so you will have to scroll down to find all of the fields.

- Change the ID Material to Copper.

- Set Dimension 1 to 240.

- Set Dimension 2 to 240, as shown in the following illustration.

- Set Name number to today's date, without dashes or slashes (08282016).

- At the bottom of the list, click Update & Close.

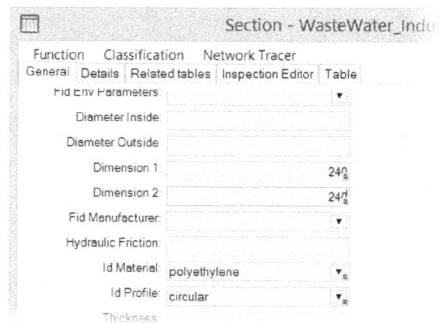

12. On the Home tab, in the Display panel, click Open Display Model, as shown in the following illustration.

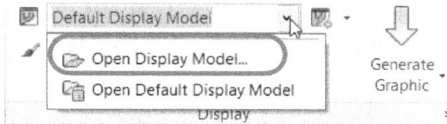

- Browse to open ...\14-Industry Models\ WasteWater_industry_model.tbdm.
- On the Home tab, in the Display panel, click Generate Graphic to redraw the map.
- Reset the view to the EDIT named view.
- Note that the pipes and manholes are now labeled including the ones just added due to an Auto-Label function built into workflows.

13. On the Home tab, in the Modify panel, click Attributes, as shown in the following illustration.

- Select the Pipe section you just created.
- Press <Enter> to bring up the attributes form.
- On the Section form, click Create Label, as shown in the following illustration.

- Checkmark the Dimension/length/Material label.
- Click OK.
- Close the form.
- Note the new labels with the values you entered in Step 10, as shown in the following illustration.

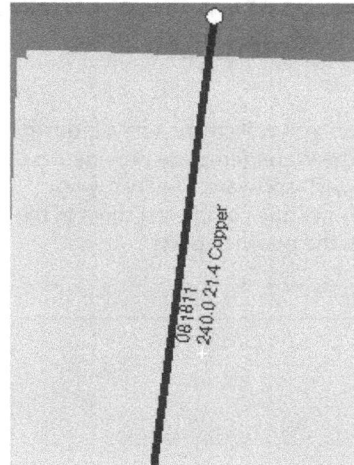

14. Under Acquisition, right-click on the Section remove option in the Workflow Explorer and choose Execute.

- Select the pipe created is Step 10.
- Click Delete then click Yes to confirm you want to delete the objects, as shown in the following illustration.

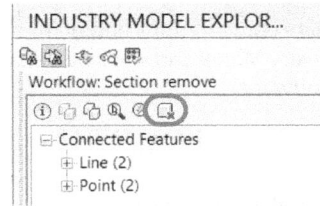

- Note the pipe section and associated manholes have disappeared both from the drawing and the database.

15. Save and close the drawing.

Exercise: Start a New Drawing from an Industry Model Template

In this exercise, you will create a new Industry Model from the Water template provided in the AutoCAD Map 3D software. The following illustration shows one completed sheet in the Map Book set with the two viewports.

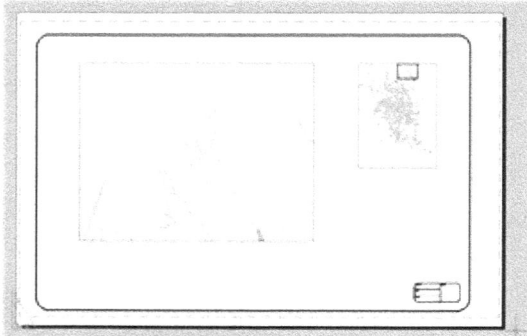

1. Start a new drawing from a template provided with the software ...\Template\ Industry Templates\IM_Water.dwt.

   The template contains a starting point for a Water Industry Model and ships by default with the software.

2. On the Display Manager tab of the Task Pane, click Data, Connect to Data.

   - Select Add SHP Connection.
   - Browse for ... 14-Industry Models\ waterlines.shp.
   - Click Connect.
   - Click Add to Map.
   - Select Assign this coordinate system, as shown in the following illustration.

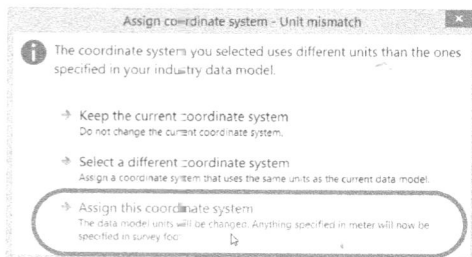

3. On the Display Manager tab of the Task Pane, select waterline.shp you just added.

   - Click Table.
   - Find FeatId 7738 and select it so that the software zooms in on the pipe. Zoom out slightly until you see pipe 7743 just above, as shown in the following illustration.

4. In the Industry Model Explorer, set the view to Workflows.

   - Under Acquisition, right-click Network pipe with fitting point creation and click Execute (or you can double-click).
   - Digitize the pipe from the endpoints of pipe 7738 and 7743, as shown in the following illustration, press <Enter>.
   - Press <Esc>.

5. Two windows appear, one for Pipe Data and one for Fitting Data.

6. On the Pipe form, fill in the following, as shown in the following illustration.

- Name number: enter today's date
- Function: **building/facility service**
- Material: **polyethylene**
- Disposition state: **proposed**
- Connection type: **glued**

At the bottom of the list, click Update & Close.

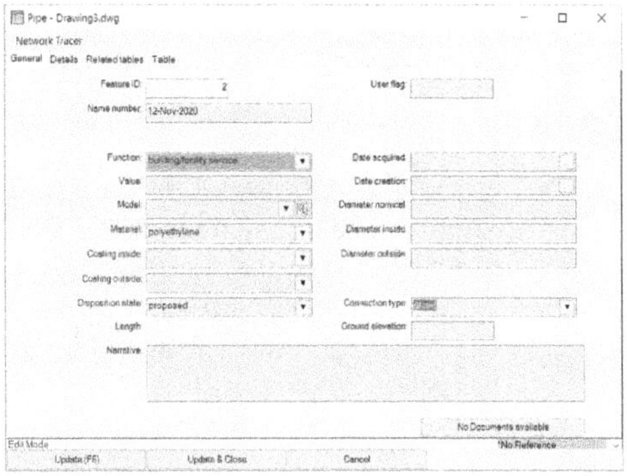

7. On the Fitting form, fill in the following, as shown in the following illustration.

- Name number: enter today's date
- Connection type: **glued**
- Disposition state: **proposed**

At the bottom of the list, click Update & Close.

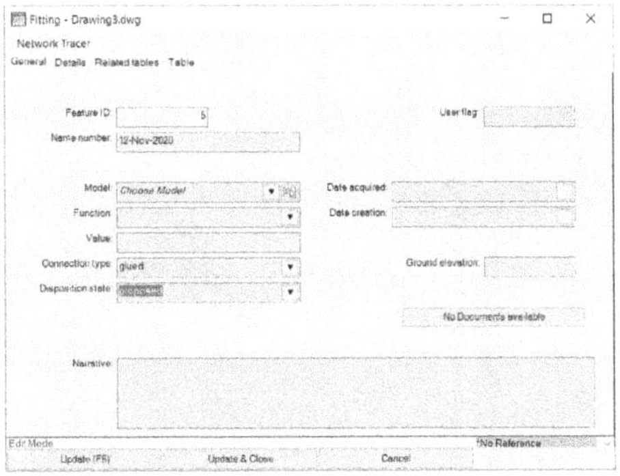

8. There is no need to save, so you can simply close the drawing.

Exercise: Import Data into the Industry Model from an FDO Data Store

In this exercise, you will create a new Industry Model from the Water template provided in the AutoCAD Map 3D software and then import a shape file to populate it. The following illustration shows one completed sheet in the Map Book set with the two viewports.

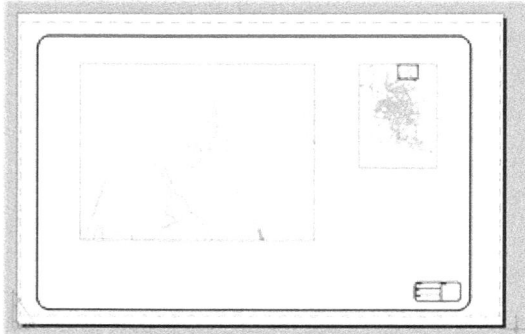

1. Start a new drawing from ...\Template\ Industry Templates\IM_Water.dwt. Ensure that the workspace is set to the Maintenance Workspace.

2. On the Insert ribbon, under the Import panel, click Convert to Industry Model.

   - Under Source Data, click Add file-based sources, as shown in the following illustration.

3. In the Open dialog box:

   - Change the file format to SHP files, as shown in the following illustration.
   - Browse for ...\14-Industry Models\ waterlines.shp.

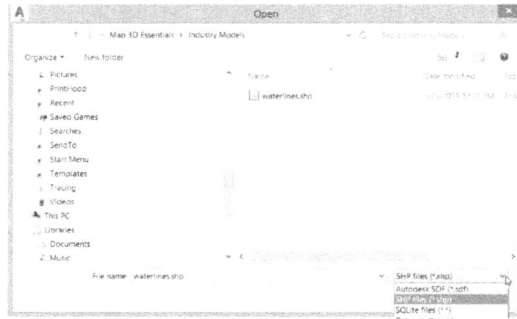

4. Under Data Mapping:

   - Expand the Waterlines on the left to show the fields available in the .DBF associated with the shape file.
   - On the right, select Water from the All Models drop-down list, as shown in the following illustration.

   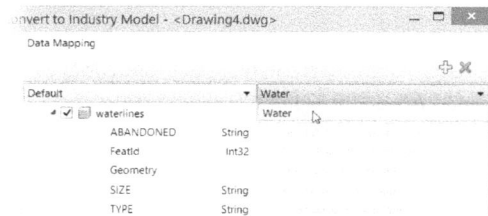

5. Under Waterlines, select Pipe from the drop-down list, as shown in the following illustration.

   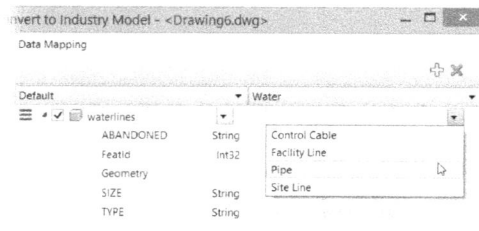

6. Click Convert at the bottom, as shown in the following illustration.

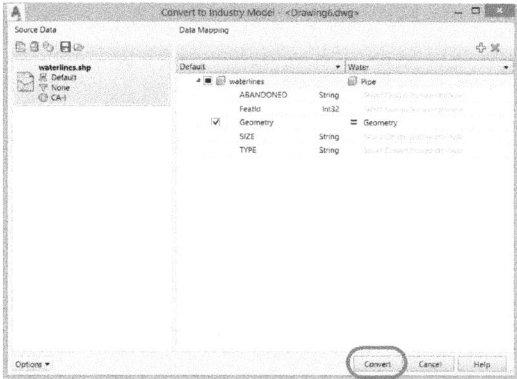

7. Click Extract, as shown in the following illustration.

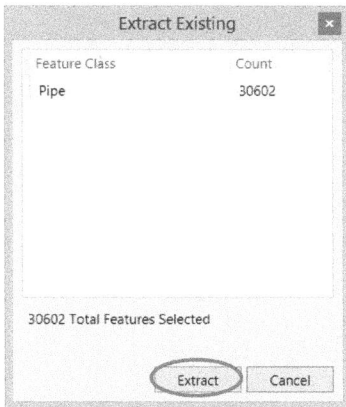

8. Save the drawing as ...\14-Industry Models\ *Waterlines_Model.dwg.*

Chapter Summary

Having completed this chapter, you can:

- Open and edit an industry model.
- Start a new drawing from an industry model template.
- Import information from an FDO data source.

Additional Exercises

In this appendix, additional exercises are provided that enable you to practice the skills that you
have learned in this learning guide. Additionally, a review of the Point Cloud content is included.

Exercise: Connect to a Feature Source

In this exercise, you will create two new SDF based layers in Display Manager, as shown in the following illustration. You will also create a new SHP based layer and view its associated data in the Data Table dialog box.

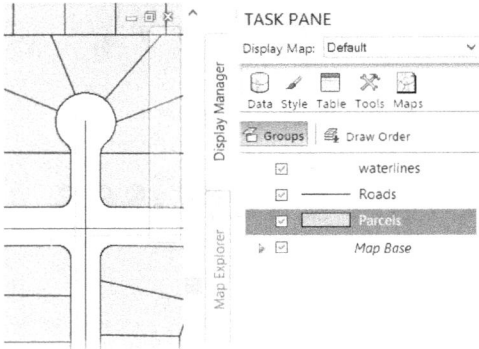

1. Open ...\Appendix\Connecting to a Feature Source\Redding-Connect.dwg.

2. Verify that Display Manager is selected in the Task Pane, as shown in the following illustration.

3. Click Data>Connect to Data, as shown in the following illustration.

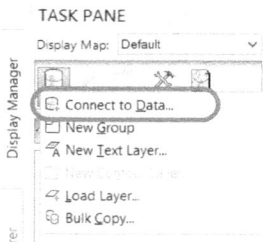

4. In the Data Connect window:
   - Click Add SDF Connection.
   - For Connection Name, enter **SDF_PARCEL**.
   - For Source File, browse to ...\Data\SDF\Parcels.sdf, as shown in the following illustration.
   - Click Connect.

5. In the Add Data to Map area:
   - Ensure the Parcels schema is selected.
   - Note that the coordinate system is CA-I.
   - Click Add to Map, as shown in the following illustration.

6. With the Data Connect dialog box still open:

- Click Add SDF Connection.
- For Connection Name, enter **SDF_ROADS**.
- For Source File, browse to ...*Data\SDF\Roads.sdf*.
- Click Connect.

7. Under Add Data to Map:

- Ensure the Roads schema is selected.
- Click Add to Map.

8. With the Data Connect dialog box still open:

- Click Add SHP Connection.
- For Connection Name, enter **SHP_WATERLINES**.
- For Source File, browse to ...*Data\SHP\waterlines.shp*, as shown in the following illustration.
- Click Connect.

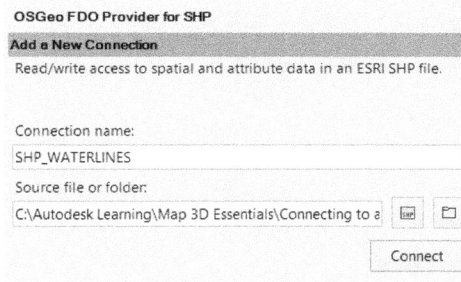

9. In the Add Data to Map area:

- Ensure the waterlines schema is selected, as shown in the following illustration.
- Click Add To Map.

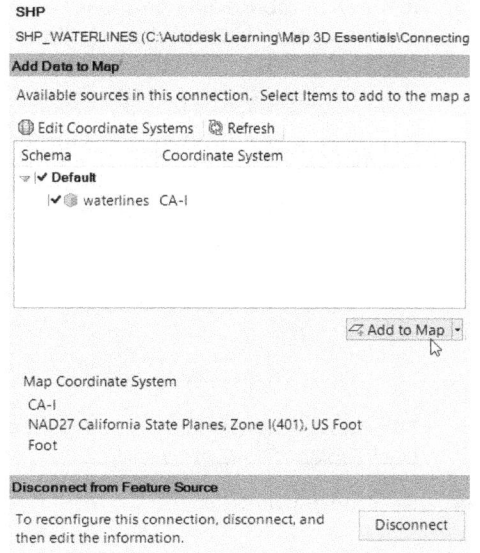

10. Close the Data Connect window.

11. In the Display Manager, select the waterlines layer, as shown in the following illustration.

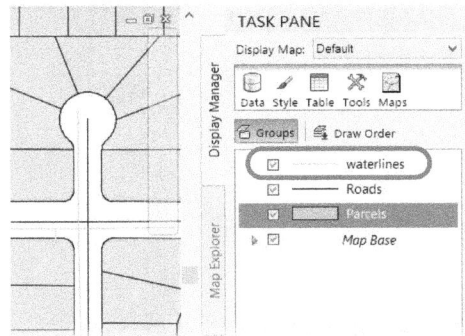

12. Click Table, as shown in the following illustration.

13. In the Data Table dialog box, select any record, as shown in the following illustration.

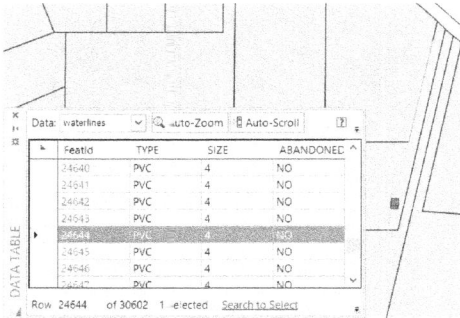

The map zooms to the objects selected in the Data Table.

14. Save the drawing.

Exercise: Use a Spatial Filter with a SHP

In this exercise, you will limit to a geographic area the number of features in a SHP file that contains valves. Only those valves that are in a drawn rectangle will display on the map, as shown in the following illustration.

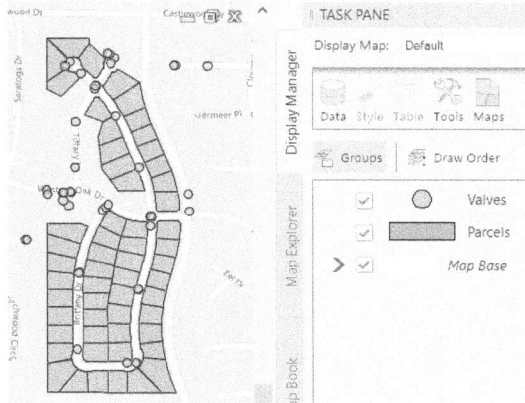

1. Open ...\Appendix\Query Features on Connect\Redding_QueryFeatures.dwg.

2. In Display Manager, click Data>Connect to Data.

3. In the Data Connect window:
   - Ensure the SDF_PARCELS_BRITTANY_DRIVE is connected.
   - Click Add SHP Connection.
   - For Connection Name, enter **SHP_VALVES_BRITTANY_DRIVE**.
   - Click SHP File Browse.

4. In the Open dialog box:
   - Browse to ...\Data\SHP.
   - Select Valves.shp.
   - Click Open.

5. Click Connect.

6. Under Schema, ensure the Valves are checked.
   - Click Add to Map with Query.

7. In the Create Query dialog box, expand Locate on Map, then select Inside Rectangle, as shown in the following illustration.

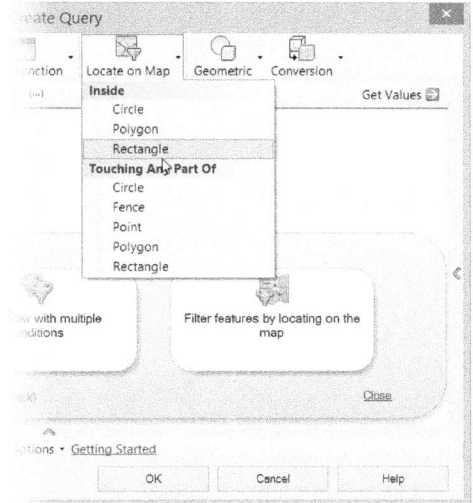

8. Create a rectangle around the parcels, as shown in the following illustration.

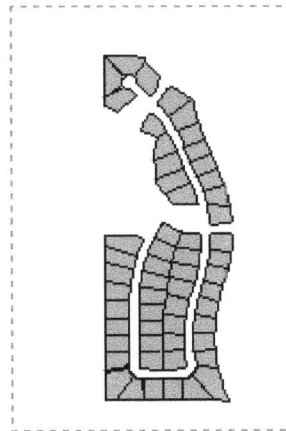

9. In the Create Query dialog box, click OK, as shown in the following illustration.

10. Close the Data Connect window.

11. Valves are filtered in the rectangle, as shown in the following illustration.

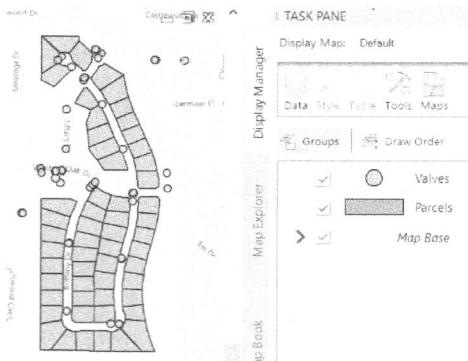

12. Save and close your drawing.

Exercise: Convert Drawings into the Current Project Coordinates

The contours reside in latitude-longitude coordinates, and the parcels are in the California State Plane coordinates. Both drawings will be attached to the REDDING project, which is in the UTM coordinates. The two drawings will be re-projected into UTM when viewed in the project drawing, as shown in the following illustration.

1. Open ...\Appendix\Working with Coordinate Systems\Parcel.dwg.

    ▪ In the Status Bar, review the Drawing Coordinates, as shown in the following illustration.

    ▪ **Note:** If the coordinates are not visible in the Status Bar, click Customize and select Coordinates.

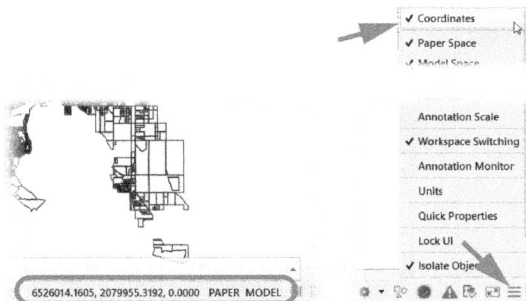

2. Open ...\Appendix\Working with Coordinate Systems\Contours_LL.dwg.

    ▪ At the bottom of the drawing editor, review the Drawing Coordinates, as shown in the following illustration.

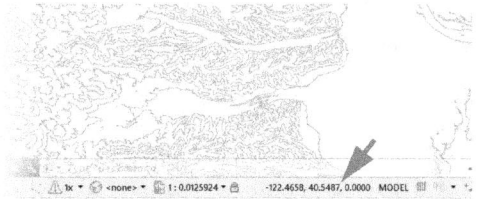

3. On the Map Setup tab, under Coordinate System, click Assign, as shown in the following illustration.

4. In the Coordinate System Assign dialog box:

    ▪ For Category, select Lat Longs.

    ▪ In the Search bar, enter **LL**.

    ▪ For Coordinate Systems in Category, select LL, No datum, Latitude-Longitude; Degrees -180 to +180, as shown in the following illustration.

    ▪ Click Assign.

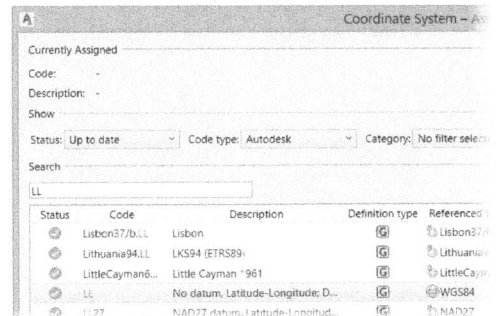

5. Save and close Contours_LL.dwg.

6. Ensure that you are working in the ...\Appendix\Working with Coordinate Systems\Parcel.dwg.

7. Repeat Steps 3 and 4 as follows:

- For Category, select USA, California.
- For Coordinate Systems in Category, select CA83-IF, NAD83 California State Planes, Zone 1, US Foot.
- Click Assign.

8. Save and close Parcels.dwg.

9. Open ...\Appendix\Working with Coordinate Systems\REDDING.dwg.

10. In Map Explorer, right-click on Current Drawing>Coordinate System, as shown in the following illustration.

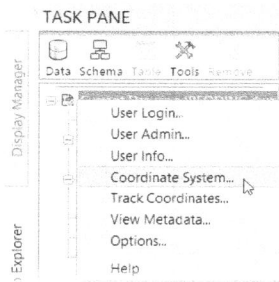

11. In the Assign Global Coordinate System dialog box:

- Note that the Coordinate System has been assigned to UTM83-10.
- Click OK.

12. In Map Explorer, right-click on Drawings> Attach, as shown in the following illustration.

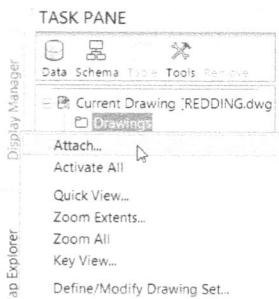

13. In the Select Drawings to Attach dialog box:

- For Look in, select the MAP_3D alias.
- Browse to ...\Appendix\Working with Coordinate Systems.
- Select Contours_LL.dwg and Parcel.dwg, as shown in the following illustration.
- Click Add.
- Click OK.

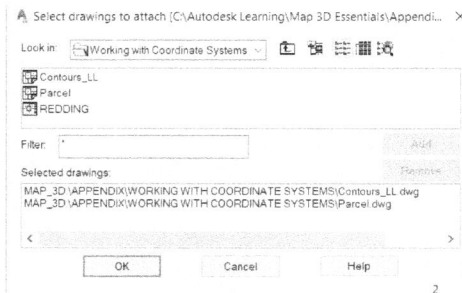

14. In Map Explorer, right-click on Drawings> Zoom Extents.

15. In the Zoom Drawing Extents dialog box, select Parcels.dwg and then click OK.

16. In Map Explorer, right-click on Drawings> Quick View.

17. In the Quick View Drawing dialog box, click OK.

18. Verify that both the Contours_LL (LL) and the Parcels (CA83-IF) drawing objects are transformed into the REDDING Project (UTM83-10) Coordinate System, as shown in the following illustration.

19. Save and close the drawing.

Exercise: Querying Objects Based on Object and SQL Data

In this exercise, you will open a drawing with two source drawings attached that contain object data and database links. You will perform a preview query of all sewer lines that are greater than 8" in diameter and an SQL query of all properties with a land value greater than $250,000, as shown in the following illustration.

1. Open ...\Appendix\Defining Data Queries\Data Query.dwg. Note in Map Explorer that Sewer.dwg and Parcel.dwg are already attached.

2. In Map Explorer:
   - Right-click on the Sewer drawing>Zoom Extents.
   - Right-click on the Sewer drawing>Quick View.

   The following illustration is a preview of the entire Sewer drawing.

3. In Map Explorer, click Data>Query Source Drawing.

4. In the Define Query of Attached Drawing(s) dialog box, under Query Type, click Data, as shown in the following illustration.

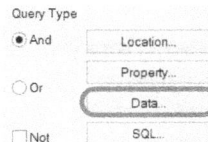

5. In the Data Condition dialog box:
   - Select Object Data.
   - Under Tables, select SEWER_PIPES, as shown in the following illustration.

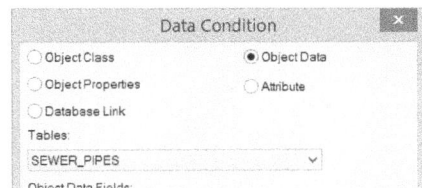

6. In the Data Condition dialog box:

- Under Object Data Fields list, select PIPESIZE.
- Under Expression, for Operator, select >.
- For Value, enter **8**, as shown in the following illustration.
- Click OK.

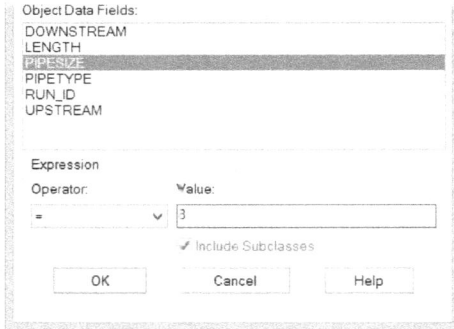

The data query displays under Current Query, as shown in the following illustration.

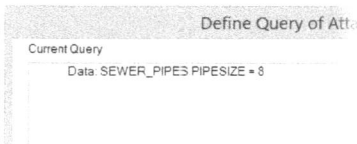

7. Confirm the Query Mode is set to Preview.

- Click Execute Query, as shown in the following illustration.

Only the sewer lines that are greater than 8" display as shown in the following illustration.

Before performing an SQL drawing query, the database connection must be established in the current drawing.

8. Using Windows Explorer:

- Browse to the ...\Appendix\Defining Data Queries folder.
- Drag Redding_Parcels_Query.mdb into Map Explorer, as shown in the following illustration.

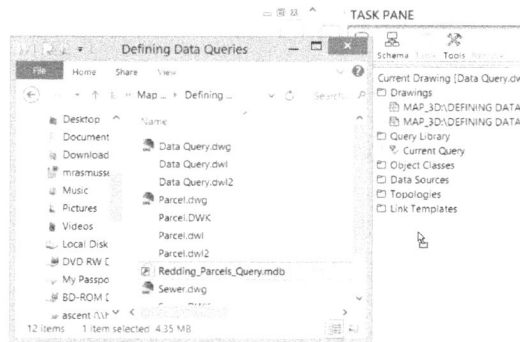

The database is attached to the current drawing and a UDL file is created to support querying linked objects from the source drawing that uses the same UDL name.

9. In Map Explorer, click Data>Query Source Drawing.

10. In the Define Query of Attached Drawing(s) dialog box, click Clear Query, as shown in the following illustration.

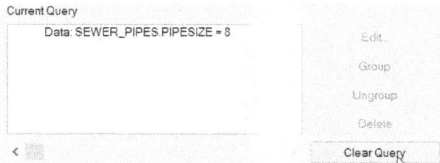

11. Under Query Type, click SQL, as shown in the following illustration.

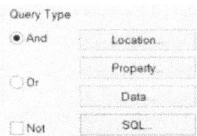

12. In the SQL Link Condition dialog box, under Column, select LAND_VALUE, as shown in the following illustration.

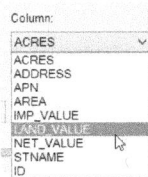

13. Under Condition:
   - For Operator, select >.
   - For Value, enter **250000**, as shown in the following illustration.
   - Click Add Condition.
   - Click OK.

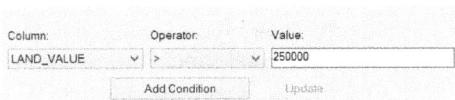

The query displays under Current Query as an SQL statement, as shown in the following illustration.

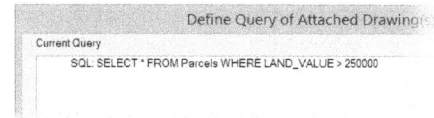

14. In the Define Query of Attached Drawing(s) dialog box:
   - Under Query Mode, select Draw, as shown in the following illustration.
   - Click Execute Query.

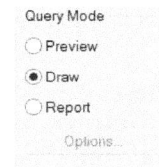

Only parcels with land values greater than $250,000 are queried from the source drawing, as shown in the following illustration.

15. Save and close the drawing.

Exercise: Performing a Compound Query

In this exercise, a compound query is applied to a drawing to retrieve a more specific set of results than could be identified with a simple data query.

1. Open ...\Appendix\Compound Queries\Query-from.dwg. Note in Map Explorer that Sewer.dwg is already attached. It might be necessary to right-click on it and select Activate.

2. In Map Explorer:

- Right-click on the Sewer drawing>Zoom Extents.
- Right-click on the Sewer drawing>Quick View.

The following illustration shows the entire Sewer drawing.

3. In Map Explorer, click Data>Query Source Drawing.

4. In the Define Query of Attached Drawing(s) dialog box, under Query Type, click Location.

5. In the Location Condition dialog box:

- Under Boundary Type, select Window, as shown in the following illustration.
- For the Selection Type, select Crossing.
- Click Define.

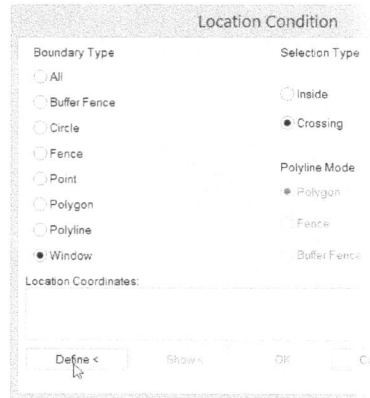

6. Make a window over approximately the top half of the map, as shown in the following illustration.

7. In the Define Query of Attached Drawing(s) dialog box:

- Under Query Type, confirm that the AND operator is selected.
- Click Data, as shown in the following illustration.

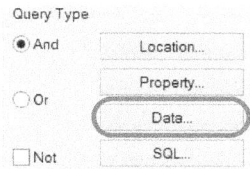

8. In the Data Condition dialog box:

- Select Object Data.
- Under Tables, select SEWER_PIPES.
- Under Object Data Fields, select PIPESIZE.
- Under Expression, for Operator select <.
- For Value, enter **10**, as shown in the following illustration.
- Click OK.

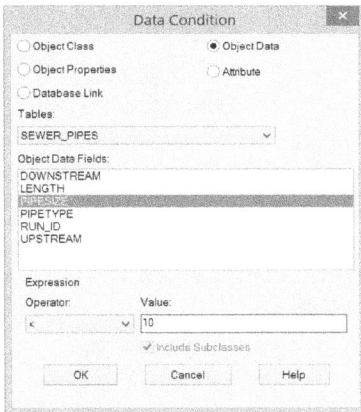

9. In the Define Query of Attached Drawing(s) dialog box:

- Note that the second query statement is added to the Current Query, as shown in the following illustration.

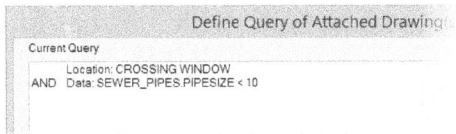

- Confirm that the AND operator is selected.
- Under Query Type, click Data.

10. In the Data Condition dialog box:

- Select Object Data.
- Under Tables, confirm that SEWER_PIPES is selected.
- Under Object Data Fields, select PIPETYPE.
- Under Expression, for Operator select =.
- For Value, enter **VCP**, as shown in the following illustration.
- Click OK.

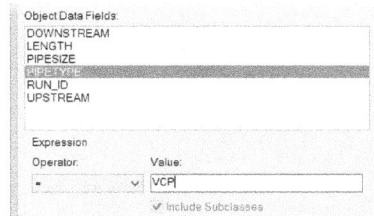

11. In the Define Query of Attached Drawing(s) dialog box:

- Note that the third query statement is added to the Current Query, as shown in the following illustration.

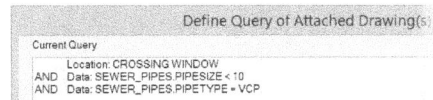

- Confirm that the Query Mode is set to Preview.
- Click Execute Query.

12. Only the sewer pipe that lies in the selected area is less than 10" diameter, and VCP material is retrieved, as shown in the following illustration.

13. Save and close the drawing.

Exercise: Create a Thematic Map

The zoning in the City of Redding is drawn as complete areas. Each area is zoned to determine what type of building is permitted per neighborhood. In this exercise, you will color code the map based on the zoning designation of each area, as shown in the following illustration.

1. Open ...\Appendix\Creating Thematic Maps\Zoning Theme.dwg.

2. In the Task Pane, click the Display Manager tab.

3. In the Display Manager, right-click on Zoning>Add Style>Theme, as shown in the following illustration.

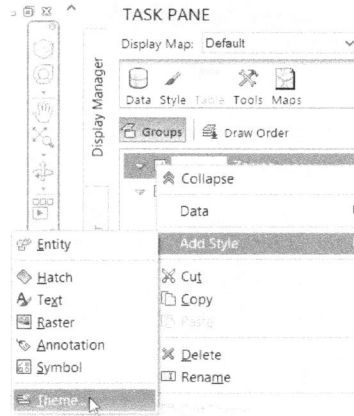

Note: If Add Style is grayed out, ensure that you have Groups selected rather than Draw Order.

4. In the Thematic Mapping dialog box:

   - Under Data Values, for Theme Type, verify that A Set of specific values is selected, as shown in the following illustration.

   - Click Values.

5. In the Thematic Values dialog box, under Data Values, for Obtain from, click the ellipses (...) icon, as shown in the following illustration.

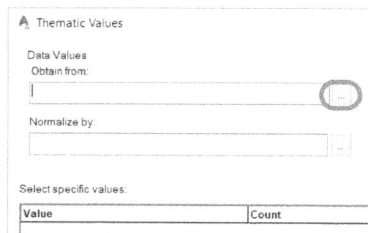

6. In the Choose Data Expression dialog box:
   - Expand Object Data and ZONING table.
   - Click ZONE_CLASS, as shown in the following illustration.
   - Click OK.

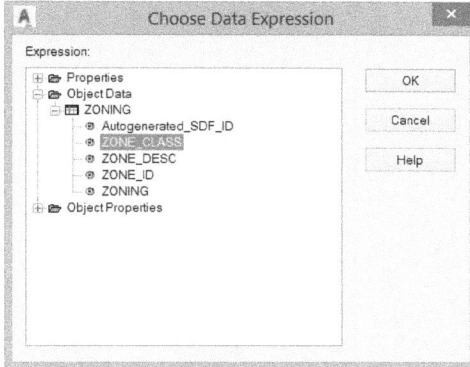

7. In the Thematic Values dialog box, click Read Data.

8. In the Thematic Values dialog box, under Select Specific Values, right-click on any value in the Value column, and select Select All, as shown in the following illustration.

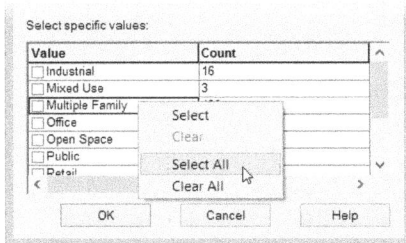

9. In the Thematic Values dialog box, click OK, as shown in the following illustration.

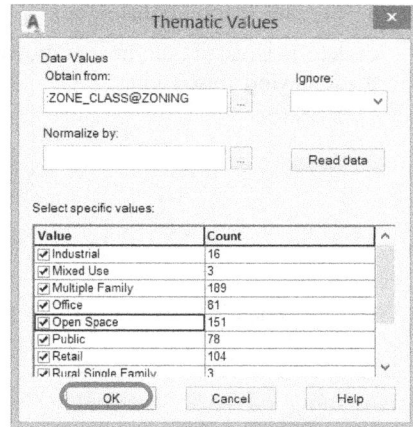

10. In the Thematic Mapping dialog box, scroll to the right and select the Hatch check box, as shown in the following illustration.

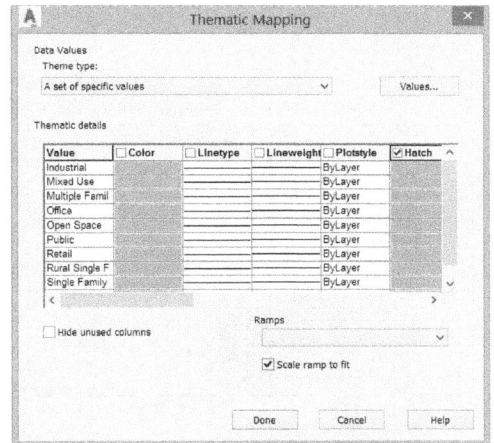

11. Under Ramps, select Solid Pastel, as shown in the following illustration.

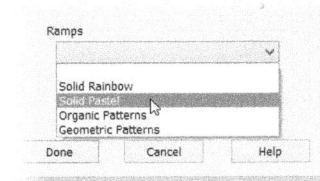

12. In the Thematic Mapping dialog box:
    - Click Hide Unused Columns, as shown in the following illustration.
    - Click Done.

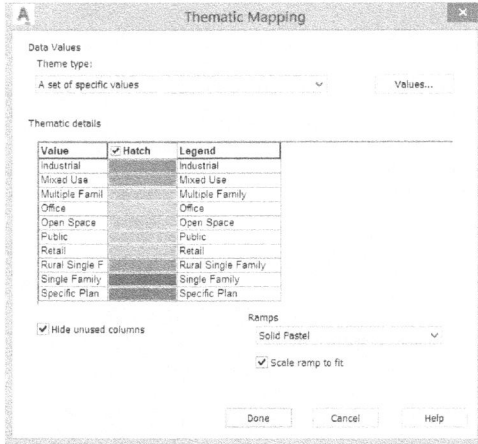

13. In the Display Manager, right-click under the layer list>Update. The following illustration shows the updated Zoning list.

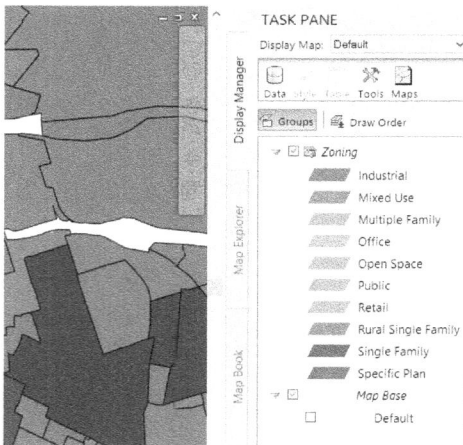

14. Save and close the drawing.

Exercise: Create a Legend

In this exercise, you will create a legend for a thematic map, as shown in the following illustration.

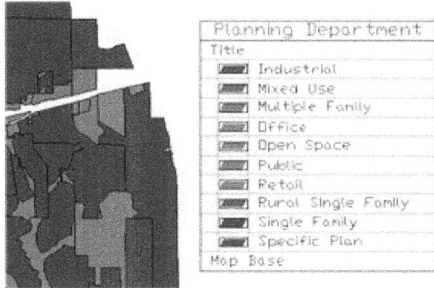

1. Open ...*Appendix\Creating Thematic Maps\Zoning Theme 2.dwg*.

2. Select Layout1 to make it the current view.

3. Right-click on Layout1, select Page Setup Manger, and then click Modify.

   - Select DWF6ePlot.pc3 for the printer.
   - Select ARCH D (36.00 x 24.00 Inches) for the paper size.
   - Click OK then Close.

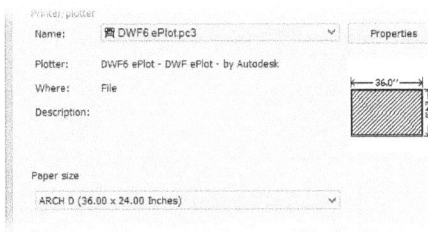

4. In the Layout Tool ribbon>Layout Elements panel, click Legend>Legend, as shown in the following illustration.

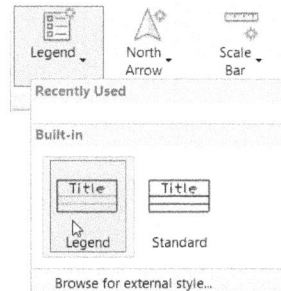

5. In Layout1, select the viewport for the new legend. Click a point to the right of the viewport to place the legend.

6. Use grips to resize the legend, as shown in the following illustration.

7. Adjust the map and legend to fit on the paper correctly, as shown in the following illustration.

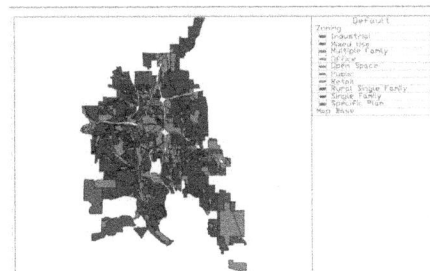

8. Save and close the drawing.

Lesson: Point Clouds

Overview

In this lesson, you import Point Cloud data. Point Clouds are extremely large groups of 3D point data created by scanning the terrain of a project. Aerial LiDAR (Light Detection And Ranging) laser scanners are the most common way to collect point cloud data, as shown in the following illustration. This lesson uses a LiDAR Aerial Survey (LAS) which has already been processed by Autodesk ReCap software for the point cloud.

Objectives

After completing this lesson, you will be able to:

- Import Point Clouds.
- Filter Point Clouds.
- Clip Point Clouds.

About Point Clouds

Point cloud data sets are large collections of 3D points (often containing millions or even billions of points), which represent the earth, high or low vegetation, buildings, and other 3D objects. Point clouds typically start out as a text file. Then, they are processed using the Autodesk ReCap software. The Autodesk ReCap software enables you to import, modify, and clean up point cloud data. It can be used to create a Point Cloud Project (.RCP) or Point Cloud Scan (.RCS) file which can be imported into the AutoCAD Map 3D software. Access to the Attach Point Cloud command and Autodesk ReCap can be found in the Insert tab>AutoCAD Point Cloud panel, as shown in the following illustration.

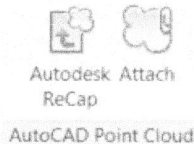

Autodesk Attach
ReCap

AutoCAD Point Cloud

Note: The Create Point Cloud command has been removed from the AutoCAD Map 3D software. You now have to take the files into Autodesk ReCap before bringing them into AutoCAD Map 3D software. If you have drawings that contain point clouds in the .PCG or .ISD file formats, they still display and can be modified.

Process of Importing Point Cloud Data

You can work with .RCP or .RCS files in the AutoCAD Map 3D software by using the AttachPoint Cloud command to import the required points.

Process: Importing Point Cloud Data

The following demonstrates the process of importing point cloud data into the AutoCAD Map 3D software.

1. In the Insert tab>AutoCAD Point Clouds panel, click Attach.

2. In the Select Point Cloud File dialog box, set the file format, browse to the .RCP or .RCS file and click Open.

3. In the Attach Point Cloud dialog box, set the Path type, Insertion point, and scale. Click Show Details to see Point cloud information in the dialog box, as shown in the following illustration. Click OK when done.

4. If you selected any of the options to Specify on screen, at the command prompt, type or click in the drawing to locate the point cloud, set its scale or rotation.

Point Clouds Contextual Tab

Once a point cloud is attached and selected, the Point Cloud contextual tab displays, as shown in the following illustration.

Display Panel

The Display panel enables you to control the size of the points in the point cloud using a Point Size slider. The Level of Detail slider controls the density of the points. Other tools in the Display panel include navigation tools such as: Perspctive, 3D Orbit, 3D Swivel, and 3D Walk.

Visualization Panel

The Visualization panel enables you to set the point cloud transparency using a slider. It also provides access to a Stylization drop-down list. This list enables you to colorize the point cloud based on the Scan Colors, Object Color, Normal direction of a point, Intensity (reflectivity), Elevation, or Classification, as shown in the following illustration.

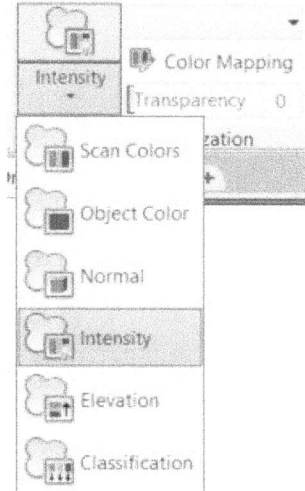

The Color Mapping command opens the Point Cloud Color Map dialog box shown in the following illustration. It can be used to customize the colorization using the options in the Intensity, Elevation, and Classification tabs.

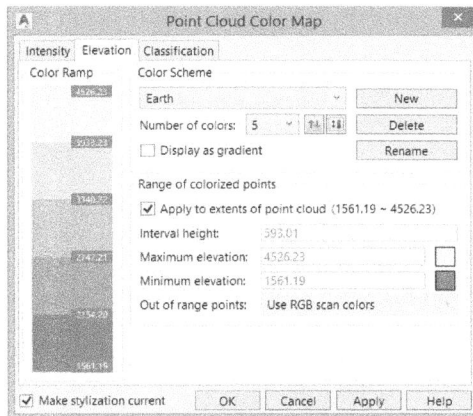

Cropping Panel

The Cropping panel enables you to control how much of the point cloud displays at any time. Named cropping states can be saved, enabling you to quickly return to specific cropping boundaries. The cropping boundary can be a rectangle, circle, or polygon, as shown in the following illustration.

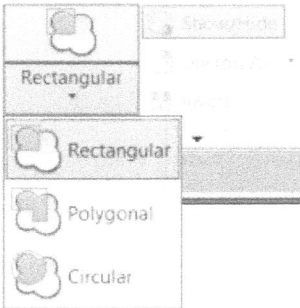

Section Panel

The Section panel enables you to create section objects for the selected point cloud using different orthogonal orientations, as shown in the following illustration.

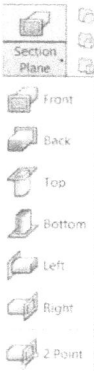

Extract Panel

The Extract panel enables you to create linework from existing sections when live sectioning is toggled on for the point cloud. You can also extract edges, corners, and center lines from point clouds. The density and alignment of the points determines when two or three point cloud planar segments intersect.

Options Panel

The Options panel enables you to open the External References Manager and the Point Cloud Manager. You can use the Point Cloud Manager to modify multiple point clouds at the same time. A list of all of the point clouds in the drawing and their regions, unassigned points, and scans displays, as shown in the following illustration. You can toggle the items on/off, rename, isolate, and highlight them in the drawing.

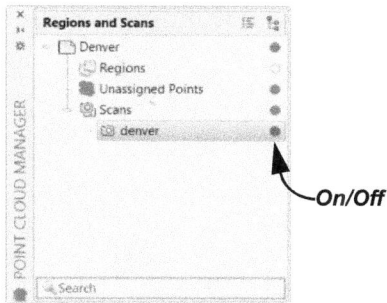

Object Snap

Point Cloud object snap modes have been added to the 3D Object Snap tab of the Drafting Settings dialog box, as shown in the following illustration. They interpret faces and edges according to the point density and alignment.

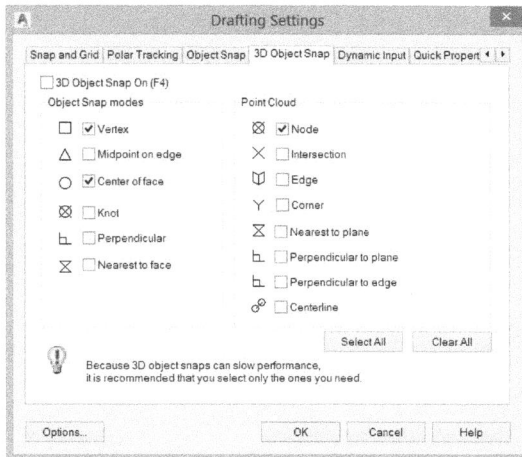